THE FANTASY FOOTBALL ABSTRACT 1993

THE FANTASY FOOTBALL ABSTRACT 1993

Rick Korch

A Perigee Book

Perigee Books
are published by
The Putnam Publishing Group
200 Madison Avenue
New York, NY 10016

ISBN 0-399-51800-2

Cover design and front cover photograph © by James L. McGuire

Printed in the United States of America
1 2 3 4 5 6 7 8 9 10

Acknowledgments

To Jacquie, whom I will marry three weeks after finishing this book. I can't wait to sit on a beach in Hawaii with you and put the last 11 months — and three books — behind me. It's going to be a long, fun summer. And thanks for your help with the statistics in this book.

Thank you to Laura Shepherd, my editor at Putnam, for letting me keep the deadline on this book later than that of any of our competitors so that this can truly be the most up-to-date book found anywhere.

To my brother Jody, a fine writer who edited the copy for this book. And to Bob Peters, who again did a great job of updating the design of the pages.

To Angela Miller, my literary agent, and to Gene Brissie, who originally had the idea for this book.

Thanks to all of the people who helped me with their fantasy football expertise: Jack Pullman of All Pro Publishing, Ian and Robert Allen of *Fantasy Football* magazine, Emil Kadlec of *Fantasy Football Pro Forecast* magazine, Patrick Hughes and Dick Giebel of the Franchise Football League, Jerry Greene of the *Orlando Sentinel* and Larry Weisman of *USA Today*.

Thank you to Bill Winkenbach, the man who invented fantasy football over 30 years ago, and to Andy Mousalimas of the King's X bar in Oakland.

Thanks to the public relations directors and their staffs on all 28 NFL teams, who helped with injury updates and other factual information, and for the photographs of the top players at the five positions — Steve Young, Barry Sanders, Jerry Rice, Keith Jackson and Chip Lohmiller.

To the members of my fantasy football league last year at *Pro Football Weekly* ...

... Michael Lev, the John Elway of fantasy football, who scored 33 points on Monday Night Football to come from behind and win our championship game 49-46.

... Ron Pollack, who hated Sundays so much last year that he's dropping out of the league this year. Maybe you can find a league in which all you have to do is draft and then declare a winner. Thanks for your many suggestions for this book over the past few years.

... Steve Silverman, the Jerry Jones/Jimmy Johnson of fantasy football who talked me into making perhaps the worst trade in the history of fantasy football, therefore knocking me out of the playoffs. I will never trade with you again.

... Jim McClevey, who went from 3-11 three years ago to first place last year. But it's the playoffs that count, Jim.

... Bob LeGere, our hard-luck player of 1992. You're going the wrong way in the standings.

... Howard Balzer, who needs to fly to Chicago for our draft so he can pick his own team.

... and Randy Bruce, our intern who knocked me out of the playoffs no matter if I had made that trade or not.

A belated thanks to everybody who wrote me last year with suggestions for this year's edition of *The Fantasy Football Abstract*. And an early acknowledgment to those of you who will write me this year so this book can be even better in 1994 (see the back of the book).

Hawaii, here I come!

Contents

Introduction

Why is fantasy football better than rotisserie baseball?

In rotisserie baseball, you don't know who's won until October. By then, the weather has not only gotten nice, it's gotten cold again.

In fantasy football, you know who's won every Monday, not too long after Hank Williams Jr. has sung the opener for Monday Night Football and your living room is full of a bunch of your best friends.

In rotisserie baseball, if a player hits a grand slam home run, it might — just *might* — give you a fraction of what it takes to win your league a whole bunch of months later.

In fantasy football, if a player goes 80 yards for a touchdown, you know right away how much it has helped you.

In rotisserie baseball, you don't have a clue how your players are doing unless you check out the box scores in the paper.

In fantasy football, all you have to do to find out how your guys are doing is turn on the TV.

In rotisserie baseball, roster maintenance is a painstaking task.

In fantasy football, you trade, cut and pick up players, just like in the NFL — and your players can immediately help you win, just like in the NFL.

Rotisserie baseball was started in 1979 by a bunch of writers.

Fantasy football was started in 1962 by a part owner of the Oakland Raiders and a bunch of sportswriters.

Nobody knows how many people play rotisserie baseball, but nobody cares, either.

Heck, I know more people who have *quit* playing fantasy football than have ever played rotisserie baseball.

The sport of baseball is just there every day. Lose a few games, and there's always next week ... and next month.

Football is an event. One loss can mean wait 'til next year.

And fantasy football is an event, too. One that is getting more and more popular every year.

But it is a pretty weird way to have fun. Fantasy insanity is what I call it.

Think about it ...

Why else do Rams fans cheer for Jerry Rice of the hated 49ers? And why do Pittsburgh fans root for Houston's Warren Moon? Only in fantasy football does that happen.

Because, if you think about it, fantasy football is really the most frustrating, inane game you can play.

It completely changes the way you watch pro football. You no longer care which teams win games; all you care is what players score.

You find yourself watching every football game on Sunday afternoons, clicking the channels back and forth for hours, or setting one television on top of the other so you can watch two games at once (if you don't do that already).

You don't care about food or water or fresh air. Your life-support system is the 10-minute ticker.

You root for a player on each team, and people look at you funny wondering which team you are really for.

You end up watching endless football reports on Sunday nights, trying to find out if the players on your fantasy team scored that day.

You know how many yards and touchdowns every player on your team had over the weekend, but you don't have any idea which teams won games.

You spend Monday mornings searching through the newspapers for game stories, summaries and statistics.

You find yourself watching Monday Night Football to the bitter end, not caring who wins, but rather hoping one of your players scores on the last play of the game.

Fantasy football has become an obsession. I mean, why else would anybody get into arguments over the productivity of the Redskins' tight ends?

Most football fans haven't even heard of the fifth wide receiver on the Chiefs' roster. But fantasy football players know his stats by heart.

That's because fantasy football is fun. And it's addicting.

Hundreds of thousands of people — millions even, because no one knows for sure — in the United States played fantasy football in 1992. It has permeated society and become a social activity. Lawyers, accountants, construction workers and cabdrivers play it. It is even played in prisons, and it has helped some bettors kick the habit, because they now can be interested in games without having to bet on them. In fact, by now, nearly everybody knows somebody who plays it.

Most football fans already feel they can build a team better than Cardinals owner Bill Bidwill. In fantasy football, they do just that.

Fantasy football participants act as the owner of their own team, with Sterling Sharpe, Barry Sanders or Dan Marino playing for them. They are the general manager, wheeling and dealing for players, signing free agents and making injury substitutions. And they are the coach, except, instead of having to decide what play to call on 3rd-and-8, they choose which running backs to play each week.

Fantasy football has become a part of the NFL. And it has changed the way millions of people watch football. Every game counts, if not for a fantasy football player, then perhaps for his opponent, or another team tied with him in the standings.

It is amazing how carefully some people will watch a what-used-to-be-meaningless game between the Cardinals and Buccaneers just because Gary Clark is on one team and Reggie Cobb is on the other. And those meaningless touchdowns on the last play of games sometimes mean the difference between winning and losing in fantasy football.

And fantasy football participants don't watch Monday Night Football just because that's what everyone else is doing, but rather because they might need three touchdown passes from Troy Aikman to pull out a last-minute victory over their opponent.

Fantasy football is sweeping the country. Pro football is the most popular sport in America, and although nearly everybody thinks he's an expert on it, there's really a lot more to be learned.

This book might seem very detailed, but don't let it scare you, because fantasy football is quite easy to enjoy.

The most common questions asked are: How do I join a league? Whom do I draft? Where do we get injury information? Read on; all of the answers are here.

At the end of this book, you won't find an address and order form trying to get you to join the author's league or to buy his fantasy football guides. This book is written for you, the fantasy football player, so that you can put together the best possible team and have the best chance to win the league in which you are playing.

Other books tell you to play fantasy football their way. But do it your way. This book tells you the most common rules and methods to play and lists the most popular variations. The idea is to have fun, and choosing your own rules is part of the fun.

This book will tell you how to play fantasy football and run your league, for both the uninitiated and the most-experienced fantasy players. But the emphasis, more than anything, is on player evaluation. That's because how you put together your team is the single most determining factor to how your team will fare during your fantasy season.

And then you'll get to sit back and see how you did.

And you, too, will soon be screaming at your TV set. "Throw it to Jerry Rice!" you'll yell. And the person next to you will shout: "No! Run it in!"

Yes, it truly is fantasy insanity.

I must be insane to keep writing this book.

Rick Korch
May 17, 1993

Chapter 1
History

On a cold, rainy fall day in New York in 1962, fantasy football was born.

Three men having lunch in a restaurant came up with the idea for what today is played by hundreds of thousands of football fans.

And we all owe a debt of gratitude to Bill Winkenbach, a limited partner of the Raiders, who is the father of fantasy football.

In those days, when pro football was striving to become the billion-dollar business that it is today, the Raiders used to take one long trip east to play the Boston Patriots, Buffalo Bills and New York Titans (now Jets). By playing all three teams in a 16-day period, the Raiders saved a lot of money on airfare.

It was on the Raiders' 1962 trip that Winkenbach and two writers for the *Oakland Tribune* — George Ross, the sports editor, and Scotty Stirling, the beat writer (and later general manager of the New York Knicks) — came up with the idea for fantasy football.

"That's practically 30 years ago, I guess," recalls Winkenbach. "We were just having lunch one day and we just kicked it around. Everybody made contributions. We were young football people, and we thought it would be a good game to pick up on — the knowledge of the players, who could score and so forth."

And thus the game of fantasy football was born.

Winkenbach, Ross and Stirling formed a league and called it the Greater Oakland Professional Pigskin Prognosticators League (GOPPPL, for short). The league still exists today, with three of the original members still playing, including Winkenbach (Stirling and Ross have dropped out).

"It was based on scoring," said Stirling. "We had a draft in which we picked two players at each of the skill positions."

Scoring in the GOPPPL was a little different than in most of today's fantasy football leagues. For instance, the original league awards 50 points for rushing touchdowns, 25 points for touchdown passes caught or thrown, 25 points for a field goal and about 200 points for touchdowns scored on returns of kicks or interceptions.

Today, the GOPPPL is still pretty much the same. "We've had a few minor changes, but it's pretty much the same," remarked Winkenbach.

From those small beginnings, fantasy football — fantasy sports, for that matter — has taken off like a rocket, with hundreds of thousands of players enjoying the game each year.

"I think fantasy football first spread in the San Francisco Bay area," Stirling remembered. "Once it got to Montgomery Street, which is to San Francisco what Wall Street is to New York, it spread like wildfire."

And it's still spreading.

Nobody knows for sure how many people played fantasy football in 1992, but estimates range from 400,000 to several million.

"It's two, two and a half million easy," said Pat Hughes, the president of the Franchise Football League (FFL), which he claims had 300,000 members last year.

"Nobody knows for sure how many people are playing it," said Jack Pullman, who owns a California-based company that offers a yearbook, weekly reports and a 900 number for fantasy football players. "My guess is that there's at least one million people playing it, but no one really knows. It's just too hard to figure."

But Steve Wulf, a writer for *Sports Illustrated* who is a member of the original Rotisserie Baseball league, said only about half a million people are playing fantasy baseball now, and that even fewer play fantasy football.

Whatever the number is, it's growing every year.

Says Ian Allen, the publisher of *Fantasy Football* magazine, "We're just touching the tip of the iceberg. The game will get bigger and bigger. There's so many people now that, if they aren't playing it, they know someone who is."

"It surprises me," said Winkenbach. "We were the first to start it, and it just mushroomed from there. There's a lot of offshoots to fantasy football. Oh yeah, I'm surprised at how big it's gotten."

In that other sport, Rotisserie Baseball was started in 1980 by writer Daniel Okrent and nine of his friends at the La Rotisserie Francaise restaurant in New York. The restaurant is now gone, but the game goes on. There were a few fantasy baseball leagues around the country before 1980, and a few can trace their origins to the '60s. Whether or not fantasy baseball predates fantasy football is anybody's guess.

However, more people play fantasy baseball, although fantasy football has had a very fast growth in the last several years.

Fans have played armchair quarterback for years. In fantasy football, they don't call the plays, but rather they are the owner, general manager and coach all at the same time. Fantasy football owners can trade, cut and bench players just like their counterparts in the NFL. They make all of the key decisions — even picking the team name.

One of the earliest leagues was begun in 1980 in Orlando, Fla., by Jerry Greene, a sportswriter for the *Orlando Sentinel*. "I remember reading an article in a magazine on fantasy football about some guys who played in Arizona," Greene recalls. "I don't even remember what magazine it was, something esoteric, like an airline magazine or *Playboy* or something like that. So I mentioned it to the other writers here and said, 'Let's give it a try.'"

Thirteen years later, Greene's group is still playing fantasy football. Some of the original members have moved to other cities, but they still get together every year, via long-distance telephone, for the annual draft. That costs quite a bit for a two- or three-hour phone call, but Greene says he's heard of even more interesting ways to conduct a draft.

"I've heard about people who go to Florida for their drafts," Greene said. "Or on an ocean cruise. Oh yeah, some people really like to turn it into a real event."

In baseball, the owners of the original rotisserie league started to make an annual pilgrimage to Clearwater, Fla., in the mid-1980s, and in 1987 they opened it up to the public. That hasn't started yet in football to anybody's knowledge, but the first fantasy football "convention" is probably just around the corner.

"The only limit to fantasy football is your imagination and the amount of money you want to put into it," Greene said. "Some leagues have team logos, T-shirts and hats. It gets really crazy. We're somewhere down the road to total lunacy, but we're not there yet."

Greene has a strong recommendation for fantasy players. His league holds an auction for players, with teams bidding rather than just drafting them.

"The first year, it's best to do a blind draw and then draft players. An auction is pretty sophisticated the first time out," he said. "Then, they should go to an auction. It's more challenging and more fun. And players have no excuses for the blind draw to blame for their (bad) picks."

Most people think that fantasy football and fantasy (or rotisserie) baseball are similar, but they really are quite different. In fantasy baseball, fantasy teams accumulate points throughout the baseball season, and the team with the most points at the end of the year is the champion. They compete against the other team owners as a group, but the outcome is not decided until the end of the six-month, 162-game season.

In fantasy football, however, teams play other teams every week; therefore, each head-to-head game yields one winner and one loser — just like in the NFL. It's that "instant gratification" that makes fantasy football better than fantasy baseball. There's also much less roster maintenance in football, which also makes it more enjoyable.

The biggest fantasy football league in the country is the Franchise Football League, which is based out of McLean, Va., and is licensed by the NFL.

"I had played the game for about 10 years," said Hughes, "and I decided it was so much fun I would try to formalize the rules for the game and market it around the country. My goal is to see the league in every office and shop across the country. My goal is ten million people playing it."

Hughes also is sponsored by Miller Brewing Company, which provides thousands of bars across the country with the materials to set up their own fantasy football leagues. At least 300,000 people played "Miller Franchise Football" in 1992 in bars.

One of the oldest fantasy football leagues in the country is played at the King's X bar and restaurant in Oakland. It dates back to 1971. The bar's owner is Andy Mousalimas, who learned the game from Winkenbach and Stirling and was an original member of the GOPPPL. "Scotty was a good friend of mine, and I remember him calling me up and telling me about it," said Mousalimas. "But it didn't catch on at all in the '60s. Rotisserie baseball caught on and it spread quicker across the country.

"But I knew we had something great back in '62," Mousalimas continued. "It's exciting to know that I helped popularize a game that went nationwide, that I was part of the group that started it.

"But Winkenbach and Scotty, they're the geniuses of the whole thing."

Chapter 2
How to Play

OVERVIEW

So, you think you know pro football? Then it's time to see how you will do. First, you have to decide how you will run your league. One of the best aspects of fantasy football is that you can make the rules any way you want them. There are thousands of fantasy leagues around the country and hundreds of variations on the scoring methods alone.

This book will tell you the basic method and detail many of the other variations, such as scoring, player transactions and playoffs. But this book is flexible. It's your league, so set it up the way *you* want to.

You will want anywhere from four to 16 people to form a fantasy football league, with each player getting his own franchise and acting as owner/general manager/coach. Each player will stock his team with players, play games, and hopefully win the championship.

First, you will have to decide on a commissioner and a deputy commissioner (who will decide on any possible disputes that may involve the commissioner, if he has a team in the league).

Your league may want to set a franchise fee, just as the NFL does when it expands. All of the money goes into a pot, which will include money that can be charged for player transactions. At the end of the season, the money is awarded to the top teams.

You will decide on a length of your league's season and then make up a schedule so the teams can play head-to-head during the season.

Team owners will gather before the start of the NFL season for the annual fantasy draft. There, they will select players in the following positions: quarterbacks, running backs, wide receivers, tight ends and kickers from actual NFL rosters.

In other variations, you may want to choose a team defense, a coach, sackers, interceptors or other variations for your league (but remember, the more complicated your scoring method, the more time-consuming it will be to tabulate scoring). Every team will have the same roster size, usually two quarterbacks, four running backs, four wide receivers, two tight ends and two kickers.

Teams will be allowed to pick up, drop and trade players after the draft, although your league will have to set rules beforehand so that nobody gains an unfair advantage.

Each team will submit a weekly lineup to the commissioner before a set deadline. The lineup usually consists of one quarterback, two running backs, two wide receivers, one tight end and one kicker, although there are many variations.

Teams will meet in head-to-head competition and score points according to a predetermined scoring method. Results and standings will be posted (or mailed to all teams) by the commissioner.

The season ends with playoffs and the championship game.

So there you have it — the basics of fantasy football. Now it's time to get a little more complicated and go a little deeper into how to play fantasy football.

JOINING A LEAGUE

There are a lot of established leagues that you can join for a fee. USA Today has a large league in which, for $99, people can draft, play and trade players by calling a toll-free 800 number.

The Franchise Football League, which started in 1988, has over 300,000 players. The Franchise Football League (FFL) is a computerized fantasy game that is licensed by NFL Properties and the NFL Players Association.

The FFL provides its players with simple, easy-to-use computer software that makes administration of the league an easy task (many other independent companies offer a similar software package). The FFL provides up-to-date NFL rosters for use on Draft Day and also charts starting lineups and trades, and allows for easy tabulation of weekly scoring.

Play-by-Mail Leagues

There are a number of other leagues that advertise in daily newspapers and sports publications called "play-by-mail" leagues.

These usually cost between $45 and $250 per year for each team, but they often have complex scoring methods that they manage with computers, so you don't have to tabulate your team's scoring. The level of competition is also noticeably higher than that in most friendly leagues.

Most play-by-mail leagues conduct their drafts through the mail. Team owners rank the players in the order they want to draft them. Each service has its own method of making sure each team gets the players it values most.

Some leagues offer phone drafts, in which every team owner gets on a conference phone call with the other members. But this method is more expensive, because drafts usually take two hours or more.

These leagues set deadlines in which you must have your starting lineup postmarked by a certain date, usually early in the week.

Since it might be difficult to get the players you want in the preseason draft, or if a player you drafted gets injured, benched or is playing poorly, you will want to play the free-agent wire often. However, it usually costs about $5 per roster move. You might even receive a few phone calls from other team owners in the league suggesting a trade.

The best way to decide if you want to join one of these leagues is to write for information, read it and then talk to the people who run the games over the telephone to see if you can trust them.

These leagues usually mail out scores, standings, up-to-date statistics, trade updates, lists of available free agents and injury reports. Many of them also offer stat services to handle your league's weekly scoring and eliminate the hassle that many league commissioners go through. Again, that costs money.

As compared to friendly leagues, weekly and year-end prizes are the main reason for fantasy football players to join these leagues, as they can be quite profitable to the winners.

STARTING A LEAGUE

Number of Teams

The best way to get involved in fantasy football is to start your own league with a group of your friends. The number of players in your league is open, and it should range from four to 16. Eight is the most common number of teams.

Remember, there are only 28 starting quarterbacks in the NFL. Since every fantasy team has two quarterbacks on its roster, if your league has more than 14 teams, some teams will have a real backup quarterback as their backup quarterback (and the same for kickers).

You will also want to have an even number of teams, because it makes scheduling easier with everybody playing head-to-head every weekend, eliminating the need for byes in your league's schedule.

The most important thing to remember in starting a league is to decide the rules first. You don't want to get into the middle of the season and have teams disputing the rules. Obviously, the rules can get complicated, so you might want to decide on the many options in this book before a situation arises in which it's too late to choose one.

Make your league's rules definitive. If there are any gray areas, there will be trouble. The best rules are the simplest ones, but you have to cover all the possible areas that can fall open to debate.

But be willing to change your rules from year to year, such as adding a new scoring variation. Too many leagues resist change over a period of years — the old "why change it if it works?" line. But change for the better is always an improvement and makes each year a little bit more fun.

Commissioner and His Duties

The commissioner is the Paul Tagliabue of your league. He manages the league, although he does not set the rules. Every team owner should have equal say in the rules.

The commissioner should have the time and organizational skills to do the job. The duties of the league commis-

sioner are to coordinate Draft Day, record rosters, keep track of roster changes, handle fees paid by teams (entry fees, player transaction fees), record the starting lineups, tabulate the scoring, distribute weekly results to the team owners and serve as the league treasurer.

In some leagues, playing rosters are distributed so that every team owner knows what players every team has activated for that game. Thus, each weekend you can keep track not only of how your players are doing but also of how your opponent's players are doing.

After compiling the weekly scores, the commissioner should revise the weekly standings, add up the total points (offensive and defensive) for every team, list all player transactions made the previous week and distribute them to every owner.

Your league should select a responsible person, perhaps somebody who does not have a team in the league. If the commissioner also has a team in the league, you should have a deputy commissioner to help settle disputes that involve the commissioner.

The commissioner should be paid at least enough to cover league expenses. If he has a team in your league, the other owners might want to waive his franchise entry fee to compensate him for his services.

Size of Rosters

Most rosters consist of approximately 14 players: two quarterbacks, four running backs, four wide receivers, two tight ends and two placekickers. One of the most common variations is for a roster to include one defensive team.

There are a lot of other variations, however, which are open to a league's preference. They are listed elsewhere in this chapter. Other books tell you to draft a number of players ranging anywhere from 12 to 26. But pick the number you feel is right. It's your league.

In most leagues, half of the players on a roster "play" during any particular week. That is, in the aforementioned 14-player roster, the active or "starting" lineup consists of one quarterback, two running backs, two wide receivers, one tight end and one kicker.

Putting Together a Roster

Your responsibilities as a fantasy team owner are much like those of the general manager and coach of an NFL team. The GM assembles the team, and the coach is the on-field leader. But first you have to put your coaching duties aside while the general manager's aspect comes to life.

There are two ways to form your roster: through a draft at the beginning of the season and, during the season, through a supplemental draft and/or by picking up free agents (and dropping one of your players).

Franchise Entry Fee

As in the NFL, most leagues have a franchise entry fee (which ranges upward from $10). The fees are collected, held and paid out at the end of the season to the best teams. If a franchise entry fee is charged, leagues should also charge a fee for all roster transactions made during the season. These entry fees usually cost more than other types of sports pools, but the entire fantasy football season lasts longer, too.

In most states, however, fee-based fantasy sports leagues that pay prize money are illegal. In Texas, players in a fantasy football league were actually charged with felony gambling. And in 1991, the state of Florida (which, by the way, operates the nation's largest lottery) ruled against fantasy sports leagues, saying they involve a form of gambling. Florida attorney general Bob Butterworth, in a nonbinding opinion requested by the state attorney, said fantasy leagues involve more chance than skill, violating state statute. Nothing has happened in other states.

It is not necessary to charge an entry fee, though, if team owners want to just play for fun.

Scheduling

Fantasy football seasons — the regular season *and* playoffs — usually begin at the start of the NFL's regular season and end on the final week of the regular season.

Some leagues also have a special fantasy playoff league that runs through the Super Bowl. This for those fantasy leaguers who can't get enough.

Since there are 18 weeks in the NFL season, you will want to shorten your regular season to 15 or 16 weeks, and then use the remaining two or three weeks for the playoffs, provided that your league intends to have playoffs.

The schedule is determined by the same order of your player draft. Team 1 plays Team 2, Team 3 plays Team 4, and so on. The order changes every week until each team has played the others once, and then the schedule is repeated.

In leagues with 12 or more teams, you way wish to split the teams into divisions of equal size, with teams playing those in its own division twice and the teams in the other division once.

Here is a typical schedule for a 10-team league in which each team plays every other twice:

Team #	1	2	3	4	5	6	7	8	9	10
Week #										
1	2	1	4	3	10	7	6	9	8	5
2	4	5	8	1	2	9	10	3	6	7
3	6	3	2	5	4	1	8	7	10	9
4	9	10	6	7	8	3	4	5	1	2
5	2	1	5	9	3	7	6	10	4	8
6	5	7	4	3	1	10	2	9	8	6
7	10	6	7	8	9	2	3	4	5	1
8	4	3	2	1	10	9	8	7	6	5
9	3	5	1	9	2	8	10	6	4	7
10	5	4	8	2	1	10	9	3	7	6
11	8	9	10	6	7	4	5	1	2	3
12	7	8	9	10	6	5	1	2	3	4
13	3	7	1	5	4	8	2	6	10	9
14	6	4	5	2	3	1	9	10	7	8
15	10	6	7	8	9	2	3	4	5	1
16	Playoffs									
17	Championship Game									
18	(Season over)									

For schedules of leagues of different sizes, see the Appendix.

Not every league will last the entire season. For example, an eight-team league that plays 14 weeks (with each team playing each other twice) and then has two weeks of playoffs will end with two weeks remaining in the NFL's regular season. If your league is set up that way, I suggest you start your league the first week of the NFL season and end it before the final week of regular-season play. It's likely that not every team will have every player signed by the season opener, but too many teams rest their starting quarterbacks in the final week of the regular season so they don't get injured before the playoffs start. Even the weaker teams often start rookie quarterbacks to see what they can do.

Thus there are always a lot of fantasy players in the final week or two who either had to play backups rather than their starters or that got no points from their starters because they didn't play at all.

In Week 1, all games count. In Week 18, you could be in your league championship but your key players might be sitting out in order to rest up for the real playoffs.

In 1993, for the first time, the NFL is using an 18-week schedule in which all 28 teams have two open dates, or byes. In the above eight-team-schedule format, you may wish to fill the remaining two weeks by reverting back to the schedule for Week 1 before starting the playoffs. Although it would eliminate the round-robin competition, it would lengthen the season to run the same as the NFL regular season. This method does, however, give unfair advantages to some teams because they might play weaker teams for the added week or two. That's why luck is such a big part of fantasy football.

If your league has 10 to 14 teams, you may wish to split the teams into two divisions. If your league has 16 teams, you may wish to split into four four-team divisions.

Playoffs

In some leagues, the traditional head-to-head style of play, with opposing teams facing off week-to-week, determines the league champion by the best win-loss record. Or, in the traditional format for fantasy baseball, cumulative season statistics (most points scored) are used to determine the winner. But fantasy leagues can — and should — use a playoff system, with the four best teams advancing to the playoffs in a single-elimination format. The team with the best record plays the fourth-best team, and the second- and third-best teams play each other. The two winners then face off in the fantasy championship. (The two losers can play to determine third place.)

Tiebreaker — If two or more teams are tied with the same record at the end of the regular season, use a tiebreaker to determine which team goes to the playoffs. There are several methods you could choose (but the method should be decided upon before the start of the season).

Option 1 — Head-to-head competition. If both teams are tied in head-to-head competition (usually one victory each), the next tiebreaker is point differential in head-to-head competition. This system is closest to the one the NFL uses. If teams are still tied, go to Option 2.

Option 2 — Most points scored during the regular season. This system better reflects how a team fared during the entire regular season and lessens the possibility that a team that got lucky in head-to-head games will advance.

Payoffs

Your league should decide before the start of the season how it will split the money paid for the franchise entry fee.

Payment is usually made to the league champion and the runner-up. Your league may wish to split some of the money among the third- and fourth-place teams that also made the playoffs. A typical breakdown might be 50 percent of the pot to the league champion, 25 percent to the second-place finisher, 15 percent to the third-place team and 10 percent to the fourth-place owner. A lot of leagues also give a "booby prize" to the last-place team.

It's best to spread the money around as much as possible. Players usually are not in it for the money so much as to have fun and share camaraderie with other football fans. More payouts keep interest going through the entire season — even for the last-place team.

A payoff to the team that scored the most points during the regular season is also wise, as that is most often the best team in the league regardless of the luck factor that goes into any one game.

Many leagues also hold back a portion of the entry fees to throw a year-end party to formally recognize the league champion and distribute the money. That's easy if your league is a close-knit group of players.

SCORING

Nowhere else in fantasy football are there more variations from league to league as there are in the scoring systems. There are as many different possibilities as one can think of.

There are three systems that are most commonly used (each with its own variations). Remember that the more complicated the system, the harder it is to determine scores each week.

You can get the official NFL scoring results out of any daily newspaper, but there will occasionally be discrepancies or missing statistics from paper to paper. The best daily sources are *USA Today* and major metropolitan newspapers, and the best weekly source is *Pro Football Weekly* (*The Sporting News* no longer lists box scores from NFL games).

Some NFL players line up at more than one position, so your league will need to clarify the position at which he will be played. For example, last year the Eagles played Keith Byars at tight end for most of the season, although they continued to list him as a running back on the roster. Select one publication to act as your league's official source, and use its designation for players' positions. *Pro Football Weekly* is the best source for this, because it lists depth charts each week (and it had Byars listed correctly).

Selecting a Scoring System

The best way to decide which scoring system your league wants to use is to poll the team owners and determine which one is most popular. The basic system is used by most fantasy leagues, but, because luck is such a big factor in it, two other systems have become popular in which performance determines the league winner more than luck.

A. The Basic System

The most widely used scoring method is the basic one — teams receive points only when one of their activated players for that week scores points in an NFL game. When a player scores a touchdown, you get six points. When a kicker converts a field goal it's worth three points, and an extra point is worth one point.

For example, if Brad Baxter dives over the goal line from the one-yard line, you get six points. Or, if Emmitt Smith runs 80 yards for a touchdown, you also get six points. It's the same way with placekickers — a 20-yard field goal is worth the same as a 55-yarder.

Scoring by Position

Quarterbacks
1. Three points for each touchdown pass thrown.
2. Six points for each touchdown scored rushing.
3. Six points for each touchdown scored receiving.

Running Backs, Wide Receivers and Tight Ends
1. Six points for each touchdown scored rushing.
2. Six points for each touchdown scored receiving.
3. Three points for each touchdown pass thrown.

Kickers
1. Three points for each field goal.
2. One point for each extra point.

Miscellaneous Scores
1. Running backs and wide receivers get six points for a touchdown on a punt or kickoff return.
2. Any player receives six points for recovering a fumble in the end zone for a touchdown.
3. Any player receives one point for an extra point scored running or receiving.

Variations to the Basic Scoring System — One of the biggest faults with the basic scoring method in fantasy football is that it rewards those players who pound the ball over from the goal line while ignoring those players who got the ball to the goal line.

For example, in 1991, the Redskins' Gerald Riggs scored 11 touchdowns, most of them from only a yard or two out after teammates Earnest Byner and Ricky Ervins had carried the ball 70 or 80 yards down the field. Byner had two 100-yard games in which he didn't score a touchdown, but Riggs had two games with less than 10 yards rushing in which he scored two touchdowns. In a 1990 game between Kansas City and New England, Chiefs running back Barry Word rushed 19 times for 112 yards but didn't score any touchdowns, while his backfield mate, Christian Okoye, carried the ball 11 times for only five yards — but he scored two touchdowns.

That is why so many leagues use variations in their scoring systems. Your league can change the scoring method any way it wants. Here are some of the most popular variations to the basic scoring system.

Passing touchdowns — Most leagues give six points to the receiver (he got the ball in the end zone) and three to the quarterback (after all, he got the ball to the receiver). But some leagues divide the points equally, with three points given to both the quarterback and the receiver (or running back) who scores. The thinking here is that the NFL gives only six points for a touchdown, so the credit should be divided equally between the two players involved. The leagues that give six points for a rushing touchdown and then split the points for a passing touchdown do so for another reason — it's harder to score on the ground. I don't necessarily believe that, however. A lot of running backs have broken free without being touched, whereas a receiver going across the middle of the end zone often gets clobbered while coming down with the ball.

Varied-point systems — Some leagues award 10 points for a touchdown (rushing or receiving), five for passing touchdowns and field goals, two points for extra points and 10 points for all defensive scores, regardless of their nature. The only difference is higher points per game, so why not just go with one, three and six points? If you use a varied-point system, be sure you do not devalue the kicking game. Points scored on field goals should be half of those scored on touchdowns. For example, don't award 10 points for a touchdown and only three for a field goal.

Yardage — Bonus points can be awarded for yards gained by running backs and receivers, passing yards or even for long plays (for example, double points for scoring plays of over 50 yards). In my league last year at *Pro Football Weekly*, we awarded three bonus points in three categories: a running back with a 100-yard rushing game, a receiver (wide receiver, tight end or running back) with a 100-yard receiving game or a quarterback with a 300-yard passing game. We also gave three bonus points to scoring plays of 40 yards or more (rushing or receiving), two points for a passing touchdown of 40 yards or more and one bonus point for field goals of 50 yards or more.

Defensive scores — In many leagues, teams draft entire defensive units from NFL teams and then award six points for every score made by that defense in a game on a touchdown return of a fumble, interception or a blocked kick. Two points are awarded for a safety.

Sacks — Leagues that draft defensive players usually award one or two points for a sack.

Interceptions — Teams can subtract one point for each interception thrown by a quarterback.

Remember, the more complicated the scoring, the harder it will be to tabulate your league's scores.

B. The Distance System
Some leagues award points according to the length of the scoring plays. This system favors the gamebreakers —

players who score on long plays, rather than those who score from a yard out. In doing so, it eliminates much of the luck factor.

There are a variety of ways to give points for long-distance scoring. The following is one of the most common methods:

Passing for a Touchdown
Length of Touchdown	Points
1 — 9 yards	1 point
10 — 19 yards	2 points
20 — 29 yards	3 points
30 — 39 yards	4 points
40 — 49 yards	5 points
50 — 59 yards	6 points
60 — 69 yards	7 points
70 — 79 yards	8 points
80 — 89 yards	9 points
90 — 99 yards	10 points

Rushing and Receiving for a Touchdown
Length of Touchdown	Points
1 — 9 yards	2 points
10 — 19 yards	4 points
20 — 29 yards	6 points
30 — 39 yards	8 points
40 — 49 yards	10 points
50 — 59 yards	12 points
60 — 69 yards	14 points
70 — 79 yards	16 points
80 — 89 yards	18 points
90 — 99 yards	20 points

Field Goals
Length of Field Goal	Points
1 — 9 yards	1 point
10 — 19 yards	2 points
20 — 29 yards	3 points
30 — 39 yards	4 points
40 — 49 yards	5 points
50 — 59 yards	6 points
60 and over	7 points

Extra points are worth one point each.

Here is a different Distance Scoring System used by the Franchise Football League:

Yardage of play	0-9 Points	10-39 Points	40-plus Points
QB pass for TD	6	9	12
RB run for TD	6	9	12
WR/TE catch for TD	6	9	12
QB run/catch for TD	12	18	24
RB catch/pass for TD	12	18	24
WR/TE run/pass for TD	12	18	24
K run/catch/pass for TD	12	18	24
ST/Defense return for TD	12	18	24
Fake field goal for TD	12	18	24

Yardage of Play	17-39	40-49	50-plus
Field Goal	3	5	10

Safety = 12 points
Point after touchdown = 1 point

C. The Performance System

Scoring under this method is based on yards gained, not points scored. The major advantage is that less luck is involved (remember the Earnest Byner-Gerald Riggs scenario?) and the true stars will stand out over the course of the season.

Here is the most common scoring method for the Performance System (although leagues can make their own variations).

Scoring By Position

Quarterbacks, Running Backs and Wide Receivers
1. One point for every 20 yards passing.
2. One point for every 10 yards rushing.
3. One point for every 10 yards receiving.

Kickers
1. Three points for each field goal.
2. One point for each extra point.
3. If a kicker passes, runs or receives for yardage, he is awarded the corresponding points as the other position players.

Points are not deducted for negative yardage. The following is a detailed chart for the Performance Scoring System just described.

Passing Yardage	Points
0 — 19 yards	0 points
20 — 39 yards	1 point
40 — 59 yards	2 points
60 — 79 yards	3 points
80 — 99 yards	4 points
100 — 119 yards	5 points
120 — 139 yards	6 points
140 — 159 yards	7 points
160 — 179 yards	8 points
180 — 199 yards	9 points
200 — 219 yards	10 points
220 — 239 yards	11 points
240 — 259 yards	12 points
260 — 279 yards	13 points
280 — 299 yards	14 points
300 — 319 yards	15 points

and so on.

Rushing Yardage	Points
0 — 9 yards	0 points
10 — 19 yards	1 point
20 — 29 yards	2 points
30 — 39 yards	3 points
40 — 49 yards	4 points
50 — 59 yards	5 points
60 — 69 yards	6 points
70 — 79 yards	7 points
80 — 89 yards	8 points
90 — 99 yards	9 points
100 — 109 yards	10 points
110 — 119 yards	11 points
120 — 129 yards	12 points

and so on.

Pass Receiving Yardage	Points
0 — 9 yards	0 points
10 — 19 yards	1 point
20 — 29 yards	2 points
30 — 39 yards	3 points
40 — 49 yards	4 points
50 — 59 yards	5 points
60 — 69 yards	6 points
70 — 79 yards	7 points
80 — 89 yards	8 points
90 — 99 yards	9 points
100 — 109 yards	10 points
110 — 119 yards	11 points
120 — 129 yards	12 points

and so on.

Another favorite performance method to award points is to develop a scoring system that includes statistics for the following: quarterback — pass-completion percentage, passing yards, passing touchdowns and negative points for interceptions; running backs — rushing yards, rushing average and touchdowns; wide receivers and tight ends — receptions, receiving yards, yards per reception and touchdowns; and kicking — field goals and points subtracted for missed field goals. For defense, a system of 1-10 points is awarded for points allowed (example: 10 points for a shutout), or 1-5 points for rushing or passing yards allowed (5 points for less than 100 yards rushing or 200 yards passing allowed). Defenses are also awarded points for sacks and interceptions. Leagues that use this type of scoring system usually devise it themselves.

Whatever scoring system you use, don't go with one that awards so many points that your game scores are 110-96. Use one with realistic scores somewhere in the range of real NFL scores.

D. The Rotisserie System

Like fantasy baseball, some league champions are the teams with the most points scored during the season. This method certainly rewards the best team overall, but it eliminates the week-to-week competition, which is the most exciting aspect of fantasy football.

The team that scores the most points is justifiably the best team in a league, but it is very possible (and even likely) that it won't win the league championship based on weekly play.

What makes the fantasy football-to-the-NFL correlation closer than the rotisserie baseball-to-the-major leagues correlation is that the highest-scoring team is not always the Super Bowl champion or the winner of a fantasy league.

THE DRAFT

Now it's time to stock your team. Your league will conduct a draft that is very much like the NFL draft, except that, instead of drafting college players, you are actually picking players from current NFL teams.

Draft Day is the most exciting event of fantasy football and also the one day that determines how well your team will fare.

Some leagues that continue from year to year with the same teams, allow owners to keep some players from the previous year's roster. It's an interesting option that a lot of leagues use, but the drawback is that everybody should have a chance to draft Jerry Rice and Barry Sanders. Keep that in mind.

Preparing for Draft Day

Study, study, study.

This book will help you immensely as you prepare for your fantasy football draft, because its emphasis is on player evaluation. But you also need to study NFL rosters and have some knowledge of each team's depth charts — who starts and who doesn't. The majority of owners in every league do their homework and prepare for Draft Day. But there are always one or two owners in every league who do not, and they are usually the ones at the bottom of the standings.

Remember, a league of eight teams will include only about 120 out of the approximately 1,600 players on NFL rosters. That leaves you with a lot of players from which to choose, making your draft picks the most crucial aspect of putting together your team.

You need to know more than just the players on your favorite team. You need more than last year's NFL statistics or a list of the All-Pro and Pro Bowl teams. You really need to know something about every team in the league — and not just who's good but rather who scores the points. You also need to know your league's rules and draft accordingly (see Draft Strategy).

But do not go strictly on last year's statistics, because most players are inconsistent, and their numbers will go up and down from year to year. Be sure to know whether or not a player's 1992 statistics were truly indicative of his abilities. Last year's statistics are useful only to the extent that they are indicative of what to expect this season. For example, Jerry Rice's numbers vary a lot from year to year, but he always ranks at the top of the list of wide receivers. But, while Herschel Walker had a great season last year, that doesn't mean he'll do it again this year, because he probably won't perform at that level on a consistent basis. The same holds true for Brett Favre, Chris Warren, Mark Jackson, Pete Metzelaars and a lot of other players.

And it's just the same for players coming off bad seasons. Mark Rypien (holdout), Eric Green (suspension) and Warren Moon (injury) all had subpar seasons in 1992 for different reasons. But all three of them are very capable of having good or great seasons again in 1993, just as they did in 1991.

Injuries have a lot to do with a player's performance, and injuries to other players often determine whether or not some players will get a chance to perform or not.

Remember, the success of your entire season largely depends on how you do in the draft. Study.

When to Hold Your Draft

It is necessary to hold your draft on a day in which every team can be represented. Do not allow an owner of one team to draft players for the owner of another team who cannot attend the draft. If a team is not represented at the draft, it must make its selections from the pool of players that remains after the draft.

You will want to hold your draft as close to the start of the NFL season as possible. The best day is anytime from Tuesday through Saturday before the NFL season starts (September 5), which is after the date that NFL teams make their final cutdown to 47 players.

A quiet environment might be the best spot to hold your draft, since you will want to be able to think. But, for some reason, bars and restaurants seem to be the most-used locations.

If your league's commissioner owns a team, you might want to have an outside friend act as the recording secretary for your draft, since the commissioner will be drafting. You need somebody to keep track of the draft order, record everyone's picks as they are made, maintain time limits between picks and leave the commissioner free to concentrate on his draft.

You might also want to have large boards made up to record the picks so everyone can see them during the draft and will know what players are no longer available.

Some leagues (especially those that have 14-week regular seasons and two weeks of playoffs) hold their drafts one or two weeks into the NFL season and then start their leagues at the same time NFL teams are playing their second game so they can run their leagues the remainder of the NFL season, rather than end a week or two before the NFL playoffs start. This gives them the advantage of seeing how certain players (especially rookies) are doing in the NFL and helps when it comes to the ever-increasing number of contract holdouts that prevent veterans and rookies from playing the first few games of every season.

Draft Order

The draft begins with each team owner drawing a number. Teams then draft players in order. In succeeding rounds, teams draft players in the reverse order. Therefore, the person with the last pick in the first round gets the first pick in the second round, giving him two picks in a row.

That's why the owner with the last pick shouldn't panic, because it all evens out in the long run. The person with the first pick in the first round does not choose again until the last pick in the second round. Then he gets two picks in a row, because, as the third round begins, he gets the first pick again. At that point, the draft returns to the original first-through-last order.

The third and fourth rounds (and all pairs of succeeding rounds) work just like the first two rounds until every owner has filled his team roster at every position up to your league's roster limit.

Here's how it works:

Team 1 —   1st pick
Team 2 —   2nd pick
Team 3 —   3rd pick
Team 4 —   4th pick
Team 5 —   5th pick
Team 6 —   6th pick
Team 7 —   7th pick
Team 8 —   8th pick
Team 8 —   9th pick
Team 7 —   10th pick
Team 6 —   11th pick
Team 5 —   12th pick
Team 4 —   13th pick
Team 3 —   14th pick
Team 2 —   15th pick
Team 1 —   16th pick
Team 1 —   17th pick

and so on.

You may want to set a time limit on each player for him to make his selection, which will keep the draft moving. A one-minute limit should be sufficient if team owners have done their homework and are prepared for the draft. In contrast to the NFL draft, when teams get 15 minutes to make their first-round pick and less in succeeding rounds, it seems like the late picks in fantasy football are the hardest to make. That's when you are trying to fill out a position, where you are looking for sleepers and players with potential and don't want to make a mistake. The early-round picks usually go quickly, because that's when the better, well-known players are selected.

An eight-team league will take at least two hours to complete a draft, but the time goes by quickly. And it's an awful lot of fun.

Drafting Players

The most important factor in fantasy football that determines who wins and who loses — other than luck — is the draft. The team with the best players scores the most points. The team with the most points wins games. So you want to put together the best (meaning highest-scoring) team possible.

You can draft players from any position in any order, but I strongly suggest you take a quarterback, a running back and a wide receiver with your first three picks. Forget about the tight ends and placekickers until the middle rounds — you want to get as many of the high-scoring players as possible early on.

There is a big disparity between the best players and the very good players at the three aforementioned positions (quarterback, running back and wide receiver), and not as much difference between the best kickers and tight ends.

In fact, in 1993 you might want to pick a running back and a wide receiver with your first two picks, because quality players at those positions are hardest to find. The pool of good quarterbacks is a bit deeper than those for running backs and wide receivers. Don't be fooled when

other team owners are drafting quarterbacks. You really will be better off taking a running back and a wide receiver first — but don't wait too long to draft a quarterback.

For example, Barry Sanders, Emmitt Smith, Thurman Thomas and Rodney Hampton are easily the four best running backs to have in fantasy football. If you don't take one of them when you have the chance, there's quite a difference between them and Chris Warren, Harold Green, Brad Baxter and Earnest Byner, four running backs who would likely be available in the fourth round. On the other hand, there is not a lot of difference between the best placekickers, many of whom are capable of kicking 100 or more points. Every team in your league will end up with a decent kicker, so the difference is not very much between them. At tight end, Keith Jackson and Eric Green are easily the best players, and they're worth an early pick, but I would always draft my second running back, wide receiver and quarterback (and perhaps my third running back and wide receiver) before picking another tight end who most likely isn't going to score a lot of points during the season.

Don't draft your second quarterback too early, even if a good one is available; instead, take a running back or wide receiver who you will use a lot during the season. Three years ago, one player in my league last year drafted Jim Kelly in the third round after already having chosen Joe Montana in the first round. The only time he played Kelly all season was the one week when Montana's 49ers had a bye. Of course, any quarterback's susceptibility to injuries warrants having a good backup quarterback on a fantasy team — much like the Oilers have a good backup to Warren Moon in Cody Carlson — but you are better off drafting players who will play and score points for you rather than having a good player on your team who you do not play much.

And, if your league uses defenses, don't draft your defensive team until the last round or two, because picking a defense is basically a crapshoot anyway.

After the draft, the commissioner should give every team owner a copy of each team's roster.

Player Auctioning

Established leagues often like to use this method, in which players are bid for rather than drafted, because it adds another dimension to the draft.

Every team spends the same amount of money to make up, or buy, their teams. This is true free agency in fantasy football, because you do actually own the player. Also, in an auction, every team has equal opportunity to get every player.

Once an order is determined for choosing the players to be bid on, owners bid for players until one owner has outbid the others for a particular player. There is no ceiling on the player bids, and the best players obviously go for the most money (perhaps as much as 40 percent of a team's limit). Since only a few players in the league are worth that percentage of a team's "salary cap," you have to be sure you make that choice wisely. Choosing players with good potential for a smaller cost will enable you to out-bid other teams for the most-sought-after players.

The auction continues until each team owner fills out his roster, and the cost of those players must not exceed the league's salary cap. In some leagues, if a team still has money left over, it can add one player at any position (usually a quarterback).

For example, one of the longest-running fantasy football leagues in the country has a $100 limit per team. Players such as Barry Sanders and Warren Moon cost over $50 each, whereas players like Eric Martin and Mark Duper can be had for $2-4. The objective is to fill out an entire roster with $100 (this league has 12 players per team). Most of the teams try to buy one or two superstars and then fill out their rosters with cheap players with good potential. For example, Barry Foster was "bought" for $6 last year. But, since every team starts with the same bankroll, the most important thing is to budget carefully.

A regular draft is much shorter than an auction, but an auction is certainly more exciting. But it's not recommended for beginning fantasy players; wait a year or two before taking the plunge into an auction.

The championship team in that Orlando, Fla., league last year had the following starting lineup: quarterback Mark Rypien, running backs Barry Foster and Earnest Byner, wide receivers Art Monk and Michael Haynes and kicker Steve Christie,

Draft Strategy

■ The rules that your league uses concerning its scoring method dictate largely the players you want to draft. If your scoring reflects only those scores made by NFL players every week, you will want to draft players who score the most points. For example, Derrick Fenner can be almost as valuable as Thurman Thomas. But if your league rewards teams with running backs who rush for 100 yards in a game or quarterbacks who throw long touchdown passes, you will want to take other factors into consideration.

If your league's scoring system gives quarterbacks six points for each touchdown pass thrown, by all means try to draft a quarterback first. And if your league gives bonus points for distance scoring, you will want to go with the gamebreakers — Terry Allen rather than Harold Green, Michael Haynes rather than Mike Pritchard, and Morten Andersen rather than Gary Anderson.

■ The most important factor in drafting is projecting a player's performance for the upcoming year. So don't place too much emphasis on last year's statistics. On the average, only about 3 of the top 10 scorers among running backs and wide receivers finish in the top 10 the following year. Quarterbacks are easier to judge, with about 70 percent finishing in the top 10 in successive years.

That is why this book lists statistics for up to the last five years of every player's career. A lot of players who were injured or had subpar seasons last year will be much better draft picks if you study their entire careers. Also, if you pick based strictly on 1992 statistics, a lot of players who had career years will never reach those marks again.

You also will want to know which of the 1992 rookies who saw little playing time last year are ready to break out in 1993.

■ Do not draft too many players from one division. During the weeks that teams have a bye (see the 1993 NFL schedule in the Appendix), you will not be able to play these players, and if too many of your best players are from the same division, you will have to play too many backups on those two weekends, almost guaranteeing that you will lose two games. So spread your picks around. Also, for the same reason, be sure to pick your two quarterbacks and two kickers from different divisions. A good suggestion is to draft your top three players (quarterback, running back and wide receiver) from three different divisions so you'll always have two of them on the bye weeks.

■ Don't draft too many players from your favorite team. If they have an off year, they will very quickly become your least-favorite players. Be objective, and even take players from a team you do not like, because they will help you win in fantasy football. And don't pass over a player like Eric Green or Johnny Johnson just because they are troublemakers. If you have a chance to "steal" either of these players in a lower round, by all means do so.

■ Don't draft too many players from bad teams. Most owners want the bulk of their players from good teams, because they'll have more scoring opportunities. Harold Green is a perfect example of a player who would accumulate some excellent statistics on a good team, but he can't do that on the Bengals.

■ Know which players are holding out, both veterans and rookies. Possible holdouts in 1993 include Steve Young, Barry Foster and Emmitt Smith.

■ Consider a player's age. Last year, several players seemed to grow old quickly, such as Art Monk and Boomer Esiason. Players who could slide this year include Herschel Walker, Henry Ellard and Anthony Carter.

■ Be aware of which players might lose their starting jobs in 1993. Some of these players are quarterbacks Chris Miller and Browning Nagle, running backs Cleveland Gary and Mark Higgs, wide receivers Mark Duper and Ricky Proehl and kicker David Treadwell.

■ Because of free agency, know the players that switched teams who could be due for outstanding years. Some of these players include running back Rod Bernstine and receivers Irving Fryar and Bill Brooks. On the other hand, receiver Gary Clark is an example of a player whose statistics probably won't be as good as they were in 1992 because he went to a weaker team.

■ Know the injury status of players you are thinking about drafting. Among the best players coming off 1992 injuries are Chris Miller, Leonard Russell and Eddie Brown (see the Injury Report in Chapter 12).

■ Don't put too much emphasis on preseason statistics, because they can be very misleading.

■ Know which teams have changed their offenses. For example, if a team goes to a one-back offense, the backups will not see much action. Kansas City is switching to a two-back offense, which means Barry Word, Christian Okoye and Harvey Williams will split the playing time unless one of them is traded. In Chicago, Neal Anderson was declared the starting running back back in March, which should help him when September comes. And be aware of possible changes on the five teams which have new head coaches in 1993 — Chicago, Denver, New England, the New York Giants and washington.

■ Know which rookies have the best chance of contributing right away. Some of these are running backs Garrison Hearst (Cardinals), Jerome Bettis (Rams) and Terry Kirby (Dolphins); wide receivers Curtis Conway (Bears), Sean Dawkins (Colts) and O.J. McDuffie (Dolphins); tight end Irv Smith (Saints); and kicker Jason Elam (Broncos).

■ When drafting, no matter what round it is, have two or three players in mind. That way, if somebody else picks the player you wanted, you will be able to make a comparable choice. In the middle rounds, many players should be even; what you are looking for is the so-called "sleeper" in every round. There's always one.

■ If you don't think the player you want will be available in the next round, now's the time to draft him.

Here's what a typical roster might look like for the 1993 season:

Round 1 — Emmitt Smith, RB, Dallas Cowboys
Round 2 — Haywood Jeffires, WR, Houston Oilers
Round 3 — Troy Aikman, QB, Dallas Cowboys
Round 4 — Fred Barnett, WR, Philadelphia Eagles
Round 5 — Reggie Cobb, RB, Tampa Bay Buccaneers
Round 6 — Brent Jones, TE, San Francisco 49ers
Round 7 — Kevin Mack, RB, Cleveland Browns
Round 8 — Flipper Anderson, WR, L.A. Rams
Round 9 — Jim Harbaugh, QB, Chicago
Round 10 — Morten Andersen, K, New Orleans Saints
Round 11 — Blair Thomas, RB, N.Y. Jets
Round 12 — Bill Brooks, WR, Buffalo Bills
Round 13 — Chris Jacke, K, Green Bay Packers
Round 14 — Houston Oilers defense
Round 15 — Derrick Walker, TE, San Diego Chargers

In this typical roster, players were chosen from all six divisions, which is the ideal spread. And, even though some of the players play for losing teams, they'll still put up some pretty good numbers. But note that most of the players play for winning teams.

ROSTER CHANGES AND TRANSACTIONS

Just like in the NFL, you are able to make changes in your roster during the season. Just because you didn't have a good draft doesn't mean you have to suffer through the season with a bad team. And when one of your players is lost to his NFL team because of an injury, you also can replace him on your roster with another player. Fine-tuning your roster is a must after the season begins.

The winner of most fantasy football leagues is not the coach who drafted the best team, but the one who did the best job working the waiver wires. There are always talented players — primarily rookies and second-year pros who didn't play much the previous year, as well as players who came out of nowhere to have good seasons — who will

be overlooked in your league's initial draft and who would be a valuable addition to a fantasy team. This is how teams catch up to the preseason favorite. In other words, don't just draft a team and sit back to see how you will do. Be active.

Some leagues do not allow roster transactions of any kind after the draft. That's wrong. A fantasy league is supposed to be fun, and flexible roster changes allow every team the opportunity to improve during the season.

There are three commonly used methods to make roster changes: trades, holding a league-wide supplemental draft or an open-waiver system in which every team is allowed to pick up and drop players at any time.

Many leagues charge a small transaction fee for any personnel move. This usually lowers the incentive to make wholesale roster changes and helps to increase the pot for the payoff.

Your roster size may never exceed the limit; for every player you add, you must drop a player. Once you drop a player, he is eligible to be picked up by any team.

Too many fantasy leagues set too many restrictive deadlines and rules for transactions (as well as drafting, weekly lineups and many other aspects of fantasy football). Be flexible. The idea is to have fun and allow every team an equal opportunity to win. You need to be sure the rules are not stretched or broken, but they should not hinder the idea of fantasy football, which is to provide enjoyment to football fans.

Remember, NFL teams change their rosters and lineups constantly throughout the season. So should you. But don't "overmanage." You want to be continuously looking for players to add to your roster, but be careful not to give up on your players too soon. Some players need time to develop, just as you knew when you drafted them.

Trades

Trading players is one of the most fascinating aspects of pro football. Fans spend weeks, if not years, trying to determine which team got the best of a trade. Remember the big trades involving Eric Dickerson and Herschel Walker in recent years?

In fantasy football, however, trades are usually a rare occurrence. In fact, some leagues do not allow them at all because of the possibility that two team owners would get together and make a trade that helps one team at the expense of another (especially at the end of the season).

If your league allows trades, you will want to set some safeguards. For example, set a deadline like the NFL does. The NFL does not allow trades after the sixth week of the season, but you will want to set your fantasy league's deadline a little later. Do not allow one team to trade a player or players for "future considerations," for obvious reasons. You can also make trades contingent on the approval of the commissioner or the other team owners to guard against hanky-panky.

Two-for-one trades (in which one team offers two players for one very good player) are allowed, as long as each team obeys the league's roster limit. The team receiving two players must drop another player on its roster, while the team receiving one player must pick up another player.

Just like in professional sports, where the commissioners have the power to veto trades that are not "in the best interests of the league," your commissioner and team owners should have the same power. If the commissioner has a team in the league, a simple majority of owners can veto a trade.

Waivers

In the NFL, teams are free to drop or *waive* players at any time and pick up or sign players at any time, and this is my suggestion. Teams should be able to improve their roster at any time. In a league of eight teams with 14 players per roster, only 112 players out of approximately 450 skill-position players (quarterbacks, running backs, wide receivers, tight ends and kickers) will be on a fantasy roster. That leaves a lot of good players undrafted; thus there should be no limit on the number of roster changes per team.

Under this method, the first team to pick up a player from the unclaimed pool of NFL players gets him. All he has to do is notify the league commissioner (and pay the appropriate fee, if there is one). For each player obtained via waivers, a player must be released.

Teams should be allowed to make roster changes whenever they want, because that's basically the way it is done in the NFL. As long as a team keeps its roster the same size for every game, it should be able to make as many changes as it wants.

Every year there are several players whose midseason addition helps fantasy teams. In 1992, Ricky Watters, Brett Favre and Pete Metzelaars came out of nowhere to star for their teams, and it's likely that they weren't even drafted before the start of the season. A few players returned from the injured reserve list a month into the season and were a nice addition for some fantasy teams. And, on September 1, how many fantasy players would have expected Rodney Culver and Tom Rathman to score nine touchdowns each? Work the waiver wires carefully and you could come up a winner.

The first two weeks of the season are an important time in the success of your team. Keep an eye on players who come out of nowhere, surprise starters or even rookies who were not expected to start or play much.

Supplemental Drafts

A league can also decide to hold a draft after four weeks (or eight weeks) to supplement rosters with players not chosen in the preseason draft (those on current rosters during the season). Team owners are able to drop as many players on their rosters as they want and replace them with new players.

The supplemental draft is conducted just like the preseason draft except that the order changes. Just like in the NFL, teams draft in reverse order of their won-lost records (that is, the team with the worst record drafts first and so on, to the team with the best record). Ties are broken by total points scored by the tied teams (with the team with the least points scored considered the weaker team). The draft then reverses order in the second round and continues back and forth until every owner has made the changes he wants to make.

Any player not on a fantasy team is available to be picked up from the supplemental pool. This is especially effective in allowing every team an almost equal opportunity to grab the latest hotshot player in the NFL, as compared to total free agency, in which the first team owner to contact the commissioner gets the player.

Not every team may wish to take part in the supplemental draft, especially if an owner is happy with his team.

If the teams in your league originally acquired players through an auction, you should hold a supplemental draft/auction at some point during the season to allow all teams to bid for new players.

No Transactions

If a league does not allow teams to make transactions, or if a deadline is put on all transactions, you still should allow teams to replace players who are injured.

The simplest way to do this is to allow teams to replace only those players who are actually placed on injured reserve by their NFL teams. No team should be forced to play without a player at a particular position or be without a capable backup. Players lost to a fantasy team because of trades or waivers would not qualify to be replaced unless your league's rules specify so.

Leagues that do not allow transactions often have larger roster sizes, which gives each team the chance to stock enough players in the draft to get through the entire season.

Injured Reserve

What do you do when one of your top players is injured and placed on injured reserve? In most leagues, you would either keep him on the bench until he is healthy again (thus taking up space that could be occupied by a healthy player), or you would drop the injured player and add another one at the same position. However, if you drop the player, he would be free to be picked up by any team when he is reactivated.

Thus, your league might want to allow teams to have an injured reserve list, so any player who is placed on injured reserve by his NFL team would be retained by the fantasy team and temporarily replaced by a pickup. Then, when the injured player is activated in the NFL, the fantasy team would either have to activate him and drop the substitute player (or another player) or drop the player on injured reserve (for example, if the substitute player is doing better).

LINEUPS

The most enjoyable week-to-week aspect of fantasy football is setting your lineup in advance of each weekend's action.

Now it's time to play coach. You are Jimmy Johnson or Don Shula. You don't decide what plays to use, but rather what players to use, and that's how you score points. If drafting is the most important part of fantasy football, then "starting" the right players is the most important decision you make once the season starts. One of the most frustrating moments of fantasy football is knowing that a player you didn't start for a particular week scored a touchdown — or even two! And it's equally frustrating to start a player who doesn't even suit up because of an injury.

Whom to Play

The starting lineup usually consists of:

1 Quarterback
2 Running Backs
2 Wide Receivers
1 Tight End
1 Kicker
1 Team Defense

Lineup variations: There are a number of variations that your league will have to decide upon before the start of the season. For example, the Franchise Football League recommends 1 quarterback, 2 running backs, 3 wide receivers, 1 tight end, 1 kicker, 1 special teams player (kick returner), 1 linebacker and 1 defensive back (or one team defense in place of the special-teams player and two defensive players). But, since NFL teams have only six skill-position players on offense, your league should, too.

Those on your team who do not "play" sit on the bench for a week (or, in some cases, all season).

Because of the advent of H-backs, run-and-shoot offenses and three- and four-wide-receiver formations, some NFL teams do not use tight ends and others use them basically for blocking. You may want to allow teams in your league the option of drafting one extra wide receiver in place of a tight end and/or playing one extra wide receiver rather than a tight end any particular week.

That's what we do in my league. Instead of drafting four wide receivers and two tight ends, we allow teams to pick five wide receivers and only one tight end *and* have the option of playing either three wide receivers or two wide-outs and one tight end each week. In 1990, some teams didn't play a tight end all season, always starting three wide receivers. So in 1991 we passed a rule in which every team had to play its tight end for at least half of the games. That is more fair to tight ends, because it doesn't totally dismiss them, and it is certainly more exciting to start players who have a better chance of scoring than a tight end who might see the end zone only three or four times all season. After all, after Keith Jackson, Eric Green, Jay Novacek and a few others, there's not much left in the NFL in the way of tight ends, and there *are* a lot of fine wide receivers.

Setting a Deadline

Be sure to set a deadline for teams to submit their starting lineups for each week, but set it as late as possible. You might want to have a deadline set for 7:00 p.m. Friday or 6:00 p.m. Saturday so that your phone is not ringing off the hook Sunday as you are sitting down to watch the NFL pregame shows on television. In the event of Thursday or Saturday games, you will need to adjust your deadlines — even if some teams don't have players involved in those games. All rosters should be turned in before the first game played each week.

Your league might want to allow teams the option to call in a lineup change anytime before 1:00 p.m. EST Sunday, when games begin, if the commissioner can be reached (or if he has a phone-answering machine). This allows teams to make last-minute changes in the event of player injury. It's not as complicated at it might seem, as it might be used only a few times in the course of the season by all of the teams.

Once the deadline has passed, changes cannot be made — even in the event of injuries to a player before a game.

If the commissioner has a team in the league, he must turn in his lineup to another league member to guard against cheating.

If a team does not turn in a lineup, its lineup from the previous week will be automatically used.

Before choosing your lineup, you should consider several factors, such as injuries, opposing defenses, whether your players are playing at home or on the road and weather. The final factor to consider is which of your players are hot and which ones are cold. But the most important factor is not to put a player in your starting lineup *after* he has had a big game. You want to put him in at the right time.

Quite often, players who are not listed on the official NFL injury list on Friday afternoon do not play in that weekend's games; thus they can't score any points for their teams. But every team is under the same disadvantage — whether it be fantasy football or real football.

Suggestion 1: One question I am often asked is whether you should play your best players against a strong defense or if you should play weaker players who are going up against easier defenses. For example, do you start Emmitt Smith against the Eagles, who have a strong run defense, or do you go with Vaughn Dunbar against the Rams, who have a weak run defense?

I prefer to start the better players, because the best players tend to play better against good teams. I offer no basis for this, other than that it works for me. Besides, take a look at the Super Bowl. That's when the best players play against the best the NFL has to offer — and the truly great players always shine in the end.

However, my rule does not hold hard and fast. I might go with Jim Harbaugh against the Buccaneers rather than Jim Everett against the Eagles, for example. In other words, when dealing with the tier of players just below the stars, it might be better to go with the player facing the weaker competition.

Also, you might want to take into consideration if a player is at home or on the road. In 1991, the Cowboys' Emmitt Smith scored 10 of his 13 touchdowns in the friendly confines of Texas Stadium and only three of them on the road. Last year, however, Smith had both of his three-touchdown games on the road. Most teams perform better at home, and so do their players, but it's not a sure thing. So go with your hunch (and hope it pays off).

Suggestion 2: Should you start a player who is listed as probable, questionable or doubtful on the official NFL injury report (which is released every Thursday)? There's nothing more frustrating during a fantasy football season than activating a player for a game and then seeing him standing on the sidelines in street clothes — or *not* starting him and watching him score three touchdowns!

Injuries are constant in the NFL; thus depth is very important for a fantasy football team. You will be guessing, however, just as NFL coaches have to guess whether or not their opponent is going to start a player listed as injured.

In the NFL, teams are supposed to list players with a 75 percent chance of playing as probable, 50 percent chance of playing as questionable and 25 percent chance of playing as doubtful. But not every team follows that guideline. Some list too many players, some don't list enough players and some don't list an injured player in an attempt to throw off their opponents.

Here's a tip: If a player is listed as probable, in all likelihood, he'll play. And you should play him (unless you have an equally talented, healthy reserve). If he's questionable and you have a pretty good backup, play the backup. And if the player is doubtful, go with your best backup, even if he has little chance of scoring. Then sit back and watch your "benched" star score two touchdowns!

How to Get Around the Byes in the NFL Schedule

As you probably know, NFL teams no longer play on every week during the season.

From 1990 to 1992, every NFL team had one bye, or one week off, without playing a game during the course of those seasons. In 1993, for the first time, all 28 teams will have *two* open dates during the season. Thus, the NFL regular season will stretch to 16 games over 18 weeks. Therefore, you will have to work around these byes when you draft your players and make up your weekly lineups.

The byes mean that every player on your fantasy team will have two weeks off in which you will not be able to play him. There were will be only 10 weeks during the 1993 season in which all 28 teams will play.

The byes don't present much of a problem, as was originally anticipated in 1990, because leagues that provide for good depth are able to deal with them.

The byes affect every team the same and balance out over the entire season. So, while you will have to bench Steve Young one game this season and play somebody like John Elway, remember your opponents have the same predicament. It's really no worse than having one of your players injured for a week when he will have to sit out a game anyway. You just have to live with it — just as the real team's coach does when one of his players is injured and out for one game.

After all, you have as many players on the bench as you normally play, so you still should be able to play a good player, especially if you drafted well before the season started (or made good roster moves).

Be sure to select a method of dealing with the byes before the start of your season. Here are the most commonly used options:

Option 1: When players on your team have a bye, you simply start other players, just as if the players whose teams do not play that week are injured.

The most important thing is not to draft too many players from the same division, because all of the teams in a division usually have an open date at the same time. Ideally, you should select your top three players (usually a quarterback, running back and wide receiver) from three different divisions.

Option 2: Expand each team's roster. Instead of a 14-man roster, you can go to a 19-man roster, adding one player at each position — quarterback, running back, wide receiver, tight end and kicker — during the draft. The bigger roster allows for more flexibility and substitution in all weeks. But, since you will find that even on a 14-man roster some players will never "play," an expanded roster is not really necessary to handle the byes.

Option 3: Allow coaches to place idle players on an "Inactive List" and pick up a replacement player for one week. But chances are that you already will have a better player sitting on your bench than you can pick up (or you better make a roster transaction right away and pick up that player for good).

Option 4: Players receive the same points during the week their teams have a bye as they will score the following week. That way your best players could play in every game. The biggest disadvantage with this method is that it delays the fantasy results for a week. Also, if the player does not score, the "goose egg" goes down on the scorecard twice. You can also use a player's score from the previous week, but, again, it can meet with the same negative consequences.

What is the effect of the byes on fantasy league scoring? In my league in 1990, the average number of points for both teams in the seven weeks without byes was 56.5 points. During the seven weeks when four NFL teams did not play, the average score was 55.8. In fact, the three highest-scoring weeks in my league that year came during weeks with the byes (although the two lowest-scoring weeks also came on bye weeks). So the byes proved to be negligible during the bye weeks because the backup players were just as capable of scoring as those players who normally would have started. In 1991, it was the opposite — 57.8 points per game during the seven non-bye weeks and only 47.9 points during the seven bye weeks. In other words, the byes have a minimal effect over the course of a year.

TABULATING THE SCORES

Since the team with the highest score in head-to-head competition each week wins, a fun part of fantasy football is tabulating the scoring. This can be a real task, however, if your league has a complicated scoring method. The league commissioner usually has the headache of putting together the stats every week, and he needs a reliable source every Monday and Tuesday to get NFL box scores from every game.

Here's my method for tabulating the scores for a game (the sample is from my league's championship game). We used a basic scoring method of six points for touchdowns rushing, receiving and defensive scores, three points for a touchdown pass thrown and field goals, two points for a safety, one point for extra points, a bonus of three points for 100-yard games rushing or receiving or 300-yard games passing. There are also bonus points for scoring plays of 40 yards or longer and field goals of 50 yards or longer.

The Vicious Wolverines	Michael's Mags
QB — Carlson - 33	QB — Aikman - 333
RB — L. White - 3	RB — E. Smith - 663
RB — Hampton - 666	RB — Higgs - 0
WR — Clayton - 6	WR — Rison - 6
WR — J. Taylor - 6	WR — Haynes - 3
TE — Jackson - 0	WR — Slaughter - 0
K — Stoyanovich - 133	K — Andersen - 3331
D — Oilers - 0	D — Chiefs - 6
TOTAL — 46	TOTAL — 49

Many leagues prefer to use the following designations for scores: T for touchdowns scored, P for touchdowns thrown (worth three points), F for field goals, X for extra points and S for safeties. That's simple enough, but I just wrote down the actual point value for each player.

What's Going On?

One of the most frustrating times for a fantasy football player is not knowing how you and your opponent are doing on Sunday afternoon. Unless your league is set up in such a way that you know what players your opponent has started, you might not even be able to tabulate his scoring.

The hardest part is trying to find out who is doing the scoring on Sunday afternoon. The halftime and postgame highlight shows and evening sports programs just don't tell you who made every score in every game — or how long the scores were or how many yards everybody gained. So you will have to wait until Monday morning when your newspaper hits your doorstep.

In my league at *Pro Football Weekly*, all eight fantasy players work Sunday nights, so as soon as games ended the scoring summaries and statistics came from the Associated Press machine and were faxed from the press boxes.

For us, it's always "Did the Dallas-Philadelphia box score come over yet?" Or "How'd Jerry Rice do? Did he catch a touchdown pass? Did he get 100 yards?" Three years ago, I heard, "How can Warren Moon throw for 527 yards and Drew Hill not catch a touchdown pass?"

I understand that ESPN has an excellent show on Sunday evenings called "Prime Time" that shows every significant scoring play and is eagerly watched by fantasy football players. I haven't seen "Prime Time," though, because I haven't had a free Sunday night during the fall in years.

Computer Software Packages

Many services advertise in daily newspapers and other sports publications that offer supposedly easy-to-use computer software packages to manage fantasy football leagues and tabulate scoring. Some of these allow leagues many different options to customize your own rules, rather than restricting you to one set of rules. Most packages are compatible with IBM computers, although a few work on Macintosh computers. The cost for these packages ranges from $40 to $125. Look in *Pro Football Weekly*, *The Sporting News* and NFL preview magazines for these kinds of ads.

Breaking Ties

Occasionally, the scores of two teams will end in a tie. Unless your league decides that ties are OK, there are two commonly used methods of breaking ties.

Option 1: Add the scores of the players on each team's reserve list (those players not activated that week). This will usually break the ties (if a tie remains, revert to Option 2). This is the best method, as the team's backups should determine a winner and a loser. When a winner is determined, the winning team receives the victory and the loser gets a loss in the standings. But only the points that led to the tie should be added to the cumulative points in the standings (in other words, the points scored by the backups are not added to the team's points in the standings).

Option 2: Teams can list their reserves in the order they would want them used in a tiebreaker. For example, teams would probably list their backup kicker first, and the team with the kicker with the most points would be a winner. If this method is used, you might want only field goals to count for kickers, as it better reflects NFL overtimes (in which there are no extra points).

In some leagues, every game has a home team and an away team. In a tiebreaker, using this method, if the home team's first reserve scores, the home team wins the game. If he fails to score, the visiting team's first player has the opportunity to break the tie. If neither player scores, the tiebreaker goes to the second players on the reserve lists (home team, then visiting team).

This method is more luck than anything, whereas Option 1 truly awards the team with the best backups (for that week, anyway). Besides, in an average season, there won't be more than two or three ties, anyway, and owners shouldn't have to spend all that time determining the order of their reserves, when they probably won't be used.

WHAT DO YOU NEED TO WIN?

An average score of 30 points per game will usually win most games and make you your league's champion for the regular season. With a poor game in the playoffs, however, all could be for naught.

Thirty points is not a lot. It could break down this way:

QB — 33		WR — 6	
RB — 6		TE — 0	
RB — 0		K — 3111	
WR — 6		Defense — 0	

That's all it takes — a good game by just a few of your players. Your quarterback throws two touchdown passes; one running back scores a touchdown, while the other doesn't score at all; both of your wide receivers score a touchdown; your kicker hits one field goal and three extra points (not much at all); and your tight end and defense don't get any scores. That's it.

Some weeks, most of your players will be hot, and you will score upwards of 50 or 60 points. Some other weeks, you might score in the teens — and still win. But it's also very possible that you can score a lot of points but your opponent's players will be even hotter and score more — and thus beat you.

VARIATIONS

Every league has its own special rules that make it unique from others. Here are some of the most common variations for fantasy football.

Drafting a Defense

Remember, football isn't just offense. The most common variation is to draft a team defense to be used as an eighth player. Unlike the skill-position players, a fantasy team drafts an entire NFL team's defense. When any member of the team's defense scores a touchdown, whether on an interception, a fumble recovery or a blocked kick, six points are awarded to the fantasy team. If a defense scores a safety, two points are awarded.

Other scoring methods include rewarding defenses for holding opposing offenses under 300 total yards, under 100 yards rushing or under 200 yards passing. Different point totals are assigned to each category.

See Chapter 9 on Defenses.

Drafting Individual Defensive Players

Some leagues, those with the most complicated rules and scoring methods, actually draft an entire defense — three linemen, four linebackers, two cornerbacks and two safeties. Points are awarded for tackles, assists, sacks and interceptions.

An option here is to subtract defensive points from your opponent's score rather than adding the defensive points to your team's score.

Remember, though, this method gets very complicated — and very few newspapers list statistics for tackles and assists. And, since statistics for tackles are unofficial anyway, they are not really an accurate measure of players' abilities. For example, the leading tacklers for the Falcons and Vikings usually have about 200 tackles a season, while teams like the Steelers, Dolphins and Bengals, who decide tackles much more conservatively, have a leading tackler with only about 100 tackles.

Drafting a Special Team

Another variation is to draft kick returners or a team's entire special teams (punt and kickoff returners). Six points are awarded whenever a player returns a kickoff or a punt for a touchdown or scores off a fake punt or a fake field goal.

Drafting a Coach

Each team can draft an NFL coach as an extra player and be awarded three points every time his team wins a game in the NFL.

Re-Drafting for Playoffs

OK, so the regular season is over and you haven't had enough. Fantasy football is in your blood and you want more. So go ahead and do it all over again during the NFL playoffs.

In the week immediately following the end of the regular season, hold a draft just as you did before the start of the season. Some leagues hold their draft the week between the four wild-card games and the first round of the divisional playoffs, because the wild-card teams will all play an extra game if they advance to the Super Bowl. I don't particularly buy this reasoning, because drafting players from a wild-card team is taking a chance since it's rare that one of those teams makes it to the Super Bowl. Most are out of the playoffs after another week.

By the end of the regular season, every fantasy owner (theoretically) will have a good feel for what players are scoring well, but the most important aspect is knowing which teams will go the furthest in the playoffs, because players can produce points only as long as their teams advance in the playoffs. That's why shrewd drafting is essential.

Unlike the regular season in fantasy football, a fantasy league held during the NFL playoffs does not feature head-to-head competition. Rather, the champion is determined by the team that scores the most points overall through the Super Bowl.

Some leagues hold their fantasy league playoffs this way but allow teams to "protect" one or two players from their rosters before beginning a new draft. Other leagues allow players to be drafted by more than one team. Scoring is the same as the method used during the fantasy season, unless you want to make alterations.

Lifelong Franchises

In rotisserie baseball, owners retain the rights to players on their fantasy teams from the previous year. You can do that in fantasy football, too, if you prefer, or you can allow each team owner to retain one player (or two).

The best part about lifelong franchises is that it is more like the NFL, where teams basically stay the same except for some changes (even teams with new head coaches don't turn over half of the previous year's roster). They provide a sense of continuity from year to year and probably foster more trades throughout the season.

But remember, if you do this you are eliminating the single most exciting part of fantasy football — Draft Day. It also denies players the opportunity to draft players like Jerry Rice, Dan Marino or Emmitt Smith if they are already on another owner's team.

But again, it's up to you and the other team owners.

SOURCES

There are several good sources for fantasy football league players to get in-depth game scores and summaries, weekly statistics, depth charts, rosters and injury updates. Here are the best:

Game Summaries and Box Scores

Good sources for game statistics are daily newspapers, with *USA Today* being the best. *Pro Football Weekly* runs game stories and box scores, but you won't receive it until late in the week.

Statistics

Most daily newspapers print individual statistics by conference, usually in the Thursday sports sections. *USA Today* runs stats by conference for each team on Wednesday and Thursday (one conference each day). *Pro Football Weekly* runs the longest lists of individual statistics, as well as the most complete team statistics and rankings.

Depth Charts

Pro Football Weekly is the only national publication that lists depth charts weekly. Its depth charts come from each NFL team's press releases and are updated each week.

Rosters

The best place to find rosters for use in the draft is any one of the reputable NFL preview magazines on the newsstands (the best being *Pro Football Weekly*'s *Preview '93*, Joe Theismann's *Pro Preview*, *Street and Smith's* and *The Sporting News*).

Injury Updates

Most daily newspapers, including *USA Today*, list the official weekly NFL injury report in the agate section of Friday's sports section. Remember that the "official" NFL injury report is not 100 accurate. Check your Saturday and Sunday newspapers, as well as the NFL pre-game shows, for last-minute updates.

NFL News

You will also need to know the latest news about what's going on around the NFL — what lineup changes are about to occur, who's playing well and when a player is about to come off the injured reserve list. The best sources for NFL news are *USA Today*, *The Sporting News* and *Pro Football Weekly*.

Fantasy Tips

There are also several 900-number services available. The best — I'm being biased here — is the one offered by *Pro Football Weekly*. Our four editors (including me) offer their best fantasy football tips, injury updates and other late-breaking news on Fridays during the season. The number is 900/407-7004, and callers are charged $1.25 per minute.

Jack Pullman, who runs All Pro Publishing in Panorama City, Calif. (818/893-5055), also has a 900 number. His service, which is probably the best around, also offers weekly newsletters during the season for fantasy football updates.

The Franchise Football League has a hotline, too. Call 703/883-0029 for details.

Chapter 3
Player Evaluations

The player evaluations in this book are the compilation of my 16 years of working in and around the National Football League. They are my opinions, based on close observation of the teams and players of the NFL over that time. They are intended as a guide to help you draft and put together your fantasy team before and during the season.

But go ahead and make your own decisions. It's your team and you should have the biggest say-so in the makeup of it.

In writing the player evaluations, I have taken into consideration such factors as player performance over an entire career (not just last year's statistics), injury status, holdouts, the improvement and decline of players, age, changes in teams' game plans (and the players' roles in them), supporting cast, the impact of the 1993 schedule, the movements of free agents and the 1993 drafts of every team.

But, since this book went to press in late spring, you will need to consider other factors, such as injuries suffered in the offseason and during training camp, depth chart changes and in-season coaching changes (for making roster transactions).

Players are ranked under a variety of headings, such as "Superstars," "Solid Picks," "Could Come On" and "Question Marks." In most cases, players are ranked under each category in order of their talents and projected contribution to a fantasy football team, but quite often a player in a later category will actually be a better pick than one in a previous category. For example, Kenneth Davis is the first running back listed under "Best of the Rest," but he is certainly a better player than Vaughn Dunbar and Blair Thomas, two players listed as "Could Come On" ahead of him.

Since each fantasy football league differs in size and makes its own rules, it is difficult to make exact evaluations and suggestions because a starting player in a 12-team league might be a backup in an eight-team league. So this book will deal with average leagues — those with 8-10 teams that draft two quarterbacks, four running backs, four wide receivers, two tight ends and two kickers and which start one quarterback, two running backs, two wide receivers, one tight end and one kicker.

This year, I have added a separate chapter ranking the top players in every position regardless of which category they are listed in throughout the player evaluations (see Rick's Picks). This is the list I will use going into my fantasy football draft (updating it, of course, with what happens during the preseason).

In the player evaluations, you will notice that there is more to each player's analysis than just a bunch of numbers and statistics. In addition to each player's statistical highlights is a description of his talents. For example, Jerry Rice is described as a receiver with "terrific hand-eye coordination and field awareness, but it's his ability to kick into some kind of otherworld, warp-speed gear in just one step that makes him so great."

No, that won't help you in fantasy football, but there's a reason why Rice has scored 107 touchdowns in eight seasons, and you'll learn that, too, in reading this book.

Besides, people who play fantasy football do so because they are big football fans — hard-core football fans. So maybe you'll run across some information that doesn't seem to pertain to fantasy football. But it does pertain to football, and that's why you play fantasy football.

Tips in Choosing Players for Your Draft

Here are some general tips for any scoring method:

■ Don't draft only big-name players.

■ Remember that other players draft foolishly when a panic occurs. Just because everybody else is drafting kickers or quarterbacks, that doesn't mean you have to follow the trend. Be like an NFL coach — don't stray from your game plan.

■ Be careful when considering injury-prone players. If one of your top draft picks misses a large portion of the season, your team will suffer.

■ Know the status of players going into the season, who's injured and who's holding out. This is very important, because you don't want to draft a player who can't play.

Here's an example of your drafting strategy for the Basic Scoring Method:

■ Round 1 — Draft the player who will score the most touchdowns, usually a running back or Jerry Rice. Remember, quarterbacks are awarded only three points for each touchdown pass thrown (in most leagues), and since quite a few of them can throw 20 touchdowns in a season, a running back or wide receiver who scores more than 10 or 12 touchdowns is very valuable — and very rare. (Suggested picks: Jerry Rice, Barry Sanders, Thurman Thomas, Emmitt Smith, Rodney Hampton or Steve Young.)

■ Round 2 — Again, try to draft a running back or wide receiver who can score 10 or more touchdowns in a season. Don't panic and take a quarterback yet, unless all the good ones are going quickly. (Suggested picks: Andre Rison, Sterling Sharpe, Ricky Watters or Terry Allen).

■ Round 3 — This is when you draft the best three-point

player, either a quarterback or the best six-point player that is still available.

■ Rounds 4-5 — If you already have a quarterback, running back and wide receiver, take another running back because there is little depth in the NFL at that position (there are a lot of good ones but only a few very good ones). But consider drafting another wide receiver, tight end Keith Jackson or a kicker like Chip Lohmiller or Pete Stoyanovich.

■ Rounds 6-8 — You will want to have all seven of your starting positions filled by the end of the eighth round, which allows you to draft one strong backup player (who will still be activated a lot if a starter is playing poorly). Take your backup quarterback here, but not too early, because you might use him only once or twice all season. Also try to get one of the top tight ends. It might also be time to draft your first kicker.

■ Rounds 9-12 — Draft your backups, but try to get players who can step into your lineup if a starter is injured or playing poorly. Take the best available players, keeping in mind that you don't want to take too many from the same division (because of the byes). Draft seriously in the late rounds, because these players often are the determining factor between winning and losing. Also consider taking a rookie as your fourth running back or wide receiver in these rounds, because they may develop into integral players on your team by the end of the season. Draft a defense in one of the final two rounds. The last round is also when you will want to gamble on a pick.

Rounds 6-10 are the most important of your draft. They are the ones that separate the contenders from the pretenders. Since most people will draft approximately the same in the early rounds, this is where you will pick up the players who will mean the difference between winning and losing. Pick some up-and-coming stars here, and, if they come through, so will your team.

Basic Scoring Method — This scoring system is the hardest to draft for, because luck more than skill determines how well your team will do.

■ Draft players solely on ability to score touchdowns.

■ Draft high-scoring running backs and wide receivers first.

■ Do not draft quarterbacks first.

■ Unless you have a chance for Keith Jackson, don't draft a tight end until the second half of the draft.

■ Fill all of your starting positions by the end of Round 8.

■ Draft wisely in the late rounds, because your backups often play a key role in the success of your team.

Performance Scoring Method — This is the easiest scoring method to draft for because it eliminates the luck factor more than the other methods, since players are awarded points based purely on yards gained.

■ Draft players strictly on potential of yards they can gain.

■ Since quarterbacks pass for 300 yards more often than running backs or wide receivers accumulate 150 yards, go for a quarterback first.

■ Draft running backs and wide receivers in Rounds 2-5. Remember to take into consideration a running back's potential to gain yards receiving.

■ Draft your second quarterback no later than the end of Round 6 (and earlier if there's a good one on the board).

■ Draft tight ends who gain yards rather than those who catch short touchdown passes at the goal line.

■ Fill all of your starting positions by the end of Round 8.

■ Draft wisely in the late rounds, because your backups often play a key role in the success of your team.

Distance Scoring Method — This method is a combination of the two above, since players are awarded points for scoring plays and the length of them. In other words, the longer the touchdown (or field goal), the more points awarded.

■ Focus on players who have big-play, long-distance abilities.

■ In the first round, draft either a running back or Jerry Rice. You want players who score from a long way out, rather than those players who only see the ball near the goal line.

■ In the second round, take your first wide receiver or one of the very top quarterbacks.

■ Wait until the third round before drafting a quarterback, and try to get one who throws to big-play receivers.

■ In the fourth round, draft the best available running back or receiver, or tight end Keith Jackson.

■ Go for a kicker in Round 5, one who has a strong leg and plays for a team that will give him a lot of opportunities for field goals.

■ Fill all of your starting positions by the end of Round 8.

■ Draft wisely in the late rounds, because your backups often play a key role in the success of your team.

Legend for Player Analyses

Injured — Player spent the entire season on injured reserve.

DNP — (Did not play) Player was not with a team during the entire season.

None — Player appeared in a game(s) but did not accumulate statistics.

Holdout — Player missed the entire season because of a contract holdout.

Chapter 4
Quarterbacks

From year to year, quarterback is probably the most consistent position with respect to production. As compared to running back and wide receiver, in which the performances of the top players fluctuate wildly every year, the top quarterbacks usually stay the same on an annual basis. On the average, of the top 10 quarterbacks in the NFL in any given season, seven of them will finish in the top 10 the following year.

The one factor that causes the biggest differences every year is injuries. In most seasons, in fact, the most important quarterbacks are those who don't get injured — and the number seems to be decreasing every year. In 1990, half of the starting quarterbacks lasted the entire season; in 1991, 11 quarterbacks started every game. And, last year, only eight quarterbacks started every game, and more than 60 different players started at least one game.

Steve Young

But don't worry too much about not getting a good quarterback. There are at least 10 quarterbacks in the NFL capable of putting up strong numbers, and, unless you blow your draft, you'll get one of them. After them, there is another group of at least eight quarterbacks who are also capable of good numbers. The talent pool is deep at quarterback, and, in an eight- or 10-team league, every team should get a good quarterback as well as a decent backup.

The most important rule in drafting a quarterback is to get a player who scores — either throwing the ball or running it in himself. Forget about completion percentage and other miscellaneous statistics that mean nothing in fantasy football.

The best quarterbacks for 1993 are Steve Young, Dan Marino, Randall Cunningham, Jim Kelly, Chris Miller, Warren Moon, Troy Aikman, Jim Everett, Mark Rypien and Brett Favre. In that group, Young, Marino, Cunningham, Moon and Kelly are definitely the top five, and then you could probably flip a coin for the next five and be just as happy. These players are all capable of throwing over 20 touchdown passes in 1993.

After that comes a group that starts with Bobby Hebert, Stan Humphries and John Elway that should be counted upon to throw about 15 TD passes in 1993.

However, there are a few other quarterbacks who had excellent seasons in past years but have slipped in the last year or two, such as Jeff George, Boomer Esiason and Bernie Kosar. Chances are one or two of them will rebound strongly this year with 15-20 TD passes. But who?

Draft Tips in Choosing a Quarterback

■ Look at past performances, especially the last two or three seasons.

■ Look for quarterbacks who play for passing teams. They'll throw the most touchdown passes (especially near the goal line). The key is to get a quarterback who will throw 20 or more touchdown passes a season. And he doesn't necessarily have to play for a winning team (Jim Everett is a good example of that).

■ Don't forget to consider a quarterback's running abilities. John Elway and Randall Cunningham score several touchdowns themselves each season. A few others, such as Stan Humphries, Rodney Peete and Jim Harbaugh, are also capable of doing that. Since a touchdown is worth six points in the Basic Scoring Method, these quarterbacks are very important. Rushing yards are also very important in the Performance Scoring Method.

■ Do not draft a quarterback from a team where the situation is unsettled. Be sure that the first quarterback you draft is going to start (and is healthy, too). If you are going to gamble, do it with your second quarterback pick.

■ Watch what is going on during training camp. Is Troy Aikman ready to move into the top echelon of superstar quarterbacks? Will Mark Rypien bounce back from an absolutely awful 1992 season? How much will the addition of Irving Fryar and Mark Ingram help Dan Marino? Is Brett Favre for real? Is John Elway ever going to throw for 20 touchdowns in a season again (he's done it only once)? Can Stan Humphries do it again? Does Phil Simms have another year or two left in him? Can Jim McMahon stay healthy (or should that be: For how many games can Jim McMahon stay healthy)? Can Chris Miller bounce back from his knee injury, and where is he going to play? If Bobby Hebert threw 19 touchdown passes last year in New Orleans, what will he do in Atlanta? And who is going to be the Saints' starter? Is Jeff George ever going to show us what he can really do? Will Jim Kelly and Warren Moon move back to the top of the quarterback pack? Can Boomer Esiason win the Jets' starting job and rebound from several subpar seasons? Is David Klingler ready? What can Randall Cunningham do with a team that seems to be losing all of its star players? Is Neil O'Donnell just going to hand the ball off to Barry Foster all season? Can Jim Everett continue his climb back into the elite of NFL quarterbacks? Can anybody do anything with the Seattle offense? Who is going to start in Detroit, Rodney Peete or Andre Ware? Who will be the Buccaneers' starter? If Jeff Hostetler is going to start for the Raiders, can he hold on to the job for the entire season? What can Steve Young do for an encore? And, finally, how good will Joe Montana be this season?

■ If your league uses a scoring method that rewards yardage or distance, try to get a quarterback who has a big-play receiver on his team, such as Steve Young with Jerry Rice, Randall Cunningham with Fred Barnett and Dan Marino with Irving Fryar.

■ Don't worry about drafting a quarterback from a losing team (if he's a good one). If his team lacks a running game, chances are he will throw a good percentage of touchdown passes, and that's what counts.

■ Make sure you have a quality backup who can take over if your starting quarterback goes down with an injury (or when your starter is out with a bye).

■ Don't pick a rookie quarterback unless you know he is going to see a lot of playing time.

SUPERSTARS

STEVE YOUNG / 49ERS

Year	Att.	Cmp.	Pct.	Yds.	TD	Int.	TD-R
1988	101	54	53.5	680	3	3	1
1989	92	64	69.6	1001	8	3	2
1990	62	38	61.3	427	2	0	0
1991	279	180	64.5	2517	17	8	4
1992	402	268	66.7	3465	25	7	4

Comments: Forget about Joe Montana — Young is now the best quarterback on the 49ers and in the NFL. In the last two years, he has proved what he had been saying for years — that he was a top NFL quarterback. He has won the NFL passing title the last two years, marking the first time

somebody has surpassed the 100.0 pass rating two consecutive years. The NFL's Most Valuable Player last year, he led the league with 25 touchdown passes and a low of seven interceptions. He threw TD's in 12 games, two or more in nine of them. He also ran for four scores and was second on the team in rushing and second among NFL quarterbacks with a league-high 8.62 yards per rush. Against Buffalo, he passed for over 400 yards, the only 49ers quarterback other than Montana to do so. In 1991, Young missed six games and the 49ers missed the playoffs. He threw touchdown passes in all but one of his starts that year, including two three-touchdown games and four with two TD's. He used to be called a running back with an underrated arm; now he's called a great quarterback who can also run well. A daring type, Young dazzles defenses with big plays. He can challenge defenses with his outside speed, because he's quick enough to outrun containment. He's smart and tough, and he knows how to stay in the pocket and buy time while waiting for his receivers to get open. Young has a 26-10 record as the 49ers' starting quarterback. With Young already having been declared the 49ers' starting quarterback for this season and considering how well he has played the last two years, he is easily the No. 1 pick among quarterbacks in fantasy football. The only thing that could go wrong is an injury (and he is quite vulnerable because of his running).

DAN MARINO / DOLPHINS

Year	Att.	Cmp.	Pct.	Yds.	TD	Int.	TD-R
1988	606	354	58.4	4434	28	23	0
1989	550	308	56.0	3997	24	22	2
1990	531	306	57.6	3563	21	11	0
1991	549	318	57.9	3970	25	13	1
1992	554	330	59.6	4116	24	16	0

Comments: The most prolific passer in the history of the NFL, Marino can still put up the big numbers. He's always a very good fantasy football pick, even though he'll probably never again reach the numbers he put up early in his career because the Dolphins have had a more balanced offense the last two years. In 1992, Marino finished second in the AFC and seventh in the NFL in pass rating, and ranks second on the all-time list. He led the league in pass attempts, completions and yards and was second in touchdowns. On the all-time passing lists, he is tied for second in career TD passes, is third in attempts and completions and is fourth in yards. He should shatter all of those records by the time he retires. He is the only quarterback ever to throw for over 4,000 yards in a season five times and he has hit 3,000 yards a record nine times. He has thrown at least one TD pass in 131 of his 151 regular-season games. He has thrown three or more touchdowns in 48 games and four or more 17 times. He hasn't thrown for more than 28 TD's since 1986, but he has thrown 20 or more all 10 seasons he has played, a record. He has led Miami to come-from-behind wins 24 times in 10 seasons. Marino went back to the long ball in 1992, with five TD passes over 40 yards.

Last year he was sacked 28 times, the highest total of his career. The ultimate franchise quarterback, Marino is very durable (although he was forced to leave two games for a few plays in '92 with injuries), having started 140 consecutive non-strike games since 1984 (the longest streak since the 1970 merger). He is a great pure passer, with the quickest release ever and a gunslinger arm. Marino is still the best and most important player on the Dolphins, but he's very frustrated by not getting back to the Super Bowl.

WARREN MOON / OILERS

YEAR	ATT.	CMP.	PCT.	YDS.	TD	INT.	TD-R
1988	294	160	54.4	2327	17	8	5
1989	464	280	60.3	3631	23	14	4
1990	584	362	62.0	4689	33	13	2
1991	655	404	61.7	4690	23	21	2
1992	346	224	64.7	2521	18	12	1

Comments: Moon missed Games 11-15 in 1992 because of a fractured arm but returned in time for the regular-season finale, playoffs and a Pro Bowl invite. He ranked first in the AFC (fourth in the NFL) in passing, fifth in yards, fifth in completions, sixth in attempts, third in touchdown passes and first in TD passes per attempt. In other words, he would have put up some excellent numbers had he played the entire season. He had four 300-yard games, giving him 35 for his career, which ranks third in NFL history behind Dan Marino and Dan Fouts. He reached the 30,000-yard mark for his career in the second-fastest time ever. Last season he threw TD passes in nine of 11 games, including five against the Bengals. In 1991, Moon set NFL single-season records for completions (404) and attempts (655) and ranked first with 4,690 passing yards, the fifth-highest total ever, becoming only the second quarterback to record back-to-back 4,000-yard seasons. It wasn't a great season, however, because of his 25-21 TD-to-interception ratio. In 1990, Moon had the second-best passing yardage day in NFL history when he threw for 527 yards against the Chiefs (with three touchdowns). Moon is a young 36 years old, custom-made to trigger the run-and-shoot offense. Although he lacks some touch on the deep ball, few quarterbacks throw the intermediate routes as well and he audibilizes as much as anyone. Moon is a leader, a mobile quarterback and can take a hit. He has an excellent arm and release, and he throws well on the run. For fantasy football, Moon is always going to be one of the top quarterback picks because he has averaged over 24 TD passes the last four years.

RANDALL CUNNINGHAM / EAGLES

YEAR	ATT.	CMP.	PCT.	YDS.	TD	INT.	TD-R
1988	560	301	53.8	3808	24	16	6
1989	532	290	54.5	3400	21	15	4
1990	465	271	58.3	3466	30	13	5
1991	4	1	25.0	19	0	0	0
1992	384	233	60.7	2775	19	11	5

Comments: Once a scrambler and a thrower, Cunningham has matured into a very accurate passer. He had a fine comeback season in 1992, finishing as the league's fifth-ranked passer. Although his statistics didn't reach those he compiled from 1988 to '90, they were respectable for an NFL quarterback. His season seemed to go in phases, ranging from spectacular to subpar. He was benched for Game 9 after four bad games before regaining his starting job and leading the team to the playoffs. He finished the season as the Eagles' third-leading rusher with 549 yards (tops among NFL quarterbacks), with a fine 6.3-yard average and five touchdowns. Cunningham missed all but one quarter of the 1991 season after suffering torn ligaments and cartilage in his left knee. He is probably the most dangerous and exciting quarterback in the NFL because of his passing and running skills (although Steve Young might give him a run for the money). Cunningham has rushed for over 500 yards every season in which he has been healthy — including 942 yards in '90 — and last season he moved ahead of Fran Tarkenton on the all-time rushing list for quarterbacks. In 1990, Cunningham accounted for 35 touchdowns (30 passing and five rushing), which was 73 percent of the team's total of 48 TD's, for the best season of his career. Teams try to contain Cunningham, but he can get away from a rush and he excels at throwing on the run, even deep. Because he is able to score both passing and running, he is extremely valuable in fantasy football (28 career rushing TD's). Don't be surprised if he throws for 25 TD's again this season and runs for five more.

JIM KELLY / BILLS

YEAR	ATT.	CMP.	PCT.	YDS.	TD	INT.	TD-R
1988	454	269	59.5	3380	15	17	0
1989	391	228	58.3	3130	25	18	2
1990	346	219	63.3	2829	24	9	0
1991	474	304	64.1	3844	33	17	1
1992	462	269	58.2	3457	23	19	1

Comments: Forget that the Bills have lost three straight Super Bowls — they have gotten there because of Kelly, one of the top quarterbacks in the league. He has averaged 26 TD passes a year the past four seasons, in which time he has been selected to the Pro Bowl every year. Only the second Bill to pass for over 20,000 yards, Kelly threw for 403 yards against San Francisco and had three consecutive 300-yard games early in the year. However, down the stretch when it counted, Kelly slipped, as he threw only five touchdowns in the last seven games (he also threw just one TD in the two postseason games in which he played). Still, Kelly tied for third in TD passes and has to be considered one of the top few quarterbacks for fantasy football. He missed the first two playoff games with a sprained knee. He runs a balanced offense and has several top receivers to throw to. He was the top-rated passer in the AFC in 1990 and the NFL in '91. His 33 TD passes in 1991 led the league, and he tossed six TD's in one game and five in another. He also set team single-season records for completions, completion percentage, yards passing, TD passes and 300-yard games. His career completion percentage is second all-time to Joe Montana. Kelly has the arm strength to throw deep and the touch to throw short. It's his ability to read defenses that is the key to his success. If teams give Kelly time to throw, he'll kill them, especially when he's throwing deep. He is the toughest quarterback in the NFL both mentally and physically. Kelly didn't play very well in the last two Super Bowls, but for an entire season, he can be counted upon for big numbers.

CAN'T MISS

TROY AIKMAN / Cowboys

Year	Att.	Cmp.	Pct.	Yds.	TD	Int.	TD-R
1989	293	155	52.9	1749	9	18	0
1990	399	226	56.6	2579	11	18	1
1991	363	237	65.3	2754	11	10	1
1992	473	302	63.8	3445	23	14	1

Comments: Aikman was the Most Valuable Player in last season's Super Bowl and one of the top quarterbacks throughout the year. He had his best season in four years as a pro, throwing more touchdown passes than in the two previous seasons combined (not including the four he threw in Super Bowl XXVII). The top pick in the 1989 NFL draft, Aikman was the third-ranked passer in the NFC. He led the conference in completions and was second in yardage and TD passes. His yardage total was fourth in Cowboys history. An extremely accurate passer (fourth on the NFL's all-time list), Aikman is 24-9 in his last 33 starts. During that time he has thrown 40 TD passes and only 28 interceptions. He didn't have a 300-yard game during the 1992 regular season, but he did have eight games with two or more TD passes. Because of too many interceptions early in his career, Aikman still has a negative touchdown-interception ratio of 54-58. He also suffered injuries in each of his first three seasons and has to continue proving his durability. Aikman is a dominating quarterback with short-to-long accuracy and a flair for last-minute heroics when they're needed. He is big, strong and tough with a good arm, and he's not afraid to run and take on blockers. He also knows how to pass the ball around to different receivers. Aikman looks like he hasn't reached his peak, so a 30-TD season this year isn't out of the question.

BOBBY HEBERT / Falcons

Year	Att.	Cmp.	Pct.	Yds.	TD	Int.	TD-R
1988	478	280	58.6	3156	20	15	0
1989	353	222	62.9	2686	15	15	0
1990	Holdout						
1991	248	149	60.1	1676	9	8	0
1992	422	249	59.0	3287	19	16	0

Comments: Hebert was released by the Saints in mid-April and signed shortly afterward by Atlanta. He ran a ball-control offense with the Saints, but now will be able to open it up wih the Falcons (he was considered a long-ball passer in the USFL). In 1992, Hebert set a career high in passing yards and ranked sixth in the NFL in touchdown passes. He was consistent, throwing TD passes in 12 games, with two 300-yard games (the third and fourth of his career) and an average of over 200 yards per game. After holding out and missing the entire 1990 season, Hebert regained his starting job at the beginning of the 1991 season, although a separated shoulder and bruised rotator cuff caused him to miss seven starts. Hebert is a gambler. He'd prefer to go downtown but is exceptional on intermediate passes and especially good against man-to-man coverage because he knows how to find open receivers. He had a 46-20 record as the Saints' starting quarterback, although he has the reputation as a streak player. Because of his durability, he could be an even better pick than Miller was the last few years.

BRETT FAVRE / Packers

Year	Att.	Cmp.	Pct.	Yds.	TD	Int.	TD-R
1991	5	0	0.0	0	0	2	0
1992	471	302	64.1	3227	18	13	1

Comments: Favre became the youngest quarterback ever to play in a Pro Bowl last year. As a rookie in Atlanta in 1991, he was considered overweight and a little irresponsible before being traded to Green Bay for a first-round draft choice during the offseason. His first blessing was going to the Packers, where Mike Holmgren knows a lot about quarterbacks, and his second blessing was having Sterling Sharpe waiting for him. He replaced Don Majkowski as the starter in Game Four and quickly became the NFL's newest young star at quarterback. By the end of the season, Favre had accumulated an impressive list of accomplishments. He tied Troy Aikman for the second-most completions in the league (302), posted the fourth-highest passing percentage (64.1, breaking Bart Starr's team record) and had the second-lowest interception percentage (13 in 471 passes). He ranked sixth in the NFL in pass rating and eighth in yardage. He set a Packers record by throwing for 200 yards in 11 games, became only the fourth Packer to pass for over 3,000 yards in a season and became the second Packer to complete 300 passes in a season. He didn't have a 300-yard game but did throw TD passes in 11 outings. The third quarterback chosen in the '91 draft, Favre saw action in only one game as a rookie, throwing five passes with no completions but two interceptions. He has a quick release and a rifle arm, although he's young and sometimes thinks he can beat any cornerback. He's a real competitor who could be the next Boomer Esiason or Neil Lomax, second-rounders who became very good quarterbacks. Time will tell, but, for now, he is already one of the league's top 10 passers.

JIM EVERETT / RAMS

YEAR	ATT.	CMP.	PCT.	YDS.	TD	INT.	TD-R
1988	517	308	59.6	3964	31	18	0
1989	518	304	58.7	4310	29	17	1
1990	554	307	55.4	3989	23	17	1
1991	490	277	56.5	3438	11	20	0
1992	475	281	59.2	3323	22	18	0

Comments: Everett had a fine comeback season in 1992 and should again be considered one of the top 10 quarterbacks in fantasy football. He passed for 22 touchdowns, and his pass rating was his highest since 1989. He had 11 more interceptions and two fewer touchdowns than his 1991 totals. He has five consecutive 3,000-yard seasons, the fourth-longest streak in NFL history. He threw TD passes in 13 games, with one 300-yard outing. Everett was pretty bad in 1991, throwing less than half the number of touchdown passes he had the previous three seasons and ranking 14th in the NFC. Everett enters 1993 118 yards shy of eclipsing Roman Gabriel's team record of 22,223 career passing yards. With 21 TD passes, he'll break another of Gabriel's records. There's no reason he can't throw 25 touchdown passes again (he led the NFL in TD passes in 1988 and '89). He doesn't throw the long ball as much as he used to, and he still gets into trouble when he reverts back to bad habits, such as throwing sidearm and off his back foot. But with Ted Tollner returning as his quarterback coach, bad habits are likely to be corrected quickly. Look for Everett to prove that he still has a lot left, because the Rams are turning it around under Chuck Knox. With protection, Everett can be very good.

MARK RYPIEN / REDSKINS

YEAR	ATT.	CMP.	PCT.	YDS.	TD	INT.	TD-R
1988	208	114	54.8	1730	18	13	1
1989	476	280	58.8	3768	22	13	1
1990	304	166	54.6	2070	16	11	0
1991	421	249	59.1	3564	28	11	1
1992	479	269	56.2	3282	13	17	2

Comments: Following a long training camp holdout last season, Rypien suffered through a nightmarish season, declining from the Super Bowl Most Valuable Player to the NFC's lowest-rated passer. He had his worst year ever, throwing for a career low in touchdowns and a career high in interceptions. He maintains he did not have an arm problem, although he did undergo minor arthroscopic surgery on his right shoulder in late February after complaining of soreness in the playoffs. Rypien was one of only eight quarterbacks who started all 16 games last year. He threw TD passes in 10 games, but more than one only three times. He didn't have any 300-yard games. In 1991, for one season at least, Rypien buried his reputation as a hot-and-cold streak passer. He led the Redskins to a 17-2 record and the Super Bowl championship. He was second in the league in passing, and he led the NFC in TD passes (28, the second most in Redskins history) and passing yards (3,564). Rypien's signature is the bomb, and some used to call him the finest deep passer in the league. He feeds off the Redskins' running threat, and he should put up big numbers because he throws to some good receivers, but he'll be hurt by the loss of Gary Clark to Phoenix. He is a stand-tall, pocket passer with poise and accuracy, and he can throw all the passes in the playbook. He is 46-22 as a starter, including playoffs. He will probably get some competition as the starter this season from Cary Conklin, though Rypien's experience will help him. But don't be surprised if he doesn't hold on to the job all year, because new head coach Richie Petitbon will be more prone to replacing Rypien if he has a slump.

QUESTION MARKS

JOE MONTANA / CHIEFS

YEAR	ATT.	CMP.	PCT.	YDS.	TD	INT.	TD-R
1988	397	238	59.9	2981	18	10	3
1989	386	271	70.2	3521	26	8	3
1990	520	321	61.7	3944	26	16	1
1991	Injured						
1992	21	15	71.4	126	2	0	0

Comments: Montana was traded to Kansas City in April, and is now that team's hope for a trip to the Super Bowl. He is supposed to be 100 percent healthy, which would seem to mean he still has what it takes to lead a team all the way. But the Chiefs' supporting cast is nowhere near as good as the one Montana had with the 49ers. After missing almost two complete seasons, he played in only the last game of '92 in one of the most anticipated moments of the season. He completed 15 of 21 passes for 126 yards and two TD's. He missed the entire 1991 season because of an injured right elbow. Montana might be the best quarterback in NFL history, and he's certainly the best of the last 25 years. In 1990, Montana carried the 49ers because they didn't have much of a running game, and he set a team record for yards passing. In one game alone he passed for 476 yards and six touchdowns. He already has four Super Bowl rings and wants a fifth, and he doesn't care if it's not with San Francisco. As a passer, Montana looks at all of his primary and secondary receivers, and he can move around. And, after 12 seasons, his touch seemed to be better than ever. He has thrown 244 touchdown passes and only 123 interceptions, an incredible 2-to-1 ratio. His arm is still good, although he rarely has to throw the ball very far to get big results. Montana is the master of the two-minute drill and the play-action pass. Although he's now 37, he can still move (three runs for 28 yards against Detroit last December). If you need a quarterback for one game, Montana is the guy; for one fantasy season, he might still be a very good early pick. See how he is playing during the preseason to determine whether or not to draft him.

CHRIS MILLER / FALCONS

YEAR	ATT.	CMP.	PCT.	YDS.	TD	INT.	TD-R
1988	351	184	52.4	2133	11	12	1
1989	526	280	53.2	3459	16	10	0
1990	388	222	57.2	2735	17	14	1
1991	413	220	53.3	3103	26	18	0
1992	253	152	60.1	1739	15	6	0

Comments: Miller was well on his way to a second straight Pro Bowl invitation when he was co-leading the NFL at the halfway point with 15 touchdown passes and only six interceptions. However, he tore a knee ligament in Game 8. He missed the remainder of the season, and his health is still in doubt heading into 1993. And that is why the Falcons signed Bobby Hebert in the offseason, which could leave Miller as the backup unless he is traded. Miller's 90.7 pass rating in 1992 ranked second in the NFL behind Steve Young, as was his 5.9 TD pass rate. He threw at least one scoring pass in every game he played, including four in a contest against the Bears. In the last four seasons, Miller has thrown 26 more TD's than interceptions (74-48) in passing for over 11,000 yards. In 1991, over the last nine weeks of the season, Miller threw 20 TD's and only six interceptions. That year he ranked third in the NFL in TD passes behind Jim Kelly and Mark Rypien, the two Super Bowl quarterbacks. He has thrown 15 or more TD passes four straight years, and he's one of the most accurate passers as far as not throwing many interceptions. With receivers like Andre Rison and Michael Haynes on the receiving end, Miller is always going to be one of the top eight picks at quarterback in any fantasy football league — if he starts. He excels in the short- and mid-range passes — only eight of his 41 TD passes the last two years have been 40 yards or more. He also has a lot of mobility, although he doesn't score on the ground himself very often, and he can make plays on his own. A more balanced offense (i.e., the running game) would help Miller immensely. And, if he can ever stay healthy a season or two, he'll be grouped among the elite of NFL passers.

SOLID PICKS

JOHN ELWAY/ BRONCOS

YEAR	ATT.	CMP.	PCT.	YDS.	TD	INT.	TD-R
1988	496	274	55.2	3309	17	19	1
1989	416	223	53.6	3051	18	18	3
1990	502	294	58.6	3526	15	14	3
1991	451	242	53.7	3253	13	12	6
1992	316	174	55.1	2242	10	17	2

Comments: OK, so what if Elway is now the highest-paid player in the NFL? He's still not a very good quarterback in fantasy football. He has thrown as many as 19 touchdown passes only once in his career, and that was six years ago. Elway's statistics don't come close to those of Marino, Kelly or Cunningham, so don't be fooled by his great talents. In 1991, Elway finished eighth in the AFC in passing, about where he usually is. But he had a very bad touchdown-interception ratio of 10-17. He missed Games 11-14 because of a bruised right shoulder, which is an indication of how good he is because Denver lost all four of those games. He had one 300-yard game last year, but he also had two with less than 100 yards. He had thrown for more than 3,000 yards and rushed for over 200 yards eight straight seasons before 1992. He passed the 30,000-yard career passing mark. He is durable, having not missed more than one game in nine years until 1992, and his career rushing yardage ranks eighth all-time among quarterbacks. The Broncos' miracle-maker, he has 17 come-from-behind victories in the final three minutes of games as a pro. Elway, who is also the NFL's winningest quarterback from 1984 to 1992, has great mobility, a cannon arm and quick release, and he's a great leader and big-play maker. He can escape the rush and throw on the run, but he has trouble in the pocket when he throws early and forces the ball. In 1991, his six rushing touchdowns were a career high, leading the team and all NFL quarterbacks.

STAN HUMPHRIES / CHARGERS

YEAR	ATT.	CMP.	PCT.	YDS.	TD	INT.	TD-R
1989	10	5	50.0	91	1	1	0
1990	156	91	58.3	1015	3	10	2
1991	None						
1992	454	263	57.9	3356	16	18	4

Comments: Humphries went from third string in Washington to first string and the playoffs in San Diego in 1992. He replaced Bob Gagliano in the season opener and led the Chargers to 11 victories in the last 12 games. That followed an 0-4 start in which he was overweight and out of shape. He also ranked dead last in the NFL in passing after four weeks with eight interceptions and only one TD pass. Then he got hot — hot enough to be selected as the first alternate to the Pro Bowl. His 3,356 yards (third in the AFC and fifth in the NFL) last year were the most by a Chargers quarterback since Dan Fouts in 1985. He threw TD passes in nine consecutive games and 11 overall, with two TD's in five of them. He suffered a dislocated shoulder in the final game but played with special padding in the playoffs. He underwent arthroscopic surgery in January, and is expected to be 100 percent this year. Humphries has a 15-6 record as an NFL starter. Once considered the Redskins' quarterback of the future, Humphries will be the incumbent in '93 in San Diego, although John Friesz will get an opportunity to win his starting job back. Humphries started five games for the Redskins in 1990 when Mark Rypien was injured, but was unable to hold on to the job after throwing 10 interceptions and only three touchdowns. He didn't take another snap until being traded to the Chargers. Humphries has a big-league arm with a football build. He likes to stay in the pocket, and he can throw long or put zip on the out passes. He's also a good runner, having scored four TD's last year.

BERNIE KOSAR / Browns

Year	Att.	Cmp.	Pct.	Yds.	TD	Int.	TD-R
1988	259	156	60.2	1890	10	7	1
1989	513	303	59.1	3533	18	14	1
1990	423	230	54.4	2562	10	15	0
1991	494	307	62.1	3487	18	9	0
1992	155	103	66.5	1160	8	7	0

Comments: Kosar broke his right ankle twice in 1992 and started only seven games the entire season. The first break came in Game 2 while he was leading the Browns to a comeback against Miami on Monday Night Football. He missed nine games, came back to start the final five, and then re-broke the same ankle in the season finale. He played well while he was in the lineup, with eight TD passes in only 155 attempts, a fine 5.2 percentage (two TD passes in four different starts). It seems like Kosar always gets injured in an even-numbered year (strained elbow ligaments in 1988 and broken thumb in 1990), which could mean he'll play all 16 games in '93. When he plays a full season, Kosar averages 18 TD passes a year. The slow-footed Kosar has taken a pounding in recent seasons. He has an accurate intermediate passing touch and brilliant ability to read defenses and audible at the line. He has won despite a bad offensive line and receivers that are average at best. In 1991, he threw 308 consecutive passes without an interception, breaking Bart Starr's league record, and was the AFC's second-ranked passer. He's a good pick for a backup quarterback in fantasy football, and when he's healthy, he is worth a fantasy start on occasion.

BEST OF THE REST

JIM McMAHON / Vikings

Year	Att.	Cmp.	Pct.	Yds.	TD	Int.	TD-R
1988	192	114	59.4	1346	6	7	4
1989	318	176	55.3	2132	10	10	0
1990	9	6	66.7	63	0	0	0
1991	311	187	60.1	2239	12	11	1
1992	43	22	51.2	279	1	2	0

Comments: McMahon signed with the Vikings as a free agent in late March and will be their starter as long as he can stay healthy. If that's the case, he could be one of the best starting quarterbacks in the league … but everyone knows he gets injured too much (and the Vikings did lose two starting linemen during the offseason). McMahon is certainly a winner, and he was tired of sitting on the bench the last three years. Last season he replaced Randall Cunningham in Game 8 and started the next week in a victory over the Raiders before Cunningham took over again. He was 8-3 as a starter in 1991 when Cunningham was injured, and he was named the Comeback Player in the NFL. He played his best football in several seasons and averaged 231 yards passing in the first four games. His record as a starter in the

NFL is 61-28. When he's on, McMahon can make things happen like few quarterbacks, although his mobility has slowed. He has a great feel for the game, good mobility and a decent arm for the short to intermediate passes.

NEIL O'DONNELL / Steelers

Year	Att.	Cmp.	Pct.	Yds.	TD	Int.	TD-R
1990	DNP						
1991	286	156	54.5	1963	11	7	1
1992	313	185	59.1	2283	13	9	1

Comments: O'Donnell was the AFC's third-ranked passer despite missing the last three games (with a broken right leg) and four overall. He returned in time for the playoffs. He broke three team records in 1992 — completion percentage, career completion and career pass rating. Two of those records had been held by Terry Bradshaw, and he became the first Pittsburgh quarterback since Bradshaw to be selected to the Pro Bowl. Last year, O'Donnell threw 12 touchdown passes in the first 10 games but did not have any 300-yard games, as the Pittsburgh offense basically consisted of Barry Foster left and Barry Foster right. He was 9-3 as the starter. O'Donnell got the starting job the second half of 1991 when he replaced Bubby Brister and led Pittsburgh to a 2-6 record. He ranked seventh in the AFC in passing that season, but his seven interceptions tied for the conference low. O'Donnell is big and strong on the difficult sideline patterns. Considered a rising star, he is a big-play quarterback with size, toughness, a good arm and fine mobility. If he could toss a few more TD passes, he would move up in the fantasy rankings.

PHIL SIMMS / Giants

Year	Att.	Cmp.	Pct.	Yds.	TD	Int.	TD-R
1988	479	263	54.9	3359	21	11	0
1989	405	228	56.3	3061	14	14	1
1990	311	184	59.2	2284	15	4	1
1991	141	82	58.2	993	8	4	1
1992	137	83	60.6	912	5	3	0

Comments: Simms has already been named the Giants' starter for 1993. New head coach Dan Reeves wants him to play for two years while tutoring Dave Brown before retiring (and perhaps becoming the team's QB coach). In 1992, Simms added to virtually all of the team's passing marks that he had already possessed. He started only the first four games before suffering an elbow injury and being sidelined the rest of the year (although he could have come back in December). He threw for an average of 228 yards per game, with five touchdown passes — not bad for somebody who was 36 at the time. In 1991, in limited time, Simms lost his starting job but actually outplayed Jeff Hostetler, who had taken over for him in December 1990 and led the Giants to the Super Bowl. Simms had led the Giants to a 10-0 start that year, and he was the top-rated passer in the NFC, throwing only four interceptions.

Simms is still tough and has a good touch, but he's not very mobile. He is adept at reading defenses, poised in the pocket and can move an offense in a disciplined manner. In other words, he's the perfect teacher for Brown. Simms is not a very good pick for fantasy football, but he might surprise some people with how he performs this year.

JIM HARBAUGH / Bears

Year	Att.	Cmp.	Pct.	Yds.	TD	Int.	TD-R
1988	97	47	48.5	514	0	2	1
1989	178	111	62.4	1204	5	9	3
1990	312	180	57.7	2178	10	6	4
1991	478	275	57.5	3121	15	16	2
1992	358	202	56.4	2486	13	12	1

Comments: After two years of progress, Harbaugh slipped in 1992 and was benched for three games near the end of the season. He threw for only 13 touchdowns and ran for just one. He also threw just four TD passes in the last 10 games. He did tie a team record with 13 consecutive completions in one game, and his interception percentage is the lowest of any Bears quarterback in history. In 1991, Harbaugh became the first Bears quarterback to start every game since 1981. He set team records in attempts (478, second most in the NFC) and completions (275) as the Bears switched from a running game to a passing attack. He was also 55 yards short of the club record for most yards in a season. Harbaugh is 28-22 as a starter. His reputation is that he throws winners through heavy traffic, then breaks your heart with a mistake. Harbaugh is a tough, gutsy, get-it-done player who has established himself as a team leader. He's very accurate, but he's not good on the deep pass and he still tends to lock on to his primary receiver for too long. He also doesn't throw very many touchdown passes because the Bears tend to run the ball from in close. Harbaugh is a very good runner, and, for that reason, he's not a bad late pick for a backup quarterback in fantasy football. The new offense being installed by Dave Wannstedt also seems to be suited more to his abilities.

STEVE BEUERLEIN / Cardinals

Year	Att.	Cmp.	Pct.	Yds.	TD	Int.	TD-R
1988	238	105	44.1	1643	8	7	0
1989	217	108	49.8	1677	13	9	0
1990	DNP						
1991	137	68	49.6	909	5	2	0
1992	18	12	66.7	152	0	1	0

Comments: Beuerlein was the hottest free-agent quarterback during the offseason before signing with Phoenix. He didn't play much in '92 as Troy Aikman led Dallas to the Super Bowl. But, in 1991, the year Dallas "stole" him from the Raiders for a fourth-round draft pick, he paid big dividends by taking over when Aikman was injured and leading them to the playoffs (he started four regular-season games and both playoff contests). Although Beuerlein

threw only five touchdown passes (one in each of his first five starts), he didn't throw an interception in his first five and a half games and only two overall. As a Raider in 1990, he didn't suit up for any games because Raiders owner Al Davis wanted to punish him for a contract holdout. Beuerlein is an accurate passer who doesn't make mistakes and has leadership abilities. While he lacks a strong arm, he can go deep and he possesses a deft touch on intermediate throws. With what appears to be a very good offense in Phoenix, Beuerlein could have a very good season.

COULD COME ON

JEFF GEORGE / Colts

Year	Att.	Cmp.	Pct.	Yds.	TD	Int.	TD-R
1990	334	181	54.2	2152	16	13	1
1991	485	292	60.2	2910	10	12	0
1992	306	167	54.6	1963	7	15	1

Comments: George will start the 1993 season as the Colts' starting quarterback, but if he falters, don't be surprised if Jack Trudeau gets the call. George had the worst season of his three-year career in 1992. He missed the first three games of the season with a torn ligament in his right thumb and three more in November and December with a broken hand, and the two injuries hampered him even when he did play. He had a 6-4 record as a starter and is 12-26 for his career. He had three 300-yard games and three two-TD games, but he failed to throw a scoring pass in six of his 12 starts. In fact, in the last two seasons, he has thrown only one more TD pass than he did as a rookie in 1990. The No. 1 pick in the 1990 draft, George was compared to Dan Marino early in his career, but he has some proving to do at this point. In 1991, George established career seasonal highs in completions, attempts (both of which are also team records) and yards. Since the 1970 merger, only seven quarterbacks (including Troy Aikman, John Elway and Terry Bradshaw) have been drafted first overall, and George has the best touchdown-interception ratio of all of them. He ranks fifth in Colts career passing yardage and attempts and fourth in completions. In 1993, George has to start showing people if his rookie season was just a fluke or if he can move up a level among NFL passers. His durability is also in question. Still, he has the potential to be a future superstar, because he has a strong arm, lightning-quick release and he throws a very catchable ball with unbelievable accuracy, especially deep. Lack of mobility is George's biggest weakness, although he has to learn to read defenses better and learn how to take a pounding.

BOOMER ESIASON / JETS

YEAR	ATT.	CMP.	PCT.	YDS.	TD	INT.	TD-R
1988	388	223	57.5	3572	28	14	1
1989	455	258	56.7	3525	28	11	0
1990	402	224	55.7	2931	24	22	0
1991	413	233	56.4	2883	13	16	0
1992	278	144	51.8	1407	11	15	0

Comments: Esiason was traded to the Jets March 17 and will either push Browning Nagle for the starting quarterback job or just take it away and maybe even lead New York to the playoffs. In his final season with the Bengals in 1992, Esiason had the worst year of his career, throwing for the fewest yards and touchdowns since he was a rookie in 1984. Esiason still has all the talent he had before his slump, but last year he seemed to lose the decision-making he used to have. Too many times he forced bad passes or made dumb calls, which was one reason he was replaced by David Klingler late in the season. He started 11 games. His high game was only 192 yards, but he did have two three-TD outings. But Esiason is only 32 years old, so he still has lots of time. He has thrown more than 20 TD's five times during his career. He ranked only 11th in the AFC in passing each of the last two seasons, and he has thrown more interceptions than TD's the last three years. He was hampered by injuries in 1990 and '91, and he led the conference in passing in 1988 and '89. In New York, he is reunited with Bruce Coslet, who was his offensive coordinator in Cincinnati. Esiason is a tough, cocky leader who can throw any pass in the book and buy time with his feet. He's a solid play-action passer, and he can turn busted plays into big plays. Does he still have it? This season will give the answer.

JEFF HOSTETLER / RAIDERS

YEAR	ATT.	CMP.	PCT.	YDS.	TD	INT.	TD-R
1988	29	16	55.2	244	1	2	0
1989	39	20	51.3	294	3	2	2
1990	87	47	54.0	614	3	1	2
1991	285	179	62.8	2032	5	4	2
1992	192	103	53.6	1225	8	3	3

Comments: Hostetler signed with the Raiders as a free agent in late March and will probably be their starter when September rolls around. He doesn't fit the team's vertical passing game as well as Jay Schroeder did, but Hostetler is probably more consistent and could lead it to the playoffs if he stays healthy. Less than two years removed from leading the Giants to a Super Bowl championship, Hostetler became the odd man out in New York when Phil Simms was named the 1993 starter. He was the success story of the NFL in 1990, going from backup to the winning quarterback in the Super Bowl. But in 1991, his first season as the full-time starter, he wasn't very impressive. He threw only five touchdown passes in 12 games before he broke three bones in his back and was placed on injured reserve (he was 7-0 as a starter before then). Hostetler began 1992 as Simms' backup, then took over in Game 4. He started seven times, then missed a month with a concussion before coming back to start the final two. His best game was in the season-ender, when he threw for 202 yards, but he also had two games with under 100 yards passing. Since the Super Bowl, Hostetler has a 12-9 record. He has run for nine TD's in the last four seasons. A high-completion passer, Hostetler threw only three interceptions in '92. He is a scrambler with a better arm than his critics say. However, unless he wants to look back at Super Bowl XXV as the highlight of his career, he had better start proving again what he can do.

COULD COME ON

WADE WILSON / SAINTS

YEAR	ATT.	CMP.	PCT.	YDS.	TD	INT.	TD-R
1988	332	204	61.4	2746	15	9	2
1989	362	194	53.6	2543	9	12	1
1990	146	82	56.2	1155	9	8	0
1991	122	72	59.0	825	3	10	0
1992	163	111	68.1	1368	13	4	0

Comments: Wilson signed with New Orleans as a free agent on April 12 and was being considered the team's starter at the time. He was the hottest quarterback in the NFL over the last three games of last season for Atlanta. He threw for over 1,000 yards and 10 touchdown passes in those three weeks, including five TD's against Tampa Bay (the season high for any quarterback) and 300-yard games in every start. They were his only starts of the season. With the Vikings in 1991, Wilson got off to a horrible start and lost his job to Rich Gannon after five games in which he had thrown 10 interceptions. He took only one snap the rest of the season. Wilson led the NFL in passing in 1988, but he's been downhill since then, except for the three-game stretch last season. He has a good arm, and he throws the intermediate routes well and can go deep. He's also a good runner, but he's not a student of the game and he can't make things happen. The 34-year-old Wilson, who has started only 51 games in 12 seasons, would be better as a backup. He'll get challenged by Mike Buck and Steve Walsh this season.

RODNEY PEETE / LIONS

YEAR	ATT.	CMP.	PCT.	YDS.	TD	INT.	TD-R
1989	195	103	52.8	1479	5	9	4
1990	271	142	52.4	1974	13	8	6
1991	194	116	59.8	1339	5	9	2
1992	213	123	57.7	1702	9	9	0

Comments: Peete is still unable to start an entire season for the Lions. Last year he started the first nine games and a 10th later on, but he was 2-8 as the No. 1 man. He will be the starter going into this season, but Andre Ware looked good in the final three games and will challenge for the starting job in training camp. Peete threw TD passes in six of the first seven games, with two in one game and three in another. But he too often failed to get the team into the end zone. He averaged only 170 yards per start. In 1991, he started the first eight games before tearing his Achilles tendon and missing the remainder of the season. His best year was in 1990 when threw 13 TD passes and ran for six touchdowns. Knee and hamstring injuries hampered him much of his first two seasons. Peete is a threat both running and passing. He's a very good athlete who can scramble away from defenders, but he seems to have more trouble with short- and medium-range passes than with the deep ball, even though he lacks arm strength. Streaky is the best word to describe him.

CHRIS CHANDLER / Cardinals

Year	Att.	Cmp.	Pct.	Yds.	TD	Int.	TD-R
1988	233	129	55.4	1619	8	12	3
1989	80	39	48.8	537	2	3	1
1990	83	42	50.6	464	1	6	1
1991	154	78	50.6	846	5	10	0
1992	413	245	59.3	2832	15	15	1

Comments: After Timm Rosenbach was injured in the second game of last season, Chandler took over and held the job the final 14 games, missing just one game with a rib injury. In that time, Chandler, a two-team castoff, seemed to have taken his game to a new level. He posted career highs in virtually every offensive category: pass attempts, completions, yards passing, completion percentage, touchdown passes and yard rushing. He engineered the Cardinals' upset victory over the Redskins. He threw seven TD passes in his first five games, but then tailed off with just four in the second half of the season. Chandler split the 1991 season in Tampa Bay and Phoenix, mostly as a backup. He was 0-6 as a starter in two years with the Buccaneers (he had cost the Bucs the No. 2 pick in the '92 draft when he was acquired). He started the last two games of '91 for Phoenix after being acquired on waivers. Chandler has a good arm, and he believes it can beat any coverage. He cut down on his interceptions last year, but still has thrown too many (31 TD's vs. 46 interceptions over his career). Chandler has lots of physical ability, but he holds on to the ball too long and struggles reading coverages. He is most effective when the running game is clicking and he can keep defenses honest with play-action passes. Steve Beuerlein will probably be the starter in 1993, although Chandler said he was going to fight for the job.

ROOKIES

See Chapter 13, The Rookie Report.

KEEP AN EYE ON

DAVID KLINGLER / Bengals

Year	Att.	Cmp.	Pct.	Yds.	TD	Int.	TD-R
1992	98	47	48.0	530	3	2	0

Comments: With Boomer Esiason gone in an offseason trade with the Jets, Klingler is now — for better or for worse — the No. 1 quarterback of the Bengals. As a rookie first-round draft choice last year, he was named to start the rest of the season before Game 12. He did miss the season finale with a hip pointer and a slight concussion. In his NFL debut against the Steelers, he lost more yards on sacks (72) than he gained on passing (68). His performances in all four games bordered on mediocre — he didn't complete 50 percent of his passes in any game — but he did throw only two interceptions. Klingler has a gun for an arm, unloads the ball on the move and scrambles for big plays. He needs to improve his mechanics, but he'll have lots of time to do that in 1993.

ANDRE WARE / Lions

Year	Att.	Cmp.	Pct.	Yds.	TD	Int.	TD-R
1990	30	13	43.3	164	1	2	0
1991	None						
1992	86	50	58.1	677	3	4	0

Comments: Ware started the last three games of 1992 and actually played the best football of his three-year career. He threw two TD's in his first start and passed for 290 starts in the next game, both victories. The 1989 Heisman Trophy winner looked like a bust his first two seasons. In 1992, he played in only one game, strictly mop-up duty. He started one game in '90 but was benched after throwing two interceptions in the first half. Ware has lots of talent, intelligence and running speed, as well as the strongest arm of the team's three quarterbacks. He improved his accuracy greatly last season and should compete with Rodney Peete for the starting job in this year's training camp.

THE BACKUPS

DAVE KRIEG / Chiefs

Year	Att.	Cmp.	Pct.	Yds.	TD	Int.	TD-R
1988	228	134	58.8	1741	18	8	0
1989	499	286	57.3	3309	21	20	0
1990	448	265	59.2	3194	15	20	0
1991	285	187	65.6	2080	11	12	0
1992	413	230	55.7	3115	15	12	2

Comments: Krieg was the only quarterback to throw all of his team's passes last season, but the addition of Joe

Montana has sent him to the bench for 1993. After joining the team as a Plan B free agent, he finished as the AFC's sixth-rated passer in '92, leading the conference in yards per attempt and ending with the fifth 3,000-yard season of his career (and only third ever for a Chiefs quarterback). On the all-time passing lists, Krieg ranks ninth in rating, 19th in yards and 12th in touchdowns. He brought the long ball back to Kansas City, as he was the only NFL quarterback last season with three TD passes of 70 yards or more. He had two 300-yard games and even ran for two TD's. From 1983 to '89, only Dan Marino threw more touchdown passes than Krieg, but those numbers have dipped the last three seasons. Krieg is a notorious up-and-downer who plays like a Pro Bowler on certain Sundays and can't even hold on to the ball on others (he has fumbled more than any player in NFL history). But he has excellent poise under pressure and could lead the Chiefs far into the playoffs with the help of a running game and a little luck if something happened to Montana.

VINNY TESTAVERDE / Browns

Year	Att.	Cmp.	Pct.	Yds.	TD	Int.	TD-R
1988	466	222	47.6	3240	13	35	1
1989	480	258	53.8	3133	20	22	0
1990	365	203	55.6	2818	17	18	1
1991	326	166	50.9	1994	8	15	0
1992	358	206	57.5	2554	14	16	2

Comments: Testaverde signed with Cleveland as a free agent on March 31 and will back up former Miami (Fla.) teammate Bernie Kosar in 1993. He was the starter in Tampa Bay most of the '92 season, starting 14 games but ranking only 10th in the NFC in passing. He was even benched for Games 8 and 9 before regaining his starting job. He threw TD passes in 11 games, but more than one only three times and never more than two. Testaverde has never thrown more touchdowns than interceptions in any of his six seasons. He had his worst season ever in 1991, and was in and out of the lineup like a yo-yo (starting in three different stints). Testaverde is 23-45 as a starter, while the Bucs are 1-11 in games he has not started since 1987. He is close to the physical prototype of an NFL quarterback, but if he gets rattled early in a game he gets thrown off his rhythm. He can throw the deep ball as well as any passer in the league, but he too often does so with too little arc on the ball, and he lacks the football smarts to be a great thinking man's quarterback (his 35 interceptions in 1988 are an NFL record). He's a good runner, but for some reason he doesn't run much. Testaverde might be one of the classic busts in pro football, but some people feel with a good QB coach he could still develop into a top quarterback. But he won't get that opportunity with the Browns as long as Kosar stays healthy.

JAY SCHROEDER / Bengals

Year	Att.	Cmp.	Pct.	Yds.	TD	Int.	TD-R
1988	256	113	44.1	1839	13	13	1
1989	194	91	46.9	1550	8	13	0
1990	334	182	54.5	2849	19	9	0
1991	357	189	52.9	2562	15	16	0
1992	253	123	48.6	1476	11	11	0

Comments: Schroeder was cut by the Raiders after they signed Jeff Hostetler and eventually signed with Cincinnati, where he will back up David Klingler and possibly take over the starting job. He started the first two and last seven games of 1992 in another season in which he was again unable to hold down the starting role. He passed for 380 yards and two TD's in Game 2, but that wasn't enough. For the season, he led the team in passing but ranked only ninth in the AFC. He had two three-TD games, but he also passed for just 93, 93, 25 and 41 yards in the last three games. In five seasons with the Raiders, he has completed exactly 50 percent of his passes — and rookies do better than that these days. Because he's the best vertical passer on the team, Schroeder will contend for the No. 1 role, but Jeff Hostetler is the favorite to take over this year. In 1991, Schroeder started the first 15 games but was benched in favor of Todd Marinovich, then an untested rookie, for the last game and the playoffs. Although he threw for the third-most touchdowns of his seven-year career that year, he also threw his second-most interceptions. Schroeder is capable of thowing for a lot of touchdowns if he can ever play consistently for 16 games. He's a big, strong-armed bomber who gives the Raiders quick-strike ability in the Daryle Lamonica style. He has prototype size and strength, but he makes too many bad reads, tries to force the ball into coverage and lacks accuracy.

RICH GANNON / Vikings

Year	Att.	Cmp.	Pct.	Yds.	TD	Int.	TD-R
1988	15	7	46.7	90	0	0	0
1989	DNP						
1990	349	182	52.1	2278	16	16	1
1991	354	211	59.6	2166	12	6	2
1992	279	159	57.0	1905	12	13	0

Comments: Gannon started the first 11 games last season, then missed four of the next five games and the playoff contest while Sean Salisbury played. As a starter, Gannon was 8-4 (19-16 for his career), but coach Dennis Green wasn't happy with his performance and Gannon most likely will be traded before the 1993 season opens. It was the same story in 1991 when he lost his starting job to Wade Wilson for a time. Gannon has had only three full seasons at quarterback, although he seemed to regress last year. In '91, he threw twice as many touchdowns as interceptions, but last year he was on the negative side. His 318 passing yards and four touchdowns against Cincinnati in September were both career highs, but he had 10 games with less than 200 yards passing. Gannon scares defenses more with his feet than with his arm — he has been the team's third-leading rusher for the last three seasons. In 1991, he threw 156 consecutive passes over seven games without an interception, to break Fran Tarkenton's team record.

CODY CARLSON / Oilers

Year	Att.	Cmp.	Pct.	Yds.	TD	Int.	TD-R
1988	112	52	46.4	775	4	6	1
1989	31	15	48.4	155	0	1	0
1990	55	37	67.3	383	4	2	0
1991	12	7	58.3	114	1	0	0
1992	227	149	65.6	1710	9	11	1

Comments: The highest-paid backup quarterback in pro football history, Carlson started the last six games of last season when Warren Moon was injured before being replaced for the playoffs. He played in five other games. Carlson was 4-2 as a starter, is 7-4 over his career and 0-1 in the playoffs. Although he completed nearly 66 percent of his passes (a team record) in his first really extended action, he threw more interceptions than touchdowns. He had two 300-yard games and threw TD's in five of his starts but never more than one in any of them. Carlson has been one of the NFL's best backup quarterbacks for several years. In 1990, he led the Oilers to a victory over Pittsburgh on 22 of 29 passing in the final game to clinch a playoff spot, but then looked miserable in the playoffs as the Oilers were knocked out. Carlson has a strong arm, poise and leadership, but he lacks consistency. The new contract gives him a lot of money and security to remain the backup, but he's not going to play unless Moon goes down again.

FRANK REICH / Bills

Year	Att.	Cmp.	Pct.	Yds.	TD	Int.	TD-R
1988	None						
1989	87	53	60.9	701	7	2	0
1990	63	36	57.1	469	2	0	0
1991	41	27	65.9	305	6	2	0
1992	47	24	51.1	221	0	2	0

Comments: Reich might not start very many games during his NFL career, but he will always be remembered as the quarterback who led the Bills to their record-setting comeback victory over Houston in last year's AFC playoffs. In that game, he threw four touchdown passes in the second half as Buffalo rallied from 32 points down to defeat Houston. Many people thought Reich should have continued starting throughout the playoffs, but he'll have to be content just being one of the top backup quarterbacks in the NFL because he plays behind Jim Kelly. Reich is a smart, well-prepared player with a quick delivery and good mobility. He has a good arm, and he plays within himself and rarely makes big mistakes. His career numbers show only six regular-season starts (and two playoff games last year), with 15 TD passes and only eight interceptions.

STEVE BONO / 49ers

Year	Att.	Cmp.	Pct.	Yds.	TD	Int.	TD-R
1988	35	10	28.6	110	1	2	0
1989	5	4	80.0	62	1	0	0
1990	DNP						
1991	237	141	59.5	1617	11	4	0
1992	56	36	64.3	463	2	2	0

Comments: A disappointment for the first six years of his career, Bono looked very impressive in six starts in 1991. Last season he backed up Steve Young, and he continued his fine play when needed. He got into six games at quarterback, completing 64 percent of his passes. In '91, Bono led San Francisco to five consecutive victories over the second half of the season. He threw back-to-back 300-yard games and passed for three touchdowns in three straight games. He placed fourth in the NFL passing race. A pure pocket passer with limited mobility, the strong-armed Bono fits the 49ers' system well. He was a journeyman early in his career with both Minnesota and Pittsburgh.

HUGH MILLEN / Cowboys

Year	Att.	Cmp.	Pct.	Yds.	TD	Int.	TD-R
1988	31	17	54.8	215	0	2	0
1989	50	31	62.0	432	1	2	0
1990	63	34	54.0	427	1	0	0
1991	409	246	60.1	3073	9	18	1
1992	203	124	61.1	1203	8	10	0

Comments: Millen was acquired by Dallas in a trade with New England in late April, so he went from starting for the worst team in the NFL to backing up for the best. He started the first five games of 1992, but then he suffered a third-degree shoulder separation and had only two starts the rest of the year. Although the Patriots were 0-7 with Millen as the starter, he was their best passer on the season. In 1991, Millen made the best of his chance as the starter, going 5-8 in 13 games. His 3,073 passing yards marked only the fifth time in team history that a quarterback had hit the 3,000-yard mark, and the first since 1986. His 246 completions were the team's third most, and his 60.1 completion percentage tied him for second on the Patriots' all-time list. Before going to New England, Millen had stints with the Falcons and Rams. He has fine size, a very good arm and decent mobility, but he's not much of a runner and has too many mental lapses during games. He throws far too many interceptions, but at least he gets a TD every now and then. He'll be a good No. 2 man for the Cowboys, but if Troy Aikman gets injured, Millen isn't good enough to get them back to the Super Bowl.

KEN O'BRIEN / PACKERS

YEAR	ATT.	CMP.	PCT.	YDS.	TD	INT.	TD-R
1988	424	236	55.7	2567	15	7	0
1989	477	288	60.4	3346	12	18	0
1990	411	226	55.0	2855	13	10	0
1991	489	287	58.7	3300	10	11	0
1992	98	55	56.1	642	5	6	0

Comments: In the last year, O'Brien lost both his starting and backup jobs with the Jets and then was traded to Green Bay, where he will back up Brett Favre. In 1992, O'Brien went into the season as the backup and tutor to Browning Nagle and started only three games. He missed the last month of the season with a fractured right arm. In limited action, he played better than Nagle, but the veteran had already been phased out of the offense and it didn't matter much. He did show, however, that he could have some very good games. In Week 8 against the Dolphins, O'Brien completed 21 of 29 passes for 240 yards and three TD's. One of the most accurate passers, O'Brien started all 16 games in 1991 and led the Jets to their first playoff appearance since 1986. A prototype dropback passer who can get very hot when he's given time to throw, he has thrown the second-most TD passes in Jets history (behind Joe Namath). His biggest negative is lack of mobility.

JACK TRUDEAU / COLTS

YEAR	ATT.	CMP.	PCT.	YDS.	TD	INT.	TD-R
1988	34	14	41.2	158	0	3	0
1989	362	190	52.5	2317	15	13	2
1990	144	84	58.3	1078	6	6	0
1991	7	2	28.6	19	0	1	0
1992	181	105	58.0	1271	4	8	0

Comments: Trudeau had a fine season last year when he replaced Jeff George for two stints, which was the eighth time he has come off the bench because of injuries to other Colts quarterbacks. Trudeau was 2-3 as a starter last year, and don't be surprised if he gets the call if George has a rough time in September. A training camp holdout last year, Trudeau also needs to learn how to stay healthy himself. He's a polished, physical quarterback, but he doesn't make things happen like George does. He is not very mobile and he lacks a strong arm and gets into trouble when he tries to take chances. But when he's on — like late in the 1989 season when he was named Player of the Week twice in a three-week span — Trudeau can be very good.

STEVE DeBERG / BUCCANEERS

YEAR	ATT.	CMP.	PCT.	YDS.	TD	INT.	TD-R
1988	414	224	54.1	2935	16	16	1
1989	324	196	60.5	2529	11	16	0
1990	444	258	58.1	3444	23	4	0
1991	434	256	59.0	2965	17	14	0
1992	125	76	60.8	710	3	4	0

Comments: Now nearing the end of his career, DeBerg might be the starter again in Tampa Bay because there's not much else on the roster. In 1992, he started Games 8 and 9, winning once and losing once, but then he was sent back to the bench and got back to the field just one time. He is 26-12 in his last 38 starts. DeBerg had a career year in 1990, then crashed in '91 and lost his starting job in Kansas City. Two years ago, he did move into 12th place on the NFL's all-time passing yardage list, and he's seventh for attempts and completions. In 1990, DeBerg threw only four interceptions, and his 0.90 interception percentage was the second-best single-season mark in NFL history. He also had a streak of 223 straight passes without an interception. He's probably still the best play-action passer in pro football. He's excellent at reading defenses and has a good arm with some zip. His biggest drawbacks are that pressure bothers him, he's not willing to stay in the pocket and he doesn't create plays when he's flushed out.

MIKE TOMCZAK / STEELERS

YEAR	ATT.	CMP.	PCT.	YDS.	TD	INT.	TD-R
1988	170	86	50.6	1310	7	6	1
1989	306	156	51.0	2058	16	16	1
1990	104	39	37.5	521	3	5	2
1991	238	128	53.8	1490	11	9	1
1992	211	120	56.9	1693	7	7	0

Comments: Tomczak always seems to be in the right place at the right time. In 1991, he replaced an injured Don Majkowski in Green Bay, and last year he took over for Bernie Kosar and Todd Philcox, Cleveland's two injured quarterbacks. Now with Pittsburgh, he'll man the bench behind Neil O'Donnell. Tomczak started eight games in 1992, going 4-4; in '91 he was 2-5. When he's on, Tomczak is one of the league's better long passers, and he can be dangerous when he doesn't gamble. But he is prone to throwing interceptions. He's a streak passer who forces too many throws into coverage and takes too many needless risks throwing downfield.

JOHN FRIESZ / CHARGERS

YEAR	ATT.	CMP.	PCT.	YDS.	TD	INT.	TD-R
1990	22	11	50.0	98	1	1	0
1991	487	262	53.8	2896	12	15	0
1992	Injured						

Comments: Friesz missed the entire 1992 season after suffering torn ligaments in his knee in the first preseason game. He will be back for '93 but might have lost his starting job to Stan Humphries, who led the Chargers to the playoffs. Friesz had assumed control of the Chargers' starting job in 1991 when he started all 16 games, although he ranked last in passing in the AFC. He did have some good moments that season, including back-to-back 300-yard games. He had three two-TD games, but went five games without a scoring pass in the second half of the season. Friesz started the final game of the 1990 season in place of Billy Joe Tolliver and played well enough to grab the starting job. The 10th quarterback taken in the 1990 draft, Friesz is an accurate passer with great poise and a strong arm. He has very good timing, anticipation and a quick release, and he can sidestep in the pocket, which helps compensate for his lack of speed. But whether or not he gets a chance to show what he can do this season remains to be seen. Chargers fans want Humphries to remain No. 1.

SCOTT MITCHELL / Dolphins

Year	Att.	Cmp.	Pct.	Yds.	TD	Int.	TD-R
1992	8	2	25.0	32	0	1	0

Comments: Mitchell took over as Miami's second-string quarterback last season. He made six appearances at quarterback, twice replacing Dan Marino when Marino was injured for short periods of time. On his first pro play, he came in for Marino and completed an 18-yard pass on 3rd-and-10 in a key situation. Mitchell is a tall lefty with a lot of finesse who might be pretty good if anything ever happens to Marino.

BROWNING NAGLE / Jets

Year	Att.	Cmp.	Pct.	Yds.	TD	Int.	TD-R
1991	2	1	50.0	10	0	0	0
1992	387	192	49.6	2280	7	17	0

Comments: After being handed the starting job last year, Nagle passed for 366 yards in his first pro start. But that was the highlight of his season, as he hit the 200-yard mark only one time the rest of the season. This year, Nagle will be pushed by Boomer Esiason for the starting job, and chances are Nagle will be sent back to the bench to learn for a couple of years. Nagle started 13 games, missing two with injuries. The jury is still out on Nagle, but the Jets believe he can develop into a top quarterback with time. A rifle-armed passer with a quick release and most of the other tools, he needs lots of refinement.

STEVE WALSH / Saints

Year	Att.	Cmp.	Pct.	Yds.	TD	Int.	TD-R
1989	219	110	50.2	1371	5	9	0
1990	336	179	53.3	2010	12	13	0
1991	255	141	55.3	1638	11	6	0
1992	DNP						

Comments: The highest-paid third-string quarterback in the NFL, Walsh didn't see any action last year, suiting up for only two games. With Bobby Hebert gone, he will compete with Wade Wilson and Mike Buck for the starting job this season. Walsh lost his starting job to Bobby Hebert before the start of the 1991 season, but still played in seven games with a 3-4 record. Even though he threw more touchdowns and fewer interceptions than Hebert, he was

banished back to the bench and slipped behind Buck on the depth chart. Walsh started 11 games in 1990 after being acquired by the Saints a month into the season. He led them to a wild-card playoff berth but was ineffective in a loss at Chicago. Walsh is a thinking man's quarterback with great touch and a strong sense of the short game. But his lack of arm strength to throw deep and outside might prohibit him from becoming more than a functional starter. If surrounded by top players, Walsh uses their abilities to enhance his own performance.

SEAN SALISBURY / Vikings

Year	Att.	Cmp.	Pct.	Yds.	TD	Int.	TD-R
1988	Played in CFL						
1989	Played in CFL						
1990	DNP						
1991	DNP						
1992	175	97	55.4	1203	5	2	0

Comments: After a career of not playing and getting cut by team after team, Salisbury moved into the Vikings' starting lineup ahead of Rich Gannon late last season and quarterbacked the Vikings in the playoffs. He had thrown only 12 passes in the NFL before 1992, but coach Dennis Green liked his poise and the effect he had on the team's offense, which had been stagnant under Gannon. In his first start, Salisbury completed 23 of 34 passes for 238 yards. He was 3-1 as a starter and 3-1 in relief of Gannon. He threw only two interceptions in 175 attempts, and his 1.1 interception percentage set a team record and led the league.

MIKE BUCK / Saints

Year	Att.	Cmp.	Pct.	Yds.	TD	Int.	TD-R
1991	2	1	50.0	61	0	1	0
1992	4	2	50.0	10	0	0	0

Comments: Buck was promoted to second string on the Saints' depth chart last season, although he played in only two games. This year, he will compete for the starting job with Wade Wilson and Steve Walsh and might have a good shot at being No. 1 because the coaches like him. The strong-armed Buck has a lot of potential but is very inexperienced.

BUBBY BRISTER / Steelers

Year	Att.	Cmp.	Pct.	Yds.	TD	Int.	TD-R
1988	370	175	47.3	2634	11	14	6
1989	342	187	54.7	2365	9	10	0
1990	387	223	57.6	2725	20	14	0
1991	190	103	54.2	1350	9	9	0
1992	116	63	54.3	719	2	5	0

Comments: Brister started four games in relief of Neil O'Donnell last season, leading the Steelers to a 2-2 record (and he's 28-29 for his career). He had a solid showing in the season finale and thinks he should be the starter, but O'Donnell is the man in Pittsburgh and Mike Tomczak will be No. 2, so Brister will be elsewhere. After having his best season in 1990, Brister lost his starting job for half of 1991 after suffering sprained knee ligaments. He had a better record than O'Donnell but was outperformed as a quarterback. In 1990, Brister's 20 TD passes were the most by a Steeler quarterback since Terry Bradshaw in 1981. He is a top athlete with agility and a rifle arm, but he doesn't always make smart decisions. He loves the deep ball, shrugs off blitzes and can rouse an offense with his toughness. Bad knees limit his mobility.

TOMMY MADDOX / Broncos

Year	Att.	Cmp.	Pct.	Yds.	TD	Int.	TD-R
1992	121	66	54.5	757	5	9	0

Comments: Maddox got a quick indoctrination into pro football last season after coming out of college as a sophomore. He played in 13 games, starting four times. Although the Broncos lost all four of those starts, he did play pretty well, completing nearly 55 percent of his passes. He's a noticeable sidearm passer with good size, a strong arm and decent mobility. Maddox might not be ready to take over yet if John Elway goes down, but he does represent the future for the Broncos. Give him time — he might be a good one.

SCOTT ZOLAK / Patriots

Year	Att.	Cmp.	Pct.	Yds.	TD	Int.	TD-R
1992	100	52	52.0	561	2	4	0

Comments: After losing two quarterbacks and their first nine games, the Patriots were forced to start Zolak in Game 10. Presto! The first-year quarterback led the team to its first victory of the season with a 20-of-29 performance for 267 yards and two touchdowns. A week later he duplicated the feat with another victory, and he quickly became a folk hero in New England. However, two losses followed, and then Zolak suffered an ankle injury, and he, too, was sent to the sidelines. While some of the team's other quarterbacks might have lost their opportunities to start, Zolak will get that chance in the future. He is big and strong-armed but very inexperienced.

MIKE PAGEL / Rams

Year	Att.	Cmp.	Pct.	Yds.	TD	Int.	TD-R
1988	134	71	53.0	736	3	4	0
1989	14	5	35.7	60	1	1	0
1990	148	69	46.6	819	3	8	0
1991	27	11	40.7	150	2	0	0
1992	20	8	40.0	99	1	2	0

Comments: Pagel is a rarely used backup with the Rams. Last season he appeared in all 16 games as the kick holder but threw passes in only two of them. Pagel has a strong arm and good mobility and might be a better athlete than Everett. He's too inconsistent to be a regular, but he's a fine backup.

STAN GELBAUGH / Seahawks

Year	Att.	Cmp.	Pct.	Yds.	TD	Int.	TD-R
1991	118	61	51.7	674	3	10	0
1992	255	121	47.5	1307	6	11	0

Comments: Gelbaugh went from third string to the starter last year. He was Seattle's highest-rated passer and the NFL's lowest-rated passer. He started eight games in two different stints, with a 1-7 record. The Most Valuable Player in the World League during its inaugural season of 1991, Gelbaugh started three games for the Cardinals that year but had a 3-10 touchdown-to-interception ratio, causing him to lose favor. He's an overachiever with a decent arm.

ERIK KRAMER / Lions

Year	Att.	Cmp.	Pct.	Yds.	TD	Int.	TD-R
1988	Played in CFL						
1990	Injured						
1991	265	136	51.3	1635	11	8	1
1992	106	58	54.7	771	4	8	0

Comments: Kramer started Games 10-12 last year, winning once, but was replaced and named the No. 3 quarterback. He threw twice as many interceptions as touchdowns, but did have one 300-yard game and two TD's in another. Ironically, those were the two losses. In 1991, Kramer took over in the eighth game when Rodney Peete was injured and led the Lions to five victories in their last five games (6-2 overall) and their first NFC Central title in eight years. Then he guided the team to an upset victory over Dallas in the divisional playoffs before his Cinderella season ended in the conference championship game against the eventual Super Bowl champion Redskins. Prior to '91, Kramer had bounced around between Atlanta and the CFL. He shows good confidence and poise and is the best pure passer on the team, though he lacks the running dimension of Peete and Andre Ware.

DAN McGWIRE / Seahawks

Year	Att.	Cmp.	Pct.	Yds.	TD	Int.	TD-R
1991	7	3	42.9	27	0	1	0
1992	30	17	56.7	116	0	3	0

Comments: Second-year quarterbacks relish the opporuntity to start for their teams. McGwire got his opportunity last year in Game 6 but fractured his left hip and missed the rest of the season. His injury could be more serious than anticipated, but Seattle is already looking for another answer anyway, because he hasn't shown he might be good enough. In two games, he threw only 30 passes, but none were for touchdowns and three were intercepted. A first-round draft pick in 1991, he started one game that season, too, playing only two quarters because he completed just three of seven passes for 27 yards. It was his only action of the season. At 6-foot-8, McGwire is the tallest quarterback ever to play in the NFL. The younger brother of Mark McGwire of the Oakland A's, he has a very strong arm and he moves pretty well for somebody his size.

TODD MARINOVICH / RAIDERS

YEAR	ATT.	CMP.	PCT.	YDS.	TD	INT.	TD-R
1991	40	23	57.5	243	3	0	0
1992	165	81	49.1	1102	5	9	0

Comments: Marinovich got the opportunity to start full-time for the Raiders last season, taking over the No. 1 role in Games 3-9. He passed for 395 yards in his first 1992 start, but he didn't play well in the rest of them, throwing nine interceptions to only five touchdowns and completing less than 50 percent of his passes. The Raiders were 3-4 in those games. Marinovich passed for just 142 yards in his last three starts and didn't get back into the lineup the rest of the year. He was demoted to third-string in mid-November. In 1991, he was inactive for the first 13 games, but he started the season finale and playoff game. He had a great pro debut against Kansas City, completing 23 of 40 passes for 243 yards and three touchdowns. Then he bombed in the wild-card playoff a week later against the same team. Marinovich is still very young, and he needs to grow up and convince Raiders owner Al Davis that he wasn't a mistake.

PETER TOM WILLIS / BEARS

YEAR	ATT.	CMP.	PCT.	YDS.	TD	INT.	TD-R
1990	13	9	69.2	106	1	1	0
1991	18	11	61.1	171	1	1	0
1992	92	54	58.7	716	4	8	0

Comments: Willis started two games last year but failed to demonstrate many of the abilties that he showed coming out of college three years ago. Although he had a fine completion percentage (58.7), he threw twice as many interceptions as touchdowns (8-4). Thus, no longer can Willis be considered the Bears' quarterback of the future. He did have one good game, with 285 yards and two touchdowns against Cleveland. Willis is a pro-style passer who is supposed to be able to read coverages well and use all of his receivers. However, Willis lacks good arm strength and mobility. He may have lost his only chance to start for the Bears last season.

SCOTT SECULES / PATRIOTS

YEAR	ATT.	CMP.	PCT.	YDS.	TD	INT.	TD-R
1988	None						
1989	50	22	44.0	286	1	3	0
1990	7	3	42.9	17	0	1	0
1991	13	8	61.5	90	1	1	1
1992	Injured						

Comments: Secules was signed by New England as a free agent on March 22 and will contend for a starting job during training camp. He had dropped to third string in Miami last season, and then he spent the entire season on injured reserve with a torn muscle in his right shoulder. From 1989 to 1991 with the Dolphins, he threw only 70 passes while playing behind Dan Marino, the most durable quarterback in the NFL. Secules is more of a runner than a passer, and he scored once in 1991 in addition to throwing a touchdown pass. He has a strong, quick arm and good potential, but he has never started a game in five NFL seasons.

BOB GAGLIANO / CHARGERS

YEAR	ATT.	CMP.	PCT.	YDS.	TD	INT.	TD-R
1988	DNP						
1989	232	117	50.4	1671	6	12	4
1990	159	87	54.7	1190	10	10	0
1991	23	9	39.1	76	0	1	0
1992	42	19	45.2	258	0	3	0

Comments: Gagliano started the first game last season but was pulled in the third quarter and saw little action the rest of the season. He has a 7-6 record as an NFL starter. But he probably won't be invited to training camp this year because Pat O'Hara has moved up to third string, forcing Gagliano out of a job. That would send him looking for his eighth NFL team. He backed up John Friesz in 1991 but played in only two games. He has a lot of mobility and seems to be a winner, but he lacks raw talent. Gagliano threw a career-high 10 touchdown passes for Detroit in 1990. He also was the quarterback of record during the Lions' five-game winning streak at the end of 1989.

DON MAJKOWSKI / PACKERS

YEAR	ATT.	CMP.	PCT.	YDS.	TD	INT.	TD-R
1988	336	178	53.0	2119	9	11	1
1989	599	353	58.9	4318	27	20	5
1990	264	150	56.8	1925	10	12	1
1991	226	115	50.9	1362	3	8	2
1992	55	38	69.1	271	2	2	0

Comments: It seems like a long time since Majkowski burst upon the scene in the NFL and threw 27 touchdown passes in 1989. Now Brett Favre is the new star quarterback in Green Bay and Majkowski is looking for a chance somewhere else to show he still has something left. He started the first two games in 1992, then strained ankle ligaments and lost his job for good because of Favre's strong performances. Four years ago, Majkowski was being considered among the best quarterbacks in the NFL. But he has since had three straight injury-plagued seasons and will probably never again be the player he was. In '89, Majkowski led the NFL in attempts, completions and passing yards. At that time, he was a tough, cocky leader with the ability to carry a team. But no longer.

BILLY JOE TOLLIVER / Falcons

Year	Att.	Cmp.	Pct.	Yds.	TD	Int.	TD-R
1989	185	89	48.1	1097	5	8	0
1990	410	216	52.7	2574	16	16	0
1991	82	40	48.8	531	4	2	0
1992	131	73	55.7	787	5	5	0

Comments: Tolliver hasn't done much in his two seasons in Atlanta and doesn't look like he'll ever be anything more than a backup quarterback, and not a very good one at that. He took over for the injured Chris Miller and started five games last year but didn't generate much offense and was benched in favor of Wade Wilson, who did. At times, Tolliver wows you with his Sonny Jurgensen-type arm, but then he brings you down with an interception at a key time. He's also too cocky for his own good. Tolliver started for the Chargers in 1990 and part of '89 but lost his job there to John Friesz. He finished 12th in the conference in passing in '90, although the Chargers were 6-8 with him as the starter. Tolliver lacks a passing touch and throws too many interceptions because he lacks patience and forces too many balls.

TOM HODSON / Patriots

Year	Att.	Cmp.	Pct.	Yds.	TD	Int.	TD-R
1990	156	85	54.5	968	4	5	0
1991	68	36	52.9	345	1	4	0
1992	91	50	54.9	496	2	2	0

Comments: After Hugh Millen was injured last year, Hodson started three of four games before he, too, was sidelined with a broken thumb. New England was 0-3 in his starts. Since Hodson started the final six games of 1990 and the first three of '91 — all losses — that gives him an 0-12 record with the Patriots. If he doesn't get another chance to start, you'll know why. A third-round draft pick, Hodson was supposed to have been one of the steals of the 1990 draft, and several opposing coaches praised his ability to read defenses as a rookie. He's good on short- to medium-range passes, but he has a weak arm on the long ball and is too erratic. More important, he hasn't been able to turn his shortcomings into big plays, something that he was noted for in college.

MARK VLASIC / Buccaneers

Year	Att.	Cmp.	Pct.	Yds.	TD	Int.	TD-R
1988	52	25	48.1	270	1	2	0
1989	Injured						
1990	40	19	47.5	168	1	2	0
1991	44	28	63.6	316	2	0	0
1992	DNP						

Comments: Vlasic didn't play at all last season when Dave Krieg took all of the snaps for the Chiefs. He signed with Tampa Bay as a free agent in May and will get a shot to be the Bucs' starter. Vlasic was signed by Kansas City in Plan B free agency two years ago and took over the starting job from Steve DeBerg in Game 15. However, his short stint (six pass attempts) as the starter was quickly cut short by sprained knee ligaments and he lost the job again. He replaced an injured DeBerg again in the playoffs but threw four interceptions. Although he is a talented passer, he has been too injury-prone and is strictly a backup.

DONALD HOLLAS / Bengals

Year	Att.	Cmp.	Pct.	Yds.	TD	Int.	TD-R
1991	55	32	58.2	310	1	4	0
1992	58	35	60.3	335	2	0	0

Comments: Hollas started the final game last season but tore ligaments in his knee. His goal was to be ready for 1993 training camp. He played in 10 games throughout the season and had the highest pass rating of the team's three quarterbacks. But, with David Klingler anointed as the starter, Hollas will have to be content with being a backup. He has decent arm strength and mobility and has been compared to Jeff Hostetler.

TOM TUPA / Colts

Year	Att.	Cmp.	Pct.	Yds.	TD	Int.	TD-R
1988	6	4	66.7	49	0	0	0
1989	134	65	48.5	973	3	9	0
1990	None						
1991	315	165	52.4	2053	6	13	1
1992	33	17	51.5	156	1	2	0

Comments: In 1991, Tupa took over and started the first 11 games for Phoenix when Timm Rosenbach was injured. However, he was mostly ineffective and eventually was demoted to third string before signing with Indianapolis a year ago. And third string is likely where he'll stay. He had opportunities to take over as the starter last year in Indianapolis because of injuries to Jeff George and Jack Trudeau, but he never got the call. In Phoenix in 1991, the Cardinals didn't score an offensive touchdown in five of the 11 games he started, which sent him to the bench. Tupa is poised, has a good arm and can scramble, but he may not get another chance to start for an extended period with the Colts.

AND THE REST

(listed in alphabetical order)

JEFF BLAKE, Jets — The No. 3 quarterback last season, Blake completed 4 of 9 passes for 40 yards as a rookie. He was a sixth-round draft pick from East Carolina.

MATT BLUNDIN, Chiefs — Blundin is the quarterback of the future in Kansas City. A second-round draft pick in 1992, he was inactive for all 16 games. A tall passer at 6-foot-6, he is accurate and poised but very inexperienced. He has a good tutor in Paul Hackett, the new offensive coordinator.

DAVE BROWN, Giants — Brown will be the Giants' second-string quarterback this season. They used a first-round pick on him in the July supplemental draft. Because of injuries to Phil Simms and Jeff Hostetler, he was rushed into action in '92, playing in two games and throwing seven passes. However, Brown suffered a broken thumb in Game 14 and missed the final two games.

JEFF CARLSON, Patriots — After two seasons on the bench in Tampa Bay, Carlson started the last two games of last year in New England because of injuries to three other quarterbacks. He didn't fare well, completing only 37 percent of 49 passes. In one start in 1991, he also looked horrible. The lefty Carlson is a hard thrower, but he's no starting quarterback in the NFL.

CARY CONKLIN, Redskins — A fourth-round draft pick in 1990, Conklin will challenge Mark Rypien for the Redskins' starting job this year. He spent the 1990 and '91 seasons on injured reserve with a knee injury and was the backup in '92. He played in one game with two completions in two attempts for 16 yards and a touchdown. Conklin is a big, strong-armed talent with lots of potential.

TY DETMER, Packers — As a rookie in 1992, Detmer suited up for two games but did not see any action. Although he lacks the size of today's pro quarterbacks and won't get many opportunities behind Brett Favre, he does show some promise.

CRAIG ERICKSON, Buccaneers — After sitting out the 1991 season, Erickson played in six games in '92. He completed 15 of 26 passes for 121 yards. He might get a chance this season to take over the Bucs' No. 1 job, but is more likely the team's long-term replacement.

VINCE EVANS, Raiders — Evans came off the bench in the season finale last year and led the Raiders to a come-from-behind victory over Washington, throwing two TD passes. But he's 38 and his best days are far behind him (like when he was in college). He saw action in the final five games of 1992.

WILL FURRER, Bears — The Bears' fourth-round draft pick a year ago, Furrer started the last game of the season, which ended up being Mike Ditka's last game as the Chicago head coach. Furrer completed only 9 of 25 passes with three interceptions on the season.

GALE GILBERT, Bills — The Bills' No. 3 quarterback, Gilbert hasn't seen any action the last two seasons. In '90, he played one half of the last game in mop-up duty, throwing two TD passes and two interceptions. That was his first action in a regular-season game since 1986. That makes his experience two quarters in six seasons.

KENT GRAHAM, Giants — An eighth-round draft pick last year, Graham played in six games and started three of them because of injuries to the teams three other quarterbacks. Graham gets rattled by pressure and changing defenses, and he threw only one TD in 97 passes.

CHUCK LONG, Lions — Long has thrown only 10 passes in the last four seasons for the Rams and Lions. He spent 1992 on injured reserve.

SHAWN MOORE, Broncos — The Broncos' third-string quarterback the last two years, Moore played in three games in '92 because of injuries to John Elway. A rollout passer, he alternated plays with Tommy Maddox in one game last season but didn't perform very well. He completed 17 of 34 passes for 232 yards with three interceptions and no touchdowns.

BILL MUSGRAVE, 49ers — Musgrave spent the entire 1992 season on injured reserve with a knee injury. He will compete with Elvis Grbac for the third-string job. Musgrave played in the last game of '91, throwing one TD pass in five attempts.

PAT O'HARA, Chargers — O'Hara earned the Chargers' No. 3 job in 1992 but did not see any action. General manager Bobby Beathard is very high on him.

TODD PHILCOX, Bengals — Philcox had one of those "what-if" seasons in Cleveland in 1992. He replaced the injured Bernie Kosar in Game 3 and threw three touchdown passes against the Raiders, but suffered a broken thumb and was knocked out of the lineup. He went back to Cincinnati, his first NFL team, in the offseason.

TIMM ROSENBACH, Cardinals — After missing the entire 1991 season with a torn ligament in his knee, Rosenbach separated his shoulder in the second game of '92 and lost his job. He came back a month later and even started one game, but later admitted he had lost a lot of confidence. He was thinking about retiring.

T.J. RUBLEY, Rams — A promising youngster who had a good preseason in 1992, Rubley might be given the opportunity to compete with Mike Pagel for the backup job to Jim Everett. He saw no action as a rookie last year.

JEFF RUTLEDGE, Redskins — The Redskins' No. 3 quarterback, Rutledge saw action in every game last year as the holder on extra points and field goals.

TONY SACCA, Cardinals — A surprise second-round draft choice a year ago, Sacca played in four games as a rookie but did not throw the ball. He's being geared more for the future than for the present.

Other Quarterbacks on Rosters

Brad Goebel, Browns
Rusty Hilger, Seahawks
Brad Johnson, Vikings
Mike Pawlawski, Buccaneers
Bucky Richardson, Oilers
Rick Strom, Steelers
Troy Taylor, Dolphins
Casey Weldon, Eagles
Erik Wilhelm, Bengals

Chapter 5
Running Backs

Quite possibly, the most important players on your fantasy teams are the running backs. That is the one position at which you need the most consistent play, because it's the one from which you will probably get the most points.

Running backs in the NFL and fantasy football are a dime a dozen, but there are several premier backs who should be among your first picks. Draft one of them and you are almost assured of a touchdown every week.

The three best running backs in the NFL are Emmitt Smith, Barry Sanders and Thurman Thomas, and it's the same in fantasy football. They'll get you 100 yards a game and usually a touchdown as well.

But running back is also the deepest position this year, as there are about a dozen other backs very capable of scoring 10 touchdowns in 1993. Two or three of them won't do much this year, but going into a fantasy draft they are certainly outstanding choices at the time.

After them, there is another group of about 15 backs who stand very good chances of coming on this year, scoring six to eight touchdowns and rushing for 600-800 yards — or more. They are great choices for your final pick at the position.

What is impossible to tell is which backs will come out of nowhere. Every year there's a Rodney Culver or Robert Delpino who doesn't get drafted but ends up being one of the highest-scoring players in the league. Try to pick them up as soon as you can determine who they are in '93.

Draft Tips in Choosing Running Backs

■ Look at past performances, especially the last two or three seasons, rather than just last season.

■ Draft running backs from run-oriented teams.

■ In the Basic Scoring Method, look for each team's designated scorers. Players such as Tom Rathman, Brad

Barry Sanders

Baxter and Rodney Culver don't gain a lot of yards but they do get into the end zone a lot. A consistent scorer is the first priority.

■ In the Performance Scoring Method, draft runners strictly by their ability to gain yards rushing and receiving. The combination of the two categories often equals one very good player, such as Thurman Thomas, Neal Anderson or Lorenzo White. But don't discount running backs who are primarily receivers, such as Ronnie Harmon or Eric Metcalf.

■ In the Distance Scoring Method, look for backs who score consistently and do so on long runs (or pass plays), such as Barry Sanders or Thurman Thomas. Under this scoring method, scatbacks are better picks than big backs. Forget about the big backs who score touchdowns but don't gain much yardage (such as Marion Butts or Tom Rathman).

■ Try to determine who will be the featured running backs for the following teams: Chiefs, Dolphins, Bears, Browns, Saints, Broncos, Raiders, Eagles, Packers, Colts, Falcons, Rams and Patriots. None of that group — half of the teams in the NFL — has a definite top running back.

■ Remember to draft rookies who might break into the starting lineup, such as Garrison Hearst, Jerome Bettis or Terry Kirby. Several rookies always have big years, and it's up to you to figure out which ones will do it in 1993.

■ Consider drafting big, durable backs rather than smaller scatbacks who often come out of the game in goal-line situations and might be more injury-prone.

■ Make sure you have capable backups who can take over if one of your starters is injured or out of the lineup on a bye.

■ Running backs who throw option passes can be good picks.

■ Know what is going on during training camp. Who is going to be the Chiefs' featured ball carrier? What is going on with Miami's Bobby Humphrey? Is the Jets' Blair Thomas ever going to reach his potential? Is Pittsburgh's Barry Foster for real? Can Emmitt Smith of the Cowboys rush for 2,000 yards? Will Seattle's Chris Warren and Cincinnati's Harold Green start turning yards into touchdowns? Can Reggie Cobb do a repeat in Tampa Bay? Who is new Patriots coach Bill Parcells looking for to be his featured back a la Joe Morris or Ottis Anderson? Does Barry Sanders have an improved offensive line blocking for him in Detroit? Is Marion Butts going to carry the load in San Diego again? Can Rod Bernstine stay healthy for an entire season in Denver? What are the Raiders going to do at halfback? Who is going to start for the Eagles, Herschel Walker or Heath Sherman? Can the Bears' Neal Anderson move back among the elite backs? Is the Cardinals' Johnny Johnson ever going to just play football? Which one of the deep corps of players in New Orleans is going to be the every-down back? Have the Falcons given up on running the ball? Is the Rams' Cleveland Gary going to keep alternating good years with bad ones?

■ If all things are equal, remember the old adage of coaches: A good big player is better than a good little player. Also, go with younger players over older or injury-prone veterans.

SUPERSTARS

BARRY SANDERS / Lions

Year	Rush	Yards	TD's	Rec.	Yards	TD's
1989	280	1470	14	24	282	0
1990	255	1304	13	35	462	3
1991	342	1548	16	41	307	1
1992	312	1352	9	29	225	1

Comments: Because the Lions acquired three good offensive linemen during the offseason, Sanders will be right back where he was from 1989 to '91 — at the top of the running backs for fantasy football. Last year, because of a weak offensive line, Sanders seemed to drop out of sight on the rushing list early in the season. He had only 367 yards in the first six games before finishing fast (985 yards in 10 games) to rank fourth in the NFL in rushing. He had six 100-yard games (seven overall) and seven touchdowns in the last 10 weeks. Sure, he didn't put up the kind of numbers Emmitt Smith did, but that was last year. Now he has a good line in front of him. Now Detroit's all-time rushing leader with 5,674 yards after only four seasons, Sanders has rushed for 100 yards in 26 of 62 career games. He has 57 touchdowns, never less than 10 in a season. In 1991, Sanders finished second in the NFL rushing. He led the league in 1990 and was second in his rookie season of '89. He led the league in touchdowns in 1990 and '91. Of the top three backs in the NFL — Sanders, Emmitt Smith and Thurman Thomas — Sanders is the worst receiver but the best pure runner. He possesses the rare ability to score

a touchdown every time he touches the ball. He has great moves, incredible vision, power to break tackles and acceleration to get to the secondary. With the Lions continuing to get him the ball as much as possible, Sanders is always going to pile up incredible statistics. But, if he ever gets injured, Detroit's prospects of winning a game would go right down the drain. And he does get the ball so much that his chances for injury are somewhat high.

EMMITT SMITH / Cowboys

Year	Rush	Yards	TD's	Rec.	Yards	TD's
1990	241	937	11	24	228	0
1991	365	1563	12	49	258	1
1992	373	1713	18	59	335	1

Comments: Smith won his second consecutive NFL rushing title with a club-record 1,713 yards and an average of 4.6 yards per carry last season. Believe it or not, that was more yards than eight AFC teams and seven NFC teams! He was the first player to win back-to-back rushing crowns since Eric Dickerson in 1983 and '84, and he also led the league with 19 touchdowns. He was second in total yards (2,048) and 100-yard games (seven). He has 18 100-yard games out of 48 total games in his career (the Cowboys are 17-1 in those games). Smith is a great runner, but he has also turned into an excellent pass receiver. Last year he finished first among NFC backs with 59 receptions. In 1991, he was second in the league in touchdowns (13) and rushing touchdowns (12). As a rookie, Smith didn't sign until a week before the regular season started, and he just missed the 1,000-yard mark with 937 yards rushing. He led all rookies in rushing, was named to every All-Rookie team and was the Offensive Rookie of the Year. The league's most dangerous back inside the 20-yard line, Smith is a great cutback runner with deceptive speed and great moves with a burst to the hole. He's also tough to tackle. Smith isn't a breakaway outside runner and he doesn't fumble much. He has carried the ball 738 times the last two years, which leaves him vulnerable to injury (although he has an uncanny knack of avoiding direct hits). The Cowboys shouldn't continue to give him the ball so much, because if he were to get hurt, their Super Bowl chances would be ruined.

THURMAN THOMAS / Bills

Year	Rush	Yards	TD's	Rec.	Yards	TD's
1988	207	881	2	18	208	0
1989	298	1244	6	60	669	6
1990	271	1297	11	49	532	2
1991	288	1407	7	62	631	5
1992	312	1487	9	58	626	3

Comments: Thomas is regarded as the best all-around running back in the NFL. While he might be a slight bit behind Barry Sanders and Emmitt Smith as a runner, he is the league's best back as a pass receiver. He has led the

NFL in combined yards from scrimmage (rushing and receiving) the last four years, breaking a league record held by the legendary Jim Brown. In 1992, Thomas gained a career-high 2,113 total yards, the ninth-highest total in NFL history, and his 1,487 rushing yards ranked third in the league. He was selected to his fourth straight Pro Bowl after rushing for 100 yards nine times in 1992, including five consecutive games. Thomas' totals would be even higher if he didn't have such a good backup in Kenneth Davis. In 1991, Thomas was named the NFL's Most Valuable Player, and only an ankle injury in the last game kept him from leading the league in rushing. In five seasons, Thomas has rushed for 6,316 yards, and he reached the 6,000-yard mark faster than even O.J. Simpson. Thomas has 29 100-yard rushing games in his career (the Bills are 27-2 in those games). Thomas scored four touchdowns in last year's season opener, but he had only three scores in the last seven regular-season games. Thomas is a terrific natural inside-outside runner and receiver with a great burst to the hole, and he's very good on draw plays. He has averaged over 4.8 yards per carry the last two years. He was a steal in the second round of the 1988 draft, a strong runner with great vision, instincts and determination. Although he lacks great moves and break-away speed, he has great balance and can single-handedly control a game.

CAN'T MISS

RODNEY HAMPTON / Giants

Year	Rush	Yards	TD's	Rec.	Yards	TD's
1990	109	455	2	32	274	2
1991	256	1059	10	43	283	0
1992	257	1141	14	28	215	0

Comments: Hampton became only the second Giants back to rush for over 1,000 yards in consecutive seasons last year, the other being Joe Morris. He also scored 14 touchdowns, third in the league. For the season, Hampton had only two 100-yard games, but he was very consistent. He scored seven touchdowns in the first six games, then was hampered later in the season after injuries played havoc with the team's quarterbacks. In other words, his stats could have been quite a bit better. With a 4.27-yard rushing average, Hampton ranks second in Giants history. In 1991, Hampton was the third-leading rusher in the NFC and tied for eighth in touchdowns with 10. He had three 100-yard games (and two others with 96 and 99 yards). In 1990, he finished second on the Giants in rushing and third in receiving. But he fractured his left ankle in the first playoff game against Chicago and missed the NFC championship game and the Super Bowl. Hampton is a big, strong runner with speed, quickness, agility and big-play ability. He's also a fine receiver (75 catches in two seasons). He should be able to continue having the kind of

seasons he has had the last two years.

BARRY FOSTER / Steelers

Year	Rush	Yards	TD's	Rec.	Yards	TD's
1990	36	203	1	1	2	0
1991	96	488	1	9	117	1
1992	390	1690	11	36	344	0

Comments: Foster had the greatest season ever for a Steelers back last season. He was second in the NFL in rushing with 1,690 yards. He led the AFC with 11 rushing touchdowns and tied Eric Dickerson's NFL record with 12 100-yard games. He also proved to be a fine receiver, as he was the team's second-leading pass-catcher last year behind fullback Merril Hoge. He scored in eight games, usually in streaks. His best game was 190 yards against the Jets. A fifth-round steal in the 1990 draft, Foster moved into the starting lineup at halfback in 1991, starting eight of 10 games. He rushed for 199 yards in the first two games and had an excellent 5.2-yard average per carry going into '92, so many people knew he was capable of a 1,000-yard season — if he could stay healthy. However, 390 carries could not have been expected out of anybody. Foster is an explosive runner with speed, balance and a burst. He has a low-to-the-ground running style that baffles tacklers, as well as deceiving speed and toughness to make tacklers miss. Don't expect Foster to come close to repeating his 1992 season this year, but there's no reason he can't hit 1,000 yards and 10 TD's again, either.

TERRY ALLEN / Vikings

Year	Rush	Yards	TD's	Rec.	Yards	TD's
1991	120	563	2	6	49	1
1992	266	1201	13	49	478	2

Comments: Allen broke Chuck Foreman's team record last season by rushing for 1,201 yards to rank third in the NFC behind Emmitt Smith and Barry Sanders. He also scored 13 touchdowns on the ground to tie Foreman's team record, and two through the air. Not bad for a ninth-round draft pick! However, there were some extenuating circumstances surrounding Allen's status in the 1990 draft. He suffered a knee injury in his junior year at Clemson in 1988 and missed the next two years of football, sitting out his rookie season in Minnesota. So, although he is now a highly regarded NFL back, many NFL observers knew it was just a matter of his getting healthy. Allen gave a preview of things to come late in the 1991 season when he rushed for 563 yards and supplanted Herschel Walker as the Vikings' top back. He had three 100-yard games, two of them in the last two weeks of the season, the first successive 100-yard games by a Vikings back since 1985. Although the Vikings offense was sporadic much of the season, Allen scored in 10 games, including two games with three TD's. He has an excellent 4.6-yard rushing average in two seasons. Allen is a slashing back who is quick to hit the hole. He can elude the first tackler with a shot at him, and he's an excellent receiver out of the backfield.

RICKY WATTERS / 49ERS

YEAR	RUSH	YARDS	TD's	REC.	YARDS	TD's
1991	Injured					
1992	206	1013	9	43	405	2

Comments: Watters gained 1,013 yards to establish a 49ers rushing record for first-year backs, surprising everybody because nobody knew what to expect. As a rookie in '91, he suffered a broken right foot at the beginning of training camp and missed the entire season. Last year he rushed for over 100 yards in his first pro game and three others. He scored 11 touchdowns, tied for sixth in the league. He did all that even though he missed two starts and almost five full games because of injuries. His 4.9-yard rushing average topped NFL backs and he proved to be a very good pass receiver. More than anything, Watters proved that any fantasy football player should check the injury list before drafting. He was an incredible find for somebody who wasn't drafted in most leagues. Watters is a sturdy, quick, open-field runner who just needs to prove his durability. If he can stay healthy for all of 1993, he might put up some numbers in the range of Barry Sanders or Emmitt Smith.

LORENZO WHITE / OILERS

YEAR	RUSH	YARDS	TD's	REC.	YARDS	TD's
1988	31	115	0	0	0	0
1989	104	349	5	6	37	0
1990	168	702	8	39	368	4
1991	110	465	4	27	211	0
1992	265	1226	7	57	641	1

Comments: White emerged as one of the NFL's top backs in 1992, rushing for 1,226 yards — fifth in the NFL — on a fine 4.6-yard average and earning his first Pro Bowl berth. He also caught 57 passes, fourth on the team, for 641 yards to total 1,867 total yards from scrimmage, fourth in the NFL. He established career highs for carries, yards, catches and receiving yards. White was the first Oiler since 1988 to amass 1,000 yards rushing and only the fifth Houston back ever to accomplish that feat. Amazingly, he did not fumble despite handling the ball 322 times. He had 10 games with over 100 rushing-receiving yards, including six straight in games 10-15. His low game rushing was 44 yards, which is pretty good. And he scored all of his touchdowns in eight different games. In 1991, White was second on the team in rushing and sixth in receiving despite not starting a game. He ran hard the second half of the season, which is why coach Jack Pardee wants him as the No. 1 back. In '90, he set personal highs with 702 yards and 12 touchdowns (four in one game), and his 1,070 rushing and receiving yards ranked 12th in the conference. White

is a slashing, tackle-to-tackle runner with good quickness and the leg power to break tackles. He isn't a breakaway threat, but he is durable and a fine receiver. As the only really good back on the Oilers, the vastly underrated White is assured of having another good season in 1993 as long as he stays healthy.

SOLID PICKS

NEAL ANDERSON / BEARS

YEAR	RUSH	YARDS	TD's	REC.	YARDS	TD's
1988	249	1106	12	39	371	0
1989	274	1275	11	50	434	4
1990	260	1078	10	42	484	0
1991	210	747	6	47	368	3
1992	156	582	5	42	399	6

Comments: Anderson has had two consecutive disappointing seasons for the Bears, although by fantasy football standards they haven't been all that bad. He has rushed for only 1,329 yards the last two years and hasn't had a 100-yard rushing game since 1990. But he scored nine and 11 touchdowns in 1991 and '92, respectively, which is very good production for fantasy football. Interestingly, last year he scored more touchdowns on pass receptions than he did running the ball. In the last two seasons, Anderson averaged only 3.6 yards per carry (his career average was 4.4 until then). Although he lost his starting job the last four games to Darren Lewis, he still led the team in rushing. He ranks second in Bears history with 67 TD's and third on the all-time rushing list with 5,520 yards. One of the best all-around backs in the NFL from 1988 to '90, Anderson needs to bounce back to show what he can do — and there are a lot of people who think he has lost it. He used to be a back who could go all the way at any time — in 1990 he had seven plays of 29 or more yards. In 1990, he finished sixth in the NFL in rushing. In '89, he led the Bears in rushing, receiving and scoring and had two games with three touchdowns. Anderson could go either way in 1993 — back to where he used to be or unused as a second stringer. Be careful when considering him on Draft Day.

MARION BUTTS / CHARGERS

YEAR	RUSH	YARDS	TD's	REC.	YARDS	TD's
1989	170	683	9	7	21	0
1990	265	1225	8	16	117	0
1991	193	834	6	10	91	1
1992	218	809	4	9	73	0

Comments: In 1992, Butts scored the fewest touchdowns of his career, but he is almost certain to be back up near double figures in '93 because of the departure of Rod Bernstine to the Broncos, although rookie Natrone Means might fill Bernstine's role. Butts and Bernstine split the duties at running back last year, and both scored four TD's. He suffered a knee injury in the season opener that caused him to miss one game and hampered him throughout the year. Still, he moved into second place on the team's career rushing list and had two 100-yard games. In four seasons, Butts averages 888 yards and seven scores. In his best season in 1990, he was second in the AFC in rushing while breaking Earnest Jackson's single-season team rushing record, even while missing the last two games. Butts is a good power fullback who's hard to bring down and a battering ram at the goal line, and he has surprising speed, balance and agility. He has good in-line quickness and he runs hard (albeit high), but he can also cut it outside and take off. He's not a fumbler, but not much of a pass receiver, either. With Bernstine gone, look for Butts to assume the Chargers' featured runner role.

REGGIE COBB / Buccaneers

Year	Rush	Yards	TD's	Rec.	Yards	TD's
1990	151	480	2	39	299	0
1991	196	752	7	15	111	0
1992	310	1171	9	21	156	0

Comments: Cobb moved into a small group that includes some of the best running backs in the NFL last season. The Bucs' first 1,000-yard rusher since James Wilder in 1985, he finished eighth in the NFL in rushing with 1,171 yards, fifth in attempts and fifth in rushing touchdowns. His rushing total ranks fourth on the Buccaneers' all-time list. Consistent, balanced and durable, he gained 50 or more yards in 13 games and more than 100 in four. He scored a single touchdown in nine games. In 1991, he led the team in rushing after stealing the starting halfback job from Gary Anderson in the fifth game. His 785 yards rushing were the most by a Bucs running back since 1985 (he got 553 of them in the second half of the season). In 1990, he played out of position at fullback but still finished third in rushing among rookies. Cobb has lots of talent. He's fullback-big and halfback-fast, with instincts and explosion. Unlike a lot of backs, he gets better as a game wears on. He's also starting to improve his skills in the passing game.

BRAD BAXTER / Jets

Year	Rush	Yards	TD's	Rec.	Yards	TD's
1989	0	0	0	0	0	0
1990	124	539	6	8	73	0
1991	184	666	11	12	124	0
1992	152	698	6	4	32	0

Comments: In the last two years, Baxter has developed into one of the best goal-line scorers in the league. In that time, he ranks fifth in the NFL with 17 rushing touchdowns. In 1992, Baxter led the Jets in rushing and was really the only back on the team that could be counted upon. He even established himself as a running threat —

not just a scorer — the second half of the season when Blair Thomas was out of the lineup and Baxter took over as the featured back. He had the team's only 100-yard game of the season, as well as two with over 90 yards. He missed the final game with a hamstring injury. And, even though his TD total dropped from the previous season, that was basically due to the Jets' lack of production at quarterback. With Boomer Esiason expected to be the starter this year, Baxter's numbers should improve. In 1991, Baxter's 11 rushing touchdowns led the AFC and tied a team record. He also finished second on the team in rushing. He is a very good blocking fullback with decent speed and moves at the line but not much out in the open.

HERSCHEL WALKER / Eagles

Year	Rush	Yards	TD's	Rec.	Yards	TD's
1988	361	1514	5	53	505	2
1989	250	915	7	40	423	2
1990	184	770	5	35	315	4
1991	198	825	10	33	204	0
1992	267	1070	8	38	278	2

Comments: Walker was the investment of the year in 1992 ($1 million for 1,000 yards rushing) after signing with Philadelphia in June. His 1,070 yards and 10 touchdowns led the team in both categories, and he became the first Eagles running back to surpass 1,000 yards since 1985. It was only the second time in his career he has hit 1,000 yards. He had five 100-yard games, including the first two contests of the season. His rushing total in the first five games surpassed the team's leader the season before. However, over the second half of the season, Heath Sherman got the ball more than Walker, so the two might split time in 1993. Walker's 1,348 yards from scrimmage were the most by an Eagle since 1981. Even when he slumped in the middle of the season, going six games with only 235 yards, he managed to score six touchdowns. All in all, for a player who draws so much criticism, Walker puts together some pretty strong numbers year after year. In 1991 he finished fifth in the NFC in rushing and scored 10 touchdowns to rank eighth. In six years in the NFL, he has rushed for 6,722 yards. He runs well straight ahead, but he does not have great moves and has never been a stylish runner. When he's getting the ball 20 times a game, Walker can be one of the NFL's best backs. He helps the offense because defenses can't tee off on Randall Cunningham.

HAROLD GREEN / Bengals

Year	Rush	Yards	TD's	Rec.	Yards	TD's
1990	83	353	1	12	90	1
1991	158	731	2	16	136	0
1992	265	1170	2	41	214	0

Comments: Green led the Bengals in both rushing and receiving in 1992 and now has to be considered one of the best running backs in the NFL. However, he scored the fewest touchdowns out of all backs who rushed for over 1,000 yards, and that doesn't help much in fantasy football (Derrick Fenner is the team's goal-line scorer). Last year he rushed for 321 yards in the first three games and ended up with 190 in Game 15. He had five 100-yard games. Those are all good totals in an offense that accomplished little with its passing game. Green replaced James Brooks as the Bengals' No. 1 halfback in late 1991. That season he led the team in rushing and had an excellent 4.6-yard rushing average. At midseason, he looked like one of the top five or six running backs in the NFL when he gained 100 yards rushing in three of four games. Green has all of the tools to be a great back, including the size to run inside and break tackles and enough speed to turn the corner. He's elusive but he has to learn not to fumble. As a receiver, he prefers to catch short dump-off passes rather than the ones downfield. He also has to continue proving his durability, which was a knock prior to 1992.

CHRISTIAN OKOYE / CHIEFS

YEAR	RUSH	YARDS	TD's	REC.	YARDS	TD's
1988	105	473	3	8	51	0
1989	370	1480	12	2	12	0
1990	245	805	7	4	23	0
1991	225	1031	9	3	34	0
1992	144	448	6	1	5	0

Comments: Okoye used to be a can't-miss pick in fantasy football, but now he's 31 years old and might have seen his best days. In 1992, he rushed for the fewest yards of his six-year career and scored fewer touchdowns than he has since 1988. He started only five of 15 games, with no 100-yard outings (he missed the opener after a training camp holdout). He did score touchdowns in each of the last three games, including a team-record 40th career TD. The Chiefs are expected to switch to a two-back offense, which would leave Okoye as the fullback. However, he thinks he can succeed in the new scheme because he can block, and he did catch 24 passes as a rookie in 1987 in a similar offense. The Chiefs' all-time leading rusher, he will also be the featured back against 3-4 defenses. In 1991, Okoye became the first Kansas City player to record two 1,000-yard seasons (he had led the NFL in 1989 with 1,480 yards) when he re-emerged as the featured back. He finished eighth in the league in rushing and tied for seventh in rushing touchdowns with nine (leading the Chiefs for the third consecutive year). In the last four seasons, Okoye has 34 rushing touchdowns, third most in the league (behind Barry Sanders and Emmitt Smith), and 3,845 yards, fifth most. "The Nigerian Nightmare" is a north-south runner who must be tackled low or else he will drag tacklers on his back. He runs high but doesn't fumble.

EARNEST BYNER / REDSKINS

YEAR	RUSH	YARDS	TD's	REC.	YARDS	TD's
1988	157	576	3	59	576	2
1989	134	580	7	54	458	2
1990	297	1219	6	26	248	1
1991	274	1048	5	34	308	0
1992	262	998	6	39	338	1

Comments: With 998 yards in 1992, Byner just missed his third consecutive 1,000-yard season. He actually hit 1,000 yards in the 16th game, then lost some yardage, was injured and never able to get back into the game. He would have been only the 11th NFL player to reach the 1,000-yard mark at age 30 or older. Still, it was another excellent season for him. The third-leading rusher in Redskins history, he scored seven times (four in the first four games) and had two 100-yard games. At 30 years old, Byner doesn't seem to be aging much. In 1991, he finished fifth in the league in rushing and fourth on the team in receiving. He scored only five times because Gerald Riggs was the goal-line runner all season. He had the best season of his career in 1990, with 1,219 yards. Byner had a few so-so seasons at the end of his tenure in Cleveland but has had a resurgence since being traded to Washington in 1989. In 1990, he got the ball more than any other NFL running back (328 times on runs and passes). Byner is a tough, instinctive runner who runs low and hard but lacks speed to go outside. However, he has a nose for the goal and he can get through a hole in a flash as well as bounce off would-be tacklers. He also makes some catches that would make a wide receiver proud, and he seems to have ended his tendency to fumble.

KEVIN MACK / BROWNS

YEAR	RUSH	YARDS	TD's	REC.	YARDS	TD's
1988	123	485	3	11	87	0
1989	37	130	1	2	7	0
1990	158	702	5	42	360	2
1991	197	726	8	40	255	2
1992	169	543	6	13	81	0

Comments: Considering he missed the first month of 1992 with a sore knee and calf, Mack had a fine season, leading the Browns in rushing. He started six of the 12 games in which he played and alternated with the team's deep corps of running backs. He scored two touchdowns in his second game in the lineup, then finished with four in the final six. In 1991, Mack tied his career season high of 10 touchdowns scored (set in 1985 and '86). Mack hasn't had a 100-yard game since 1988, but he usually gets 60 or 70 an outing. At 31, Mack remains the catalyst of the Browns' running game, a tough, inside runner with tackle-breaking power. However, he hasn't had an injury-free season since '87, and other backs are going to start seeing the ball more. Still, look for Mack to be Cleveland's most dependable back again in '93, which makes him a good pick as a backup back in fantasy football.

TOM RATHMAN / 49ERS

Year	Rush	Yards	TD's	Rec.	Yards	TD's
1988	102	427	2	42	382	0
1989	79	305	1	73	616	1
1990	101	318	7	48	327	0
1991	63	183	6	34	286	0
1992	57	194	5	44	343	4

Comments: Rathman doesn't run for very many yards these days, but he still scores a lot of touchdowns. In 1992, he scored nine times, on five runs and four passes, although he compiled only 537 yards from scrimmage. He doubled his career reception TD total, and he can be a real weapon as the fifth player out on passes. Rathman started 15 games at fullback, missing the last one with an injury. In 1991, he had his poorest year since he was a rookie in 1986. Although he started 16 games and scored six touchdowns, all of them on goal-line plunges, he was largely bypassed while the 49ers looked for somebody to be their every-down back. Until 1991, he was an integral part of the 49ers' offense, an outstanding, aggressive blocker, a fine inside and short-yardage runner and a strong receiver with subtle moves and instincts. Rathman knows his role, and he plays it to perfection. He's worth a late pick in fantasy football because he usually pays good dividends.

ROD BERNSTINE / BRONCOS

Year	Rush	Yards	TD's	Rec.	Yards	TD's
1988	2	7	0	29	340	0
1989	15	137	1	21	222	1
1990	124	589	4	8	40	0
1991	159	766	8	11	124	0
1992	106	499	4	12	86	0

Comments: Bernstine signed with Denver as a free agent on March 13, the first skill-position player to change teams under the new rules. With San Diego in 1992, he had just taken over the starting job in Game 6 and rushed for 150 yards when he separated a shoulder in the fourth quarter and missed the next seven games. He returned in Game 14 but then injured his right ankle the following week, although he continued to play. Then, in the playoffs, he injured his left ankle. In 1991, Bernstine also finished second on the Chargers in rushing with more yards than he had in his first four seasons combined. He also had a fine 4.8-yard average per carry and scored eight touchdowns, tops on the team. He also threw a TD pass. He had consecutive 100-yard games early in the season, and later in the year he had a 104-yard, three-TD game. Bernstine made a rapid transition from tight end to running back in 1990. A big, strong back, he is an excellent all-around player whose only knock is that he can't stay healthy. He heads to Denver as the starter, but he has never been a team's featured back for an entire season, and more work might mean more injuries.

MARK HIGGS / DOLPHINS

Year	Rush	Yards	TD's	Rec.	Yards	TD's
1988	0	0	0	0	0	0
1989	49	184	0	3	9	0
1990	10	67	0	0	0	0
1991	231	905	4	11	80	0
1992	256	915	7	16	142	0

Comments: Higgs might be the least-appreciated running back who has rushed for over 900 yards each of the last two seasons, the reason being that few people think he should be a featured back in the NFL. His 1,820 yards in that time ranks fourth among AFC backs. He rushed for a career-best 915 yards in 1992, the most by a Miami back since 1978 and the seventh most in team history. His seven rushing touchdowns (out of the team's total of nine) tied for the team lead and for third in the conference and were also a personal best. Higgs scored six of his seven TD's in the first seven games of the season. He started in 15 games and led the team in rushing in 13 of them. But he suffered torn cartilage in his right knee in the final game and missed the playoffs. Higgs has five 100-yard games during his career, including two last season. Two others came in his first two NFL starts in '91, when he gained more yards in those games than in his previous three years in the league. Higgs has averaged only 3.8 yards per carry during his career, and he isn't much of a pass receiver. But he is a fine inside runner with a low center of gravity, balance, speed and power.

BRAD MUSTER / SAINTS

Year	Rush	Yards	TD's	Rec.	Yards	TD's
1988	44	197	0	21	236	1
1989	82	327	5	32	259	3
1990	141	664	6	47	452	0
1991	90	412	6	35	287	1
1992	98	414	3	34	389	2

Comments: Muster signed with the Saints as a free agent on April 19 and might be their featured back this season. In 1992, Muster was again the Bears' second-leading rusher. He could be a dangerous run-catch threat, but his former team, the Bears, never featured him that way. Muster started all 16 games in 1992 but had only one game with more than 54 rushing yards. He scored all five touchdowns in the first half of the season. He had his first career 100-yard rushing day in 1991, and it is the Bears' only one of the last two seasons. Muster really came into his own in 1990, rushing for 664 yards, leading the Bears in receiving with 47 catches and scoring six touchdowns. He isn't a prototype fullback, as he's more comfortable taking a pitch than heading straight into the pile, but he can go between the tackles (although he lacks speed and runs high). Muster's forte is receiving, not blocking. Since the Saints have lots of talent in their backfield, be careful when choosing where to draft Muster, although he could produce nice benefits.

BARRY WORD / Chiefs

Year	Rush	Yards	TD's	Rec.	Yards	TD's
1988	0	0	0	0	0	0
1989	DNP					
1990	204	1015	4	4	28	0
1991	160	684	4	2	13	0
1992	163	607	4	9	80	0

Comments: Word started 11 of 12 games last year, leading the Chiefs in rushing for the second time in three years, but had his fewest yards in three seasons. He missed two games near midseason because of a knee injury, and then he didn't play in Games 14 and 15. He had the team's only two 100-yard rushing games, on consecutive weeks in September. In the last three seasons, Word has the most yards of any Kansas City back (2,306), with a 4.3-yard average and 14 touchdowns. Since Word had only 38 yards rushing in the last five games, he isn't happy about returning this year, and he isn't sure where he fits into the new offense that is being planned. In 1991, he rushed for 429 yards and three touchdowns in the final four games after gaining only 255 yards and scoring one TD in the first 12. Word also holds the team record with a 200-yard day in 1990, when he had his best season. He was named the NFL's Comeback Player of the Year that season after rushing for 1,015 yards with a 5.0-yard average per carry. Word has the ability to break away from tacklers and take the ball downfield. He has speed, power and a fluid running style. He might be traded before the start of the '93 season, and he might be worth a high fantasy pick if he goes to the right team (although he has never scored more than four touchdowns in a season).

DERRICK FENNER / Bengals

Year	Rush	Yards	TD's	Rec.	Yards	TD's
1989	11	41	1	3	23	0
1990	215	859	14	17	143	1
1991	91	267	4	11	72	0
1992	112	500	7	7	41	1

Comments: Fenner very quietly had a fine comeback season in 1992 after being acquired by Cincinnati. He was the team's No. 2 rusher and leading touchdown scorer. He started only one of 16 games, playing mostly in short-yardage situations. He had come out of nowhere in 1990 to score 15 touchdowns in Seattle, which tied for the NFL lead. But in 1991 he lost his starting job after six games because he was averaging only 3.1 yards per carry. He gained only 10 yards on nine carries in the last nine games. Fenner is a big, athletic, upright runner who lacks moves in the open field. He's not much of a pass catcher, but there's no reason he can't repeat his 1992 rushing and scoring stats in '93.

CHRIS WARREN / Seahawks

Year	Rush	Yards	TD's	Rec.	Yards	TD's
1990	6	11	1	0	0	0
1991	11	13	0	2	9	0
1992	223	1017	3	16	134	0

Comments: Warren was a remarkable success story in 1992. He went from being the Seahawks' No. 3 halfback to becoming only the second player in team history to reach the 1,000-yard rushing mark, joining Curt Warner. He finished the year with 1,017 yards. He passed 1,000 yards on a 30-yard run in the season finale, then suffered a concussion two plays later and missed the rest of the game. For the season, he had three 100-yard games and 1,927 all-purpose yards (including kick returns) but only three touchdowns. In 1991, Warren made one start but rushed for only 13 yards on 11 carries. He is big with tremendous speed, but he lacks instincts (which is why he is used as a kick returner). There's no reason Warren can't rush for 1,000 yards again this year, but don't be surprised if he turns out to be a one-season wonder, too.

COULD COME ON

JOHNNY JOHNSON / Jets

Year	Rush	Yards	TD's	Rec.	Yards	TD's
1990	234	926	5	25	241	0
1991	196	666	4	29	225	2
1992	178	734	6	14	103	0

Comments: Johnson was traded to the Jets on Draft Day and might be a nice surprise this season. Because of a protracted contract holdout and early-season shoulder and chest injuries, Johnson had little playing time over the first seven games of 1992 when he played for the Cardinals. But he came on strong in November and December, gaining all but 22 of his team-leading 734 rushing yards in eight of the Cardinals' final nine games (missing one with a groin injury). He cracked the 100-yard barrier in Games 14 and 15 with a career-best 156 yards and then 146 yards before finishing with 91 yards in the season-ender. He also had games of 102 and 91 yards after midseason. The seventh-round draft choice made a huge impact in 1990, when he led all rookies in rushing until missing most of the last four games with an ankle injury. He finished with 926 yards rushing, 11 behind Dallas' Emmitt Smith, but he may have had about 1,200 yards without the injury. He also became only the third Cardinals rookie to be voted to the Pro Bowl. In 1991, though, Johnson didn't do much, slumping to a team-high 666 yards on a poor 3.4-yard average per carry. He is a power back with deceptive speed who can break shoulder and arm tackles and juke defenders with his legs. If he's forced laterally, he struggles. He's also a good receiver, and he has been compared to former Viking Chuck Foreman. Although he has loads of talent, Johnson shouldn't be counted upon for a high pick in fantasy football because one never knows if he has his mind in the game. In other words: buyer beware.

HEATH SHERMAN / Eagles

Year	Rush	Yards	TD's	Rec.	Yards	TD's
1989	40	177	2	8	85	0
1990	164	685	1	23	167	3
1991	106	279	0	14	59	0
1992	112	583	5	18	219	1

Comments: Over the second half of last season and in the playoffs, Sherman carried the load rather than Herschel Walker. He gained only 94 yards in the first eight games, then started seven games down the stretch alongside Walker and rushed for 497 yards over the second half of the season. He had one 100-yard game and scored six touchdowns, proving to be a good pass receiver, too. His 5.2-yard average on the ground was one of the league's best marks. Sherman followed up a solid 1990 season by not doing much in 1991; a holdout and too much weight contributed. But he came back in '92 with a strong preseason. If he does the same in '93, he might become a permanent starter. In 1990, Sherman burst onto the scene at midseason with two 100-yard rushing games and led the Eagles' backs in rushing (quarterback Randall Cunningham led the team) with 685 yards. He was the first Eagles back in nine years to gain 100 yards in successive games, but he scored only one rushing touchdown in 164 carries. Sherman has strong leg drive and breakaway capabilities, but he's a halfback-sized fullback who has trouble with blitzing linebackers.

HARVEY WILLIAMS / Chiefs

Year	Rush	Yards	TD's	Rec.	Yards	TD's
1991	97	447	1	16	147	2
1992	78	262	1	5	24	0

Comments: Williams has yet to reach the potential expected of him as a first-round pick in 1991. However, he did lead the Chiefs in rushing the last eight games of last year and will go into 1993 as the starter. He should also benefit from the new offense being installed by the Chiefs. Last year he was the Chiefs' third-leading rusher for the second year in a row. He didn't start a game during the regular season, but did open in the playoffs. In 1991, he led the Chiefs in all-purpose yardage with 1,118 (447 rushing, 147 receiving and 524 on kickoff returns). He was the only player on the team to score both rushing and receiving. A big back with speed and body lean, he adds versatility to the offense, and the Chiefs think he can develop into a Thurman Thomas-type back. He has explosive speed and can turn the corner.

VAUGHN DUNBAR / Saints

Year	Rush	Yards	TD's	Rec.	Yards	TD's
1992	154	565	3	9	62	0

Comments: Dunbar led the Saints in rushing as a rookie and was named to the All-Rookie team. But he did not have an exceptionally strong year and lost his starting job the second half of the season. He finished 14th in the NFC in rushing with 565 yards, second among rookies. His best outing was 91 yards and a touchdown on 13 carries in Game 15 against Buffalo. Dunbar is a durable, inside runner with cutback ability and a burst to the corner. His problem last year was that he missed too many holes which he should've run through. He'll get the first opportunity in 1993 to start for the Saints and could hit the 1,000-yard mark and score quite a few TD's.

TOMMY VARDELL / Browns

Year	Rush	Yards	TD's	Rec.	Yards	TD's
1992	99	369	0	13	128	0

Comments: Vardell was called "Touchdown Tommy" in college, but he didn't get into the end zone as a rookie in the NFL. He looked very impressive in Game 2 with 84 yards against Miami, but he never did become Cleveland's featured ball carrier the entire season. He missed the last two games with a calf injury. Still, he was the team's No. 2 rusher with 369 yards. Vardell is a tough inside runner with great receiving skills (which also weren't used much in '92). Look for Vardell to get a big opportunity to become the Browns' No. 1 back this year. If so, he would be a good fantasy pick.

ERIC BIENIEMY / Chargers

Year	Rush	Yards	TD's	Rec.	Yards	TD's
1991	3	17	0	0	0	0
1992	74	264	3	5	49	0

Comments: Bieniemy was finally able to get some playing time last season behind Marion Butts and Rod Bernstine, although he was hampered all year long by an ankle injury. He played in 15 games with a single-game high of 48 rushing yards. With Bernstine gone to Denver, Bieniemy might move up to No. 2 and pick up the slack. He's a change-of-pace runner with the best quickness on the team, especially outside. Only 5-7, he is a strong goal-line runner. Bieniemy has been waiting for his shot, so this is put-up or shut-up time for him.

TONY SMITH / Falcons

Year	Rush	Yards	TD's	Rec.	Yards	TD's
1992	87	329	2	2	14	0

Comments: As a rookie first-round draft choice in 1991,

Smith was the Falcons' second-leading rusher. However, he showed a horrible penchant for being injured — five different injuries nagged him throughout the season and he ended up on injured reserve with a knee injury. In other words, he proved to be another Steve Broussard. When he was healthy and in the lineup — he started six of 14 games — Smith had a decent 3.8-yard average and was OK on kick returns. His best game was an 81-yard outing on 10 carries against New England. Smith has speed, elusiveness and receiving ability, although he didn't show much of the latter as a rookie. If he can stay healthy in 1992, Smith will get the first chance to be Atlanta's No. 1 back.

BLAIR THOMAS / JETS

YEAR	RUSH	YARDS	TD's	REC.	YARDS	TD's
1990	123	620	1	20	204	1
1991	189	728	3	30	195	1
1992	97	440	0	7	49	0

Comments: This might be the last year Thomas is on the list of players that "could come on." If he doesn't improve in 1993, he'll probably be classified as a bust. In fact, former Cardinal Johnny Johnson might replace him as the starter this season. Last year, Thomas missed seven of the last nine games because of a groin pull and a sprained left knee. In other words, he still hasn't learned to play with pain. He finished the year with only 440 yards rushing and seven receptions. The No. 2 pick in the 1990 draft, Thomas hasn't been the impact player he was expected to be. As a rookie, he averaged five yards a carry after a prolonged holdout. In 1991, he led the team in rushing and was third in receiving. He played well early in the season, but a fumble against Chicago seems to have affected him mentally, and he no longer has the confidence he once had. Thomas occasionally flashes great moves, instinct and power, but he lost some speed. This season will probably be his last in New York to prove what he can do.

NICK BELL / RAIDERS

YEAR	RUSH	YARDS	TD's	REC.	YARDS	TD's
1991	78	307	3	6	62	0
1992	81	366	3	4	40	0

Comments: Bell has yet to have the kind of season many people think he is capable of having. Last year he started only the last game, but he ran for 72 yards and a touchdown on 21 carries against the Redskins. He also had a 97-yard performance and a score vs. the Seahawks. In '91, Bell had an off-and-on rookie season. He missed the first four games with a hamstring injury, then he played five games and started to challenge for a starting job. In his first start, he was knocked back onto injured reserve and missed three more games. But, in limited action, he scored three touchdowns both years. Bell gives the Raiders the power runner they need. He has all the tools, but there are a lot of questions about his durability and heart. He's big and fast

with moves, but he runs upright, which leaves him vulnerable.

RICKY ERVINS / REDSKINS

YEAR	RUSH	YARDS	TD's	REC.	YARDS	TD's
1991	145	680	3	16	181	1
1992	151	495	2	32	252	0

Comments: Ervins had a very disappointing second season, especially to people who expected so much out of him based on his fine rookie year. Although he carried the ball six more times than he did in 1991, he had a bad 3.3-yard average last year and rushed for almost 200 yards less than he did in '91. Ervins had 10 games in 1992 with less than 30 yards rushing (16, 10, 29, 26, 29, 17, 17, 6, 0 and 1 yards). He did develop into a pretty good receiver, and more will be expected out of him in that phase of the offense. Ervins was the NFC's top rookie rusher in 1991. Until Game 7 that season, he had rushed only 11 times for 86 yards before becoming a featured element of the offense the second half of the season (including an excellent 4.7-yard average per carry). Ervins is a fast, little fireplug who shows the ability to be a breakaway back. He's built like Barry Sanders and is always looking to cut back.

DARREN LEWIS / BEARS

YEAR	RUSH	YARDS	TD's	REC.	YARDS	TD's
1991	15	36	2.4	0	0	0
1992	90	382	4	18	175	0

Comments: Lewis became the Bears' starting halfback late last season, opening five games (including the final four). However, he actually played better coming off the bench than he did in those starting roles (only 36.8 yards a game). As a sub, he scored four of his five touchdowns (including a kickoff return), showing speed, moves and instincts that were lacking in the Bears' offense. He was the Bears' third-leading rusher and top kickoff returner. He didn't play much as a rookie, but in a 1991 playoff game against Dallas he gained 65 yards on nine carries. Lewis signed a three-year $1.65 million contract during the offseason and will be given the opportunity to become the No. 1 back on a full-time basis. If that happens during training camp, he might be a good sleeper pick.

JOHN STEPHENS / PACKERS

YEAR	RUSH	YARDS	TD's	REC.	YARDS	TD's
1988	297	1168	4	14	98	0
1989	244	833	7	21	207	0
1990	212	808	2	28	196	1
1991	63	163	2	16	119	0
1992	75	277	2	21	161	0

Comments: Stephens was acquired by Green Bay in a trade with New England on March 30 and he'll get a good opportunity to earn a starting job. He started 16 games at fullback for the Patriots in 1992 but was used mostly as a blocker for Leonard Russell and Jon Vaughn, the half-backs, which is Stephens' natural position. After three excellent seasons to begin his career, Stephens has rushed for only 440 yards the last two years. He was the Rookie of the Year in 1988, but he let success go to his head and lost his starting job at halfback after an ill-advised holdout in '91. Some people think Stephens hasn't lost anything. Moody but talented, he prefers to run over tacklers because he lacks the moves to get past them. He might be the fastest fullback in the league, but Green Bay will use him more wisely.

AMP LEE / 49ERS

YEAR	RUSH	YARDS	TD's	REC.	YARDS	TD's
1992	91	362	2	20	102	2

Comments: As a rookie second-round draft choice last year, Lee started three games at the end of the season and finished third on the team in rushing, second among backs. Backing up Ricky Watters, he carried the ball only 21 times in the first 11 games. Then, when Watters was injured, Lee took over for three games. He scored four touchdowns, two both rushing and receiving, and had a 134-yard game vs. Minnesota. He also proved to be an excellent receiver. Lee doesn't have great speed, but he possesses good vision, freezes tacklers with his elusive moves and doesn't fumble. However, Watters will start again this year, with Lee backing him up. But if Watters goes down, look for Lee to take over.

DAVID LANG / RAMS

YEAR	RUSH	YARDS	TD's	REC.	YARDS	TD's
1991	0	0	0	0	0	0
1992	33	203	5	18	283	1

Comments: Lang had a career game in the season finale last year, rushing for three touchdowns against the Falcons, giving his six TD's for the year. He also had the two longest plays from scrimmage for the Rams in 1992, a 67-yard pass reception and a 71-yard run. He started 11 of 16 games and will be given a shot at the starting job in '93. A 12th-round draft choice in 1990, Lang has potential to be a big-play runner in the Rams' offense of the future. He has speed and innate running ability and is tough.

ROOKIES

See Chapter 13, The Rookie Report.

BEST OF THE REST

KENNETH DAVIS / BILLS

YEAR	RUSH	YARDS	TD's	REC.	YARDS	TD's
1988	39	121	1	11	81	0
1989	29	149	1	6	92	2
1990	64	302	4	9	78	1
1991	129	624	4	20	118	1
1992	139	613	6	15	80	0

Comments: Davis is the best backup running back in the NFL, and he regularly rushes for more yards than a lot of starters on other teams. After being let go by Green Bay after the 1988 season, Davis has found a home with the Bills. He set career single-season highs for rushing and receiving in 1991, and he nearly equaled them last season. Against Atlanta last year he rushed for 181 yards and scored twice, and he also outplayed Thurman Thomas in the Super Bowl again. He is usually the ball carrier in Buffalo's goal-line offense, which is why he scores on the ground almost as much as Thomas. Davis has a quick, slashing running style. He's fast through a hole and might be the closest thing the Bills have to a breakaway runner. In fact, Davis had a 78-yard run that was the longest run from scrimmage in the NFL in 1991. He had two 100-yard rushing games in '91, and he gained 208 yards on the ground in the final two games. In 1990, he scored four TD's during the regular season, then added three more in the AFC championship game, tying a league playoff record.

ERIC METCALF / BROWNS

YEAR	RUSH	YARDS	TD's	REC.	YARDS	TD's
1989	187	633	6	54	397	4
1990	80	248	1	57	452	1
1991	30	107	0	29	294	0
1992	73	301	1	47	614	5

Comments: Following two subpar seasons, Metcalf made a fine comeback in 1992. He was the Browns' second-leading receiver with 47 catches and third-leading rusher with 301 yards. He had his best game of the season in Week 3 when he scored four touchdowns against the Raiders (three on pass receptions). He started five of 16 games off and on throughout the season. He also scored a touchdown on a punt return, giving him seven for the season. As a rookie in 1989, Metcalf scored 10 touchdowns. But, two years later, he didn't score at all before bouncing back in '92. As a runner out of the backfield, Metcalf can't run between the tackles, and he's also a fumbler. He is, however, one of the NFL's best kick returners, running back two kickoffs for touchdowns in '90, and he's a dangerous receiver (he averaged 13.1 yards per catch last year). When he's on, Metcalf is a lightning-quick scatback with speed, acceleration and riveting change of direction. If the Browns continue to use him as a role player, he could again surprise as a fantasy sleeper.

DALTON HILLIARD / Saints

Year	Rush	Yards	TD's	Rec.	Yards	TD's
1988	204	823	5	34	335	1
1989	344	1262	13	52	514	5
1990	90	284	0	14	125	1
1991	79	252	4	21	127	1
1992	115	445	3	48	465	4

Comments: Seven touchdowns is pretty good production for any back, and that's what Hilliard scored in 1992 in limited action. He started four of 16 games, and finished second on the team in rushing. The best fantasy football player in 1989, he has never been able to get back to his former self because of repeated knee and other injuries. After major knee surgery in 1990, he is just a shadow of what he once was. When he was 100 percent, Hilliard hit the hole faster than any back in the league. He was a great cutback runner with vision, balance and lean. His big thighs and strong shoulders literally punished would-be tacklers, and he had the speed to break through the line. He still has a place on the team, however, although Vaughn Dunbar and Brad Muster will carry the load this season.

GASTON GREEN / Raiders

Year	Rush	Yards	TD's	Rec.	Yards	TD's
1988	35	117	0	6	57	0
1989	26	73	0	1	-5	0
1990	68	261	0	2	23	1
1991	261	1037	4	13	78	0
1992	161	648	2	10	79	0

Comments: Green was traded to the Raiders in mid-April and will compete for a starting job, although they seem to be loaded at halfback. Although Green didn't approach his statistics of the previous season in 1992, he did have another fairly strong year. He led Denver in rushing and was 10th in the AFC with 648 yards, although he scored only two touchdowns. Green surprised the football world in 1991 when he replaced holdout Bobby Humphrey and rushed for over 1,000 yards, which ranked second in the AFC and sixth in the NFL. He had been viewed as a bust in his first three seasons with the Rams. Green has excellent speed, moves, quickness and acceleration. When he was in Los Angeles, he too often seemed to want to turn every play into a sweep instead of just hitting the hole. That changed in Denver, where he proved he could play in the NFL. Now that he's back in L.A. — although with the other team in town — his playing time is not a sure thing again. He's also not much of a touchdown scorer.

VINCE WORKMAN / Buccaneers

Year	Rush	Yards	TD's	Rec.	Yards	TD's
1989	4	8	1	0	0	0
1990	8	51	0	4	30	1
1991	71	237	7	46	371	4
1992	159	631	2	47	290	0

Comments: Workman signed with Tampa Bay s a free agent in early May. Although he scored only two touchdowns for Green Bay in 1992 as compared to his output of 11 scores the year before, he actually had a better season. Until separating his shoulder in the 10th game, he ranked first in receiving among NFL running backs and had surprisingly gained 631 yards on the ground. His 631 yards were the most by a Green Bay back since 1989 and led the squad. His 101-yard game against Detroit was the team's first 100-yard outing in three years. A slashing, physical runner, Workman can get tough yards inside. In 1991, he went from a rarely used back to the fifth-leading scorer among NFC nonkickers. He was the Packers' third-leading rusher and second-leading receiver.

CRAIG HEYWARD / Bears

Year	Rush	Yards	TD's	Rec.	Yards	TD's
1988	74	355	1	13	105	0
1989	49	183	1	13	69	0
1990	129	599	4	18	121	0
1991	76	260	4	4	34	1
1992	104	416	3	19	159	0

Comments: Heyward signed with the Bears as a free agent on April 11, giving them two players who are both overweight and very talented. He is reunited with Ron Turner, the Bears' offensive coordinator, who recruited him to the University of Pittsburgh a decade ago. Heyward started 13 games at fullback for New Orleans last season, finishing third on the team in rushing and first with a 4.0-yard average per carry. He is an extremely talented player who may never reach his potential because he doesn't always have the right attitude (he was suspended for the final three games of 1991 for repeated violations of unspecified team rules). Occasionally, Heyward flashes his brilliance, and he's a great blocker. But he plays at a weight so high that he can't cut. In other words, if the hole isn't in front of him, he won't find it. When he's lighter, he's a pile driver with great agility and moves. Heyward wasn't happy with the Saints, so the change of teams might be good for him. He might also turn into a top goal-line runner, something the Bears need.

JARROD BUNCH / Giants

Year	Rush	Yards	TD's	Rec.	Yards	TD's
1991	1	0	0	2	8	0
1992	104	501	3	11	50	1

Comments: Bunch is starting to show signs of being a

real bruiser. Last year he ranked second on the Giants in rushing, and he had a 4.8-yard average, which is great for a fullback. He started 13 of 16 games, and, although he didn't make the headlines, he took some pressure off Rodney Hampton as a runner. The best big back in the 1991 draft, Bunch didn't do much as a rookie, when he backed up Maurice Carthon. The 250-pounder is a strong goal-line runner and a decent receiver.

JOHN L. WILLIAMS / Seahawks

Year	Rush	Yards	TD's	Rec.	Yards	TD's
1988	189	877	4	58	651	3
1989	146	499	1	76	657	6
1990	187	714	3	73	699	0
1991	188	741	4	61	499	1
1992	114	339	1	74	556	2

Comments: Although he's not a game-breaking threat, Williams continues to be the most consistent player on the Seattle offense. In fact, only five backs in NFL history have caught more passes than he. And, since entering the NFL in '86, no other back has more receptions (413) for more yards (3,701) than Williams. He led the team in receiving in 1992 (for the third time in five years) and was second in rushing. His 74 receptions were second among NFL running backs (behind San Diego's Ronnie Harmon), and his 11 in one game was the league high for 1992. His best rushing game last season was only 48 yards, but he bested that in receiving yards four times. One of the best runner-receivers among NFL backs, he had more than 1,000 combined yards four of the last five seasons, averaging 1,334 yards a year, before falling short with 895 last season. Williams is the most complete fullback in the NFL. As a runner, he can make tacklers miss or run over them. As a receiver, he uses his size to get free and has good speed downfield. However, because of the emergence of Chris Warren, Williams doesn't figure to be back near 700 or 800 yards rushing in a season again.

1992 SURPRISE

RODNEY CULVER / Colts

Year	Rush	Yards	TD's	Rec.	Yards	TD's
1992	121	321	7	26	210	2

Comments: Culver scored nine touchdowns as a rookie but averaged only 2.7 yards per carry on the ground and isn't being counted upon as an every-down back. However, he will probably continue to be the team's goal-line ball carrier. His best game was in the 1992 season finale; he rushed for 92 yards and a score and caught seven passes for 51 yards. Eight of his touchdowns came from inside the 10-yard line (the other was a 36-yard run). Culver's nine touchdowns were the most by a Colts back since Eric

Dickerson in 1988 and tied for the second most by a rookie in team history. He started only two games.

QUESTION MARKS

CLEVELAND GARY / Rams

Year	Rush	Yards	TD's	Rec.	Yards	TD's
1989	37	163	1	2	13	0
1990	204	808	14	30	150	1
1991	68	245	1	13	110	0
1992	279	1125	7	52	293	3

Comments: Gary led the Rams in both rushing and receiving in 1992, when he had the best season of his career, but the addition of No. 1 draft pick Jerome Bettis could spell the end for Gary in Los Angeles. Last year, he was 10th in the NFL in rushing with 1,125 yards, eighth with 1,418 total yards from scrimmage and 11th in scoring with 10 touchdowns. He set career highs for rushing yards, receptions (52) and yards in a game (144). He had four 100-yard games and scored eight of his TD's in Games 6-10. After a great 1990 season in which he scored 15 touchdowns, Gary sat on the bench most of the time in '91, finishing second on the team in rushing but scoring only one time while being hampered by hamstring and knee injuries. Gary is still a chronic fumbler, but he's a big back with great hands and a superior blocker. He's a better runner inside than outside because of a lack of top speed. Chuck Knox says he is going to give David Lang a chance to start this season. But, if Gary gets the job and can keep from dropping the ball, he'll hang on to the job and would again be a pretty good choice in fantasy football.

BOBBY HUMPHREY / Dolphins

Year	Rush	Yards	TD's	Rec.	Yards	TD's
1989	294	1151	7	22	156	1
1990	288	1202	7	24	152	0
1991	11	33	0	0	0	0
1992	102	471	1	54	507	1

Comments: The Dolphins' leading receiver and No. 2 rusher in 1992, Humphrey could be at a crossroads in his NFL career. In January, he was arrested for cocaine possession and aggravated assault. Eight days later he was shot in the right thigh by a supposed friend. The Dolphins appeared to have gotten the better of their 1992 trade of Sammie Smith to Denver for Humphrey, but Humphrey's troubles can't be overlooked. He faces a six-game suspension because of the drug charge. During the '92 season, Humphrey wasn't able to earn a starting position, but he did turn into a valuable player on passing downs (his 54 receptions ranked seventh in the NFL among backs). He had his best game of the season in the last one, when he replaced an injured Mark Higgs and rushed for 88 yards and compiled 139 total yards. He also started throughout the playoffs. In 1991, Humphrey held out 97 days over a contract dispute and played in only four games. In 1989 and '90, he was one of the best backs in the league, becoming only the ninth player in NFL history to rush for 1,000 yards in each of his first two seasons. Humphrey is a strong, quick runner who makes good cuts with his exceptional balance, as well as an excellent pass receiver. In 1990, he was leading the NFL in rushing, was averaging 5.2 yards per carry and had just finished his fourth straight 100-yard game when, in Week 5, he suffered a badly sprained ankle that hampered him the rest of the season. Those are numbers he is capable of achieving again if he is able to get his troubles behind him and get his act together.

MARCUS ALLEN / RAIDERS

YEAR	RUSH	YARDS	TD'S	REC.	YARDS	TD'S
1988	223	831	7	34	303	1
1989	69	293	2	20	191	0
1990	179	682	12	15	189	1
1991	63	287	2	15	131	0
1992	67	301	2	28	277	1

Comments: Allen was demoted to third downs and short-yardage situations late last season, and he accused Raiders owner Al Davis of trying to ruin his career. There are still many people who think Allen has a year or two left in him, if given the opportunity. In 1991, he suffered sprained ligaments in the season opener and missed eight games before returning in a backup role. His best season in quite a while was 1990, when he rushed for 682 yards and scored 13 times. In 11 seasons, Allen has been one of the league's best all-around backs, and he might make it to the Hall of Fame someday. He has great run vision, elusive moves, quick feet and is tough to tackle, and he's a good blocker and receiver (he's the only AFC back to catch 400 passes in his career). Allen never had great feet, but he's been able to pick and slide with the best. While he no longer is a threat to go the distance, Allen still can cut back against the grain and make tacklers miss. He has rushed for 8,545 yards during his career and scored 97 times.

SAMMIE SMITH / CUT BY BRONCOS

YEAR	RUSH	YARDS	TD'S	REC.	YARDS	TD'S
1989	200	659	6	7	81	0
1990	226	831	8	11	134	1
1991	83	297	1	14	95	0
1992	23	94	0	0	0	0

Comments: The Broncos had a lot of high hopes for Smith after acquiring him from Miami for Bobby Humphrey last year. However, Smith played in only four games, starting once, in an injury-filled campaign and he was not offered a contract for 1993. He started the season on injured reserve, played four games and then went back on I.R. because of a torn stomach muscle. In other words, he didn't do much, carrying the ball just 23 times for 94

yards. Smith showed a lot of promise his first two seasons with the Dolphins in 1989 and '90 before falling apart the last two seasons. The 1991 season was when he fumbled two balls on the goal line and another on the six-yard line. In 1990, Smith's 831 yards were 13th in the NFL, and his 1,490 yards in two seasons were the most ever for a second-year player on the Dolphins. He also tied for 13th in the NFL with nine touchdowns (eight rushing). The knocks against Smith are his fumbling and that he doesn't play with injuries. But he has loads of talent, speed, quickness, moves and power, and he still could bounce back if he gets his head together with the right team.

ALLEN PINKETT / CUT BY SAINTS

YEAR	RUSH	YARDS	TD'S	REC.	YARDS	TD'S
1988	122	513	7	12	114	2
1989	94	449	1	31	239	1
1990	66	268	0	11	85	0
1991	171	720	9	29	228	1
1992	Injured					

Comments: Pinkett suffered torn knee ligaments in a scrimmage in July and missed the entire season after being acquired by the Saints in a trade from Houston in the offseason. New Orleans did not offer him a contract for 1993, but he will probably be signed by another team. In 1991, he had the best season of his six-year career, starting all 16 games for the Oilers and leading the team in rushing with a career-best 720 yards. His team-best 10 touchdowns ranked fifth in the AFC among nonkickers. In 1990, he backed up White and failed to score a touchdown all season for the first time in his career. Pinkett is a good, small, third-down back with cutback moves who excels on screens and draws. Pound for pound, he's very strong player, but he isn't an every-down back.

FADING VETERANS

ERIC DICKERSON / RAIDERS

YEAR	RUSH	YARDS	TD'S	REC.	YARDS	TD'S
1988	388	1659	14	36	377	1
1989	314	1311	7	30	211	1
1990	166	677	4	18	92	0
1991	167	536	2	41	269	1
1992	187	729	2	14	85	1

Comments: Dickerson led the Raiders in rushing last year and had his best season since 1989. But nobody includes him among the best running backs in the NFL anymore because he has lost a lot. In 1992, he started 15 games. He had consecutive 100-yard games in November, but they were his only real good outings all year. He did become the league's second-leading career rusher during the season. In 1991, Dickerson had the worst year of his career, playing in only 10 games and rushing for only 536 yards. That year he was hampered by injuries and he even was suspended by the Colts for insubordination and forced to miss three games. In 1990, he missed the first five weeks because he was suspended after holding out in a contract dispute and then failed a physical. Until the 1990 season, he had missed only one game due to injury. Dickerson rushed for a league-record seven straight 1,000-yard seasons from 1983 to '89, and he has 64 100-yard games (second to Walter Payton). Dickerson can still be a very good runner with decent speed and slashing ability, but now he tends to overread at the line of scrimmage rather than just attacking the holes.

JOHNNY HECTOR / Cut By Jets

Year	Rush	Yards	TD's	Rec.	Yards	TD's
1988	137	561	10	26	237	0
1989	177	702	3	38	330	2
1990	91	377	2	8	72	0
1991	62	345	0	7	51	0
1992	24	67	0	2	13	0

Comments: Hector played in only five games at the end of last season, rushing for a career-low 67 yards. Like Freeman McNeil, Hector's best days are behind him, although he can probably still fill a role as a capable backup. In fact, starting the final game of 1991 for the injured Blair Thomas, Hector responded with 13 carries for 132 yards. Hector is the team's fourth all-time leading rusher with 4,280 yards, and he's only five yards behind Matt Snell for the No. 3 spot. He was not offered a contract for the 1993 season.

OTTIS ANDERSON / Giants

Year	Rush	Yards	TD's	Rec.	Yards	TD's
1988	65	208	8	9	57	0
1989	325	1023	14	28	268	0
1990	225	784	11	18	139	0
1991	53	141	1	11	41	0
1992	10	31	0	0	0	0

Comments: Anderson carried the ball more in the Super Bowl two and a half years ago than he did all of last season. After 14 seasons, Anderson is sticking around just for the money. In 1991, he made just one start and rushed for only 141 yards. Last year, he played in 13 games but carried only 10 times (eight of them in Game 15). And, after scoring 25 touchdowns in 1989 and '90, he has seen the end zone only once since. The NFL's eighth all-time leading rusher with 10,273 yards, Anderson might still be productive if given the opportunity, especially as a goal-line runner.

SLIPPED IN 1992

LEONARD RUSSELL / Patriots

Year	Rush	Yards	TD's	Rec.	Yards	TD's
1991	266	959	4	18	81	0
1992	123	390	2	11	24	0

Comments: After a Rookie of the Year season in 1991, the sophomore jinx hit Russell hard last year. He had a lousy 3.2-yard average and missed five games with a sprained ankle and a hip pointer. He started off with games of 71 and 81 yards, but once the injury bug hit, he didn't gain over 39 yards. He was an almost-unheard-of junior in the 1991 draft who took the starting job from holdout John Stephens in training camp and kept it all season. He led all rookie rushers with 959 yards in 15 games (missing one start), and ranked fourth overall in the AFC. He had six games with 75 or more yards and two 100-yard games, but he did fumble too much. If he can go 100 percent, he should be able to bounce back this year. Russell has the size and power of a fullback with the moves of a halfback. He has speed and good instincts catching passes.

ROBERT DELPINO / Broncos

Year	Rush	Yards	TD's	Rec.	Yards	TD's
1988	34	147	0	30	312	2
1989	78	368	1	34	334	1
1990	13	52	0	15	172	4
1991	214	688	9	55	617	1
1992	32	115	0	18	139	1

Comments: Delpino was acquired by the Broncos in mid-April and will compete with Rod Bernstine for playing time in Denver. After an excellent 1991 season in which he scored 10 touchdowns, he was one of the "fantasy busts" of '92, scoring only once. He started off the season pretty well, with 17 carries, seven pass receptions and one touchdown in the first two games. But then Cleveland Gary took over as the featured ball carrier and Delpino was pretty much forgotten. He also missed six games with ligament damage in his left knee. He's not a heavy-duty, every-down back, so he's mostly used as a third-down, multipurpose player. In 1991, Delpino led the Rams in rushing, although his average per carry was only 3.2 yards, and he was second in receiving. His 10 touchdowns tied for eighth in the conference, and he gained 1,359 total yards. Delpino is a tough plugger with some quickness and elusiveness. He could be a good goal-line runner.

LEROY HOARD / Browns

Year	Rush	Yards	TD's	Rec.	Yards	TD's
1990	58	149	3	10	73	0
1991	37	154	2	48	567	9
1992	54	236	0	26	310	1

Comments: In 1992, Hoard was the classic fantasy bust. After scoring 11 touchdowns in 1991, he got into the end zone just one time in '92. Hoard did have a fine 4.4-yard average running the ball, but he didn't get the ball much on passes because the Browns' top two quarterbacks were injured last year. With Bernie Kosar back this year, Hoard might rebound nicely. Last year, he started nine games, and he gained 101 of his 236 rushing yards in the final two games. In 1991, Hoard came out of nowhere to score 11 touchdowns, and his nine TD catches were the most in one season by an NFL running back since official statistics were first recorded in 1932. An excellent receiver out of the backfield, he shows a big-play ability to take short, dump-off passes all the way for scores.

SPECIALISTS

RONNIE HARMON / Chargers

Year	Rush	Yards	TD's	Rec.	Yards	TD's
1988	57	212	1	37	427	3
1989	17	99	0	29	363	4
1990	66	363	0	46	511	2
1991	89	544	1	59	555	1
1992	55	235	3	79	914	1

Comments: The Chargers' leading receiver in 1992, Harmon is the best pass-catching specialist in the league. He led all NFL backs last year with his 79 catches, most of them coming on third downs (35 netted a first down), and a career-high 914 receiving yards. He had a team-high 1,149 combined yards and was voted the first alternate running back to the Pro Bowl. He caught six or more passes in a game eight times and scored four touchdowns. Harmon was voted the Chargers' Most Valuable Player the last two seasons by his teammates. In 1991, he led the team with 1,099 yards from scrimmage and was third in rushing with 544 yards and a 6.1-yard average that led NFL running backs. He is a skilled player in third-down and long-yardage situations. He does his best running in the open field after the catch (he dances too much behind the line on running plays). With Rod Bernstine gone, Harmon's reception total could get close to 100.

DAVE MEGGETT / Giants

Year	Rush	Yards	TD's	Rec.	Yards	TD's
1989	28	117	0	34	531	4
1990	22	164	0	39	410	1
1991	29	153	1	50	412	3
1992	32	167	0	38	229	2

Comments: Meggett doesn't carry the ball from scrimmage much, but he is one of the best pass-receiving specialists in the league. In 1991, he led the team in receptions, and last year he was second. He also scored a TD on a kickoff return in '92 and on a punt in '91. In 1990, he led the NFC in kickoff returns and was second in punt returns. The versatile Meggett is an excellent scatback. He has great acceleration to go with quick feet, but he is used mainly in passing situations and on kick returns. The Giants try to get him the ball in the open field on screens or isolated against a linebacker, and that's when he is most dangerous. He could also be a decent runner if given the chance; fans who remember Super Bowl XXV know that much.

TONY PAIGE / Dolphins

Year	Rush	Yards	TD's	Rec.	Yards	TD's
1988	52	207	0	11	200	0
1989	30	105	0	2	27	0
1990	32	95	2	35	247	4
1991	10	25	0	57	469	1
1992	7	11	1	48	399	1

Comments: Miami's third-leading receiver in '92, Paige carried the ball from scrimmage only seven times but was third on the team with 48 catches. He started all 16 games, with a high game of eight catches for 71 yards. Paige is one of the best blocking fullbacks and receivers out of the backfield in the NFL. He has to be, or else no team would start a back who barely ever ran the ball. He didn't have a carry in 12 games. He is a superb lead blocker and pass protector. In '91, Paige finished third on the Dolphins in receiving (and fifth in the NFL) and third in receiving yards. In 1990, he was called the key to the Dolphins' 12-4 season. Prior to the 1990 season, he had spent six years as a little-used, journeyman backup for the Jets and Lions.

TODD McNAIR / Chiefs

Year	Rush	Yards	TD's	Rec.	Yards	TD's
1989	23	121	0	34	372	1
1990	14	61	0	40	507	2
1991	10	51	0	37	342	1
1992	21	124	1	44	380	1

Comments: Kansas City's leading receiver in '92, McNair is one of the best third-down specialists in the NFL (he plays primarily as the lone setback on passing downs). He set personal highs for receiving in 1992, but also ranked as the team's fourth-leading rusher. He had at least three catches in 10 games, and, from 1988-92, he leads all Chiefs players in receiving. When McNair is in the game, you know it's third down and the Chiefs are going to pass, because that's how he gets the ball. In four years, he has rushed for only 357 yards and one touchdown, but he has caught 155 passes for 1,601 yards and five TD's. He's also a terror on special teams.

LARRY CENTERS / CARDINALS

YEAR	RUSH	YARDS	TD's	REC.	YARDS	TD's
1990	0	0	0	0	0	0
1991	14	44	0	19	176	0
1992	37	139	0	50	417	2

Comments: Centers is an excellent third-down back whose 50 catches last year equalled Terry Metcalf's 1975 total that ranks fifth in team history. He ranked sixth in the league among running backs in receiving. Centers caught a pass in 15 of 16 games, getting seven receptions in a game on three occasions. He started one time.

GARY ANDERSON / BUCCANEERS

YEAR	RUSH	YARDS	TD's	REC.	YARDS	TD's
1988	225	1119	3	32	182	0
1989	Holdout					
1990	166	646	3	38	464	2
1991	72	263	1	25	184	0
1992	55	194	1	34	284	0

Comments: Anderson's best days are behind him, as Reggie Cobb is fully entrenched as the starting fullback, and he is in danger of losing his role as the team's third-down back to Anthony McDowell. He was the Buccaneers' fourth-leading receiver, although he caught only 14 passes in the last seven games. He started four games. In 1991, he lost his starting job to Cobb. Still an acrobatic player, Anderson possesses some of the best breakaway moves in the NFL. He's still a fine pass receiver with excellent speed and moves. But he's too fragile for full-time duty and might be starting to show some age.

HARRY SYDNEY / PACKERS

YEAR	RUSH	YARDS	TD's	REC.	YARDS	TD's
1988	9	50	0	2	18	0
1989	9	56	0	9	71	0
1990	35	166	2	10	116	1
1991	57	245	5	13	90	2
1992	51	163	2	49	384	1

Comments: Sydney started 10 games at fullback last season and finished third on the team in receiving and first among backs after being acquired from the 49ers in the offseason. In 1991, he was the 49ers' No. 2 fullback, although he led the running backs in touchdowns with seven (five rushing and two receiving). Sydney is a tough, hard-nosed, versatile back who can catch and block OK, but he doesn't do anything special. But coach Mike Holmgren likes him coming out of the backfield, which means he should catch a lot of passes again in 1993.

DARYL JOHNSTON / COWBOYS

YEAR	RUSH	YARDS	TD's	REC.	YARDS	TD's
1989	67	212	0	16	133	3
1990	10	35	1	14	148	1
1991	17	54	0	28	244	1
1992	17	61	0	32	249	2

Comments: Johnston started all 16 games at fullback during the Cowboys' Super Bowl season last year. He has developed into a fine receiver, especially on circle routes, but he doesn't carry the ball much from scrimmage (only seven carries in the last 11 games). He finished fifth on the team in receiving and first among the team's backs. But, more important, he is an effective lead blocker for Emmitt Smith — and that's what keeps him in the lineup. However, he ignored some shoulder problems last year and had shoulder surgery this March. He should be ready to go by the start of training camp, with full range of motion.

ANTHONY McDOWELL / BUCCANEERS

YEAR	RUSH	YARDS	TD's	REC.	YARDS	TD's
1992	14	81	0	27	258	2

Comments: McDowell came out of nowhere as an eighth-round draft pick last year. A fullback, he turned into an excellent pass receiver out of the backfield in 1992, and he averaged 5.8 yards per rush. He caught 27 passes, almost twice as many as the number of times he carried the ball. He missed the first eight games of the season, then started eight of the last 12.

STEVE SEWELL / BRONCOS

YEAR	RUSH	YARDS	TD's	REC.	YARDS	TD's
1988	32	135	1	38	507	5
1989	7	44	0	25	416	3
1990	17	46	3	26	268	0
1991	50	211	2	38	436	2
1992	Injured					

Comments: Sewell missed the entire 1992 season with a broken ankle. Although he's listed as a running back, he is used mainly as a receiver. He'll run a few draws and an occasional sweep, but he's best scooting up the middle in short-yardage situations. One of the most versatile Broncos, he can also get downfield and make tough catches (he has six catches of 50 yards or more as a pro). In 1991, he was one of only two players in the NFL to run for a touchdown, catch a pass for a score and throw a TD pass (teammate John Elway was the other).

OTHERS

CARWELL GARDNER / Bills

Year	Rush	Yards	TD's	Rec.	Yards	TD's
1990	Injured					
1991	42	146	4	3	20	0
1992	40	166	2	7	67	0

Comments: At one time, Gardner was viewed as the Bills' fullback of the future. But, although he played in all 16 games last year and started seven times, he is used mostly as a blocker and doesn't get the ball very much because he is prone to fumbling. A strong pile-mover at the goal line, Gardner might improve if he ever gets much of a chance. A former defensive end who led the University of Louisville in rushing and receiving in 1989, his rookie season of 1990 was a washout because of a knee injury. In 1991, he started off quickly, with four touchdowns in the first seven games, but the Bills went to more of a one-back offense and he saw little action down the stretch (only 10 carries for 36 yards in the last eight games).

ANTHONY JOHNSON / Colts

Year	Rush	Yards	TD's	Rec.	Yards	TD's
1990	0	0	0	5	32	2
1991	22	94	0	42	344	0
1992	178	592	0	49	517	3

Comments: Johnson is one of the best pass-receiving backs in the NFL, and last year he showed he can also run with the ball. He led the Colts in rushing and was third in receiving last year for a career-best 1,109 total yards from scrimmage that ranked seventh in the AFC and 20th in the NFL. He started 13 games, getting 240 total yards in one of them against New England (77 rushing and 163 receiving) to break Eric Dickerson's team record. Only five Colts have eclipsed the 200-yard mark in a single game. Johnson's three touchdowns surpassed his career total of two heading into last season. But he has yet to score a rushing TD in 200 carries (for 686 yards). In 1991, before he suffered an eye injury, his 42 receptions led all NFL running backs and ranked seventh in the league. Although he missed seven games, he finished third on the team in receiving. Johnson is also a proven blocker.

JON VAUGHN / Patriots

Year	Rush	Yards	TD's	Rec.	Yards	TD's
1991	31	146	2	9	89	0
1992	113	451	1	13	84	0

Comments: Vaughn was the Patriots' leading rusher in 1992, despite starting only five games. His 4.0-yard average per carry was the best of the starters. After a slow start, only 31 carries in the first nine games, he came on like gangbusters, rushing for 268 yards in the next three, including the team's first 100-yard game of the season. Then he slumped again, gaining only 84 yards in the last month. The exciting Vaughn shouldn't be expected to be an every-down back, but he could develop into a fine off-the-bench role player. He's very fast and talented, with power, speed and elusiveness, and he is starting to develop as a pass receiver. In 1991 he returned a kickoff 99 yards for a touchdown and also threw a TD pass.

ROGER CRAIG / Vikings

Year	Rush	Yards	TD's	Rec.	Yards	TD's
1988	310	1502	9	76	534	1
1989	271	1054	6	49	473	1
1990	141	339	1	25	201	0
1991	162	590	1	17	136	0
1992	105	416	4	22	164	0

Comments: With his third team in three years, Craig no longer gains 1,000 yards a season, but he was a valuable backup to Terry Allen after being acquired in the old Plan B free agency. At 33, he has slowed more than just a step, although he should have another year or two left in him. He had scored only two touchdowns in 1990 and '91 before getting four TD's last year. At his best, he has an explosive start and an uncanny ability to let his blocking develop, read the gap and then burst through the hole with his trademark high-knee action. Receiving is still where Craig shines. He became the NFL's all-time leading receiver among running backs in 1990, breaking Walter Payton's career record. In 1991, Craig started 13 games for the Raiders. In 1990, he culminated the worst season of his career with a fumble that led to the 49ers' loss to the eventual Super Bowl champion Giants in the NFC championship game. During the season, he gained only 540 yards rushing and receiving and averaged just 3.1 yards per carry. Just two years before, he had gained over 2,000 total yards from scrimmage.

DARRELL THOMPSON / Packers

Year	Rush	Yards	TD's	Rec.	Yards	TD's
1990	76	264	1	3	1	0
1991	141	471	1	7	71	0
1992	76	255	2	13	129	1

Comments: Potential and promise have yet to turn into performance for Thompson, a first-round draft choice in 1990 who has rushed for less than 1,000 yards in three seasons. He spent the first half of 1992 on injured reserve after tearing a quadriceps muscle during training camp. He played only seven games all year, starting only the last four games following another injury, this time an ankle. His best games were 72 and 84 yards, which would be fine performances if he could produce them a number of times a year rather just twice. The Packers still hope he can turn into their featured back, but that looks unlikely at this stage. Thompson started 13 games at fullback in 1991, leading the Packers in rushing, but he had a poor 3.3-yard average and scored only one touchdown. Thompson is a big runner with great acceleration through the hole and good balance, but he's not overly instinctive and doesn't have very good moves. He's also not much of a pass catcher.

GREG LEWIS / Broncos

Year	Rush	Yards	TD's	Rec.	Yards	TD's
1991	99	376	4	2	9	0
1992	73	268	4	4	30	0

Comments: Lewis put together another solid season in 1992, scoring four more touchdowns. He started two of 16 games, with all of his scores coming in the second half of the season when he got more playing time. He was third on the team in rushing. Lewis had a fine rookie season in 1991, when he was second in rushing. He started four times and averaged 74 yards per game in those starts. He's a quick inside runner who's strong at the goal line.

MERRIL HOGE / Steelers

Year	Rush	Yards	TD's	Rec.	Yards	TD's
1988	170	705	3	50	487	3
1989	186	621	8	34	271	0
1990	203	772	7	40	342	3
1991	165	610	2	49	379	1
1992	41	150	0	28	231	1

Comments: Hoge started 12 games last year but was used mainly as a blocking fullback for Barry Foster. He carried the ball one-fourth of the time he did in the previous few seasons, and he scored just once, meaning he's no longer a decent fantasy football pick. Hoge used to be one of the most underrated and consistent workhorse running backs in the NFL. He's a tough, hard-nosed player who led the Steelers in rushing three times in four seasons from 1988 to '91. His 50 and 49 receptions in recent seasons are the most in team history for a running back. A classic overachiever, Hoge runs inside well and is tough near the goal line.

REGGIE RIVERS / Broncos

Year	Rush	Yards	TD's	Rec.	Yards	TD's
1991	2	5	0	0	0	0
1992	74	282	3	45	449	1

Comments: Rivers was a pleasant surprise for Denver last season, when he ranked as the team's No. 2 rusher and No. 3 pass receiver. A multiposition player who doesn't make many mistakes, he was the Broncos' go-to player early in the season. He set career and season highs for rushing attempts, yards and touchdowns as well as receptions. His high game was 66 yards on eight carries in Game 4.

STEVE BROUSSARD / Falcons

Year	Rush	Yards	TD's	Rec.	Yards	TD's
1990	126	454	4	24	160	0
1991	99	449	4	12	120	1
1992	84	363	1	11	96	1

Comments: Broussard has been a disappointment for the Falcons for three straight seasons after being drafted in the first round in 1990. He led the Falcons in rushing the last two years, although his total of 812 yards over that time isn't anything to get excited over. Last year Broussard missed too much game time because of several injuries and started just once in the 15 games he played. And he had only two games in which he rushed for more than 40 yards. As a rookie in '90, Broussard started off very well, but then he ran tentatively the rest of the season while nursing the first of many injuries that have hounded him. He did start 10 games, finishing second on the Falcons in rushing. The 5-6 1/2 Broussard moves like a bowling ball, but he doesn't like to take a hit and goes out of bounds too easily. That and the injuries have kept him in Jerry Glanville's doghouse, and he might not have many more opportunities to play his way out of it. When healthy, Broussard has quickness, balance and change of direction, and he's also supposed to be a good pass receiver (although the Falcons don't use him much on third downs).

AARON CRAVER / Dolphins

Year	Rush	Yards	TD's	Rec.	Yards	TD's
1991	20	58	1	8	67	0
1992	3	9	0	0	0	0

Comments: Craver spent most of the 1992 regular season on injured reserve with a pulled hamstring, playing in just the first six games. At the time he was injured, he ranked ninth in the league in kickoff returns. He returned for the playoffs and showed how talented he is, rushing for 72 yards and a touchdown on eight carries against San Diego. Craver was supposed to be one of the steals of the 1991 draft. Instead, he has shown little as a pro except for the one playoff game. He's a big back who can run and catch coming out of the backfield. He will get another opportunity to show his stuff this year.

LEROY THOMPSON / Steelers

Year	Rush	Yards	TD's	Rec.	Yards	TD's
1991	20	60	0	14	118	0
1992	35	157	1	22	278	0

Comments: Thompson is the Steelers' first running back off the bench. He ranked second on the team in rushing with a club-best 4.7-yard average per carry. In 1991, he carried 20 times for 60 yards as a rookie third-stringer.

EDGAR BENNETT / PACKERS

YEAR	RUSH	YARDS	TD's	REC.	YARDS	TD's
1992	61	214	0	13	93	0

Comments: Bennett showed strong promise in his first pro start when he rushed for 107 yards against Chicago. He became the first Packers rookie to register a 100-yard game since 1979. For the season, he ranked third on the team in rushing, starting two of 16 games. Bennett is a versatile fullback who could move into the starting lineup this year, although he'll never be a featured back. He could, however, score a few touchdowns in short-yardage situations.

KEITH HENDERSON / VIKINGS

YEAR	RUSH	YARDS	TD's	REC.	YARDS	TD's
1989	7	30	1	3	130	0
1990	6	14	0	4	35	0
1991	137	561	2	30	303	0
1992	44	150	1	5	64	0

Comments: Henderson was acquired in a trade with San Francisco before Game 3, but he wasn't much more than a backup in Minnesota. In 1991, he led the 49ers in rushing and was fourth in receiving, despite missing two games with an ankle injury. He was the 49ers' third-round draft pick in 1989, but he played in only eight games his first two seasons because of injuries and a steroid suspension. Henderson is a combination halfback/fullback, a big back with tackle-breaking power, but he has a knack of fumbling and he's too inconsistent.

MARK GREEN / BEARS

YEAR	RUSH	YARDS	TD's	REC.	YARDS	TD's
1989	5	46	1	5	48	0
1990	27	126	0	4	26	1
1991	61	217	3	6	54	0
1992	23	107	2	7	85	0

Comments: Green didn't play much again in 1992, but he still scored two touchdowns. In 1991, he started four games when Neal Anderson was battling hamstring problems. He had a career-high 82 yards and two touchdowns on 18 carries late in the season, and three TD's for the season. He doesn't get much playing time behind Anderson and Darren Lewis. He's a slashing runner who can catch the ball, but he doesn't stand out.

JOHNNY BAILEY / CARDINALS

YEAR	RUSH	YARDS	TD's	REC.	YARDS	TD's
1990	26	86	0	0	0	0
1991	15	43	1	0	0	0
1992	52	233	1	33	331	1

Comments: An excellent kick returner with great speed and moves, Bailey got a chance to show what he could do as a running back last year. He was the Cardinals' second-leading rusher and No. 5 receiver in 1992, making more of a contribution in the passing game. He missed the last two games with an ankle injury but played in the Pro Bowl as the alternate kick returner. Bailey was signed by Phoenix in Plan B free agency after two years as Chicago's No. 3 halfback. Even though he has lots of skill, he is too small to be an every-down back in the NFL. He led the NFL in punt returns last year.

SCOTT LOCKWOOD / PATRIOTS

YEAR	RUSH	YARDS	TD's	REC.	YARDS	TD's
1992	35	162	0	0	0	0

Comments: An eighth-round draft pick a year ago, Lockwood rushed for 123 yards against Miami in the final game. He was seldom used, playing in only four games and carrying the ball in just the last two (he also looked good in Game 15 with five carries for 39 yards). New coach Bill Parcells might be tempted to give him a chance based on those performances. He has a lot of speed for a fullback.

FRED McAFEE / SAINTS

YEAR	RUSH	YARDS	TD's	REC.	YARDS	TD's
1991	109	494	2	1	8	0
1992	39	114	1	1	16	0

Comments: The Saints' leading rusher as a rookie in 1991, McAfee carried the ball only six times for four yards in the first 11 games in '92. Then, because Vaughn Dunbar and Dalton Hilliard were too often ineffective, he got a chance to jump-start the offense. He took over for Hilliard in Game 14, but suffered a shoulder injury and was lost for the rest of the season. A sixth-round draft pick, he rushed for 494 yards in '91 — all of them in the final eight games of the season. His average per carry of 4.5 yards was also a team high. McAfee is very instinctive, with speed and quickness, but he isn't much of a pass receiver.

ERIC BALL / BENGALS

YEAR	RUSH	YARDS	TD's	REC.	YARDS	TD's
1989	98	391	3	6	44	0
1990	22	72	1	2	46	1
1991	10	21	1	3	17	0
1992	16	55	2	6	66	2

Comments: Four touchdowns is excellent production for a back who touched the ball just 20 times in 1992. Ball started 14 games at fullback, playing mostly as a blocker. He scored three of his four touchdowns in the first three games but wasn't used much afterward. Ball is a big back with lots of ability, but, since 1989 when he had a fine rookie season, he hasn't shown what he can do when given the opportunity. He also hasn't shown much durability.

IVORY LEE BROWN / CARDINALS

YEAR	RUSH	YARDS	TD's	REC.	YARDS	TD's
1992	68	194	2	7	54	0

Comments: A big back at 6-2, 245 pounds, Brown started five games last year but missed a month with a knee injury. He had turned a lot of heads in 1992 by leading the World League in rushing with 726 yards and a 4.7-yard average. If he can stay healthy, he might surprise if he gets the chance.

STEVE SMITH / RAIDERS

YEAR	RUSH	YARDS	TD's	REC.	YARDS	TD's
1988	38	162	3	26	299	6
1989	117	471	1	19	140	0
1990	81	327	2	4	30	3
1991	62	265	1	15	130	1
1992	44	129	0	28	217	1

Comments: Smith started 15 games at fullback last year. He is a strong inside runner and good pass receiver, but it's his blocking that keeps him on the field. He is arguably the AFC's best lead blocker. That won't help you in fantasy football, but it will help the halfback he's blocking for.

KEITH JONES / FALCONS

YEAR	RUSH	YARDS	TD's	REC.	YARDS	TD's
1989	52	202	6	41	396	0
1990	49	185	0	13	103	0
1991	35	126	0	6	58	0
1992	79	278	0	12	94	0

Comments: Jones started eight of 16 games last season, mostly at fullback when the Falcons used a two-back set. He was the team's third-leading rusher, although he didn't score all year. As a rookie in 1989, Jones scored six touchdowns, but he hasn't been in the end zone since. He missed 11 games in 1991 with a back injury. While he does everything OK and is best in short-yardage situations, he lacks the size and speed that is needed to be a top back and is used mostly as a blocker.

DEXTER CARTER / 49ERS

YEAR	RUSH	YARDS	TD's	REC.	YARDS	TD's
1990	114	460	1	25	217	0
1991	85	379	2	23	253	1
1992	4	9	0	1	43	1

Comments: Carter spent the first 10 games of 1992 on injured reserve with a shoulder injury. He played only three games after returning, with his only good play being a 43-yard touchdown reception. Then he suffered a knee injury and went back on injured reserve. Three years after joining the 49ers as a first-round draft pick, Carter has yet to prove that he is an NFL-caliber back. In 1991, he placed third on the team in rushing and seventh in receiving. In '90, Carter led the 49ers in rushing because both Roger Craig and Tom Rathman had subpar seasons. He is a quick, little scatback who showed elusiveness and receiving abilities as a rookie. Since then he has proven to be too small to be an every-down back.

ANTHONY THOMPSON / RAMS

YEAR	RUSH	YARDS	TD's	REC.	YARDS	TD's
1990	106	390	4	2	11	0
1991	126	376	1	7	52	0
1992	18	65	1	5	11	0

Comments: Thompson was waived by the Cardinals after two games and quickly claimed by the Rams. Thus, he escaped the shadow of Johnny Johnson in Phoenix but got lost in the shuffle in Los Angeles. He played in seven games and didn't suit up for the other seven. Thompson carried the ball only 18 times all season, and he scored his only touchdown for the Cards. He has been a disappointment since being drafted in the second round in 1990 and holding out. Thompson doesn't have great speed and hasn't proven to be much of an inside or goal-line runner.

LEWIS TILLMAN / GIANTS

YEAR	RUSH	YARDS	TD's	REC.	YARDS	TD's
1989	79	290	0	1	9	0
1990	84	231	1	8	18	0
1991	65	287	1	5	30	0
1992	6	13	0	1	15	0

Comments: At one time, Tillman was considered a top backup who would push Rodney Hampton for playing time. That isn't so any longer. Last season, he barely even saw the ball, even though he played in all 16 games. Tillman, who broke most of Walter Payton's records at Jackson State, is a slasher with power and speed, although he has a poor 3.5-yard average on runs.

JAMES JOSEPH / EAGLES

YEAR	RUSH	YARDS	TD's	REC.	YARDS	TD's
1991	135	440	3	10	64	0
1992	0	0	0	0	0	0

Comments: After leading the Eagles in rushing in 1991, Joseph played all 16 games last season but didn't carry the ball from scrimmage. He is being groomed to be the kind of multifaceted back that Keith Byars is, and he filled in some at tight end in '92. Joseph was the main ball carrier the second half of 1991. He calls himself the slowest running back in the NFL, but he shows some ability to break tackles and get outside.

WARREN WILLIAMS / Steelers

Year	Rush	Yards	TD's	Rec.	Yards	TD's
1988	87	409	0	11	66	1
1989	37	131	1	6	48	0
1990	68	389	3	5	42	1
1991	57	262	4	15	139	0
1992	2	0	0	1	44	0

Comments: Williams used to be a factor at halfback in Pittsburgh, but the emergence of Barry Foster has sent him to the bench. He is the team's special-teams star, however. In 1991, he started four games when Foster was injured and finished third on the team in rushing. He also led the team with four rushing touchdowns, which was half of the team's total, because he's an excellent goal-line runner. Williams is a between-the-tackles, slashing runner who can't run outside.

KEN CLARK / Colts

Year	Rush	Yards	TD's	Rec.	Yards	TD's
1990	7	10	0	5	23	0
1991	114	366	0	33	245	0
1992	40	134	0	5	46	0

Comments: Clark started two of 13 games last season but was used mostly as a blocking back. He started seven games in '91, usually in a two-man backfield. Clark is a fine receiver out of the backfield and short-yardage runner, but he's too slow to do much else.

PAT CHAFFEY / Jets

Year	Rush	Yards	TD's	Rec.	Yards	TD's
1991	29	127	1	0	0	0
1992	27	186	1	7	56	0

Comments: The Jets' backup fullback, Chaffey played in 14 games last year. He missed the final two with a rib injury. He had a fine 6.9-yard rushing average, finishing third on the team with 186 yards. He played for Atlanta in 1991, starting twice.

ERRIC PEGRAM / Falcons

Year	Rush	Yards	TD's	Rec.	Yards	TD's
1991	101	349	1	1	-1	0
1992	21	89	0	2	25	0

Comments: After coming out of nowhere in 1991 as an unknown rookie from North Texas State, Pegram didn't get the ball much in '92, although he did play in all 16 games. In '91, he led the Falcons in rushing attempts (101) and was third in yards (349). But the promise he showed as a rookie has faded and he isn't expected to be much of a factor this season. Pegram's biggest problem is that he dances too much at the line of scrimmage instead of just

hitting a hole or making one.

TOMMIE AGEE / Cowboys

Year	Rush	Yards	TD's	Rec.	Yards	TD's
1990	53	213	0	30	272	1
1991	9	20	1	7	43	0
1992	16	54	0	3	18	0

Comments: Agee is a backup fullback for Dallas who doesn't see much action except as an occasional blocker for Emmitt Smith. He's a good receiver who was the Cowboys' No. 2 rusher in 1990. His playing time has slipped the last two years.

GARY BROWN / Oilers

Year	Rush	Yards	TD's	Rec.	Yards	TD's
1991	8	85	1	2	1	0
1992	19	87	1	1	5	0

Comments: The backup to Lorenzo White, Brown played in all 16 games and ranked third on the team in rushing last year. A sixth-round draft pick, he looked impressive as a rookie in 1991. He's a load who can run, block and catch.

KEVIN TURNER / Patriots

Year	Rush	Yards	TD's	Rec.	Yards	TD's
1992	10	40	0	7	52	2

Comments: Turner played in all 16 games as a rookie in 1992, starting once. He scored two touchdowns on pass receptions. He has good speed, catches the ball well and can block. In time, he should develop into a solid fullback.

AND THE REST

(listed in alphabetical order)

KIMBLE ANDERS, Chiefs — Anders played in 11 games last year, including two starts. Injuries forced him to miss all but two games in '91. He caught five passes for 65 yards and had one rush for one yard. He missed five weeks with a knee injury. He fits well into the Chiefs' new offense because he is a prototype halfback.

RANDY BALDWIN, Browns — A big back who might see more playing time this season, Baldwin played in 15 games in 1992, rushing for 31 yards and catching two passes. He was the team's top kickoff returner.

A.B. BROWN, Jets — Brown carried 24 times for 42 yards last season — a lousy 1.8 yards per rush — all in the final three games of the season. Because Freeman McNeil retired and and Johnny Hector was released, Brown might be a backup.

THE FANTASY FOOTBALL ABSTRACT 1993

MAURICE CARTHON, Colts — Carthon started six games last season but carried the ball only four times for nine yards, because he's mainly a blocker.

DERRICK GAINER, Cowboys — Gainer played in five games for Dallas last year after being acquired from the Raiders. He was Emmitt Smith's backup in the playoff run.

SAM GASH, Patriots — Gash played mostly on special teams as a rookie (one of three first-year backs on the team) in 1992. He rushed five times for seven yards and scored one touchdown.

SCOTTIE GRAHAM, Jets — As a rookie, Graham rushed for 29 yards on 14 carries. He saw action only in the final two games of the season.

ROBERT GREEN, Redskins — A rookie free agent, Green rushed for 46 yards on eight carries last year. He could see more playing time in 1993 because he showed a lot of potential.

ALONZO HIGHSMITH, Chiefs — A former No. 1 draft pick whose career has been downhill ever since because of injuries, Highsmith has rushed for only 69 yards the last three seasons. He had knee surgery last November and is attempting a comeback. But Kansas City is his fourth team in the last four years, and this will be his final chance t show he has something.

IVY JOE HUNTER, Patriots — Hunter missed the entire 1992 season with a knee injury. In '91, he started 11 games as a blocking fullback but carried the ball only 18 times for 53 yards. He did better as a receiver, catching 11 passes for 97 yards.

TRACY JOHNSON, Seahawks — A decent fullback, Johnson rushed only three times for 26 yards last year. He's a good blocker.

JAMES JONES, Lions — Jones was signed by Detroit as a free agent in May. He played both fullback and tight end in 1992. He didn't run the ball from scrimmage but did catch 21 passes for 190 yards. In 1991, he started the last six games, scoring three touchdowns in the final three in short-yardage situations. He might be Barry Sanders' backup this season.

MARC LOGAN, 49ers — Logan was primarily a kickoff returner for San Francisco last year. He had his best seasons with Miami in 1989 and '90 when he rushed for 201 and 317 yards, respectively.

RUEBEN MAYES, Seahawks — Mayes, who rushed for 1,353 yards as a rookie for New Orleans in 1986 before blowing out his knee, came out of voluntary retirement last year but shouldn't have because he doesn't have much left. He rushed for only 74 yards on 28 carries. He'll probably be cut.

NAPOLEON McCALLUM, Raiders — The Raiders' No. 2 fullback, McCallum played in 13 games last year with no carries and one reception. He was used mainly as a kick returner. In '91, he ran the ball 31 times for 110 yards.

DEXTER McNABB / Packers — McNabb played in all 16 games as a rookie but didn't get the call very much. He gained 11 yards on just two carries. He could see more time this year.

BRIAN MITCHELL, Redskins — Mitchell hasn't been used much at running back the last two seasons, but he showed his talents in a playoff game against Minnesota last season when he rushed for 109 yards and a touchdown. He's an excellent kick returner who will play more if Earnest Byner slows down or Ricky Ervins doesn't come on.

DARRIN NELSON, Vikings — These days Nelson is a fine kick returner who doesn't get the ball from scrimmage much. He lacks the speed he once had but knows how to follow his blockers on kickoffs. Last year he rushed 10 times for only five yards.

JAMES SAXON, Dolphins — Saxon is a seldom-used backup fullback for Miami who played in all 16 games as mostly a special-teams performer. In the last three years in Kansas City and Miami, he has rushed only 13 times for 35 yards.

JOHN SETTLE, Redskins — Settle has spent the last two seasons on injured reserve with rib and knee injuries. His best season was 1988, when he came out of nowhere to rush for 1,024 yards and catch 68 passes for the Falcons. But he hasn't done much since then and might be cut before the start of training camp.

SPENCER TILLMAN, Oilers — Tillman was the Oilers' No. 3 back in 1992. He played in all 16 games but carried the ball only one time.

ROBERT WILSON, Packers — Wilson didn't play in 1992 after getting cut by Tampa Bay before the start of the season. As a rookie in '91, he started 15 games and ran 42 times for 179 yards and caught 20 passes for 121 yards. Don't be surprised if he surprises in Green Bay this season as a blocking back.

RON WOLFLEY, Browns — Wolfley is just a special-teams star and not much of a runner (only one carry last year).

Other Running Backs on Rosters

Jeff Alexander, Broncos
Latin Berry, Packers
Eric Blount, Cardinals
Tony Brooks, Eagles
Bob Christian, Bears
Derrick Douglas, Browns
Terrence Flagler, Chiefs
Eddie Fuller, Bills
Mike Gaddis, Vikings
Victor Jones, Broncos
Tim Lester, Rams
Derek Loville, 49ers
Eric Lynch, Lions
Ostell Miles, Bengals
Ty Montgomery, Raiders
Don Overton, Bengals
Bernie Parmalee, Dolphins
Mazio Royster, Buccaneers
Chris Samuels, Chargers
Siran Stacy, Eagles

Craig Taylor, Saints
Ed Tillison, Lions
Ed Toner, Colts
Peter Tuipulotu, Chargers

Adam Walker, 49ers
Marcus Wilson, Packers
Tim Worley, Steelers

Chapter 6
Wide Receivers

San Francisco's Jerry Rice is again the preeminent wide receiver in the NFL, which comes as no surprise. At no other position in pro football does one player so clearly dominate his peers as Rice does. It is for that reason that Rice should again be strongly considered for the No. 1 overall pick in many fantasy drafts.

A year ago, wide receiver was the deepest of the five main positions in fantasy football, but that's not the case this year, because many of the best receivers are coming off subpar seasons. Thus it is this year the thinnest of positions. There are perhaps a dozen who are capable of scoring at least 10 touchdowns a season, with the most likely being Andre Rison, Michael Haynes, Sterling Sharpe, Haywood Jeffires, Michael Irvin and Ernest Givins.

After them comes a small group of solid receivers that includes Fred Barnett, Andre Reed, Gary Clark and John Taylor before you get to a large group of players who could get anywhere from eight touchdowns to only one or two. And that is the group of receivers that is going to be so important this year. The team that drafts one or two of them who comes through will be in contention for a fantasy league championship.

Draft Tips in Choosing Wide Receivers

■ Look at past performances, especially the last two or three seasons, rather than just last season.

■ Draft receivers from pass-oriented teams, such as the Oilers, Falcons, Redskins and Dolphins. Forget about running teams like the Steelers, Giants and Vikings.

■ Draft receivers who are favorite targets of a good quarterback, such as Jerry Rice, Andre Reed, Andre Rison, Haywood Jeffires and Irving Fryar.

■ Don't overlook the secondary receivers, such as John Taylor, Calvin Williams, Willie Anderson and Mike

Jerry Rice

Pritchard, because they occasionally play better over an entire season (and certainly in stretches) than the main receiver. Also, if the primary receiver gets injured, the secondary receiver becomes the main target.

■ Remember that in today's era of three- and four-wide-receiver formations, a receiver does not have to be a starter to make a big contribution. Many backup wideouts catch half a dozen touchdown passes each season, which is as many — or more — as a lot of the good starters will catch.

■ Remember to draft rookies who might break into the starting lineup, such as Curtis Conway, Sean Dawkins and O.J. McDuffie. Several rookies always have big years, and it's up to you to determine which ones will do it in 1993. And, because this year's wide receivers are so average, one or two rookies might come through in big ways.

■ Look for speed receivers who make the big plays, rather than possession receivers (especially in the Performance Scoring Method).

■ Make sure you have capable backups who can take over if one of your starters is injured or out of the lineup on a bye.

■ If a team has just made a quarterback change, or it looks like a team will have inconsistent quarterbacking throughout the season, take that into consideration. Last year's Vikings and Raiders were a perfect example. With two or three quarterbacks starting during the season, the statistics of those teams' receivers were affected. In other words, stay away from quarterback controversies.

■ Take into consideration that receivers are often double-teamed, so you will want to know which players will be affected by that and which ones can beat the double-team.

■ Be aware of what is going on during training camp. Are Andre Reed, John Taylor and Mark Clayton ready to make comebacks from subpar seasons? Can Mark Jackson and Sterling Sharpe do it again, or were their 1992 seasons career years? Do Art Monk and James Lofton have another good season left in them? Who is going to replace Gary Clark as the Redskins' star receiver? What will Clark do in Phoenix? How much is Desmond Howard going to play for the Redskins? Who is going to replace Irving Fryar in New England? Which of Dan Marino's new receivers will have the bigger year, Fryar or Mark Ingram? Where is Mark Clayton going to play in 1993? Is Rob Moore ever going to move into the elite of NFL receivers? Are Anthony Carter and Mervyn Fernandez past their prime? Is Eddie Brown going to make a comeback in Cincinnati? Can Andre Rison and Michael Haynes keep catching 10-plus touchdowns a season?

THE BEST

JERRY RICE / 49ERS

Year	Rec.	Yards	Avg.	TD's
1988	64	1306	20.4	9
1989	82	1483	18.1	17
1990	100	1502	15.0	13
1991	80	1206	15.1	14
1992	84	1201	14.3	10

Comments: Rice is the greatest receiver in pro football today and maybe the best of all time. He can do it all — catch short passes or deep ones and make the big runs after catching the ball. In 1992, he continued to register his place in team and league history, and he's on pace to shatter every career receiving record in the NFL record books. Rice is now the 49ers' all-time leading receiver (609 catches), he extended his team records for receiving yardage (10,273) and total touchdowns (108), and he became the NFL's all-time touchdown reception leader (103), moving ahead of Don Hutson and Steve Largent. He finished the season as the No. 3 receiver in the NFC with 84 receptions for 1,201 yards, tying Lance Alworth's league record for most consecutive 1,000-yard receiving seasons (seven). He has caught at least one pass in every game during his career, 111 straight games, dating back to 1985. Rice is a touchdown waiting to happen. He has terrific hand-eye coordination and field awareness, but it's his ability to kick into some kind of otherworld, warp-speed gear in just one step that makes him so great. He's also a threat on end-arounds, as he scored on running plays in 1986, '87, '88 and '92. In one of the most memorable performances of the 1990 season, Rice caught 13 passes for 225 yards and five touchdowns against the Falcons. Opponents have found that there is no one way to stop Jerry Rice — that's how good he is. Pick him first among wide receivers; no one else should even be considered.

SUPERSTARS

ANDRE RISON / FALCONS

Year	Rec.	Yards	Avg.	TD's
1989	52	820	15.8	4
1990	82	1208	14.7	10
1991	81	976	12.0	12
1992	93	1121	12.1	11

Comments: Rison is the only player in NFL history to catch over 300 passes in his first four seasons. His 33 TD passes in the last three years trails only Jerry Rice, and he and Rice are the only two players in the league to have three straight seasons of 80 or more receptions and 10 or more touchdowns. Rison holds the Falcons' three highest single-season receiving marks in his three years with the team (he broke into the NFL with the Colts). In 1992, Rison ranked second in the NFL in receiving and fourth in yards. Rison doesn't break too many long ones, as he has averaged just a tad over 12 yards a catch the last two years, but he's one of the game's top scorers and he's practically impossible to stop near the goal line. Rison missed the season opener last year over a contract squabble and didn't start the next two games because he was still in the doghouse. For the season, he had two 100-yard games and two others with 99 yards. In the last two years, Rison has caught five or more passes in 22 games and three or more in 28 of 31. He had three-TD games in both seasons. Rison seems to go in streaks, and when he's hot, he's one of the top few players in fantasy football. Rison specializes in underneath and crossing routes, relying on great quickness, elusiveness and running precise routes rather than straight-out speed. He can make acrobatic catches, and he has great hands, which make him Atlanta's go-to receiver in clutch situations. The man in motion from the left slot position, Rison has one shortcoming: he's impatient. If he doesn't get his share of passes early in a game, he complains and starts to free-lance. Still, he's one of the best receivers in the NFL, and, in fantasy football, the second-best receiver.

STERLING SHARPE / PACKERS

Year	Rec.	Yards	Avg.	TD's
1988	55	791	14.4	1
1989	90	1423	15.8	12
1990	67	1105	16.5	6
1991	69	961	13.9	4
1992	108	1461	13.5	13

Comments: Sharpe reaffirmed that, if he has a good quarterback throwing to him (such as Brett Favre), he is one of the best receivers in the NFL. In 1992, Sharpe set the all-time NFL record with 108 receptions. He became the first Packer to lead the league in receiving, yards (1,461) and touchdowns (13) since Don Hutson in 1944. His fantastic totals pushed him to fourth place on the team's all-time receiving list and fifth for yardage. He also became the first Packer to catch 50 or more passes in five consecutive seasons, the second to catch 60 in four seasons and the second to catch 70 in two seasons. He also has three 1,000-yard receiving seasons. With 389 receptions, he has caught more than any other receiver ever in his first five seasons. Last year, he extended his consecutive game reception streak to 71, dating back to 1988. He caught five or more passes in 14 games, he had seven 100-yard games and he scored in 11 games (only two two-TD games). Whereas most receivers specialize in either short or long passes, Sharpe scored from every distance — four from inside the 10-yard line, six from 10-39 yards and three from over 40. Even when he doesn't have somebody good throwing to him, Sharpe is a very consistent player who ranks among the top 10 in receptions but far down the list in touchdowns (he had only 10 in 1990 and '91). Built like a halfback, Sharpe has everything it takes — size, speed, strength, moves, great hands and durability. He seems immune to double coverage, and he has a quick burst after the catch in addition to being a hard-nosed blocker. With Favre and coach Mike Holmgren around, there's no reason Sharpe's statistics can't be as good as those of Jerry Rice.

HAYWOOD JEFFIRES / Oilers

YEAR	REC.	YARDS	AVG.	TD's
1988	2	49	24.5	1
1989	47	619	13.2	2
1990	74	1048	14.2	8
1991	100	1181	11.8	7
1992	90	913	10.1	9

Comments: Jeffires had another outstanding season in 1992, catching 90 passes to lead the AFC in receptions for the third consecutive year. Although he gained only 913 yards (10.1-yard average), he scored nine touchdowns to tie for fifth in the league. His 190 receptions the last two years is the third-highest total ever. Jeffires led the team in receiving six times and in receiving yards five times. He had one 100-yard game and scored in seven games, including a three-TD outing against Cincinnati (the first game of his career with more than one TD catch). He had 11 games with five or more receptions, and he has caught at least one pass in 48 consecutive games. In 1991, he became only the fifth player in pro football history to amass 100 receptions in one season, joining an exclusive club that includes only Washington's Art Monk, Houston's Charley Hennigan, Denver's Lionel Taylor and San Francisco's Jerry Rice (Green Bay's Sterling Sharpe did it in '92). He also had 1,181 receiving yards, which was first in the AFC and third in the NFL. Jeffires is the ultimate possession receiver, but, believe it or not, Jeffires still has a reputation for dropping passes. He's clearly the Oilers' most gifted athlete, a long strider who has the speed to go deep and can outjump smaller corners on fade routes.

CAN'T MISS

MICHAEL IRVIN / Cowboys

YEAR	REC.	YARDS	AVG.	TD's
1988	32	654	20.4	5
1989	26	378	14.5	2
1990	20	413	20.7	5
1991	93	1523	16.4	8
1992	78	1396	17.9	7

Comments: In 1992, Irvin became the first Dallas player to surpass 75 receptions and 1,300 receiving yards in consecutive seasons. He finished the year ranked second to Green Bay's Sterling Sharpe in receiving yards, and his 17.9-yard average was easily the best of any player with at least 55 catches. In his last 21 regular-season games, Irvin has averaged 5.5 receptions and 98 yards per game, with 10 100-yard games and 11 touchdowns. He averages a touchdown every 9.2 receptions, although last year he scored his seven TD's in only four games, being shut out of the end zone in the other 12. He has caught at least one pass in 33 straight games. Because of injuries, Irvin missed one-third of Dallas' games from 1988 to '90. In 1991, he finished second in the NFL in receptions (93, tied for the eighth most in NFL history) and first in receiving yards (1,563, sixth best ever). He shattered the Dallas records for catches by 17 and yards by 331. Irvin does it all — he can be a possession receiver or a deep threat. He doesn't have the type of deep speed that makes cornerbacks quiver, but he explodes out of his cuts and can burst open after he makes a catch. He creates big sideline plays, and although he may be a hotdog, he's big, fearless over the middle, has good hands, and breaks tackles. As long as Irvin can continue to stay healthy, he will continue putting up big numbers, and even more so with Troy Aikman developing into one of the NFL's best quarterbacks.

MICHAEL HAYNES / Falcons

YEAR	REC.	YARDS	AVG.	TD's
1988	13	232	17.8	4
1989	40	681	17.0	4
1990	31	445	14.4	0
1991	50	1122	22.4	11
1992	48	808	16.8	10

Comments: Over the last two seasons, Haynes has scored 21 touchdowns on 98 receptions, a fantastic 21 percent, higher than anyone else in the league. In fact, only teammate Andre Rison and San Francisco's Jerry Rice have more TD catches the last two years. Haynes had two 100-yard games in 1992, giving him eight for his career, and his lifetime average of almost 18 yards per reception ranks him among the top active players. He missed Games 3 and 4 last year with a separated shoulder after scoring three times in the first two games. Only one of his touchdowns in 1992 was less than 10 yards (that's where Rison gets the ball). Haynes was a seventh-round draft pick in 1988 who had only moderate success in his first three seasons. In 1991, the only season in which he stayed healthy, Haynes emerged as one of the NFL's top deep threats with 11 touchdowns and a league-best 22.4-yard average per catch (he also scored two TD's in the playoff opener). A former Olympics Trials speedster, Haynes might be the fastest player in the league in pads. He was fifth in the league in receiving yards and fourth in receiving TD's in '91. That year he had 12 catches of 30-plus yards — 80, 75, 67, 57, 55, 52, 46, 44, 43, 43, 41 and 30 — and he averaged 44.9 yards per score. Haynes specializes on fly patterns, mostly avoiding the middle of the field where he would meet contact. He stretches defenses, which helps his teammates get open. He has proven he can control a game by himself, if given the chance.

ERNEST GIVINS / OILERS

YEAR	REC.	YARDS	AVG.	TD's
1988	60	976	16.3	5
1989	55	794	14.4	3
1990	72	979	13.6	9
1991	70	996	14.2	5
1992	67	787	11.7	10

Comments: Year in and year out, Givins is one of the most consistent receivers in the NFL. Although he didn't come close to gaining 1,000 yards receiving last year (he always seems to fall short by a few yards), he set a personal high with 10 touchdown catches. That figure led the AFC and was third-most in the NFL. He caught only 13 passes for 143 yards in the first four games of the '92 season because of double coverage, then came on like gangbusters with six TD's in the next five games. Givins has caught 50 or more passes in seven consecutive seasons and at least one pass in 52 straight games. He should move ahead of Drew Hill on the club's career receiving list this year (he is only 42 behind). He started all 16 games last year and has missed only two due to injury in his seven-year career. In 1991, Givins ranked third on the Oilers in receptions (tied for seventh in the AFC) and receiving yards (ninth in the conference), second in TD's receiving and first in average yards per catch. Givins is tough to jam at the line and he has excellent quickness and change of direction. He has deceptive speed and great cutting ability to make tacklers miss, and he's one of the league's best after-the-catch receivers. Since cornerbacks play so far off him, he catches a lot of short hitches.

FRED BARNETT / EAGLES

YEAR	REC.	YARDS	AVG.	TD's
1990	36	721	20.0	8
1991	62	948	15.3	4
1992	67	1083	16.2	6

Comments: Barnett has quietly turned into one of the best receivers in the NFL, and he might be the most underrated. In 1992, Barnett led the Eagles in receiving and receiving yards, ranking 13th and fifth in the NFL, respectively, in those categories. His 16.2-yard average was the second-best of all receivers with 55 or more catches. A true long-ball threat, Barnett was the first Eagle to surpass 1,000 yards receiving since 1985. He was the only player on the team to catch passes in all 16 games, and he had three 100-yard outings (and nine in three years). He had a career-high 193 yards in Game 2. Four of his six touchdowns were scored in the first month of the year. In three seasons, 18 of Barnett's 165 receptions have gone for touchdowns, including eight of 35 yards or more. He tied for the team lead in receptions in 1991, when injuries put five different quarterbacks in the lineup and contributed to his low total of only four scores. Barnett has great athleticism. He can outjump most cornerbacks or beat them with his speed on deep passes, and he's improving on shorter patterns. This could be the year Barnett moves into the elite of NFL receivers.

JOHN TAYLOR / 49ERS

YEAR	REC.	YARDS	AVG.	TD's
1988	14	325	23.2	2
1989	60	1077	18.0	10
1990	49	748	15.3	7
1991	64	1011	15.8	9
1992	25	428	17.1	3

Comments: Taylor had an injury-marred season in 1992. He missed six games with a broken left leg suffered in the third game and had the fewest receptions he's had since his 1988 rookie year. He scored three touchdowns, two in Game 2 against Buffalo when he caught five passes for 112 yards. After returning in Game 10, he scored only one more time before missing the last game with a leg injury. He returned for the playoffs. If Jerry Rice weren't on the 49ers, Taylor might catch 90 passes and score 15 touchdowns a season, because he is that good. His trademark is the big play; he uses exceptional strength to shrug off defenders. The consummate over-the-middle receiver, he might be the most dangerous after-the-catch end in pro football. Taylor might have more speed than Rice, and he can break into a long-striding sprint in just a few steps. In 1991, he caught a career-high 64 passes, and his yardage and touchdown totals were just off his personal bests set in 1989. He scored in eight games and had three 100-yard games despite the team's quarterbacking woes. Taylor is an excellent punt returner, too, scoring twice on returns in 1988. As long as he's healthy in 1993, Taylor's performances will be back where they were from 1989 to '91.

ANDRE REED / BILLS

YEAR	REC.	YARDS	AVG.	TD's
1988	71	968	13.6	6
1989	88	1312	14.9	9
1990	71	945	13.3	8
1991	81	1113	13.7	10
1992	65	913	14.0	3

Comments: Reed is usually one of the most consistent receivers in the NFL, although he didn't have his usual 70-catch, nine-TD season in 1992. Over the last 10 games of the season, Reed caught only 27 passes. However, he showed that he hasn't lost anything in the AFC wild-card game against Houston when he caught three TD passes in the second half in Buffalo's amazing come-from-32 points-behind victory. Reed started off strong in '92, with both of his 100-yard receiving games and two of his three TD's in the first five games. That's also when he had his career-best 168-yard day. In 1991, Reed scored touchdowns in nine games (including two in one of them), and his 10 receiving TD's tied a team record. He also had four 100-yard games. The secret to Reed is his ability to quickly get off the line of scrimmage, and he runs precise routes and knows how to come back to the quarterback, something a lot of top receivers don't know. He lacks sprinter's speed, but he is very strong with good hands. Reed excels in traffic and he's at his best after getting the ball. He's best on the deep sideline routes. He's also a fine runner on end-arounds (20 carries for 201 yards the last two years). Reed became the Bills' all-time leading receiver in 1990, for yardage and touchdowns. He has led the team in receiving seven straight years and owns the team's top four single-season receiving marks. He has had 11 multi-touchdown games and 51 total TD's in his career. He became the 31st NFL player to catch 500 passes, and his 7,379 yards ranks 43rd all-time.

ANTHONY MILLER / CHARGERS

YEAR	REC.	YARDS	AVG.	TD's
1988	36	526	14.6	3
1989	75	1252	16.7	10
1990	63	933	14.8	7
1991	44	649	14.8	3
1992	72	1060	14.7	7

Comments: With a good quarterback throwing to him, Miller proved again last season that he is one of the best wide receivers in the NFL. He earned his third trip to the Pro Bowl after catching 72 passes for a team-high 1,060 yards and seven touchdowns (he scored another on a fumble recovery in the end zone). In the first four games of '92, Miller caught only 12 passes for 158 yards. Then, at the same time the team got hot (winning 11 of 12 games), Miller came on strong. He quickly became Stan Humphries' favorite receiver, with four 100-yard games and anywhere from two to nine receptions a game. In 1991, he was the victim of bad quarterbacking, bad coaching and

nagging injuries. In 1989 and '90, Miller caught 138 passes for 2,185 yards and 17 touchdowns. Miller may not yet be in a class with John Jefferson and Wes Chandler, but he has led the Chargers in receiving twice, something neither of them did even once. A faster, less physical version of Buffalo's Andre Reed, Miller has great speed (4.4), and when the ball is in his hands, he's the ultimate big-play receiver. He likes deep routes and comebacks, and he makes good adjustments. He can also turn short flips into long gains by breaking tackles. If Humphries can come anywhere close to his 1992 stats, so will Miller.

SOLID PICKS

IRVING FRYAR / DOLPHINS

YEAR	REC.	YARDS	AVG.	TD's
1988	33	490	14.8	5
1989	29	537	18.5	3
1990	54	856	15.9	4
1991	68	1014	14.9	3
1992	55	791	14.4	4

Comments: Fryar was traded to Miami on April 1 and might turn into one of the NFL's top receivers this year with Dan Marino throwing to him. New England's leading receiver in '92, he became the first player on the team to catch more than 50 passes in three consecutive seasons. He also set a career high with 165 receiving yards on eight catches against the Jets. His 55 catches was the second-best total of his career, and after several seasons of unrealized potential, Fryar has played very well the last three years. In 1991, he became just the third player in Patriots history to have over 1,000 yards receiving in a season, and his 68 catches — fourth most in one season in team history — moved him into second place on the team's all-time receiving list. His 1991 receptions and yards were both career highs. Scouts point to his poor work habits and off-field distractions as key reasons behind his mediocre career, but he continues to be a solid home-run threat because he's very dangerous after the catch. Fryar is big, fast, tough, fearless over the middle and has great moves. But he runs stiff, predictable routes and hasn't been consistent until lately. He no longer has great speed, but he's finally playing the way he was supposed to as the first pick in the 1984 draft. He also might be the best blocker of NFL wideouts.

CRIS CARTER / VIKINGS

YEAR	REC.	YARDS	AVG.	TD's
1988	39	761	19.5	6
1989	45	605	13.4	11
1990	27	413	15.3	3
1991	72	962	13.4	5
1992	53	681	12.8	6

Comments: These days it's Cris Carter, not Anthony,

who is the key to Minnesota's passing game, and he'll become even more important whenever the team finds a consistent quarterback. He was the team's leading receiver in 1992, despite missing the last four games because of a broken collarbone. In six games in the middle of the season, Carter caught 39 passes for 474 yards and four touchdowns, which are clearly the numbers of a player who can dominate a game. Only in the last two years has Carter lived up to the billing that made him a first-round pick in the 1987 supplemental draft by the Eagles. In 1991, he led the Vikings in all three receiving categories (receptions, yards and touchdowns) and, for the first time, had other teams realizing that *he* was the Carter to worry about. He has caught at least one pass in 26 of his last 28 games, and in '91 he had all four of the team's 100-yard receiving games. Twice in the last two years he has caught 11 passes in a single game. He is a fine possession receiver who runs well after the catch, but it's his abilities as a tremendous leaper that makes Carter one of the league's best receivers near the goal line. He doesn't have great speed, but he makes tough catches in traffic and is adept at getting open deep.

RICKY SANDERS / REDSKINS

YEAR	REC.	YARDS	AVG.	TD's
1988	73	1148	15.7	12
1989	80	1138	14.2	4
1990	56	727	13.0	3
1991	45	580	12.9	5
1992	51	707	13.9	3

Comments: Because of the departure of Gary Clark to Phoenix and the expected move of Art Monk to the bench, Sanders is no longer overshadowed and should take over as Washington's main pass receiver this season. After two excellent seasons in 1988 and '89, he has been just another guy the last three years, averaging 51 catches for 671 yards and four touchdowns a season. Last year, Sanders ranked second on the team in receiving and tied for third in TD's. He started just five of 15 games, missing the season finale. He had a lot of off-field problems in 1990 which contributed to his slipping statistics, but they seem to be behind him. Sanders excels after the catch with a strong cutback move and a straight-ahead burst. He has a preference for speed routes and literally can run under passes, but he can be challenged physically and knocked off the line of scrimmage. If Mark Rypien bounces back, look for Sanders to benefit more than any of the team's other receivers.

CALVIN WILLIAMS / EAGLES

YEAR	REC.	YARDS	AVG.	TD's
1990	37	602	16.3	9
1991	33	326	9.9	3
1992	42	598	14.2	7

Comments: Williams rebounded nicely in 1992, lead-

ing the Eagles with seven touchdown receptions and finishing third in receiving. He scored five of his touchdowns in the first half of the season, including two against Denver when he caught five passes for 108 yards. He's more of a possession receiver, so that was his only 100-yard game during the season. A dislocated left shoulder sidelined him for a month in 1991, when he had the lowest figures of his three-year career and a poor 9.9-yard average per catch that was the lowest in the league for starting wide receivers. In '90, Williams started 15 of 16 games as a rookie, with nine touchdowns to set a team record for rookies. He's fast, fearless over the middle, reads routes well and has outstanding body control. He just needs to learn how to separate from defenders better.

GARY CLARK / CARDINALS

YEAR	REC.	YARDS	AVG.	TD's
1988	59	892	15.1	7
1989	79	1229	15.6	9
1990	75	1112	14.8	8
1991	70	1340	19.1	10
1992	64	912	14.3	5

Comments: Clark signed with the Cardinals as a free agent on March 22, which means he probably won't come close to having the kind of seasons he has had in recent years because Phoenix is nowhere near the caliber of team Washington is. Last year with the Redskins, he failed to reach 1,000 yards receiving after three consecutive seasons of doing so, but he broke into the top 20 on the league's all-time receiving list. He caught at least one pass in every game but had just one 100-yard game and scored only one touchdown in the final 10 games. In the last eight seasons, Clark is second to Jerry Rice in yards receiving and touchdown receptions, and he's third to Rice and Art Monk in catches in that time. He has caught at least 50 passes for eight straight seasons, a Redskins record. In 1991, he finished second in the NFL in receiving yardage (1,340) and second with a 19.1-yard average (he had seven of the Redskins' 10 longest pass receptions). One of the toughest wideouts in the NFL, Clark can make any catch because he has the speed of a sprinter and the nerve of a tight end. His trademark route is the deep post on a stop-and-go pattern, but he's great on tough catches over the middle, too. He makes up for his height (5-9) with 4.5 speed. Clark remains a dangerous receiver and home-run threat, and Steve Beuerlein, the team's new quarterback, should be able to hook up with him a few times.

ROB MOORE / JETS

YEAR	REC.	YARDS	AVG.	TD's
1990	44	692	15.7	6
1991	70	987	14.1	5
1992	50	726	14.5	4

Comments: Moore started 15 of 16 games last season,

finishing second on the Jets to Chris Burkett in receiving but first in touchdown catches. His reception total dropped last season because of the team's problems at quarterback; his best outing, in the season opener (five catches for 99 yards), was also Browning Nagle's best game. Moore caught passes in 15 games. But, in three NFL seasons, he has yet to turn into the kind of gamebreaker he was expected to be after being drafted in the 1990 supplemental draft. Moore made most of the All-Rookie teams in 1990 and followed that up with a fine second season in which he ranked second on the Jets with 70 receptions. In '92, he scored five of the team's 12 receiving touchdowns. Moore has been called the second coming of Art Monk. He has rare leaping ability and body control and makes tough catches look easy, but he can also go deep. He could really flourish this year with Boomer Esiason getting the ball to him.

WEBSTER SLAUGHTER / Oilers

Year	Rec.	Yards	Avg.	TD's
1988	30	462	15.4	3
1989	65	1236	19.0	6
1990	59	847	14.4	4
1991	64	906	14.2	3
1992	39	486	12.5	4

Comments: Slaughter signed with the Oilers as an unconditional free agent on September 29 and played in 12 games, starting the last nine, immediately making a huge impact. He scored touchdowns in each of the second, third and fourth games he played for Houston, and he ended up fifth on the team in receiving with 39 catches for 486 yards and four touchdowns. He also emerged as the team's punt returner. Slaughter is very durable, having not missed a game due to injury since 1988. One of the NFL's most underrated wide receivers, he always knew he would be a star on a passing team, which is why he wanted out of Cleveland. The Browns' sixth all-time leading receiver, Slaughter has 15 career 100-yard games. When he does score, it's usually a long one; of his 31 career touchdowns, 12 have been over 40 yards. Slaughter lacks outstanding speed, but he makes good cuts off the line of scrimmage, adjusts to coverages well and can separate from a defender. He's also fearless, and might be the NFL's finest downfield blocker.

TIM BROWN / Raiders

Year	Rec.	Yards	Avg.	TD's
1988	43	725	16.9	5
1989	1	8	8.0	0
1990	18	265	14.7	3
1991	36	554	15.4	5
1992	49	693	14.1	7

Comments: The Raiders' leading receiver in 1992, Brown has fully recovered from a 1989 knee injury that almost ended his career and has turned into a very productive player. He moved into the starting lineup ahead of Mervyn Fernandez in Game 3, missed a game with a pulled hamstring, and then started the rest of the year. He had only one 100-yard game, but he spread his touchdowns out, scoring in seven different games. In 1991, Brown led the team's wide receivers with five touchdowns on only 36 receptions (he also had one TD on a punt return). He ended the season with three TD's in the last three games and one 100-yard performance. Brown has lost some speed, but he still has enough of it to run by defenders to go along with explosive open-field running abilities. He was one of the NFL's best punt and kickoff returners as a rookie in 1988. In '91 he tied for the AFC lead in punt returns; last year he was fifth. With better quarterbacking, Brown could catch 60 passes and score 10 TD's in a season.

MIKE PRITCHARD / Falcons

Year	Rec.	Yards	Avg.	TD's
1991	50	624	12.5	2
1992	77	827	10.7	5

Comments: Pritchard has quickly become one of the league's best possession receivers, and he has caught a pass in all 32 games in which he has played. His 77 catches in 1992 is the fifth highest in Falcons history and ranked eighth in the NFL. He had six games with seven or more catches, and his total of 127 in 32 games is an average of four per game. Although teammates Andre Rison and Michael Haynes get more notice, Pritchard looks like he's going to keep getting better as he turns raw ability into veteran talent. He was named to the All-Rookie team in 1991, when he finished second among first-year wide receivers in catches. He started 26 games in two seasons, with one 100-yard game. An inside receiver in the run-and-shoot, he complements Rison well because of his good hands. The speedster from Colorado has been called a poor man's Rocket Ismail coming out of college and could turn into a home-run hitter.

ERIC MARTIN / Saints

Year	Rec.	Yards	Avg.	TD's
1988	85	1083	12.7	7
1989	68	1090	16.0	8
1990	63	912	14.5	5
1991	66	803	12.2	4
1992	68	1041	15.3	5

Comments: Martin is another one of those players who turn in consistent performances year after year (even after a 42-day holdout in 1992). Last season he tied for seventh in the NFC with 68 receptions and sixth in yards. He caught at least one pass in all 16 games, upping his streak to 89 straight and 125 of 127 games over his career. He scored four times in the first seven games of the season, then only once the rest of the way. He had two 100-yard games, doing it in consecutive games near midseason. In 1991, he was overshadowed by Floyd Turner, who scored eight touchdowns compared to Martin's four. The Saints' career receiving leader, Martin is too often used as a possession and third-down receiver. He's a big, physical target in the Art Monk mold. He has sneaky speed and great hands, and he is adept at breaking first tackles. He toils in relative obscurity in New Orleans, despite averaging 70 catches and 986 yards from 1988 to '92. Those numbers are good for a No. 2 or 3 receiver on a fantasy team.

HERMAN MOORE / LIONS

YEAR	REC.	YARDS	AVG.	TD's
1991	11	135	12.3	0
1992	51	966	18.9	4

Comments: Moore had an excellent season in 1992 and might be ready to move into the elite of NFL receivers. He missed four games early in the season because of a torn thigh muscle but still put up some very good numbers (over a 16-game season, they would translate to 67 catches and 1,265 yards). He demonstrated big-play ability and had the highest average per catch in the NFC for players with 50 or more receptions. He caught at least one pass of 18 or more yards in every game he played and seven passes of 40 or more. He had three 100-yard games. In 1991, Moore started one game and he responded with five catches for 70 yards. His progress was hindered somewhat because — like most top draft picks — he missed the early part of training camp due to a holdout. Then he had trouble with his eyes, finally being fitted with contact lenses before Week 3. Moore is a big, physical receiver with size, speed, hands, and leaping ability. He has been compared to James Lofton because of his big-play potential. He can run over or around defenders, and is both a deep threat and good on short patterns. He should continue to improve in 1993.

WILLIE "FLIPPER" ANDERSON / RAMS

YEAR	REC.	YARDS	AVG.	TD's
1988	11	319	29.0	0
1989	44	1146	26.0	5
1990	51	1097	21.5	4
1991	32	530	16.6	1
1992	38	657	17.3	7

Comments: Anderson scored seven touchdowns last year when he scored once for every 5.4 receptions. He had only 10 TD's for his four-year career prior to 1992. His average yards per catch dropped to 21.3 for his career (176 catches), but that mark is still the highest among active players in the NFL with at least 100 receptions. He appeared in 15 games with 10 starts, catching at least one pass in every one. He scored all of his touchdowns in Games 3-5 and 12-15 but was very inconsistent due to injuries. One of these days Anderson is going to put together a truly fantastic season. He is one of the league's most explosive

receivers. In 1990, he combined with Henry Ellard to make the Rams the third team in NFL history to have two receivers enjoy back-to-back 1,000-yard receiving seasons. Anderson runs deep patterns to perfection with outstanding acceleration, and he's fluid with great leaping ability. He's also physical; he can beat bump-and-run coverage and also come down with the ball over the middle. His biggest problems are his tendency to sometimes run poor routes and his desire to always go deep. Anderson burst onto the scene in 1989 with 15 receptions for a league-record 336 yards in one game against New Orleans.

MARK DUPER / DOLPHINS

YEAR	REC.	YARDS	AVG.	TD's
1988	39	626	16.1	1
1989	49	717	14.6	1
1990	52	810	15.6	5
1991	70	1085	15.5	5
1992	44	762	17.3	7

Comments: Duper led the Dolphins with seven touchdowns receiving last year, tied for fourth in the conference in that category. He ranked fourth on the team and first among wide receivers with 44 catches, and first in yardage. He tied or led the team in receiving in five games, and he has caught at least one pass in 138 of his 152 career games. Miami's second-leading career receiver, Duper had one 100-yard game in 1992, giving him 28 for his career. He also has four 1,000-yard seasons. In 1991, he showed he hadn't gotten too old with 70 catches for the second-highest total of his career and 1,085 yards for the third highest. For his career, he has caught 511 passes for 8,869 yards and 59 TD's. Duper is still the lone long-ball threat in the Miami offense, with three of his scores last year going for over 40 yards. In 1988 and '89, Duper caught a lot of passes but scored only one touchdown in each season. Though he doesn't have the speed he once had, his deceptive quickness and great routes make him one of the toughest receivers to cover. These days he specializes more as an intermediate receiver, setting up defensive backs rather than running by them. The Dolphins don't throw long as much as they used to, but Duper should always be considered as a later-round fantasy pick.

MICHAEL JACKSON / BROWNS

YEAR	REC.	YARDS	AVG.	TD's
1991	17	268	15.8	2
1992	47	755	16.1	7

Comments: Jackson might be the least recognized No. 1 receiver in the NFL, although he certainly is not a bad one. Cleveland's leading receiver last year, Jackson was the only really feared member of the Browns' receiving corps. He started 14 of 16 games in 1992, catching at least one pass in 14 of them. His seven touchdown receptions led the team and ranked fourth in the AFC. And his 16.1-yard average was the best of any receiver in the conference with more than 45 catches. A sixth-round draft pick in 1991, Jackson is a long-strider who excels on fly patterns and outjumps defenders with good height and speed. If Bernie Kosar can stay healthy, don't be surprised if Jackson develops into one of the league's best wideouts.

HENRY ELLARD / RAMS

YEAR	REC.	YARDS	AVG.	TD's
1988	86	1414	16.4	10
1989	70	1382	19.7	8
1990	76	1294	17.0	4
1991	64	1052	16.4	3
1992	47	727	15.5	3

Comments: After four consecutive 1,000-yard seasons, Ellard's numbers fell way off in 1992 despite Jim Everett's revival, and Ellard might be showing signs of age. He led the Rams' wide receivers in catches and receiving yards but scored only three times (all in the second half of the season). And, after leading the team in receptions eight straight years, he finished second in '92. He started 15 games and moved into second place behind Elroy Hirsch on the team's list for career TD receptions. He's already the team leader for receptions (532) and yards (8,816), and is one of only 33 receivers in NFL history to record at least 500 receptions. With a fine average per catch over the last few seasons, Ellard remains one of the NFL's most dangerous receivers. He had four consecutive 1,000-yard seasons from 1988 to '91, something only Jerry Rice had done. Ellard is a textbook receiver. He doesn't have great speed; instead, he lulls cornerbacks to sleep and then bursts by them with sneaky acceleration. He might have the quickest first-pivot move after the catch in the NFL. However, his 1992 season could have showed that he is starting to age (he's 32).

WILLIE GREEN / LIONS

YEAR	REC.	YARDS	AVG.	TD's
1990	Injured			
1991	39	592	15.2	7
1992	33	586	17.8	5

Comments: Green had another solid season in 1992 and has developed into a pretty good touchdown scorer. In '91, he came out of nowhere to score seven times during the regular season and three more in two playoff games. Last year, he followed that up by scoring in each of the first three games. He had two 100-yard games but caught only four passes in the last six games. He was suspended for Game 14 for "conduct detrimental to the team." He spent 1990 on injured reserve (shoulder), and had to beat out highly touted rookies Herman Moore and Reggie Barrett for a starting job in '91, which he earned by the season opener. Green caught TD passes in five of the first six games and

six of the first eight. Quickness and precision of routes — especially end zone fade patterns — are Green's forte. He still has a reputation for dropping easy passes and catching the difficult ones.

JAMES LOFTON / RAIDERS

YEAR	REC.	YARDS	AVG.	TD's
1988	28	549	19.6	0
1989	8	166	20.8	3
1990	35	712	20.3	4
1991	57	1072	18.8	8
1992	51	786	15.4	6

Comments: Lofton was signed by the Raiders on May 10, shortly after being released by the Bills. He hasn't lost it yet, but he did have a bad habit of dropping passes in 1992. Lofton might be headed to the Pro Football Hall of Fame someday. Last year he became the NFL's all-time leader in receiving yardage, and he has caught 50-plus passes nine times, tying a record held by Steve Largent and Charlie Joiner. Over his career, Lofton has caught 750 passes for 13,773 yards. He will be 36 when the '93 season rolls around and everybody keeps waiting for him to slow down, but he isn't cooperating. He's still dangerous on fly and corner routes, and he lulls defenders to sleep with his smooth stride before kicking into second gear when the ball is in the air. In 1991, he became the oldest player in league history to record 1,000 yards receiving in a season, and his 46 career 100-yard receiving performances (but only one of them last year) rank second behind only Don Maynard's NFL mark of 50. One of the game's ultimate big-play receivers, Lofton joins a deep corps of wide receivers with the Raiders and he doesn't have a top quarterback throwing to him. But don't be surprised if he surprises everybody again.

COULD COME ON

TIM McGEE / REDSKINS

YEAR	REC.	YARDS	AVG.	TD's
1988	36	686	19.1	6
1989	65	1211	18.6	8
1990	43	737	17.1	1
1991	51	802	14.7	4
1992	35	408	11.7	3

Comments: McGee has a fresh start with the Redskins after signing with them as a free agent in April, and his stats could improve a lot with Mark Rypien throwing to him. Last year, because of the Bengals' problems at quarterback, he had his worst season in five years. McGee started all 16 games but really tailed off the second half of the season (only seven receptions the last seven games). He has always been inconsistent for a player who could rank among the elite of the league's receivers. In 1991, he was the Bengals' second-leading receiver and he topped the team in receiving touchdowns. In 1990, McGee's numbers were almost exactly the same as those of teammate Eddie Brown, yet Brown caught nine touchdown passes to McGee's one. McGee was the featured receiver in 1989, his best season, when Brown was slowed by injuries, but the results weren't the same in '92, when Brown was again injured. McGee is a burner, a big-play receiver with good moves, but he also has the courage and toughness to go over the middle. However, cornerbacks have learned they can sometimes take McGee out of a play at the line of scrimmage, and he doesn't have good hands.

MARK INGRAM / DOLPHINS

YEAR	REC.	YARDS	AVG.	TD's
1988	13	158	12.2	1
1989	17	290	17.1	1
1990	26	499	19.2	5
1991	51	824	16.2	3
1992	27	408	15.1	1

Comments: Ingram signed as a free agent with Miami on March 18 after six mostly unproductive seasons with the Giants. He has a new lease on life and could really flourish with the Dolphins and with Dan Marino throwing to him. Ingram had the best season of his career in 1991, leading the Giants with 51 receptions. The season before, he had scored five touchdowns, his career high. In 1992, he started 12 games, missing four at midseason with a knee injury. He caught only 27 passes and scored just once. Ingram is a quick receiver with a burst out of his cuts that separates him from tight coverage. He has the acceleration to leave cornerbacks behind, and his best routes are outs and posts. He's sure-handed and aggressive. If he can stay healthy — durability has been a problem in the past — he could be a real surprise this year.

ALVIN HARPER / COWBOYS

YEAR	REC.	YARDS	AVG.	TD's
1991	20	326	16.3	1
1992	35	562	16.1	4

Comments: Last season, Harper developed into a fine complementary receiver to Michael Irvin. He started 13 games and caught passes in 15, setting career highs for receptions, yards and TD's. He scored three times in the final six games, when he caught 18 passes. Harper moved into the Cowboys' starting lineup nine games into the '91 season, although it took him almost another year to start making an impact. He takes some pressure off Irvin with his big-play ability. Harper is a big, deep burner with great leaping ability. He is starting to beat bump-and-run coverage and quit tipping off his routes. He has been compared to former Jet Al Toon, but is more of a threat. Harper could be a real sleeper this season.

DESMOND HOWARD / REDSKINS

YEAR	REC.	YARDS	AVG.	TD's
1992	3	20	6.7	0

Comments: Howard played in all 16 games last season, starting once, but was not much of a factor. He caught only three passes, all of them late in the season. He scored his only pro touchdown on a punt return. Howard will probably inherit a starting job this year because of the departure of Gary Clark to Phoenix as a free agent. Howard is an electrifying big-play receiver who excels around the goal line. Draft him as your fourth wide receiver and he might be the best one on your team by the end of the season.

WILLIE DAVIS / CHIEFS

YEAR	REC.	YARDS	AVG.	TD's
1992	36	756	21.0	3

Comments: Davis came out of relative obscurity last season to become one of the NFL's most electrifying wide receivers, leading the league in yards per catch with a lofty 21.0-yard average. In 16 games (14 starts), he had 36 catches (third on the team) for 756 yards and three touchdowns. He had a three-game run in October with a team-record-tying three straight 100-yard games. Altogether, he had 13 catches of 20-plus yards, six of 40-plus and four of 50-plus. Opposing defenses might learn to stop Davis, but he has the kind of blazing speed that will occasionally allow him to have explosive games.

MIKE SHERRARD / GIANTS

YEAR	REC.	YARDS	AVG.	TD's
1988	Injured			
1989	Injured			
1990	17	264	15.5	2
1991	24	296	12.3	2
1992	38	607	16.0	0

Comments: Sherrard was signed by the Giants as a free agent on April 2 and might be the team's No. 1 receiver this year. He has rebounded nicely from a twice-broken leg that kept him out of action for three years. San Francisco's No. 3 receiver last year, Sherrard had totals for receptions and yards that were his best since his rookie season in Dallas. He scored his only TD on a recovered fumble in the end zone. Against Buffalo in Game 2, he caught six passes for 159 yards. That was his best performance of the season, but he did catch passes in 14 of 16 games. Sherrard first broke his leg in 1987 and then again in '88, missing three seasons. In 1990, he broke his right leg for the third time in late October but made an extremely quick recovery and returned for the playoffs, catching a touchdown pass in the first game. Sherrard once had great speed and hands to go with his tremendous size. In his rookie season of 1986, he caught 44 passes for 744 yards and five touchdowns.

CARL PICKENS / BENGALS

YEAR	REC.	YARDS	AVG.	TD's
1992	26	326	12.5	1

Comments: Although Pickens' statistics were merely average in 1992, he was one of the two wide receivers on most All-Rookie teams. He started 10 of 16 games, catching a pass in 13 of them. A great natural athlete, Pickens was sometimes compared to Jerry Rice before his rookie season. You'll get an idea how good he can be this year if the Bengals can get some consistent quarterbacking.

COURTNEY HAWKINS / BUCCANEERS

YEAR	REC.	YARDS	AVG.	TD's
1992	20	336	16.8	2

Comments: Hawkins made most of the All-Rookie teams last year. He started off fast, catching 18 passes in the first nine games. His best outing was five receptions for 102 yards and a TD against Chicago. He also started five of 16 games. Hawkins is an acrobatic, big-play receiver who could improve considerably if given the opportunity to play and better quarterbacking.

ODESSA TURNER / 49ERS

YEAR	REC.	YARDS	AVG.	TD's
1988	10	128	12.8	1
1989	38	467	12.3	4
1990	6	69	11.5	0
1991	21	356	17.0	0
1992	9	200	22.2	2

Comments: A free-agent pickup a year ago, Turner started off the season in a flurry but caught only two passes after midseason. With Mike Sherrard gone, Turner moves up to No. 3 receiver in San Francisco this year. He was the Giants' No. 3 wideout prior to signing with San Francisco. In 1990, Turner played only the first four games before being cut because of attitude problems. He led the Giants in receiving in '89. His size and quickness allow him to separate from defenders at the line of scrimmage. He's a hybrid wide receiver/tight end who can make the big catch.

JEFF QUERY / BENGALS

YEAR	REC.	YARDS	AVG.	TD's
1989	23	350	15.2	2
1990	34	458	13.5	2
1991	7	94	13.4	0
1992	16	265	16.6	3

Comments: Query was picked up in October by Cincinnati. He played in 10 games, replacing rookie Carl Pickens as the starter for two contests before missing the final two with an ankle injury. While he was in the lineup, he seemed to be David Klingler's favorite target. Query finished seventh on the team in receiving but scored three touchdowns, which tied for the team lead. A speed receiver whose best assets are his great hands (he rarely drops a ball), the frail-looking Query is small but tough and extremely fast (4.32 in the 40). He'll probably be the team's possession receiver this year.

LAWYER TILLMAN / BROWNS

YEAR	REC.	YARDS	AVG.	TD's
1989	6	70	11.7	2
1990	Injured			
1991	Injured			
1992	25	498	19.9	0

Comments: After missing 37 games with stress fractures in his lower left leg, Tillman finally made it back into the lineup in mid-October last season. He started nine of the last 11 games, but then broke his right ankle in the last game. It was healing well in the offseason, although his stress fractures started to bother him again. Tillman was the Browns' fourth-leading receiver in 1992. His best game was eight receptions for 148 yards against San Diego four weeks after he returned. The Browns' No. 2 pick in 1989, Tillman missed the entire 1990 and '91 seasons, and his rookie season was a near washout because of a prolonged holdout. He has the talent and potential to be a real star, especially near the goal line, where his great leaping ability could get him a lot of touchdowns.

ANTHONY MORGAN / BEARS

YEAR	REC.	YARDS	AVG.	TD's
1991	13	211	16.2	2
1992	14	323	23.1	2

Comments: The fastest receiver on the Bears, Morgan scored touchdowns on two of his first three receptions last season. He missed the first four games of the season with an injury but started the final four in place of the injured Tom Waddle. In those four games, he caught 10 passes for 171 yards and ran two times for 51 yards, showing good versatility. In '91, he started two games and also scored two times. Morgan shows flashes but is too inconsistent. If he can learn how to turn his speed into production, he could earn a starting job. At the least, he gives the Bears the speed receiver they so dearly need.

1992 SURPRISES

MARK JACKSON / GIANTS

YEAR	REC.	YARDS	AVG.	TD's
1988	46	852	18.5	6
1989	28	446	15.9	2
1990	57	926	16.2	4
1991	33	603	18.3	1
1992	48	745	15.5	8

Comments: Jackson signed with the Giants and his former coach, Dan Reeves, in late March as a free agent and could become that team's leading receiver. In 1992, his last in Denver, he had one of the best seasons of his career. He scored on one out of every six receptions, eight in all, which tied for sixth in the NFL. That's his career high. He was the only Bronco with at least one catch in every game. In 1990, he had the best year of his career and led the team in receiving for the first time. Jackson has a fine 17.4-yard average per catch over his career. He's a shifty runner with a burst to get by a defender, and he was also the Broncos' most reliable receiver in traffic. Jackson is a speed merchant with a strong upper body, and he's tough to jam at the line. John Elway looked to him when he was flushed out of the pocket. But don't expect Jackson to score eight TD's again in 1993.

ED McCAFFREY / GIANTS

YEAR	REC.	YARDS	AVG.	TD's
1991	16	146	9.1	0
1992	49	610	12.4	5

Comments: Despite starting only three games last year when Mark Ingram was injured, McCaffrey led the Giants with 49 catches and five receiving touchdowns in 1992. In fact, after four games, he had as many catches as the two starters had combined. He caught at least one pass in 14 games, including a season high of six for 105 yards in Game 12 against Dallas. A third-round draft choice in 1991 — he was called the steal of the round by Bill Walsh — McCaffrey was the Giants' No. 4 wide receiver as a rookie in 1991. He has been called a larger, faster Dwight Clark. In other words, the 6-foot-5 McCaffrey is good, but he won't scare anyone. He will be hurt this year by the addition of Mark Jackson and Mike Sherrard to the team and will most likely be relegated to the role of possession receiver.

QUINN EARLY / SAINTS

YEAR	REC.	YARDS	AVG.	TD's
1988	29	375	12.9	4
1989	11	126	11.5	0
1990	15	238	15.9	1
1991	32	541	16.9	2
1992	30	566	18.9	5

Comments: With Floyd Turner injured nearly all of last season, Early had a lot of opportunities to shine in New Orleans, and that's just what he did. He started all 166 games and caught five touchdown passes in 30 receptions. He caught at least one pass in all 16 games. He was obtained in a trade before the 1991 season from San Diego, where he failed to excite anyone. Early has a lot of speed, he knows how to work the middle and he's a great leaper. But he is not a smooth route runner, and he cradles too many catches. He was also bothered by too many injuries before the last two seasons.

1992 SURPRISES

ART MONK / REDSKINS

YEAR	REC.	YARDS	AVG.	TD's
1988	72	946	13.1	5
1989	86	1186	13.8	8
1990	68	770	11.3	5
1991	71	1049	14.8	8
1992	46	644	14.0	3

Comments: Now the NFL's all-time leading receiver with 847 catches, Monk has been dropped to No. 4 on the team's depth chart at wide receiver. He didn't have one of his better seasons in 1992 and might be slowing (at age 35 he has every right to do so). Monk did extend his consecutive game receiving streak to 148, third all-time, but he also posted the lowest stats of any full season in his 13-year career. He didn't have a touchdown until Game 12, and no 100-yard games. In '91, he led the team with 71 catches for 1,049 yards and equaled a career-best eight touchdown receptions and three 100-yard games. Monk is the best possession receiver in the NFL, tough enough to muscle past coverage at the line of scrimmage and still fast enough to go by them. He excels on deep sideline catches and is a great leader who gets overlooked because he doesn't score 10 touchdowns a season. With Gary Clark gone to Phoenix, Monk could again be a focus in the Washington offense, but other players are going to get the opportunity first.

ANTHONY CARTER / VIKINGS

YEAR	REC.	YARDS	AVG.	TD's
1988	72	1225	17.0	6
1989	65	1066	16.4	4
1990	70	1008	14.4	8
1991	51	553	10.8	5
1992	41	580	14.1	2

Comments: Carter is coming off the two most disappointing seasons of his eight-year career and is mostly a possession receiver these days. He's no longer the No. 1 threat in Minnesota, having passed that moniker to Cris Carter two years ago. Last year, Carter set a personal low with only two touchdowns, although he did improve his average per gain from the season before (his average had decreased every year since 1987). Even his streak of consecutive games with a pass reception was stopped at 105 last year. These days, the best Carter has to look forward to is moving up in the record books. He holds team records for career 100-yard games (19), yards (6,861), and most rushing attempts, yards and touchdowns by a wide receiver (40-271-2). Carter had three consecutive 1,000-yard seasons from 1988 to '90, and he averaged nearly seven touchdowns a season until 1992. Still sure-handed with great body control, Carter is no longer a burner and he doesn't do much after the catch. This year should tell if Carter has anything left.

MERVYN FERNANDEZ / 49ERS

YEAR	REC.	YARDS	AVG.	TD's
1988	31	805	26.0	4
1989	57	1069	18.8	9
1990	52	839	16.1	5
1991	46	694	15.1	1
1992	9	121	13.4	0

Comments: Fernandez was traded to the 49ers on May 8. He started the first two games last season but then was benched and then demoted to fourth string. He had his worst season since joining the Raiders out of the CFL in 1987. Until last year, Fernandez was the team's most productive wideout. In 1989, he caught nine touchdown passes and had developed into one of the better receivers in the league. He led the Raiders in receptions and receiving touchdowns in '89 and '90, and in '91 he was second behind tight end Ethan Horton. Fernandez is a possession receiver with great hands. He's more polished than a lot of receivers, but he lacks great speed, instead relying on deceptive moves to set up a defender. A change of scenery will certainly refresh him, and he could be a valuable backup to Jerry Rice and John Taylor.

QUESTION MARKS

MARK CLAYTON / DOLPHINS

YEAR	REC.	YARDS	AVG.	TD's
1988	86	1129	13.1	14
1989	64	1011	15.8	9
1990	32	406	12.7	3
1991	70	1053	15.0	12
1992	43	619	14.4	3

Comments: Clayton was very disgruntled in 1992, which resulted in a subpar season for him. He missed the first three games with a neck sprain and became the Dolphins' career reception leader in Game 4 after coming off injured reserve. But then Miami signed free-agent tight end Keith Jackson, and Clayton started complaining about not getting the ball thrown his way often enough. By the end of the season, most people knew that Clayton was nearing the end of his days in Miami. He did, however, catch a pass in all 13 games in which he played to increase his streak to 92 consecutive games with at least one reception dating back to 1986. He currently ranks 18th on the NFL's all-time reception list with 550 catches and eighth on the TD reception list with 81. He's also second on Miami's receiving yardage list with 8,643. He has 22 career 100-yard games (none in 1992), and he's only the 10th player in NFL history to have five or more 1,000-yard seasons. He holds Miami's top three slots for receiving touchdowns in a season, and he averages 8.1 touchdowns a year. Clayton is getting up in years (32), but he's one of the league's truly great touchdown scorers. He set the NFL record (since broken by Jerry Rice) with 18 TD receptions in 1984. Dan Marino's favorite target, he led the NFL in TD catches twice. Clayton never has been a true burner, but he's quick and one of the best receivers going over the middle and finding holes in a zone. He'll have a much-needed new start wherever he ends up.

EDDIE BROWN / BENGALS

YEAR	REC.	YARDS	AVG.	TD's
1988	53	1273	24.0	9
1989	52	814	15.7	6
1990	44	706	16.0	9
1991	59	827	14.0	2
1992	Injured			

Comments: Brown missed the entire 1992 season with a neck injury suffered early in the preseason. One of the league's biggest gamebreakers just a few years ago, Brown is going to have to prove what he can still do. In 1991 he had perhaps the least effective season of his career. Although his team-high 59 receptions were also a career high, his two touchdowns were a career low. He also wasn't much of a deep threat, and he had only one 100-yard game, while missing three games with injuries. When Brown is 100 percent, he's a threat to go all the way every time he touches the ball. He has tremendous acceleration off the line of scrimmage — cornerbacks used to play off him farther than nearly every other receiver — and great leaping ability. But what set him apart from others is that he ran like a halfback after making a catch. Brown's negatives are inconsistency and a tendency to drop passes. Check his status during training camp to determine if he should be drafted.

ERNIE JONES / CARDINALS

YEAR	REC.	YARDS	AVG.	TD's
1988	23	496	21.6	3
1989	45	838	18.6	3
1990	43	724	16.8	4
1991	61	957	15.7	4
1992	38	559	14.7	4

Comments: A big-play receiver, Jones was arrested on charges of possession of marijuana and crack cocaine in February and will face an NFL suspension if he is convicted, which could be the beginning of the end for him in Phoenix. He missed four games with a separated shoulder last year and didn't return to the starting lineup after his rehab for the final six games. He does put up good numbers season after season. In 1991, he led the Cardinals with 61 catches for 957 yards, including back-to-back eight-catch games. He is one of the more underrated receivers in the NFL, and is good on the catch-and-run. He's big and strong and can take a crossing pattern all the way. But whether or not he gets back onto a football field is now in doubt because of his arrest.

HART LEE DYKES / Patriots

Year	Rec.	Yards	Avg.	TD's
1989	49	795	16.2	5
1990	34	549	16.1	2
1991	Injured			
1992	Injured			

Comments: Dykes has missed the last two seasons because of a broken right kneecap, and in mid-May it was announced he would sit out 1993 with a left knee injury. He had a strong rookie season in 1989, when he was the first receiver picked in the draft, but then he didn't play as well in '90 and really needs to bounce back and show he can still play. He missed six games in the middle of the '90 season with an eye injury. Dykes has good quickness for a big receiver, and he could turn into a good power-oriented one. Some people have compared him to former Jet Al Toon as a short-to-intermediate receiver. But he doesn't have great speed and he drops too many passes.

BEST OF THE REST

BILL BROOKS / Bills

Year	Rec.	Yards	Avg.	TD's
1988	54	867	16.1	3
1989	63	919	14.6	4
1990	62	823	13.3	5
1991	72	888	12.3	4
1992	44	468	10.6	1

Comments: Brooks was signed as a free agent by Buffalo on April 1 and will probably take over James Lofton's starting job opposite Andre Reed. Thus he could provide big value for a late fantasy pick. After six solid seasons with the Colts, Brooks was demoted to second string behind Reggie Langhorne late last year as his role in the Indianapolis offense diminished drastically. He caught his only touchdown pass of the season in the final game of the season, and it was the first for any wide receiver on the team since the fifth game. Prior to '92, Brooks had led Colts receivers in receiving four times in six years. He is the second most prolific receiver (411 catches) in team history behind Hall of Famer Raymond Berry. Brooks has quietly produced solid numbers since being drafted in the fourth round in '86. Although he doesn't have great speed, he is a complete receiver, with quickness off the line, acceleration to get past a defender, great hands and the ability to turn a short flip into a big play. He's built like a halfback and he's best when running intermediate routes over the middle. He has caught at least one pass in 103 of 106 career games.

CURTIS DUNCAN / Oilers

Year	Rec.	Yards	Avg.	TD's
1988	22	302	13.7	1
1989	43	613	14.3	5
1990	66	785	11.9	1
1991	55	588	10.7	4
1992	82	954	11.6	1

Comments: Duncan enjoyed the best season of his career in 1992, catching 82 passes, fifth in the league and the sixth-highest total in team history. He had a team-best 954 yards but he scored only once, and that was in the next-to-last game of the year. That was his first score in 108 catches, one of the longest streaks in NFL history. In a loss at Denver, he had a career-best 133 yards, including a 72-yard catch that was the team's high for the season. He led the Oilers in receptions in seven games. He has not missed a game since his rookie season of 1987. Duncan always seems to be overshadowed by the team's other receivers, although it's probably because he doesn't score much. He's a long-striding outside receiver who is largely used as a possession receiver because of his good hands. He runs the inside routes best and has a flair for the spectacular. He's not as quick as the other receivers on the Oilers, but he is stronger, has better straight-ahead speed and he reads coverages well.

JESSIE HESTER / Colts

Year	Rec.	Yards	Avg.	TD's
1988	12	176	14.7	0
1989	DNP			
1990	54	924	17.1	6
1991	60	753	12.6	5
1992	52	792	15.2	1

Comments: Although he scored only one touchdown last season, Hester has had three consecutive solid seasons since signing with the Colts. In that time, he averaged 55 receptions for 823 yards and four TD's. He has caught at least one pass in 46 straight games (the only Colt to do so in 1992), and he has caught more than one in 38 of 41 games. In the two seasons prior to 1992, Hester set personal highs for catches and yards. He is a speedster who knows how to get open and is shifty after the catch. He is better along the sidelines than over the middle. He was forced into retirement in 1989 after failing with the Raiders and Falcons, but the Colts saw something in him (and they were also desperate at the time they signed him). Hester is one of the more underrated receivers in the NFL and a player who is a threat to go all the way every time he catches the ball.

BRIAN BLADES / SEAHAWKS

YEAR	REC.	YARDS	AVG.	TD's
1988	40	682	17.1	8
1989	77	1063	13.8	5
1990	49	525	10.7	3
1991	70	1003	14.3	2
1992	19	256	13.5	1

Comments: Blades played in only six games last season. Following a training camp holdout, he was injured on his first play in the first game (which he didn't start). A broken collarbone kept him out of the lineup for the next 10 weeks. After returning, he became the team's only receiving threat, although the team's passing was pretty bad. He caught a TD pass in his first game and had two games with six catches, one with over 100 yards. In 1991, he finished with 70 receptions and over 1,000 yards for the second time in three years. He had three games with 100 receiving yards, and three other times he just missed that mark (97, 99 and 99). He scored just two times. Blades' biggest problem is that he is too often double-covered because other Seahawk receivers can't take the pressure off him. He's a smooth runner who can separate from a defender and isn't afraid to go over the middle. Although he's considered a deep threat, Blades' average per catch hasn't reflected that in recent years. He would also welcome a good quarterback in Seattle.

RANDAL HILL / CARDINALS

YEAR	REC.	YARDS	AVG.	TD's
1991	43	495	11.5	1
1992	58	861	14.8	3

Comments: Hill and his blazing speed led the Cardinals in receiving yardage with 861, and he finished as the team's second-leading receiver in 1992. That put to rest any doubts that he might be a bust, as some people thought after his inconsistent rookie season that included an early-season trade from Miami. He was traded to Phoenix for a first-round draft choice in 1992 that ended up being the seventh pick in the draft. Hill finished last season with a 28-game streak of consecutive games with receptions, and he also posted lengthy catches of 45, 44, 42, 40, 40, 37 and 34 yards. In 1991, Hill started only five games but was a passing-down regular and was the team's third-leading receiver. He adds much-needed speed — which he isn't

always in control of — to the Cardinals' lineup, and he is a legitimate deep threat. The Cardinals like to use him on short crossing patterns, enabling him to run after the catch. However, he does have a reputation for showboating and shying away from contact. With better quarterbacking, Hill could develop into a truly outstanding receiver.

FLOYD TURNER / SAINTS

YEAR	REC.	YARDS	AVG.	TD's
1989	22	279	12.7	1
1990	21	396	18.9	4
1991	64	927	14.5	8
1992	5	43	8.6	0

Comments: In 1991, Turner went from the Saints' third or fourth wide receiver to the team's top pass catcher. He caught a career-high 64 passes for 927 yards and a personal-best eight touchdowns. All three figures were more than he had in his first two seasons combined (figures he surpassed by the 12th game). However, last year he broke his left thigh against Chicago in Game 2 and will have to earn back his job. Despite so-so speed, Turner makes big plays and has good hands. If he recovers from the injury, don't draft him too high, because he might never match his 1991 numbers again.

MARK CARRIER / BROWNS

YEAR	REC.	YARDS	AVG.	TD's
1988	57	970	17.0	5
1989	86	1422	16.5	9
1990	49	813	16.6	4
1991	47	698	14.9	2
1992	56	692	12.4	4

Comments: Carrier signed as a free agent with the Browns on April 7, and the new scenery should be good for him. Cleveland needs some good receivers, and although Carrier won't repeat the excellent season he had in 1989 in Tampa Bay (86 catches for 1,422 yards and nine touchdowns), he should turn into a solid starter. The Bucs' second-leading receiver in 1992, Carrier's mark is consistency and he remains a threat at any time. He started 11 of 14 games last season, missing two with a knee injury. Three times he caught seven passes in one game. Carrier has caught 47 or more receptions five straight years. He runs precise routes and has great hands (he rarely drops a pass). He's capable of making acrobatic catches and is a good blocker on running plays. His biggest negative is a lack of blazing speed.

WENDELL DAVIS / Bears

Year	Rec.	Yards	Avg.	TD's
1988	15	220	14.7	0
1989	26	397	15.3	3
1990	39	572	14.7	3
1991	61	945	15.5	6
1992	54	734	13.6	2

Comments: Davis led the Bears in receiving in 1992, although by most standards he didn't have an exceptionally strong season — and certainly not as good as he had in '91. He caught at least one pass in 15 games and had a high of eight catches for 106 yards in one game (his only 100-yard outing all year). In 1991, Davis started 16 games for the first time in his career and led the Bears with 61 catches for 945 yards — both totals were the highest by a Bear since in 1971. Davis has deceptive speed and very good hands. He could benefit from a new offense this year that will rely more on intermediate passes (the famous Bill Walsh scheme). He's probably a good pick for a fourth wide receiver in fantasy football.

DREW HILL / Falcons

Year	Rec.	Yards	Avg.	TD's
1988	72	1141	15.8	10
1989	66	938	14.2	8
1990	74	1019	13.8	5
1991	90	1109	12.3	4
1992	60	623	10.4	3

Comments: Hill has decided to return for a 13th NFL season. Although his numbers slipped somewhat in 1992, his first season in Atlanta, Hill is always a threat because he knows how to get open and burn defenses, even on the short stuff. Besides, he's only two years removed from the best season of his career, and in the final two games of 1992, Hill caught 17 passes for 191 yards and one TD. The 10th player in NFL history to catch 600 passes, Hill has eight consecutive seasons with 45 or more receptions. He also ranks 10th in history in receiving yards (9,447) and has 60 career scoring receptions. In 1991, Hill became the first NFL receiver to have four 1,000-yard receiving seasons after the age of 30. That year he combined with Haywood Jeffires for 190 catches, which is more than any other duo in NFL history (surpassing the record of 171 by San Diego's Kellen Winslow and John Jefferson in 1980). The Oilers' all-time leading receiver with 540 catches, Hill is overshadowed on the Falcons because of Andre Rison and Michael Haynes, but he shouldn't be overlooked. Although he has lost some speed and quickness in recent years, only San Francisco's Jerry Rice had more receiving yards from 1987 to '91. He started 14 games last year.

VANCE JOHNSON / Broncos

Year	Rec.	Yards	Avg.	TD's
1988	68	896	13.2	5
1989	76	1095	14.4	7
1990	54	747	13.8	3
1991	21	208	9.9	3
1992	24	294	12.3	2

Comments: Johnson has had two consecutive disappointing seasons and might not get too many opportunities to pull out of his slump. The third-leading receiver in Broncos history, he started seven of 11 games last year, taking over for Derek Russell, after missing the first four with a shoulder injury. He was used sparingly in the offense. Earlier in his career, Johnson was John Elway's favorite scoring target. He likes to play inside the red zone (the 20-yard line to the end zone), and is the fastest and most polished of Denver's wideouts. He hits full speed quickly, but he can be intimidated over the middle and he produces in spurts.

REGGIE LANGHORNE / Colts

Year	Rec.	Yards	Avg.	TD's
1988	57	780	13.7	7
1989	60	749	12.5	2
1990	45	585	13.0	2
1991	39	505	12.9	2
1992	65	811	12.5	1

Comments: Acquired from Cleveland a year ago, Langhorne was the Colts' leading pass-catcher in 1992, setting personal season bests for both catches and yards. He started 12 of 16 games, replacing Bill Brooks in the starting lineup for the final five contests. He had career reception highs of eight catches in two games. He caught at least one pass in all but one game, with 14 multiple-reception games, including the last 13. Langhorne rebounded from a subpar 1991 season in which he did everything he could to get out of Cleveland, including getting suspended for insubordination. He was the Browns' second-leading receiver from 1988 to '91, with 201 catches. Langhorne lacks great speed, but he has good size and great hands, and he can shake free after a catch. He's one of the toughest receivers in the league.

BRETT PERRIMAN / Lions

Year	Rec.	Yards	Avg.	TD's
1988	16	215	13.4	2
1989	20	356	17.8	0
1990	36	382	10.6	2
1991	52	668	12.8	1
1992	69	810	11.7	4

Comments: Without much fanfare, Perriman has led the Lions in receiving the last two seasons. His 69 catches in 1992 were the third-highest single-season total in Detroit history. He ranked sixth in the NFC in receptions and 11th in yards. He was the only Lion player to catch a pass in all 16 games and has a streak of 33 consecutive games with at least one catch. Perriman was acquired from New Orleans — where he was considered a bust — in a preseason trade before the start of the '91 season. Perriman is a blazer, though it's strictly straight-line. He has been mostly a possession receiver the last three seasons, when he has had marginal averages per catch. He can outmuscle and outjump defenders, but he can't block at all (though that won't keep him out of the lineup).

NATE LEWIS / CHARGERS

YEAR	REC.	YARDS	AVG.	TD's
1990	14	192	13.7	1
1991	42	554	13.2	3
1992	34	580	17.1	4

Comments: The Chargers' No. 2 wide receiver, Lewis started 10 games last year (missing two with injuries) and finished third on the team in receiving (34), second in TD receptions (four) and first in average yards per catch (17.1). In doing so, he proved wrong many critics who said he was just a possession receiver who dropped too many passes. A fine kick returner, he totaled 1,016 all-purpose yards. He caught 42 passes in 1991, also third on the team, and he led the AFC with a 25.1-yard average on kickoff returns, including a 95-yard return for a TD. He is still somewhat inconsistent, but he's strong and fast and could still develop into a big-time player.

WILLIE GAULT / RAIDERS

YEAR	REC.	YARDS	AVG.	TD's
1988	16	392	24.5	2
1989	28	690	24.6	4
1990	50	985	19.7	3
1991	20	346	17.3	4
1992	27	508	18.8	4

Comments: Gault started all 16 games last year, although he wasn't productive because of the team's troubles at quarterback. Four touchdowns on 27 catches and 18.8 yards per catch are indications Gault still has a lot of talent, so it's too bad he doesn't get the opportunity to use it. He didn't catch more than three passes in a game all year. In 1991, he caught only seven passes for 81 yards in the final nine games (including the wild-card playoff). But he continues to hold down a starting role because his world-class speed opens lanes for other receivers and he does have the ability to score every time he gets a pass thrown his way. He doesn't have great hands. In five seasons since being acquired in a trade with Chicago, Gault has caught only 141 passes.

RICKY PROEHL / CARDINALS

YEAR	REC.	YARDS	AVG.	TD's
1990	56	802	14.3	4
1991	55	766	13.9	2
1992	60	744	12.4	3

Comments: Proehl was the Cardinals' leading receiver in '92 for the second time in his three-year career. His streak of 33 consecutive games with receptions was snapped in November, but then he came back with consecutive 100-yard games. He logged a career-high nine receptions against the Rams and had his career-longest reception, a 63-yarder, against the Chargers. He had three 100-yard games in all and started 14 of 16 games. In 1991, Proehl started all 16 games and ranked second on the team in receiving. He is a typical possession receiver — not a burner, but he can sneak deep, and he has great hands and hand-eye coordination. He runs great routes, is a fine blocker and is fearless over the middle. He has been compared to former Seahawks receiver Steve Largent, the future Hall of Famer (except Proehl doesn't score as much). In 1990, despite not starting a game, he was the first Cardinals rookie since Bob Shaw in 1950 to lead the team in receiving.

HASSAN JONES / CUT BY VIKINGS

YEAR	REC.	YARDS	AVG.	TD's
1988	40	778	19.5	5
1989	42	694	16.5	1
1990	51	810	15.9	7
1991	32	384	12.0	1
1992	22	308	14.0	4

Comments: Jones was released by Minnesota in May after asking for too much money but will catch on with another team. He is one of the better backup wideouts in the NFL, but he was sidelined twice with a back injury last year. However, he did score four touchdowns — second on the Vikings — on 22 catches, which is an excellent ratio. Jones is a long-ball threat who had the best season of his career in 1990, setting career highs in receptions, yards and touchdowns, despite being hampered by injuries. He has only average speed, but he has superior hand-eye coordination and he's a great jumper. If he can stay healthy for a season, he might put up some outstanding numbers and surprise a lot of people.

ROOKIES

See Chapter 13, The Rookie Report.

OTHERS

LAWRENCE DAWSEY / BUCCANEERS

YEAR	REC.	YARDS	AVG.	TD's
1991	55	818	14.9	3
1992	60	776	12.9	1

Comments: Dawsey led the Buccaneers in receiving again in 1992, although he scored only one touchdown. He missed one game and three other starts, but caught passes in 14 games. He showed promise of things to come in his first pro game in 1991 when he caught a 65-yard touchdown pass against the Jets (the longest ever by a Bucs rookie). A steal in the third round, he made the All-Rookie team when he led all first-year receivers in catches (55) and yards receiving (818). Dawsey is a big, physical player, although he is a bit slow. He has great leaping ability and can turn short passes into long gains. Dawsey could develop into one of the best wideouts in the league, but it's going to take a better passing game in Tampa Bay for that to happen.

JEFF GRAHAM / STEELERS

YEAR	REC.	YARDS	AVG.	TD's
1991	2	21	10.5	0
1992	49	711	14.5	1

Comments: Graham had a fine sophomore season in 1992 after doing nothing as a rookie the season before. He was Pittsburgh's leading receiver with 49 catches, although he scored only one touchdown. In the first game of the season he caught seven passes for 89 yards and the one score. A week later, Graham caught six balls for 146 yards and looked like he might contend for the NFL receiving title. That didn't happen, but he did continue to look outstanding in spurts (15 catches for 202 yards in consecutive games later in the season). He missed two games with an ankle injury. The sixth wide receiver drafted in 1991, Graham could be a star receiver. He has deceptive speed and soft hands. Although he's not a burner, he is a deep threat.

STEPHEN BAKER / GIANTS

YEAR	REC.	YARDS	AVG.	TD's
1988	40	656	16.4	7
1989	13	255	19.6	2
1990	26	541	20.8	4
1991	30	525	17.5	4
1992	17	333	19.6	2

Comments: With Mark Ingram gone to Miami, Baker could take over as New York's biggest threat at receiver. He started 11 games last year but didn't do a whole lot, much of it due to the team's numerous injuries at quarterback. With only two TD catches last year, few people are calling Baker "The Touchdown Maker" anymore. For the fourth straight season, Baker led New York receivers with a fine average per catch. The diminutive Baker is an exciting player who's also a good jumper and can break a big play with his 360-degree spin move. He's fast, but he's frail and telegraphs his routes, so the Giants' quarterbacks often have to dump the ball off to backs. He'll get the chance this year to take over, so he might be worth a late fantasy pick.

TIM BARNETT / CHIEFS

YEAR	REC.	YARDS	AVG.	TD's
1991	41	564	13.8	5
1992	24	442	18.4	4

Comments: Barnett's second NFL season was slowed by a hamstring injury, but he still finished fourth on the Chiefs with 24 catches and a team-high four receiving touchdowns. He averaged 18.4 yards per catch, while starting three of 12 games, missing a month with a hamstring injury. He had his best game of the season against the Redskins, with six catches for 148 yards and two TD's. In two years, Barnett's nine TD's lead the Chiefs. He finished his rookie season with 41 catches (second on the team) for 564 yards (first) and five touchdowns (also first). He started eight of 16 games. His reception and yardage totals are the most for a Chiefs rookie since 1960. Barnett is a downfield receiving threat. He has elusive quickness, great leaping ability, fine size and speed and an uncanny knack for getting open. He probably won't be as good as his cousin, Fred, who plays for the Eagles, but Tim still could be a solid receiver.

CHRIS BURKETT / JETS

YEAR	REC.	YARDS	AVG.	TD's
1988	23	354	15.4	1
1989	24	298	12.4	1
1990	14	204	10.2	1
1991	23	327	14.2	4
1992	57	724	12.7	1

Comments: Burkett has really come on since joining the Jets in 1989. Last year, he was the team's leading receiver with 57 catches. He took over a starting job in mid-November when Al Toon was forced to retire, and he's the first player other than Toon to lead the team in catches since 1985. In 1991, Burkett was voted the team's Most Valuable Player by his teammates because of his play on special teams. But he has also proven to be a top receiver if he's in the lineup. That year he had four touchdowns among his 23 catches. Burkett sometimes reminds people of Toon because he is a big target at 6-4 (although he can't do much after the catch and he drops too many passes). In 1986, his average of 22.9 yards per catch led the NFL while he was with Buffalo.

DON BEEBE / Bills

Year	Rec.	Yards	Avg.	TD's
1989	17	317	18.6	2
1990	11	221	20.1	1
1991	32	414	12.9	6
1992	33	554	16.8	2

Comments: Buffalo's No. 3 receiver, Beebe set personal highs last season with 33 catches for 554 yards, including a 65-yard TD reception against the Colts. He also had four 100-yard games, which was the most on the team — and not bad for a player who missed four games because of a hamstring injury and started only eight times. His 16.8-yard average also led the Bills. Beebe's problem is that he always seems to get injured. But, when he's in a game, he can make things happen. In a 1991 game against Pittsburgh, he caught four touchdown passes and finished with 10 catches for 112 yards to tie a team single-game record. A slender speedster, the aggressive Beebe has exceptional speed and a knack for splitting a zone. If James Lofton slips, Beebe might move into the starting lineup, but the addition of Bill Brooks to the team could lessen his chances of playing, too.

TOM WADDLE / Bears

Year	Rec.	Yards	Avg.	TD's
1989	1	8	8.0	0
1990	2	32	16.0	0
1991	55	599	10.9	3
1992	46	674	14.7	4

Comments: The last two seasons, Waddle has been one of the favorite players for the NFL's blue-collar fans. He's a free agent find and a gutsy overachiever who is one of the league's best possession receivers. He was the Bears' leading receiver until injuring his hip in the 12th game and missing the rest of the season. In 1991, he was the only Bear to catch a pass in every game, and he finished second in receptions (55) and yards (599) — all that after having been waived in the final cutdown before being brought back. He also set a team record with nine catches in the playoff loss to Dallas. Waddle has great hands and knows how to split zones and find a seam. His greatest attribute is delivering in the clutch (he dropped only one catchable pass in '92). But, at 6-foot-1, 190 pounds, he's not built to play every down, and new head coach Dave Wannstedt wants to use Waddle as a third-down specialist in 1993. Thus, his numbers will probably decrease this season.

J.J. BIRDEN / Chiefs

Year	Rec.	Yards	Avg.	TD's
1990	15	352	23.5	3
1991	27	465	17.2	2
1992	42	644	15.3	3

Comments: Birden continues to improve after three seasons. Starting 11 games in 1992, he led the Chiefs' wide receivers with 42 catches, which matched his career totals going into the year. His 15.3-yard average was sixth in the AFC. A true deep threat, he had TD catches of 72, 43 and 24 yards in 1992, and his eight career scores average 54.3 yards in length. His best game last season was three catches for 79 yards and two TD's vs. Philadelphia. Birden led the team in average yards per catch his first two seasons. A speedster with a 4.3 40-time, he is quick off the line but tends to fumble because of his small size.

DWIGHT STONE / Steelers

Year	Rec.	Yards	Avg.	TD's
1988	11	196	17.8	1
1989	7	92	13.1	1
1990	19	332	17.5	1
1991	32	649	20.3	5
1992	34	501	14.7	3

Comments: A converted running back, Stone started 13 games last season, finishing third on the team in receiving and tying for the team lead with three touchdown receptions. He had one 100-yard game. Stone had the most productive year of his career in 1991 when he led the team's wideouts with five touchdowns (all of them were for more than 40 yards). The former 10th-round draft pick has great speed but shaky hands and he does not run precise routes. He's a big-play receiver who doesn't get the ball enough to make enough big plays.

TOMMY KANE / Seahawks

Year	Rec.	Yards	Avg.	TD's
1988	6	32	5.3	0
1989	7	94	13.4	0
1990	52	776	14.9	4
1991	50	763	15.3	2
1992	27	369	13.7	3

Comments: Believe it or not, with 27 catches, Kane was Seattle's No. 2 receiver in 1992. He started only 11 games, missing a month with a knee injury. He came on at the end of the season, catching 21 passes in the final six games, with two touchdowns. Kane was remarkably consistent in 1990 and '91, hitting the 50-reception and 700-yard marks both times. He was the Seahawks' top wide receiver in '90, surpassing Brian Blades. Kane has the blazing speed to complement Blades and stretch defenses, giving Seattle two home-run hitters. He has good hands and excellent change of direction after the catch.

TONY JONES / Falcons

Year	Rec.	Yards	Avg.	TD's
1990	30	409	13.6	6
1991	19	251	13.2	2
1992	14	138	9.9	1

Comments: After a very promising rookie season with the Oilers, Jones hasn't done much the last two seasons. He started the first four games of the year when Andre Rison and Michael Haynes were out of the lineup, and that's when he had 11 of his 14 receptions (which ranked fifth on the team). He had two stints on injured reserve last season, missing October with an ankle injury and the last game again with a bad ankle. The smallest player in the NFL (5-foot-7, 145 pounds), Jones is strictly a downfield speedster. He did show a lot in 1990, when he came on late to catch six TD passes, despite not starting.

KELVIN MARTIN / Seahawks

Year	Rec.	Yards	Avg.	TD's
1988	49	622	12.7	3
1989	46	644	14.0	2
1990	64	732	11.4	0
1991	16	243	15.2	0
1992	32	359	11.2	3

Comments: Martin was signed as a free agent by Seattle on April 1 and should be used more as a receiver than he was in Dallas the last two seasons. He is a solid possession receiver who scored three times in 1992 on 32 receptions. But he is a better kick returner than receiver. Last year he scored two TD's on punt returns and finished second in the league in punt return average. He led the Cowboys in receiving in 1990 with a career-high 64 catches for 732 but dropped back to the third or fourth receiver the last two seasons. Martin lacks great speed, instead specializing in outs and curls.

JEFF CHADWICK / Rams

Year	Rec.	Yards	Avg.	TD's
1988	20	304	15.2	3
1989	9	104	11.6	0
1990	27	478	17.7	4
1991	22	255	11.6	3
1992	29	362	12.5	3

Comments: Chadwick finished 1992 tied for second on the Rams with three receiving touchdowns and fifth with 29 receptions. He started two games, but played mostly in multiple-wide-receiver formations. The dependable Chadwick will probably never repeat his 1986 numbers (53 catches for 995 yards and five TD's). He is a possession receiver who has a little trouble getting off the line against a press, but he has fine hands and can read coverages.

ERNIE MILLS / Steelers

Year	Rec.	Yards	Avg.	TD's
1991	3	79	26.3	1
1992	30	383	12.8	3

Comments: A third-round draft pick in 1991 who didn't

do much as a rookie, Mills had a fine sophomore season. He was the team's fourth-ranked receiver with 30 catches, although he started only four games. He caught at least one pass in 14 of the last 15 games and has turned into a decent possession receiver. Mills has terrific speed but stiff hands. He should continue to improve.

FRED BANKS / Dolphins

Year	Rec.	Yards	Avg.	TD's
1988	23	430	18.7	2
1989	30	520	17.3	1
1990	13	131	10.1	0
1991	9	119	13.2	1
1992	22	319	14.5	3

Comments: Banks played in all 16 games in 1992 with no starts but finished with 22 catches for 319 yards and three touchdowns. His best game was four receptions for 85 yards and a TD against Houston in Week 11. Banks played in only seven games in 1991 because of a right knee injury and then a fractured right leg. He also missed half of 1990 with a fractured left foot. Now healthy, Banks has the speed and talent to be a big-play receiver. If Mark Clayton leaves the team and Banks can stay healthy, he could be a factor in 1993.

DEREK RUSSELL / Broncos

Year	Rec.	Yards	Avg.	TD's
1991	21	317	15.1	1
1992	12	140	11.7	0

Comments: Russell started six of the first 12 games last season. He lost his starting job in Week 9, then missed the final four games with a thumb injury. He wasn't very productive when he was in the lineup, catching only 10 passes — all of them in the first eight games — to finish seventh on the team. Russell had a good rookie campaign in 1991. After going the first five games without a reception, he caught 10 passes for 164 yards and his only touchdown in the next four games. Then he caught at least one pass in every game the rest of the season. Russell is quick and elusive and can turn a short pass into a long gain by spinning and weaving through traffic. He has big-play speed, something the Broncos need.

ARTHUR MARSHALL / Broncos

Year	Rec.	Yards	Avg.	TD's
1992	26	493	19.0	1

Comments: Marshall was a true free-agent find in 1992. An unknown receiver in September, he made most of the All-Rookie teams by the end of December. He started only one game and scored just one touchdown, but he caught passes in 11 games. He's very versatile — he carried the ball on 11 end-arounds for 56 yards and even threw an 81-

yard TD pass. Marshall also proved to be an excellent punt returner, finishing sixth in the NFL with a 10.6-yard average.

WESLEY CARROLL / Saints

Year	Rec.	Yards	Avg.	TD's
1991	18	184	10.2	1
1992	18	292	16.2	2

Comments: Carroll has been a disappointment in two seasons, with only 18 catches each year. In '92, he caught touchdown passes in each of the first two games, then was shut out of the end zone the rest of the season. Although he was regarded as a gamebreaker coming out of college, he doesn't have great speed. He is a very aggressive underneath receiver who has great concentration in a crowd and won't be intimidated. He should develop into a very productive and consistent go-to receiver in clutch situations, but that can be said for a lot of players who never quite do it.

GREG McMURTRY / Patriots

Year	Rec.	Yards	Avg.	TD's
1990	22	240	10.9	0
1991	41	614	15.0	2
1992	35	424	12.1	1

Comments: McMurtry has turned into a solid receiver in New England, starting 29 games the last two seasons. He finished third on the team in receptions both years. His high game in '91 was eight catches for 199 yards; last year he had two games with seven catches. McMurtry is a big, fluid receiver with good hands, but his speed and separation quickness are just average. He's at his best as a possession receiver coming in on third downs.

RON LEWIS / Packers

Year	Rec.	Yards	Avg.	TD's
1990	5	44	8.0	0
1991	Injured			
1992	13	152	11.7	0

Comments: Lewis was claimed off waivers from San Francisco before Game 11 and moved into the starting lineup a week later, benching Sanjay Beach, who hasn't done much. In those six games, he caught 13 passes for 152 yards and provided a decent complement to Sterling Sharpe. His best outing was four catches for 57 yards in his first start. With the 49ers, he was a rookie backup in 1990 and he missed the entire '91 season with a back injury. Lewis has quickness, speed, hands and blocking ability. If he holds on to the starting role, Lewis could surprise with some good numbers.

TONY MARTIN / Dolphins

Year	Rec.	Yards	Avg.	TD's
1990	29	388	13.4	2
1991	27	434	16.1	2
1992	33	553	16.8	2

Comments: The Dolphins' No. 3 receiver, Martin ranked sixth on the team with 33 catches last year, and it seems he scores two touchdowns every season. His average of 16.8 yards per catch was second on the team, and a 55-yarder was the season long. Martin started in place of the injured Mark Clayton the first three games of 1992, making 10 catches. His high game was five receptions for 90 yards against the Colts. In 1991, Martin had two 100-yard games and tied both Mark Clayton and Mark Duper, each of whom had nearly three times as many catches. Martin is super fast, but he runs uncertain routes and has shaky hands. Too often he follows a great catch by dropping an easy pass. If Mark Clayton leaves the team as a free agent, Martin will most likely assume a starting role.

MICHAEL TIMPSON / Patriots

Year	Rec.	Yards	Avg.	TD's
1989	0	0	0.0	0
1990	5	91	18.2	0
1991	25	471	18.8	2
1992	26	315	12.1	1

Comments: Timpson started two games last year and played in the other 14, ranking fourth on the Patriots in receiving. He has loads of speed and big-play potential, but he has yet to develop into much of a threat. His best game in 1992 was six catches for 74 yards and his only touchdown. In '91, he caught seven passes for 150 yards and one TD in his best outing. He caught only nine passes over the second half of 1992.

AARON COX / Colts

Year	Rec.	Yards	Avg.	TD's
1988	28	590	21.1	5
1989	20	340	17.0	3
1990	17	266	15.6	0
1991	15	216	14.4	0
1992	18	261	14.5	0

Comments: Cox was signed by the Colts as a free agent in mid-April, but he will probably never reach his potential in a career that seems to be injury-plagued. Last year he missed the last six games because of a hamstring injury. Twice he caught five passes in one game. The Rams' No. 3 wide receiver, Cox stayed relatively injury-free in 1991 but caught only 15 passes. In five NFL seasons, he has yet to put together the type of season you would expect of a first-round draft pick. Cox has a lot of ability and can flat-out fly, but he flat-out gets injured too much.

SHAWN JEFFERSON / Chargers

Year	Rec.	Yards	Avg.	TD's
1991	12	125	10.4	1
1992	29	377	13.0	2

Comments: Jefferson started the final two games last season, turning into a valuable No. 3 receiver after getting over a hamstring injury suffered in training camp. He ranked fifth on the team in receiving, but could move up to a starting role this year. He has tremendous deep speed but needs to get tougher. He joined the Chargers two weeks before the start of the 1991 season from Houston.

TERANCE MATHIS / Jets

Year	Rec.	Yards	Avg.	TD's
1990	19	245	12.9	0
1991	28	329	11.8	1
1992	22	316	14.4	3

Comments: Mathis ranked fourth among Jet wide receivers in catches in 1992, after finishing second the two previous seasons. He had three touchdowns among his 22 receptions, and he scored once on a 10-yard run. Mathis was a prolific collegiate receiver at New Mexico who set NCAA records for career receptions, yardage and games catching a TD pass. He's quick and elusive, but doesn't have the size to start. He usually plays in multiple-receiver sets. He did lead the team in punt and kickoff returns in 1991, and he returned a kickoff for a TD in '90.

ROBERT BROOKS / Packers

Year	Rec.	Yards	Avg.	TD's
1992	12	126	10.5	1

Comments: As a rookie third-round draft choice last year, Brooks didn't do very much. He started the season opener in a three-wide-receiver alignment, but was best used as a kick returner. He has possibilities as a deep threat as he develops. He's extremely quick and separates well from defenders.

ALEXANDER WRIGHT / Raiders

Year	Rec.	Yards	Avg.	TD's
1990	11	104	9.5	0
1991	10	170	17.0	0
1992	12	175	14.6	2

Comments: After two years as a big bust in Dallas, Wright was acquired by the Raiders in an early-October trade and actually started to show some of his talents. He caught touchdown passes in the last two games of the season, his first two NFL scores. A second-round draft pick in 1990 who has tremendous speed, Wright needs to develop his skills. His problem is he can't separate from defenders, nor can he read coverages. In 1991, he caught only 10 of 24 passes thrown his way. Don't expect much out of Wright, but Raiders owner Al Davis does have a way of turning rejects into prospects.

ROBB THOMAS / Seahawks

Year	Rec.	Yards	Avg.	TD's
1989	8	58	7.3	2
1990	41	545	13.3	4
1991	43	495	11.5	1
1992	11	136	12.4	0

Comments: Cut by Kansas City in the final cut, Thomas was signed by Seattle and played in the final 15 games of the season. He caught only 11 passes, far off his totals of the two previous seasons. He led the Chiefs in receiving with 43 catches and ranked second with 495 receiving yards. The son of former Giants receiver Aaron Thomas, he is a fine possession receiver. Thomas looks small and he doesn't have blazing speed. He has good but inconsistent hands because he drops too many easy passes.

REGGIE REMBERT / Bengals

Year	Rec.	Yards	Avg.	TD's
1990	Injured			
1991	9	117	13.0	1
1992	19	219	11.5	0

Comments: Rembert finished the 1992 season on the fast track following a slow start. He was placed on the reserve/non-football illness list Sept. 29 for alcohol dependency, missing nine games. After returning, he had 12 receptions for 125 yards over the last three games, two of which he started. He played in all 16 games in '91 as the Bengals' fourth wideout after missing the entire '90 season with a hamstring injury that left people questioning his attitude. Rembert is big, tall and fast — the kind of player who should be making a big impact. But he has terrible work habits — and, obviously, some other terrible habits as well.

CHRIS CALLOWAY / Giants

Year	Rec.	Yards	Avg.	TD's
1990	10	124	12.4	1
1991	15	254	10.9	1
1992	27	335	12.4	1

Comments: Calloway started just one game last season but finished sixth on the Giants in receiving. He caught at least one pass in 14 games. His best game was four catches for 54 yards and a touchdown in Game 15 against Kansas City. In 1991, Calloway played in 12 games for Pittsburgh, where he was a backup. He isn't big or fast, and has been described as a poor man's Louis Lipps.

SHAWN COLLINS / Browns

Year	Rec.	Yards	Avg.	TD's
1989	58	862	14.9	3
1990	34	503	14.8	2
1991	3	37	12.3	0
1992	3	31	10.3	0

Comments: Collins was obtained in a trade with Atlanta last September, playing in nine games and starting twice. He caught only three passes and ended the year on injured reserve with a rib injury. Thus, in three years, Collins has gone from the All-Rookie team to oblivion. In 1989, he led every rookie in receiving. If he gets his act together again, he could still be a productive receiver because he has size, strength and good hands.

ROY GREEN / Eagles

Year	Rec.	Yards	Avg.	TD's
1988	68	1097	16.1	7
1989	44	703	16.0	7
1990	53	797	15.0	4
1991	29	364	12.6	0
1992	8	105	13.1	0

Comments: Green will be 36 when the 1993 season begins and he no longer has the speed and moves he did years ago. However, he still possesses the experience and craftiness needed to be a backup receiver, which is why the Eagles keep him around. In 1992, Green missed the first seven games of the season with an elbow injury. He ranks 15th all-time in both receptions and receiving yards. He joined the Eagles three games into the 1991 season when Calvin Williams was injured and immediately started three games. In his first game with the team, Green caught six passes for 114 yards to show he wasn't washed up. So, if Fred Barnett or Williams were to get injured, Green would get the call and probably play good ball.

EMILE HARRY / Broncos

Year	Rec.	Yards	Avg.	TD's
1988	26	362	13.9	1
1989	33	430	13.0	2
1990	41	519	12.7	2
1991	35	431	12.3	3
1992	6	57	9.5	0

Comments: Harry was signed as a free agent in the offseason. He joined the Rams for the last month of 1992 after five seasons with the Chiefs. Harry is a small possession receiver. He started eight games in 1991, missing four weeks with an injury, and finished fourth on the team in receptions. In the final six games, he had 27 catches for 361 yards and two touchdowns. In 1990, Harry set personal bests with 41 catches and 519 receiving yards, when he was used primarily as a third-down receiver.

RON MORRIS / Bears

Year	Rec.	Yards	Avg.	TD's
1988	28	498	17.8	4
1989	30	486	16.2	1
1990	31	437	14.1	3
1991	8	147	18.4	0
1992	4	44	11.0	0

Comments: Morris has had two straight years that he would like to forget — and most football fans have already forgotten him. He has played in only seven games the last two years because of a knee injury that hasn't come around yet. In 1991, he was rushed back into the lineup and caught five passes for a career-high 106 yards against the Redskins. That's proof that he has talent. Now he just has to get it into games on a consistent basis. Morris is more of a power receiver than a speedster.

LOUIS CLARK / Seahawks

Year	Rec.	Yards	Avg.	TD's
1990	None			
1991	21	228	10.9	2
1992	20	290	14.5	1

Comments: Clark started nine of the first 10 games last season when Brian Blades was injured. Then he suffered a rib injury and missed the rest of the season. Still, he was fourth on the team with 20 catches. He's a good No. 3 or 4 receiver in the NFL, but he's certainly not a starter.

BRIAN BRENNAN / Chargers

Year	Rec.	Yards	Avg.	TD's
1988	46	579	12.6	1
1989	28	289	10.3	0
1990	45	568	12.6	2
1991	31	325	10.5	1
1992	19	188	9.9	1

Comments: Brennan was claimed off waivers from Cincinnati prior to Game 10 last season. He caught three passes for San Diego, all for first downs. With Cleveland from 1984 to '91, he was considered one of the league's best possession receivers, with 315 receptions.

TORRANCE SMALL / Saints

Year	Rec.	Yards	Avg.	TD's
1992	23	278	12.1	3

Comments: A great fifth-round draft pick a year ago, Small was a pleasant surprise as a rookie, catching 23 passes and scoring three touchdowns. He started one game. Small has size and speed, catches the ball well and should get better.

CEDRIC TILLMAN / Broncos

Year	Rec.	Yards	Avg.	TD's
1992	12	211	17.6	1

Comments: Tillman played in nine games as a rookie last season, catching 11 of his 12 passes in the final four games. His second pro reception was an 81-yard touchdown catch in Game 13. He shows a lot of promise and should see more playing time in '93.

CHARLES DAVENPORT / Steelers

Year	Rec.	Yards	Avg.	TD's
1992	9	136	15.1	0

Comments: The Steelers have been looking for a top receiver for years, and Davenport will get his oportunity one of these days. A fourth-round pick last season, he played in 15 games, mostly as a backup. He's a big, athletic wide receiver with good hands but not a lot of speed.

MIKE FARR / Patriots

Year	Rec.	Yards	Avg.	TD's
1990	12	170	14.2	0
1991	42	431	10.3	1
1992	15	115	7.7	0

Comments: Farr signed with New England as a free agent during the offseason. He has started 23 games the last two years, although his statistics slipped in '92 when the ball didn't come his way very much. In '91, he finished third on the Lions in receiving, although he scored just one time. Although he'll never be a star like his father, Mel, Mike excels on third downs.

GEORGE THOMAS / Buccaneers

Year	Rec.	Yards	Avg.	TD's
1990	18	383	21.3	1
1991	28	365	13.0	2
1992	6	54	9.0	0

Comments: Thomas joined the Buccaneers for the last five games last year, starting the season finale. He compiled all of his statistics in Atlanta, where he played the first half of the season, starting one game. Thomas has great speed, which accounted for his 21.3-yards-per-catch average in 1990. But he's still learning and has trouble staying healthy.

LEONARD HARRIS / Oilers

Year	Rec.	Yards	Avg.	TD's
1988	10	136	13.6	0
1989	13	202	15.5	2
1990	13	172	13.2	3
1991	8	101	12.6	0
1992	35	435	12.4	2

Comments: Harris replaced Drew Hill and started the first seven games of the season before being benched in favor of free-agent signee Webster Slaughter because he averaged barely 11 yards per catch at the time. He caught only 10 passes the rest of the season. Harris is a quick, little receiver with very good hands. But he won't catch 35 passes again this season unless somebody gets injured.

CLARENCE VERDIN / Colts

Year	Rec.	Yards	Avg.	TD's
1988	20	437	21.9	4
1989	20	381	19.1	1
1990	14	178	12.7	1
1991	21	214	10.2	0
1992	3	37	12.3	0

Comments: Verdin is primarily a kick returner, although he is certainly one of the best in the NFL. Last year he ran two punts back for touchdowns, and he also had a 20.9-yard average on kickoffs, earning his second Pro Bowl berth. He is the only Colts player ever to score on both kickoffs and punts and the first to score on two punts in one season. In 1991 he ranked sixth on the Colts in receiving (third among wide receivers). He used to be strictly a home-run hitter (he averages 50.8 yards on nine career receiving TD's), but he has yet to reach his 1988 numbers because he can't find the hole in a zone and is plagued by dropped balls.

JOE JOHNSON / Vikings

Year	Rec.	Yards	Avg.	TD's
1989	0	0	0.0	0
1990	3	36	12.0	0
1991	0	0	0.0	0
1992	21	211	10.0	1

Comments: After three years in Washington where he was unable to get the opportunity to show what he can do, Johnson (formerly Joe Howard) became a valuable third-down receiver in Minnesota. A fine kick returner and end-around runner, Johnson spent the 1991 season on injured reserve with a wrist injury.

TONY HARGAIN / Chiefs

Year	Rec.	Yards	Avg.	TD's
1992	17	205	12.1	0

Comments: Hargain came on late last season, catching 16 passes for 192 yards in the final seven games. He had caught just one for 13 yards in the first nine games. Hargain had not played football since fracturing a kneecap early in his senior season in college in 1990.

JASON PHILLIPS / Falcons

Year	Rec.	Yards	Avg.	TD's
1989	30	352	11.7	1
1990	8	112	14.0	0
1991	6	73	12.2	0
1992	4	26	6.5	1

Comments: Phillips played in 12 games last season, missing a month with a knee injury, but didn't get the ball thrown his way much because the Falcons throw strictly to their four starters. A real smurf who spent his first two seasons in Detroit, Phillips was expected to flourish in Atlanta's run-and-shoot, but that hasn't been the case. He has good hands but he doesn't run good routes.

JEFF CAMPBELL / Lions

Year	Rec.	Yards	Avg.	TD's
1990	19	236	12.4	2
1991	2	49	24.5	0
1992	8	155	19.4	1

Comments: Campbell started the last eight games of 1990, but was used little in '91 and '92. He was used mostly as a kick returner. Campbell is a quick, gutty little receiver who makes things happen, although he doesn't have a lot of speed.

AL EDWARDS / Bills

Year	Rec.	Yards	Avg.	TD's
1990	2	11	5.5	0
1991	22	228	10.4	1
1992	2	25	12.5	0

Comments: Fourth wide receivers on some teams see a lot of action. But, after a fine season in 1991, Edwards didn't play much at wideout in '92. He missed the first nine games of the season with a rib injury and was used mostly on kickoff returns when he came back. In 1991, he had nine catches for 78 yards in vs. the Jets, and he also became the first Bills player since 1978 to return a kickoff for a TD.

ANTHONY EDWARDS / Cardinals

Year	Rec.	Yards	Avg.	TD's
1989	2	74	37.0	0
1990	0	0	0.0	0
1991	0	0	0.0	0
1992	14	147	10.5	1

Comments: A special-teams standout, Edwards capably replaced Ernie Jones during his absence and caught his first touchdown as a pro. He started two games, one at wide receiver and another at H-back.

SANJAY BEACH / Packers

Year	Rec.	Yards	Avg.	TD's
1989	0	0	0.0	0
1990	DNP			
1991	4	43	10.8	0
1992	17	122	7.2	1

Comments: Beach started the first 11 games last season until Ron Lewis arrived. Still, he caught only 17 passes all season with a very poor 7.2-yard average per catch. He's a quick receiver who lacks deep speed. He'll probably slip down to fourth on the team's depth chart this year behind Robert Brooks.

AND THE REST

(listed in alphabetical order)

MIKE BARBER, Buccaneers — Barber played in only two games last year, finishing the season on injured reserve with a shoulder injury. He caught just one pass for 32 yards. A quick and agile receiver, he caught 37 passes in Cincinnati in 1990 and '91.

REGGIE BARRETT, Lions — In two years, Barrett slipped from No. 1 on a scouting combine's list of the top wide receivers in the 1991 draft to the third round of the draft to an unused player with the Lions. He caught only four passes last season, although he does have potential if he ever gets his head together. He has missed 22 games in two seasons because of injuries.

ROB CARPENTER, Jets — Carpenter played in all 16 games last year, catching 13 passes for 161 yards and one touchdown. In the season opener, he caught six passes for 109 yards.

PAT COLEMAN, Oilers — Coleman has caught only 13 passes in two seasons, although he is supposed to have the kind of talent that would have him competing for playing time.

DAVID DANIELS, Seahawks — Daniels was considered a steal in Round Three of the 1991 draft, but he has been unimpressive since then, catching only nine balls in two years. He's big and fast but very raw.

SAM GRADDY, Raiders — Graddy had the best season of his career in 1992, catching 12 passes for 205 yards and one TD. He was developing into a big-play receiver and started Game 4 before breaking an arm and missing 10 weeks. He has world-class speed and seems to have turned into a pretty good football player.

MEL GRAY, Lions — Gray sees very little action as a receiver, but he's the best kick returner in the NFL. In 1991, he was the first player in NFL history to lead the league in both punt and kickoff returns in the same season. Last season, he ranked fifth in kickoff returns and ran back both a punt and a kickoff for touchdowns. He has played in the Pro Bowl the last three years.

COREY HARRIS, Packers — Harris split last season between the Oilers and Packers. He is an excellent kickoff returner and special-teams player. He might be moved to defensive back.

STEPHEN HOBBS, Redskins — Hobbs played in only the first two games of last season before going on injured reserve with a knee injury and missing the rest of the season. He is mainly a special-teams player.

JOHN JACKSON, Cardinals — Jackson is a possession receiver who has caught only nine balls in three seasons.

FRED JONES, Chiefs — Jones played in 14 games last year, missing the final two with a knee injury. He had career highs with 18 receptions for 265 yards. He is considered one of the NFL's best blocking wide receivers, but he hasn't proven to be very durable, missing almost half of the last three seasons.

TODD KINCHEN, Rams — A third-round draft pick a year ago, Kinchen raised eyebrows when he returned two punts for touchdowns in the final game of the season, only the sixth time that has occurred in NFL history. As a receiver, he has shown little ability to adapt to NFL schemes, too often running wrong routes.

GLEN KOZLOWSKI, Bears — Chicago's No. 5 wideout and special-teams kamikaze doesn't have much speed (after reconstructive knee surgery when he was in college) but loves to go over the middle. He has caught only 12 passes in the last three years.

BRAD LAMB, Bills — Lamb played in the first seven games last year, catching seven passes for 139 yards. He finished the season on injured reserve.

LOUIS LIPPS, Steelers — Seemingly out of football in 1992, Lipps is attempting a comeback with the team that released him only one year ago.

AUBREY MATTHEWS, Lions — Matthews doesn't play much. He ranked third among Detroit wideouts in receptions in 1990, but caught only 12 balls the last two seasons. He's fast but has inconsistent hands.

PAT NEWMAN, Saints — Newman caught three passes for 21 yards in 10 games last season, but he's been around and never seems to reach his potential.

STEPHONE PAIGE, Saints — The former Chiefs star sat out 1992 in a contract dispute and will attempt a comeback. He could help the Saints' receiving corps.

JAKE REED, Vikings — Reed was a highly regarded third-round draft pick in 1991 who hasn't shown much (six receptions for 142 yards in two seasons). A converted running back, he still has solid potential with speed and size.

VAI SIKAHEMA, Eagles — Sikahema is one of the best kick returners in the NFL. Last year he ranked third in punt returns. He also played quite a bit at wide receiver last year, catching 13 passes for 142 yards. Both figures were the second best of his career.

JIMMY SMITH, Cowboys — A second-round draft choice last year, Smith played in only seven games, missing the first month with a leg injury. He was the team's No. 4 wideout, although he failed to catch a pass. That will improve this season because he moves up to the No. 3 job after Kelvin Martin's departure to Seattle.

RICO SMITH, Browns — Smith started one of 10 games as a rookie in 1992, catching five passes for 64 yards. He was a sixth-round draft pick.

MILT STEGALL, Bengals — A rookie in 1992 who played in all 16 games, Stegall caught three passes for 35 yards. He was the Bengals' leading kickoff returner.

DOUG THOMAS, Seahawks — Thomas is another third-year receiver for the Seahawks who hasn't done much (see David Daniels). He has only 11 receptions in two seasons. He's all speed, but he hasn't learned what to do with it.

VERNON TURNER, Rams — The Rams' top kick returner, Turner caught five passes for 42 yards in 1992. He led the team in punts and kickoff returns. In 1991, he caught three passes for one touchdown.

MICHAEL YOUNG, Chiefs — The ex-Bronco signed with Kansas City during the offseason. He had retired midway through the 1992 season.

Other Wide Receivers on Rosters

Michael Bates, Seahawks
Robert Claiborne, Buccaneers
Dale Dawkins, Jets
Mark Didio, Steelers
Floyd Dixon, Redskins
Marcus Dowdell, Saints
Willie Drewrey, Oilers
Shane Garrett, Bengals
Carl Harry, Redskins
Jamie Holland, Browns
Barry Johnson, Broncos
Troy Kyles, Packers
Sammy Martin, Saints
Damon Mays, Oilers
Keenan McCardell, Browns
Eddie Miller, Colts
Scott Miller, Dolphins
James Milling, Falcons
James Pruitt, Browns
Patrick Rowe, Browns
Joey Smith, Giants
Michael Smith, Chiefs
Jeff Sydner, Eagles
Steve Tasker, Bills
Kitrick Taylor, Broncos
Yancey Thigpen, Steelers
Brian Treggs, Seahawks
Gary Wellman, Oilers
Ronnie West, Vikings
Mike Williams, Dolphins
Walter Wilson, Buccaneers
Eric Wright, Bears

Chapter 7
Tight Ends

Tight ends score fewer points in fantasy football than any other position, but they still can mean the difference between winning and losing any particular week. And that's why drafting the right tight ends is so valuable.

Keith Jackson is clearly the best tight end because of his consistency over the years and his ability to score from anywhere on the field. He could be joined among the elite by Eric Green, but Green had personal troubles in 1992 and will have to show that he has put them behind him. They are the only two tight ends capable of having truly great years — as much as 10 touchdowns in a season.

However, after Green and Jackson, there is a tier of about a half-dozen tight ends who are capable of making 40 or so receptions and scoring five or six touchdowns each season. They are Jay Novacek, Jackie Harris, Marv Cook, Brent Jones, Shannon Sharpe and maybe Keith McKeller. These players might not score as much as Jackson and Green, but some might catch as many or more passes.

Johnny Mitchell and Derek Brown are the two second-year tight ends who didn't do much as rookies but who have the talent to join Jackson and Green as outstanding players at the position. And Irv Smith, a rookie this year, also shows possibilities of being that good. Steve Jordan is past his time, and Ethan Horton and Ferrell Edmunds are what you might term "boom-or-bust" tight ends.

So, although the selection is limited at the top, there are enough good tight ends available for every team in a fantasy league, even in today's era of sophisticated offenses and multiple-receiver formations when tight ends are too often relegated to blocking duties.

Keith Jackson

end might be the one position where last year's performance should weigh heaviest).

■ Draft tight ends from predominantly passing teams that spread the ball around, because they are likely to catch more passes. And on these teams, look for tight ends who are integral parts of a team's passing attack. Those teams are Buffalo, Miami, San Francisco, Indianapolis, Pittsburgh, Green Bay, Denver, Dallas, New England and the Los Angeles Raiders and Rams. Stay away from teams like Chicago, Seattle, Atlanta and Houston (which doesn't even have a tight end on its roster).

■ Draft tight ends who catch the most passes, because they are most likely to get into the end zone.

■ At the same time, if a tight end is on a team with two very good wide receivers, he might be more apt to catch more passes because those other players will draw more double coverage.

■ Don't draft tight ends who are basically blockers. Know which tight ends are receivers and which ones are blockers.

■ Know which tight ends can go long and which ones catch the short passes. But sometimes the ones who catch the short passes near the goal line are the best ones.

■ Consider matching a tight end with your quarterback when putting together your team. It's worth more points if you have both players from one team when they score.

■ Take into consideration tight ends on teams that are likely to have a quarterback change during the season (or did so in training camp). The switching of quarterbacks often means a change in a team's offensive scheme, and thus it could change the production of the player you want to pick.

■ A tight end you draft in the last round won't be much different in terms of scoring capability than one you might draft in the middle rounds, so don't choose one too early if you can stock up on other positions.

Draft Tips in Choosing Tight Ends
■ Look at past performances, especially the last two or three seasons, rather than just last season (although tight

■ Watch what is going on during training camp. Are there any holdouts among the top tight ends? What can Keith Jackson accomplish after a full training camp with the Dolphins? Can the Raiders' Ethan Horton repeat his fine 1991 season or is 1992 more indicative? Will Jay Novacek again lead all tight ends in receptions? Can Marv Cook score a little more often for the Patriots? Is Ferrell Edmunds ever going to start living up to his abilities now that he has a fresh start in Seattle? Will Rodney Holman and Keith McKeller bounce back from subpar 1992 seasons? Did Pete Metzelaars have a career year in 1992, or can he do it again? Does Eric Green have his personal troubles behind him? Depending on that answer, how will it affect Adrian Cooper? Will the Redskins throw the ball more often to Terry Orr? When are Derek Brown and Johnny Mitchell going to start producing? Will Kerry Cash and Charles Arbuckle provide a solid 1-2 punch in Indianapolis? Is Shannon Sharpe ready to move up to the top group of tight ends? Does the Eagles' Mark Bavaro have anything left? Has the Vikings' Steve Jordan gotten too old? Is Jackie Harris the next Brent Jones?

SUPERSTARS

KEITH JACKSON / Dolphins

Year	Rec.	Yards	Avg.	TD's
1988	81	869	10.7	6
1989	63	648	10.3	3
1990	50	670	13.4	6
1991	48	569	11.9	5
1992	48	594	12.4	5

Comments: Jackson was Miami's second-leading receiver in 1992 despite missing the first three games of the season while holding out from the Eagles. He signed with Miami on September 29, five days after being declared an unrestricted free agent following four years with the Eagles. He caught a TD pass in his first game and all five of his TD's in the first six. He was held without a catch in only one game, and he finished second on the Dolphins in receiving TD's and third in yards. A four-time Pro Bowler, Jackson has been the most productive tight end in the NFL over the last five years, with 290 receptions and 25 TD's. In 1991, Jackson finished third on the Eagles in receiving and first in TD's, although he missed the Pro Bowl for the first time in his career. As a rookie in 1981, his 81 catches ranked second in league history for a rookie tight end. Jackson is a wide receiver with a tight end's body. He can line up tight and still go deep and beat a defensive back. He has tremendous hands, good speed and never gets intimidated. He gives Miami a dangerous presence going across the middle and a threat at tight end, two things the team has lacked. No longer is Jackson the consensus best tight end in the NFL, but with Dan Marino throwing to him and Mark Clayton almost certain to leave the team, Jackson could be in for a huge season.

ERIC GREEN / Steelers

Year	Rec.	Yards	Avg.	TD's
1990	34	387	11.4	7
1991	41	582	14.2	6
1992	14	152	10.9	2

Comments: Green could be and should be the best tight end in the NFL. However, last year he had so many problems that his future has to be considered questionable. He suffered a bruised shoulder in the first game and missed the next three games. He came back for a month, then was suspended by the NFL for six weeks for substance abuse. He finally returned for the season finale and the playoffs. Green caught all of his passes in Games 5-9 last year, scoring twice. In 1991, he played in only 11 games because of a broken right ankle. He caught at least one pass in all 11 games, and he scored in four straight games. In 1990, he missed the first three games of his rookie season because he was the last first-round draft pick to sign a contract. Once he got into the lineup, he caught five touchdown passes in his first two games, and finished with seven TD's, tops among NFL tight ends. His 34 catches were the most for a Pittsburgh tight end since 1983, and his TD total set a team record for the position. Green is huge — 6-5, 280 pounds — yet he blocks like a tackle and catches like a wide receiver. He can run a 4.7 40-yard dash. Green is considered the prototype tight end, but he has to learn how to stay in the lineup if he is to realize his enormous potential.

CAN'T MISS

JAY NOVACEK / Cowboys

Year	Rec.	Yards	Avg.	TD's
1988	38	569	15.0	4
1989	23	225	9.8	1
1990	59	657	11.1	4
1991	59	664	11.3	4
1992	68	630	9.3	6

Comments: Novacek was the best tight end in the NFL last season. He led the position with 68 receptions (a team record) and tied with Buffalo's Pete Metzelaars with six touchdowns. He has led NFC tight ends in receptions the last three years. He caught only nine passes in the first three games, then had 59 (4.6 per game) in the next 13. In 1991, Novacek had two of the four 100-yard games turned in by NFL tight ends. His 59 receptions were second in the NFL behind New England's Marv Cook, and he led Cook late in the season before missing three starts because of a knee injury. He caught his four TD passes in the first seven games of the season, and his 11-catch outing against Green Bay was an NFC single-season high. A bulked-up wideout who drives to get open and catches everything despite only modest speed, Novacek thrives on mismatches. He isn't much of a run blocker, but that doesn't matter in fantasy football. Consistency does, and Novacek is Mr. Consistent when it comes to tight ends.

BRENT JONES / 49ERS

YEAR	REC.	YARDS	AVG.	TD's
1988	8	57	7.1	2
1989	40	500	12.5	4
1990	56	747	13.3	5
1991	27	417	15.4	0
1992	45	628	14.0	4

Comments: The 49ers' second-leading receiver in 1992, Jones earned his first Pro Bowl invitation. He has been one of the steadiest tight ends in the NFL for the last four years. Last year he didn't catch any passes in the first three games (missing one with a hamstring injury) but caught anywhere from two to six passes a game the rest of the season. He had his best game near midseason against New Orleans when he caught two touchdown passes. Jones missed six games with a knee injury in 1991. In the two seasons before then, he had caught 96 passes for 1,247 yards and nine touchdowns, although he is greatly overshadowed by Jerry Rice and John Taylor. A free-agent signee in 1987, Jones is a fine receiver who lacks speed but knows how to work his way into areas left open by Rice and Taylor, especially those across the middle. A clutch player, he catches everything in his vicinity and has the speed to beat a defensive back deep.

JACKIE HARRIS / PACKERS

YEAR	REC.	YARDS	AVG.	TD's
1990	12	157	13.1	0
1991	24	264	11.0	3
1992	55	595	10.8	2

Comments: In 1992, Harris turned into one of the top receiving tight ends in the NFL. An up-and-coming star, he finished second on the Packers in receiving, and the team is convinced he'll turn into a Pro Bowler in Mike Holmgren's offense. He moved ahead of Ed West as the starter in mid-October and started the last 11 games of the season. Harris caught at least one pass in all 16 games, and had a season high of nine catches for 87 yards against the Giants. His 55 catches ranked second only to Dallas' Jay Novacek among tight ends, and he became only the second Packer tight end to catch 50 in a season. He scored only twice, but that should improve in time. In fact, his numbers should parallel those of San Francisco's Brent Jones. A fourth-round pick in 1990, Harris is a gifted receiver who can get away from defenders and run after the catch. He's also a downfield threat.

MARV COOK / PATRIOTS

YEAR	REC.	YARDS	AVG.	TD's
1989	3	13	4.3	0
1990	51	455	8.9	5
1991	82	808	9.9	3
1992	52	413	7.9	2

Comments: Although Cook's statistics slipped from the previous season, he made the Pro Bowl for the second consecutive year and became the second Patriots player to catch 50 passes in three consecutive seasons. The team's second-leading receiver in 1992, he caught at least one pass in 15 games, the same number as he started. His best outings were in Games 3 and 4 when he caught 13 passes for 95 yards and two TD's. In 1991, Cook led all tight ends in receptions and finished fourth among all players. In '90 he led AFC tight ends with 51 catches, and his five touchdowns led his team. He doesn't average many yards per catch, but he has quietly emerged as one of the league's top tight ends. Cook was considered just a good blocker coming out of college, but has proven quickly that he can catch the ball well. The athletic Cook runs precise routes, knows how to get open and will catch over the middle without flinching.

SOLID PICKS

SHANNON SHARPE / BRONCOS

YEAR	REC.	YARDS	AVG.	TD's
1990	7	99	14.1	1
1991	22	322	14.6	1
1992	53	640	12.1	2

Comments: Sharpe swings between tight end, H-back and wide receiver for the Broncos. He started 11 games at all three positions in 1992. He led the team in receiving and finished with 640 yards and two TD's, all career highs. The younger brother of Green Bay's Sterling Sharpe, Shannon caught passes in 13 games with two 100-yard days. He is a strong, physical receiver with sure hands who should improve even more this year.

KEITH MCKELLER / BILLS

YEAR	REC.	YARDS	AVG.	TD's
1988	None			
1989	20	341	17.1	2
1990	34	464	13.6	5
1991	44	434	9.9	3
1992	14	110	7.9	0

Comments: McKeller is one of the better tight ends in the NFL, but last year he was overshadowed by Pete Metzelaars after missing five games and eight starts because of a knee injury. Even after returning and moving back into the starting lineup, McKeller didn't see the ball come his way very often. Still, look for him to be the team's go-to tight end in 1993. McKeller's five touchdowns in 1990 tied a team record for the position (that was broken last year by Metzelaars). And, although McKeller didn't score last season, Jim Kelly likes to throw to his tight ends in scoring position. In the last three years, the Bills have thrown 22 TD's to tight ends. Kelly calls McKeller "a wide receiver in a tight end's body." He's best on short to intermediate passes over the middle, but he can occasionally sneak deep. The knock is that he sometimes drops passes. In 1991, he had a 10-catch, one-TD game against the Raiders.

ETHAN HORTON / RAIDERS

YEAR	REC.	YARDS	AVG.	TD's
1988	3	44	14.7	1
1989	4	44	11.0	1
1990	33	404	12.2	3
1991	53	650	12.3	5
1992	33	409	12.4	2

Comments: Horton started all 16 games last season but didn't put up the kind of statistics he did the year before. He caught passes in 14 games, but didn't have a touchdown the first half of the season (causing a lot of fantasy football players to quit playing him). Still, he was the Raiders' second-leading pass-catcher. A Pro Bowler in 1991, Horton is a true success story. A first-round draft pick of the Chiefs in 1985, he was a bust as a running back. The Raiders signed him in 1989 and converted him into a tight end. He struggled early on with dropped passes and too many holding penalties. In '91, he led the Raiders in receiving and scored five touchdowns. Horton is a talented athlete with good speed, skills and versatility. He can beat coverages, and he runs well after the catch. But he lacks strength against linebackers and is not a good blocker. Like the rest of the Raiders' receivers, he would be aided by better quarterbacking.

COULD COME ON

DEREK BROWN / GIANTS

YEAR	REC.	YARDS	AVG.	TD's
1992	4	31	7.8	0

Comments: Brown started seven of 16 games last season and was not much of a factor after having been chosen in the first round of the draft. He is a very good receiver, with size, hands and moves. Don't be surprised if he takes the starting job away from Howard Cross this year and catches 40 passes. Phil Simms, who started only four games in '92, likes to go to his tight ends.

JOHNNY MITCHELL / JETS

YEAR	REC.	YARDS	AVG.	TD's
1992	16	210	13.1	1

Comments: Mitchell was drafted for his big-play reputation in college, but, after playing in the first game, he spent the beginning of last season on injured reserve with a sprained left shoulder. After missing five games, he played in the final 10, starting three times. His 16 receptions ranked sixth on the team. Mitchell is a great raw talent who has been compared to Keith Jackson.

PETE HOLOHAN / BROWNS

YEAR	REC.	YARDS	AVG.	TD's
1988	59	640	10.8	3
1989	51	510	10.0	2
1990	49	475	9.7	2
1991	13	113	8.7	2
1992	20	170	8.5	0

Comments: Holohan could have been a pleasant surprise last year if he hadn't missed seven games with a foot injury. He caught 10 passes in the first four games before being injured. After returning, he caught nine balls in Games 14 and 15. With Mark Bavaro gone to Philadelphia, Holohan might have a solid season in 1993. The Browns were Holohan's fourth team in six years. From 1984 to '90, he had caught at least 40 passes in five of seven seasons. One of the best tight ends on third-and-short, he is just an average blocker. He specializes on 12-yard hooks and goal-line plays such as crosses and delay patterns.

1992 SURPRISE

PETE METZELAARS / BILLS

YEAR	REC.	YARDS	AVG.	TD's
1988	33	438	13.3	1
1989	18	179	9.9	2
1990	10	60	6.0	1
1991	5	54	10.8	2
1992	30	298	9.9	6

Comments: Metzelaars had an excellent season in 1992 after a few years in which he didn't contribute much. He tied with Dallas' Jay Novacek for the league lead with six TD receptions for tight ends, and he now has 16 for his career, making him Buffalo's all-time leader in the category. In the season's second game against San Francisco, he caught four passes for 113 yards and two TD's, including a 53-yarder. A big target at 6-foot-7, 251 pounds, Metzelaars is an underrated tight end who saw most of his playing time in recent seasons in short-yardage situations. Heading into his 12th season, the Bills' all-time leading receiver among tight ends is a blocker first. Don't expect him to score six touchdowns again in 1993.

QUESTION MARKS

KEITH BYARS / EAGLES

YEAR	REC.	YARDS	AVG.	TD's
1988	72	705	9.8	4
1989	68	721	10.6	0
1990	81	819	10.1	3
1991	62	564	9.1	3
1992	56	502	9.0	2

Comments: After Keith Jackson held out and then signed with Miami as a free agent last year, Byars moved full time to tight end and was very productive. He started the last six games at tight end, and the Eagles went 5-1 in that time. Previously as a running back, even though he averaged over 400 yards rushing per season, he was always more of a receiver than a runner, so the move fitted him well. Byars missed one game in 1992 because of a hand injury but caught at least one pass in every other game, moving his streak to 86 consecutive games with one or more receptions dating back to 1987. He has caught at least 56 passes in five straight seasons. He has also proven to be an effective run blocker. In 1991, he tied for both the Eagles' lead in receiving and the NFL title among running backs. Byars is a terrific third-down specialist. In the course of a game, he sometimes plays as many as six positions — halfback, fullback, tight end, wide receiver, wingback and in the slot. He is also a threat on option plays, having thrown five touchdown passes during his career.

FERRELL EDMUNDS / SEAHAWKS

YEAR	REC.	YARDS	AVG.	TD's
1988	33	575	17.4	3
1989	32	382	11.9	3
1990	31	446	14.4	1
1991	11	118	10.7	2
1992	10	91	9.1	1

Comments: Edmunds was signed as a free agent by Seattle on March 12. After three pretty good seasons in Miami, he hasn't been very good the last two years, having been beset with personal problems that have lessened his concentration. But he has a new lease on life in Seattle, which needs a good tight end. But, even if Edmunds gets his act together, he'll find out that his quarterbacks aren't nearly as good as Dan Marino. He played in only 10 games last year, missing the middle part of the season. Edmunds could be one of the best tight ends in the NFL. He has a rare combination of size, speed and ability which allows him to go deep down the middle and run away from defenders, and he's a load to bring down.

MARK BAVARO / EAGLES

YEAR	REC.	YARDS	AVG.	TD's
1988	53	672	12.7	4
1989	22	278	12.6	3
1990	33	393	11.9	5
1991	Retired			
1992	25	315	12.6	2

Comments: Bavaro signed with Philadelphia in late March after playing in Cleveland in 1992. He had been forced to retire in 1991 after an excellent career with the Giants which saw him win two Super Bowl rings. Bavaro is not the threat he used to be, but he can be a dependable receiver, and he's one of the toughest players around. Randall Cunningham, who likes to throw to his tight ends, needs one to replace the departed Keith Jackson, so Bavaro could yet surprise. He started all 16 games for the Browns last year.

BEST OF THE REST

RON HALL / BUCCANEERS

YEAR	REC.	YARDS	AVG.	TD's
1988	39	555	14.2	0
1989	30	331	11.0	2
1990	31	464	15.0	2
1991	31	284	9.2	0
1992	39	351	9.0	4

Comments: Hall is one of the most consistent tight ends in the NFL. Last year he started 11 of 12 games, missing the last three with a sprained knee. He was the Buccaneers' third-leading receiver, though he tied for the team lead with four receiving touchdowns. He caught at least one pass in every game in which he played. One of the best deep threats among NFL tight ends, Hall is very underrated and sure-handed. He has good size and speed, is a tackle-breaker and is a good blocker. His drawback is an inability to stay healthy.

ADRIAN COOPER / STEELERS

YEAR	REC.	YARDS	AVG.	TD's
1991	11	147	13.4	2
1992	16	197	12.3	3

Comments: Cooper started 14 of 16 games last season, taking over as the Steelers' No. 1 tight end when Eric Green was out of the lineup. He caught only 16 passes but scored three touchdowns, a good total for a tight end. In 1991, he was voted the team's Rookie of the Year. He started eight games and tied for third on the team in TD receptions with two. The second tight end drafted that year, he should continue seeing a lot of time in '93. Cooper is big and physical with surprising speed and quickness.

KERRY CASH / Colts

Year	Rec.	Yards	Avg.	TD's
1991	1	18	18.0	0
1992	43	521	12.1	3

Comments: Cash had a surprisingly good season in 1992, catching passes in the last 15 games and becoming the first Colts tight end since Tom Mitchell in 1972 to surpass 40 in a season. His 521 yards was also a team high since Reese McCall in 1979, and his three touchdowns was the team best since Pat Beach in 1985. He and teammate Charles Arbuckle had 100-yard games in 1992. Cash started all 16 games, and the Colts like to throw to him in short-yardage situations. He has good hands and some downfield speed. In 1991, Cash started two of the first four games but was knocked out the rest of the season with a broken leg.

TERRY ORR / Redskins

Year	Rec.	Yards	Avg.	TD's
1988	11	222	20.2	2
1989	3	80	26.7	0
1990	0	0	0.0	0
1991	10	201	20.1	4
1992	22	356	16.2	3

Comments: Orr had the best season of his career in 1992. In six previous seasons, he had caught only 30 passes, but last year he caught 22 more. Perhaps the best deep threat among all tight ends in the NFL, Orr scored three touchdowns and averaged an excellent 16.2 yards per catch. The Redskins' motion tight end, he started seven of 16 games. In 1991, after being cut by San Diego, he was one of the Redskins' unheralded stars. He caught only 10 passes but averaged a team-high 20.1 yards per catch. Four of his 10 receptions were for touchdowns, and six of them were for 22 yards or longer. If your league requires you to draft two tight ends, Orr is a certain bet to be one of them. And, if he gets the ball a few more times in '93, he might be a good pick for your starter. He underwent knee surgery in January but will be ready to go in September.

BEN COATES / Patriots

Year	Rec.	Yards	Avg.	TD's
1991	10	95	9.5	1
1992	20	171	8.6	3

Comments: Coates keeps improving every year and has turned into one of the best backup tight ends in the NFL. Last year he doubled his output of his rookie season with 20 receptions. He scored one more touchdown than Marv Cook, the starter, and ranked second among the team's receivers. A fifth-round draft pick, Coates started two games but played a lot in the others. He is bigger, stronger and faster than Cook, but he has to work on his blocking.

JIM PRICE / Rams

Year	Rec.	Yards	Avg.	TD's
1991	35	410	11.7	2
1992	34	324	9.5	2

Comments: Price is an underrated and unknown tight end who would be a good backup in fantasy football. He started only three games but caught at least one pass in all but two of the 15 in which he played. He finished fourth on the team with 34 catches and two touchdowns. After spending the 1990 season on the Rams' developmental squad, Price led the Rams' tight ends in receptions (and was third on the team) in '91 despite playing in only 12 games (three starts). He is the best receiver among the Rams' tight ends.

DERRICK WALKER / Chargers

Year	Rec.	Yards	Avg.	TD's
1990	23	240	10.4	1
1991	20	134	6.7	0
1992	34	393	11.6	2

Comments: Walker had a very good season last year, with 34 catches for 393 yards and two TD's — all career highs and pretty good numbers for a tight end these days. He has started 46 of 49 NFL games. In 1991, he finished second among Charger tight ends in receptions, although his 6.4-yard average per catch was hardly worth bragging about. He was considered a blocker in college, but he surprised the Chargers as a rookie in 1990 with his pass-catching skills. He's a good short-to-intermediate receiver.

PAT CARTER / Rams

Year	Rec.	Yards	Avg.	TD's
1988	13	145	11.2	0
1989	0	0	0.0	0
1990	8	58	7.3	0
1991	8	69	8.6	2
1992	20	232	11.6	3

Comments: Carter started all 16 games last year, having the finest season of his career with 20 catches for 232 yards and three touchdowns. He has all the tools to be a fine tight end — he's a good blocker with good hands and speed — but he was an underachiever until 1992.

ROOKIES

See Chapter 13, The Rookie Report.

FADING VETERANS

STEVE JORDAN / Vikings

Year	Rec.	Yards	Avg.	TD's
1988	57	756	13.3	5
1989	35	506	14.5	3
1990	45	636	14.1	3
1991	57	638	11.2	2
1992	28	394	14.1	2

Comments: The Vikings' all-time leading receiver, Jordan slipped considerably last year and is no longer considered among the top tight ends in the NFL. Even his streak of six consecutive Pro Bowls was snapped. He had his worst season since 1983, and only a six-reception, one-TD game in the season finale gave much hope of what he can still do. He missed Games 7 and 8 with knee and ankle injuries. He still might be able to bounce back, but don't expect 50 catches this year. Jordan has always had a high yards-per-catch average for a tight end. He can block, catch and get deep, but it's his brains that help him the most. Jordan can read the soft spots in a zone and has enough speed to get away.

RODNEY HOLMAN / Lions

Year	Rec.	Yards	Avg.	TD's
1988	39	527	13.5	3
1989	50	736	14.7	9
1990	40	596	14.9	5
1991	31	445	14.4	2
1992	26	266	10.2	2

Comments: After being cut by Cincinnati, Holman was signed by Detroit, where he takes over as the Lions' top tight end—if he still has anything left, that is. Holman was the best tight end in the AFC in 1989 and '90, but he had bad seasons in '91 and '92 and his best days are certainly behind him. He started 13 games in 1992. In 1989, Holman's stats were as good as you would hope to get from any wide receiver. Few players have the receiver's touch and offensive lineman's blocking skills that Holman once possessed. Now, however, he's just an aging veteran.

SLIPPED IN 1992

DAMONE JOHNSON / Rams

Year	Rec.	Yards	Avg.	TD's
1988	42	350	8.3	6
1989	25	148	5.9	5
1990	12	66	5.5	3
1991	32	253	7.9	2
1992	0	0	0.0	0

Comments: Johnson played only the first four games of 1992, spending the last 12 on injured reserve with a partial tear of the rotator cuff in his left shoulder. The starter since 1987, he is a notch below the league's best tight ends as both a blocker and receiver. But, from 1988 to '91, only Keith Jackson and Rodney Holman scored more touchdowns than Johnson, who had 16. He's a good goal line receiver with decent deep speed, and he's a good in-line blocker in the two-tight-end offense.

ED WEST / Packers

Year	Rec.	Yards	Avg.	TD's
1988	30	276	9.2	3
1989	22	269	12.2	5
1990	27	356	13.2	5
1991	15	151	10.1	3
1992	4	30	7.5	0

Comments: West was the forgotten man in Mike Holmgren's offense last season. Normally one of the steadiest tight ends in the NFL, he caught just four passes all season, despite starting eight games, as Jackie Harris moved ahead of him. In fact, after catching three balls in the first three weeks, he was shut out until the final game. In the four years from 1988 to '91, only Keith Jackson and Rodney Holman had scored more touchdowns than West's 16, which was excellent production for a tight end. Unless he gets the ball a few times near the goal line, West will be relegated to blocking duties. He's a physical run blocker and adequate short receiver who runs well after the catch and is tough to bring down.

OTHERS

HOWARD CROSS / Giants

Year	Rec.	Yards	Avg.	TD's
1989	6	107	17.8	1
1990	8	106	13.3	0
1991	20	283	14.2	2
1992	27	357	13.2	2

Comments: Cross had a solid season in 1992, starting all 16 games and finishing fifth on the team in receiving. He scored touchdowns in Games 2 and 3, then was shut out of the end zone the rest of the year. His best game was six catches for 77 yards and one TD against Dallas. Cross is a very good blocking tight end, but he has trouble shaking a defender as a receiver and he drops too many passes. Derek Brown is destined to be New York's tight end of the future, so Cross might not match his 1992 totals again.

CRAIG THOMPSON / Bengals

Year	Rec.	Yards	Avg.	TD's
1992	19	194	10.2	2

Comments: A fifth-round draft pick a year ago, Thompson started three of 16 games last year and had the most receptions of the team's tight ends who are back for 1993 (Rodney Holman was released in February). Thompson caught five passes in two different games last year. He shows flashes of Holman's ability and is built along the same lines.

BUTCH ROLLE / Cardinals

Year	Rec.	Yards	Avg.	TD's
1988	2	3	1.5	2
1989	1	1	1.0	1
1990	3	6	2.0	3
1991	3	10	3.3	2
1992	13	64	4.9	0

Comments: A touchdown machine in Buffalo from 1986 to '91, Rolle failed to get into the end zone with the Cardinals last season after signing as a free agent. A third-string tight end with Buffalo, he had an amazing streak of 10 consecutive receptions for touchdowns that lasted from 1987 to '91. With the Bills, he scored touchdowns on 10 of his 15 receptions, none of them more than three yards. That wasn't the case in Phoenix for a team that didn't score all that often in 1992. Rolle started 13 games at H-back last season. He caught eight passes in the first four games, but didn't get involved in the passing game much the rest of the year. Look for him to score once or twice in '93.

KEITH CASH / Chiefs

Year	Rec.	Yards	Avg.	TD's
1991	7	90	12.9	1
1992	12	113	9.4	2

Comments: A Plan B pickup from Pittsburgh, Cash played in 15 games and got two starts in two-tight-end formations in 1992. He had 12 catches for 113 yards and two TD's, both on two-yard plays. He has good hands and the speed to separate from defenders.

ANDREW GLOVER / Raiders

Year	Rec.	Yards	Avg.	TD's
1991	5	45	9.0	3
1992	15	178	11.9	1

Comments: Glover keeps improving every year. As a rookie in 1991, he caught only five passes for 45 yards, but three of them were for touchdowns. Last season, he started one game and set personal bests for receptions and yards. At nearly 6-foot-7, Glover is great near the goal line

because he can jump and outmuscle defensive backs for the ball. He has loads of potential because of his size, speed and hands.

JIMMIE JOHNSON / Lions

Year	Rec.	Yards	Avg.	TD's
1989	4	84	21.0	0
1990	15	218	14.5	2
1991	3	7	2.3	2
1992	6	34	5.7	0

Comments: Johnson started five of 16 games last season but was used infrequently as a pass receiver and didn't turn into the touchdown scorer that he has the ability to be. With the Redskins in 1991, he scored touchdowns in the first two games and looked like he was on the verge of having a great season. But he was dropped to second string when the team went to a ground game, and then he was placed on injured reserve for the final 10 games with a pinched nerve in his neck. Johnson is a gifted receiver who catches everything and can run away from defenders. He's not much of a blocker.

REGGIE JOHNSON / Broncos

Year	Rec.	Yards	Avg.	TD's
1991	6	73	12.2	1
1992	10	139	13.9	1

Comments: With Clarence Kay gone, the Broncos will count on Johnson to assert himself more. He moved into the lineup late in 1992 when Kay was slowed by a knee sprain. He caught six of his 10 receptions in the final two games, with his only touchdown coming in the season finale. The first tight end chosen in the 1991 draft (second round), Johnson is a fine blocker who is often compared to Kay as a tight end. He scored a touchdown on his first reception in his first pro game, but that was the highlight of his rookie season. He has good speed and is an adequate receiver and a tenacious blocker.

KEITH JENNINGS / Bears

Year	Rec.	Yards	Avg.	TD's
1991	8	109	13.6	0
1992	23	264	11.5	1

Comments: Jennings started 14 games last year in place of the injured Jim Thornton, putting up pretty good numbers for a Bears tight end. He caught passes in 12 games, including eight in the first three. He's big and athletic and is a natural receiver who should improve.

CHARLES ARBUCKLE / COLTS

YEAR	REC.	YARDS	AVG.	TD's
1992	13	152	11.7	1

Comments: Arbuckle was one of two Colt tight ends to have 100-yard receiving games in 1992 (Kerry Cash was the other). He started three games, catching nine passes for 106 yards in his first start. Arbuckle caught the game-deciding 23-yard TD pass to beat the Jets for his first career touchdown. Although Cash will continue to start, Arbuckle's statistics should improve in 1993.

MARK BOYER / JETS

YEAR	REC.	YARDS	AVG.	TD's
1988	27	256	9.5	2
1989	11	58	5.3	2
1990	40	334	8.4	1
1991	16	153	9.6	0
1992	19	149	7.8	0

Comments: Boyer led the Jets' tight ends in receptions last year with 19. He started all 16 games, but his playing time should diminish with the development of Johnny Mitchell and the signing of James Thornton. Boyer is a good blocker and a dependable short-to-intermediate receiver. In 1990, he caught 40 passes to finish third on the team and second among AFC tight ends and was the only Jet to catch a pass in all 16 games. He missed five games with various injuries in 1991.

JONATHAN HAYES / CHIEFS

YEAR	REC.	YARDS	AVG.	TD's
1988	22	233	10.6	1
1989	18	229	12.7	2
1990	9	83	9.2	1
1991	19	208	10.9	2
1992	9	77	8.6	2

Comments: A dominating blocker who is a key ingredient in the success of Kansas City's ground game, Hayes has started 76 of the last 88 games, including 32 straight the last two years. He caught only nine passes all year, but got four of them — and both touchdowns — in the season finale against Denver. A marginal receiver, Hayes lacks confidence in his hands and will body-catch. He's never caught more than 22 passes in a season.

MIKE TICE / VIKINGS

YEAR	REC.	YARDS	AVG.	TD's
1988	29	244	8.4	0
1989	1	2	2.0	0
1990	0	0	0.0	0
1991	10	70	7.0	4
1992	5	65	13.0	1

Comments: Tice is a solid blocker and not much of a receiver. Tice joined Minnesota in Plan B free agency from Seattle last year but missed Games 3-7 with a back injury. He had started 15 of 16 games in 1991 for the Seahawks when he caught 10 passes and scored four times because he knows how to get open in the end zone. Prior to that year, he had scored only five times in 10 seasons.

PAUL GREEN / SEAHAWKS

YEAR	REC.	YARDS	AVG.	TD's
1992	9	67	7.4	1

Comments: Prior to last season, Green's only NFL experience was in Super Bowl XXIV three years ago. He started the first four games of the season, catching nine passes for 67 yards and a touchdown. But he broke his left shoulder blade in practice and missed the rest of the season.

JAMES THORNTON / JETS

YEAR	REC.	YARDS	AVG.	TD's
1988	15	135	9.0	0
1989	24	392	16.3	3
1990	19	254	13.4	1
1991	17	278	16.4	1
1992	Injured			

Comments: Thornton started 55 straight games at tight end for the Bears until missing the last three of 1991 and then all of '92 with an arch injury. He had surgery again January 28 and will be 100 percent healed in time for training camp. He signed with the Jets as a free agent on April 5. Although Thornton doesn't see a lot of passes, he is a good receiver and runner after the catch. He's a big, fast, strong bruiser (his nickname is Robocop).

HOBY BRENNER / SAINTS

YEAR	REC.	YARDS	AVG.	TD's
1988	5	67	13.4	0
1989	34	398	11.7	4
1990	17	213	12.5	2
1991	16	179	11.2	0
1992	12	161	13.4	0

Comments: Brenner started 14 games last year but caught only 12 passes because the Saints don't throw much to their tight ends. In '91, he started all 16 games for the second consecutive season. The Saints' all-time receiving leader at tight end, he is used mainly as a blocker, although he is a good downfield receiver. Irv Smith, the Saints' first-round draft pick, will probably replace Brenner as the starter this year.

TYJI ARMSTRONG / Buccaneers

Year	Rec.	Yards	Avg.	TD's
1992	7	138	19.7	1

Comments: Part of a strong rookie class for the Buccaneers, Armstrong started eight of 15 games and proved to be a decent receiver. Considered a blocker coming out of college, he caught an 81-yard touchdown pass against the Rams.

DON WARREN / Redskins

Year	Rec.	Yards	Avg.	TD's
1988	12	112	9.3	0
1989	15	167	11.1	1
1990	15	123	8.2	1
1991	5	51	10.2	0
1992	4	25	6.3	0

Comments: Warren started 10 of the first 11 games last season, then went on injured reserve with a shoulder injury. He also missed six games in 1991 with a fractured ankle. Blocking has been Warren's calling card for 14 seasons.

JOHN TICE / Cut by Saints

Year	Rec.	Yards	Avg.	TD's
1988	26	297	11.4	1
1989	9	98	10.9	1
1990	11	113	10.3	0
1991	22	230	10.5	0
1992	0	0	0.0	0

Comments: Tice played just three games at midseason last year because of a shoulder injury. He underwent surgery in January. He is the Saints' second-string tight end behind Hoby Brenner, but led the position in receiving in 1991 with 22 receptions. Tice is a blocker first, receiver second. Although he's a load to tackle at 250 pounds, he no longer possesses the speed he once did. He was cut by New Orleans in early May.

PAT BEACH / Eagles

Year	Rec.	Yards	Avg.	TD's
1988	26	235	9.0	0
1989	14	87	6.2	2
1990	12	124	10.3	1
1991	5	56	11.2	0
1992	8	75	9.4	2

Comments: After 10 years with the Colts, Beach was signed by the Jets and then cut before being picked up by Philadelphia during Keith Jackson's holdout. He started seven games at tight end the first half of the season before Keith Byars moved there permanently. Beach scored both of his touchdowns in Game 5 against the Chiefs, which was the only game in which he had more than one reception. He started 10 games in 1991 for the Colts while having the worst season of his career. Beach is mainly a blocker because he lacks the speed and quickness to be much of a receiver. He has good hands and will catch in a crowd.

SCOTT GALBRAITH / Browns

Year	Rec.	Yards	Avg.	TD's
1990	4	62	15.5	0
1991	27	328	12.1	0
1992	4	63	15.8	1

Comments: Galbraith lost his starting job last season to Mark Bavaro but might regain it this year because Bavaro signed with Philadelphia as a free agent during the offseason. Galbraith played in 14 games in '92 but caught only two passes. He emerged as the Browns' starter in 1991, replacing Ozzie Newsome. He is more of a blocker than a receiver, and he'll remain in that role.

WALTER REEVES / Cardinals

Year	Rec.	Yards	Avg.	TD's
1989	1	5	5.0	0
1990	18	190	10.6	0
1991	8	45	5.6	0
1992	6	28	4.7	0

Comments: Reeves started all 16 games last year but is used mostly as a blocker. With 33 career receptions, he has yet to score a touchdown. He's an excellent power-blocking run-blocker who is more like a 265-pound tackle, but he does struggle on pass protection.

JAMIE WILLIAMS / 49ers

Year	Rec.	Yards	Avg.	TD's
1988	6	46	7.7	0
1989	3	38	12.7	0
1990	9	54	6.0	0
1991	22	235	10.7	1
1992	7	76	10.9	1

Comments: Williams is basically a third tackle because of his superb blocking abilities. He played in all 16 games last year, starting once when Brent Jones was injured. In 1991, he was forced into the role of a pass receiver for six games when Jones was injured.

AND THE REST

(listed in alphabetical order)

ROB AWALT, Bills — A Plan B signee, Awalt was cut by the Broncos before the start of last season and joined the

Bills one game into the season. He played in 14 games with one start. His receiving totals still haven't come close to matching what he did his first three seasons of 1987-89 (114 receptions), because he has caught only nine passes for 91 yards in the last two years.

GREG BATY, Dolphins — Baty played in all 16 games last season with only three catches but one touchdown. He doesn't look like he'll ever catch 37 passes in a season again, as he did as a rookie in 1986 in New England. Baty started eight games in 1991, which were his first starts since '86), and was the Dolphins' leading receiver among tight ends. Miami was looking for another tight end during the offseason, which could mean the end for Baty.

KELLY BLACKWELL, Bears — As a free-agent rookie backup in 1992, Blackwell caught five passes for 54 yards.

JOHN BRANDES, Giants — Brandes was claimed off waivers by the Giants for the last month of the season after spending six seasons in Washington. He's basically a blocker.

MIKE DYAL, Chiefs — Dyal has been beset by injuries the last three years and might never develop into the player he once had the abilities to be. After not playing since 1990, last year he played in three games before returning to injured reserve with a broken forearm.

RON HELLER, Seahawks — Heller missed the 1991 season but was signed by Seattle after it ended. He started 11 of the last 12 games in '92 after Paul Green was injured. He caught 12 passes for 85 yards, but will probably not be around in '93.

STEVE HENDRICKSON, Chargers — The Chargers' jack-of-all-trades, Hendrickson is a superb blocker in short-yardage situations who is known mostly for his special-teams prowess. He started his pro career as a linebacker and was switched over in 1991, when he rushed one time for a touchdown and caught four passes with another TD. He didn't catch a pass in '92, but still played a lot of tight end as an extra blocker..

MAURICE JOHNSON, Eagles — Johnson started during the preseason last year but an injury kept him out for the first month of the regular season. He started three games in 1992, catching two passes for 16 yards. He is regarded mostly as a blocker.

TIM JORDEN, Steelers — Jorden started four games last year in two-tight-end formations, catching six passes for 28 yards with two touchdowns. His playing time during the upcoming season will diminish if Eric Green is back in the lineup.

THOMAS McLEMORE, Lions — McLemore missed the first month of last season with a shoulder injury but played in 11 games. He caught only two passes for 12 yards and will need some time to develop.

TRAVIS McNEAL, Rams — Cut by Seattle in September after a training camp holdout, McNeal signed with the Rams before Game 5 and played in the final 12 games. He saw most of his action in three-tight-end sets. His 17 receptions led Seattle tight ends in 1991.

RON MIDDLETON, Redskins — Middleton started 12 of 16 games last season at tight end and H-back, with seven receptions for 50 yards. He's a key factor in the success of the Redskins' running game because he's a top-notch blocker, but he is also developing into a good pass receiver.

AARON PIERCE, Giants — The second rookie tight end on the Giants last year, Pierce played in only the last game after spending the first 15 weeks on injured reserve. A former decathlon star with speed, he and Derek Brown represent the future at tight end for the Giants, not Howard Cross.

JIM RIGGS, Bengals — Riggs started two games in 1992 but missed the last four with a sprained ankle. He caught 11 passes for 70 yards but is mainly a blocker. He will have a hard time making the team this season.

ALFREDO ROBERTS, Cowboys — The Cowboys' No. 2 tight end, he played in all 16 games before suffering a severe knee injury and missing the playoffs. He had reconstructive knee surgery in January and should be ready by mid-August. He's a good run-blocker but not much as a receiver.

DEREK TENNELL, Vikings — Tennell was signed by Dallas for the playoffs last year and earned a Super Bowl check. He caught a touchdown pass in the first playoff game, which was his first NFL catch since 1989. He signed with Minnesota in April.

JEFF THOMASON, Bengals — A free-agent signee with Cincinnati in 1992, Thomason caught two passes for 14 yards.

FRANK WAINRIGHT, Saints — Wainright played in 13 games last year, starting four times, because of an injury to John Tice. He caught nine passes for 143 yards, a nice 15.9-yard average.

WESLEY WALLS, 49ers — Walls missed the entire 1992 season because of a shoulder injury. Mostly a blocker, he will be the team's No. 3 tight end in '93, though he has quite a bit of potential.

DEREK WARE, Cardinals — As a rookie seventh-round draft choice in 1992, Ware played in 15 games without making a start. He caught one pass for 13 yards in Game 14.

KEN WHISENHUNT, Jets — Whisenhunt started six of the last 10 games last year after missing the first six weeks of the season. He caught only two passes for 11 yards.

DUANE YOUNG, Chargers — A powerful blocker, Young caught four passes in the first half of 1992 but none afterward, although he started 14 games. He plays mostly in three-tight-end formations.

Other Tight Ends on Rosters
Jesse Anderson, Packers
Russ Campbell, Steelers
Todd Harrison, Buccaneers
Darryl Ingram, Packers
James Jenkins, Redskins
David Jones, Raiders
Trey Junkin, Seahawks

Brian Kinchen, Browns
Harper LeBel, Falcons
Deems May, Chargers
Orson Mobley, Dolphins
Dave Moore, Buccaneers
Keith Neubert, Eagles

Brent Novoselsky, Vikings
Alfred Pupunu, Chargers
Ray Rowe, Redskins
Kevin Smith, Raiders
Ed Thomas, Bills
Nate Turner, Bills

Chapter 8
Kickers

Kickers play an enormously big role in pro football. Nearly half of all games in the NFL are decided by less than a touchdown, and kickers are almost always a team's leading scorer.

Kickers are also very valuable in fantasy football. However, there are a lot of very good ones in the NFL, with close to a dozen scoring 100 or more points every season.

Most years one kicker far outdistances the pack in scoring, and it's usually a different kicker every year. But last year was different, with several players all within a field goal or two from the scoring lead.

The best kickers are not necessarily those who score the most points. The best kickers really are probably Nick Lowery and Morten Andersen. But those two play for teams that don't score a very high number of points, and they usually don't score as many points as some of their competitors.

In fantasy football, points count the most, and the kickers who score the most points are Chip Lohmiller, Steve Christie, Pete Stoyanovich, Nick Lowery, Morten Andersen, Lin Elliott, Gary Anderson, Al Del Greco, David Treadwell, Norm Johnson and Mike Cofer. That's a lot of kickers, so you can't help but have a good one on your fantasy team.

The best long-distance kickers are Nick Lowery, Pete Stoyanovich, Morten Andersen, Steve Christie, Norm Johnson and Chip Lohmiller.

The best kickers in the clutch are Jeff Jaeger, Nick Lowery, Morten Andersen and Chris Jacke.

And the best kickers to be your backup are Fuad Reveiz, Roger Ruzek, John Carney, Kevin Butler, Tony Zendejas, Matt Bahr and Jim Breech.

However, kickers are probably the least reliable players in the NFL. Every year, two or three of them have bad seasons, and the key to a fantasy season could be not having

Chip Lohmiller

one of the bad kickers on your team (or having a good backup). The kickers who had off years in 1992 were Jeff Jaeger, Dean Biasucci, Roger Ruzek, Greg Davis and John Kasay.

Draft Tips in Choosing Kickers

■ Look at past performances, especially the last two or three seasons, rather than just last season. Far too often, a kicker's most recent season is not indicative of his true abilities (whether he had a good season or a poor one).

■ The biggest consideration for a kicker is the team he plays on. Therefore, be sure to draft those kickers who will get the most opportunities to score. The best guide here is a team's performance from the previous season.

■ Be sure to have a very good backup kicker who can take over if your starter is injured or is having a bad season. Don't be forced to go through the season with a kicker having an off year.

■ A kicker's longevity with a team is important, because many teams don't have any continuity at the position and thus change kickers often (even in midseason). If a kicker has played for the same team for several years, that team obviously has a lot of confidence in that kicker.

■ If your league's scoring system rewards long field goals, know which kickers are reliable on the long kicks (40 yards or longer).

■ Kickers are ranked according to their ability to score points — not on how good they are.

■ Know what is going on during training camp. What kickers have been cut? (Yes, every year fantasy players draft NFL players who have been cut by their teams.) Can Chip Lohmiller continue to score an average of 125 points a season? Is Lin Elliott going to continue kicking the way he did the second half of 1992? Can Jeff Jaeger rebound from a miserable 1992? Will David Treadwell get back into the 100-point column? Can John Carney kick as well as he did in 1992? Can Gary Anderson have another strong year? Is Jim Breech starting to slip? Is Norm Johnson ever going to age? Can Nick Lowery continue hitting 90 percent of his field goals as he has the last three seasons? Can Matt Bahr hold on to his job with the Giants and stay healthy? Will Roger Ruzek get more opportunities to kick field goals? Is Pete Stoyanovich going to quit missing clutch extra points? If Greg Davis misses half of his field goals again, will he be cut before the end of the season? Who's going to be the Buccaneers' kicker? Can Dean Biasucci keep his job in Indianapolis? Will Al Del Greco do the same in Houston? And will the 49ers ever provide some competition for Mike Cofer?

SUPERSTARS

CHIP LOHMILLER / Redskins

Year	XP	XPA	FG	FGA	Points
1988	40	41	19	26	97
1989	41	41	29	40	128
1990	41	41	30	40	131
1991	56	56	31	43	149
1992	30	30	30	40	120

Distance	1-19	20-29	30-39	40-49	50+
1992	2/2	9/9	9/15	8/12	2/2

Comments: Lohmiller has averaged 125 points a season since entering the NFL in 1988, more than any other player in NFL history after five years in the league. Last year, his 120 points tied with Morten Andersen for the NFC scoring lead and was second in the league behind Pete Stoyanovich. His 30 field goals tied Stoyanovich for the NFL lead. He kicked at least one field goal in 14 of the games, including three games with three three-pointers and one game with five field goals. His 75 percent accuracy rate ranked seventh in the conference, and he has a career mark of 73.5 percent. He improved on his longer kicks in '92, hitting 10 of 14 attempts over 40 yards, but he missed 40 percent of his kicks from 30-39 yards. In 1991, he led the NFL in scoring with 149 points, the second most in Redskins history, and actually outscored the entire Indianapolis Colts team 149-143 (the last time a player outscored another team was back in 1945). In one game in 1991, he had two 50-yarders in the same quarter, tying a league record, and four kicks over 45 yards, setting a record. On the usually high-scoring Redskins, Lohmiller will always rank among the top scorers in the league, which again makes him the No. 1 pick among placekickers in fantasy football.

PETE STOYANOVICH / Dolphins

Year	XP	XPA	FG	FGA	Points
1989	38	39	19	26	95
1990	37	37	21	25	100
1991	28	29	31	37	121
1992	34	36	30	37	124

Distance	1-19	20-29	30-39	40-49	50+
1992	0/0	9/9	14/16	4/4	3/8

Comments: The NFL's scoring leader in 1992, Stoyanovich set a Dolphins record with 124 points. In four seasons in the NFL, he has averaged 110 points a year and has surpassed 100 points in three seasons, tying a team record. He also tied for the league lead with 30 field goals. Now with 101 career field goals in 125 attempts (80.8 percent), Stoyanovich ranks as the NFL's all-time most accurate field goal kicker, moving ahead of Nick Lowery, Morten Andersen and everybody else. He kicked field goals in all but two games last year, getting 13 in the first four games and more than one in 10 games. Stoyanovich did miss two key extra points last season, which may not mean much in fantasy football but keeps him from being regarded as the best placekicker in the game. In 1991, he missed the first two games over a contract holdout, but he still finished first in the AFC and second in the NFL in scoring with 121 points. He also ranked first in the AFC and tied Washington's Chip Lohmiller with 31 field goals for the NFL lead. Stoyanovich already has 10 career field goals of 50 yards or longer (a team record), including a 59-yarder in 1989, which is the fourth-longest in NFL history, and an NFL playoff-record 58-yarder in the 1990 playoffs. In '90, he hit 14 straight field goal attempts before missing his first, a 53-yarder into a 27-mph wind. He has never hit on less than 73 percent of his field goal tries in a season. Look for another big year — easily 100 points — out of Stoyanovich in 1993.

STEVE CHRISTIE / Bills

Year	XP	XPA	FG	FGA	Points
1990	27	27	23	27	96
1991	22	22	15	20	67
1992	43	44	24	30	115

Distance	1-19	20-29	30-39	40-49	50+
1992	2/2	9/9	3/6	7/8	3/5

Comments: Playing for the high-scoring Bills, Christie is always going to be one of the top kickers in fantasy football. Last year, his first in Buffalo after two in Tampa Bay, Christie continued his consistent performances, hitting 80 percent of his field goal attempts. For his career, he has kicked 81 percent, which would place him in the top three in NFL history if he had the required 100 successful kicks. He is 19 of 24 from 40 yards or more over his career. His 115 points set a personal high and ranked second in the AFC and fourth most in team history. His 43 extra points was the highest in the conference. Christie kicked field goals in 14 of 16 games last year, including four in one game against Miami. He has missed only one of 93 career extra point attempts. His 24 field goals were the third most by a Buffalo kicker. Christie left Tampa Bay and had no trouble adapting to the cold, blustery conditions at Rich Stadium because he's a native of nearby Canada. In two seasons with the Buccaneers, he connected on 38 of 47 field-goal attempts (81 percent). Christie has a very strong leg, and he regularly boots his kickoffs into the end zone, which assures his status in Buffalo.

MORTEN ANDERSEN / SAINTS

YEAR	XP	XPA	FG	FGA	POINTS
1988	32	33	26	36	110
1989	44	45	20	29	104
1990	29	29	21	27	92
1991	38	38	25	32	113
1992	33	34	29	34	120

Distance	1-19	20-29	30-39	40-49	50+
1992	0/0	10/10	8/10	8/11	3/3

Comments: For the seventh time in the last eight seasons, Anderson reached the century mark in points, falling short only in 1990. He finished tied for first in the NFC and second in the NFL in scoring with 120 points (one point shy of his career high). His 29 field goals were second in the conference, and his 85.3 percent accuracy mark was best in the NFC and second in the league. There probably isn't much dispute that Andersen is the best kicker in the NFL. However, playing for the ball-control Saints keeps him from scoring an enormous number of points. He has a streak of 20 consecutive field goals intact going into 1993, tying his previous best. Early last season he was bothered by tendonitis in his kicking knee (he missed four field goals in the first five games). He had hit 120 consecutive extra points until a late 1992 miss. Andersen holds the NFL record with 21 field goals of 50 yards or longer (breaking Nick Lowery's mark last year), and his 60-yarder in 1991 is tied for the second-longest in NFL history. Anderson ranks third in career field goal accuracy, trailing only Pete Stoyanovich and Nick Lowery. He has kicked 246 of 315 field goals (78.1 percent). Andersen kicked at least one field goal in 15 games in 1992, and he has scored in 142 consecutive games. Andersen kicks indoors, which gives him an edge most of the season over a lot of other kickers, especially since he has the strongest leg in the league.

NICK LOWERY / CHIEFS

YEAR	XP	XPA	FG	FGA	POINTS
1988	23	23	27	32	104
1989	34	35	24	33	106
1990	37	38	34	37	139
1991	35	35	25	30	110
1992	39	39	22	24	105

Distance	1-19	20-29	30-39	40-49	50+
1992	0/0	9/10	9/9	3/4	1/1

Comments: Lowery led the NFL again in field goal percentage in 1992, hitting 22 of 24 attempts for 91.7 percent. All-time, he is 306 of 382 for 80.1 percent, the second-best mark ever (behind Pete Stoyanovich, who hit his 100th field goal in the season finale to quality for the record). He's also the second-most accurate extra point kicker behind Tommy Davis with 449 of 453 for 99.1 percent. He extended his NFL record for 100-point seasons to 10, despite missing Game 8 with a groin injury. And he moved into third place on the all-time field goal list with 306, trailing only Jan Stenerud and George Blanda. He's also the league's seventh-leading career scorer with 1,367 points. The 37-year-old Lowery hasn't slowed with age. He easily leads all NFL kickers in field goal percentage the last three years with an 89 percent success rate. He has 19 career field goals from 50 yards or more, a record that was broken in 1992 by Morten Andersen. In both 1990 and '91, he has had streaks of 21 consecutive field goals made (the NFL record is 24). In 1990, Lowery scored 139 points and hit 34 of 37 field goal attempts for the fourth-best single-season accuracy mark in NFL history (91.9 percent). Lowery has also scored more than 100 points nine of the last 10 full seasons (not including the strike-shortened 1982 season). So, considering all of these statistics and records, even though Lowery might not lead the NFL in scoring year after year, he is the league's most consistent kicker and maybe best ever. For fantasy football, he will always be one of the best picks.

CAN'T MISS

LIN ELLIOTT / COWBOYS

YEAR	XP	XPA	FG	FGA	POINTS
1992	47	48	24	35	119

Distance	1-19	20-29	30-39	40-49	50+
1992	0/0	6/7	10/14	5/10	3/4

Comments: Elliott was handed the Cowboys' place-kicking job in training camp and nearly lost it by midseason because he had converted only 8 of his first 16 field goal attempts. Then he got hot, hitting a team-record 13 straight and 18 of 21, including two 53-yarders. Altogether he hit 24 of 35 three-point tries for 68.6 percent, 10th in the conference. He finished as the NFC's third-leading kick scorer with 119 points, a Cowboys record for rookies. He proved to be very good from 50 yards and out, hitting 3 of 4 attempts. As long as he doesn't have a prolonged slump, Elliott promises to be one of the highest-scoring kickers in the league because of the team he plays on. He just needs to improve his accuracy on the shorter kicks.

MIKE COFER / 49ERS

Year	XP	XPA	FG	FGA	Points
1988	40	41	27	38	121
1989	49	51	29	36	136
1990	39	39	24	36	111
1991	49	50	14	28	91
1992	53	54	18	27	107

Distance	1-19	20-29	30-39	40-49	50+
1992	0/0	7/8	5/8	6/10	0/1

Comments: It's hard to believe that the 49ers place their fortunes on Cofer year after year, because he is one of the worst kickers in the NFL. However, as long as he *is* their kicker, he is always going to be a very good one for fantasy football, because he scores a lot of points. His 107 points led the team in scoring for the fifth straight year. He was successful on 67 percent of his field goal attempts, which was considerably better than the year before but still one of the lowest percentages for a pro kicker. In 1991, he missed half of his 28 field goals — the worst mark in the NFL — and he scored only 91 points. In Cofer's defense, he did have a new holder and snapper that season, and those problems seemed to have been solved. No matter what, he still doesn't have a long leg. He attempted the most field goals in the NFL in 1988, scored the most points in '89 and had the longest field goal (56 yards) during the regular season in '90. In the last three years, he is only 19-of-41 from 40 yards and beyond.

AL DEL GRECO / OILERS

Year	XP	XPA	FG	FGA	Points
1988	42	44	12	21	78
1989	28	29	18	26	82
1990	31	31	17	27	82
1991	16	16	10	13	46
1992	41	41	21	27	104

Distance	1-19	20-29	30-39	40-49	50+
1992	3/3	8/9	5/6	4/8	1/1

Comments: Del Greco scored a career-best 105 points last season and seems to have solidified his position as the Oilers' kicker after a shaky career with Green Bay and Phoenix. He scored in all 16 games in 1992, kicking field goals in 13 of them, with two three-FG games. He ranked fifth in the AFC and eighth in the NFL in scoring, becoming only the fourth Oiler to eclipse 100 points. Del Greco's 77.8 percent field goal percentage tied for 10th in the league and was much better than his 66 percent mark heading into '92. He has made 115 consecutive extra points, last missing in 1989. He enters 1993 ranked ninth among active scorers with 674 points. Del Greco was signed by the Oilers before Game 10 in 1991 to replace an ineffective Ian Howfield. In his first game with Houston, Del Greco kicked four field goals in five attempts to give the team a 26-23 overtime victory over Dallas. He has mediocre leg strength and is usually not very consistent. However, anybody who kicks for the high-scoring Oilers is going to score a lot of points. That's what makes Del Greco a high pick among kickers in fantasy football.

GARY ANDERSON / STEELERS

Year	XP	XPA	FG	FGA	Points
1988	34	35	28	36	118
1989	28	28	21	30	91
1990	32	32	20	25	92
1991	31	31	23	33	100
1992	29	31	28	36	113

Distance	1-19	20-29	30-39	40-49	50+
1992	0/0	12/13	12/15	4/6	0/2

Comments: Anderson went from 19th to 15th on the NFL's all-time scoring list last season when he posted the sixth 100-point season of his career. He is one of the most accurate kickers in NFL history (257-of-336 all-time, for a 76.5 percentage), and he's considered one of the best because he kicks outdoors in Pittsburgh. In 1992, Anderson scored in every game and kicked at least one field goal in 14 of them. He had four games with three field goals. He used to have a streak of 57 consecutive field goals made from 35 yards or less, but he has missed a few from that range in the last two seasons. And, although he has seven career field goals of 50 yards or longer, he doesn't have a long leg anymore and the Steelers don't let him try too many from that distance (he was 0-2 from 50 yards out last season). Also, he had missed only two extra points in the first 10 years of his career, but he missed two last September alone. In 1990, he became only the second kicker to hit 200 field goals in less than 10 seasons (Jan Stenerud was the other). Anderson might be starting to show some age, but as long as the Steelers continue to win, he will be one of the highest-scorers. He's always a good bet for a backup fantasy kicker, but don't draft him as your No. 1 guy.

DAVID TREADWELL / BRONCOS

Year	XP	XPA	FG	FGA	Points
1989	39	40	27	33	120
1990	34	36	25	34	109
1991	31	32	27	36	112
1992	28	28	20	24	88

Distance	1-19	20-29	30-39	40-49	50+
1992	1/1	9/10	6/8	4/5	0/0

Comments: Treadwell scored more than 100 points in each of his first three seasons in the league before slipping to 88 last season, ranking only eighth in the AFC. His 20 of 24 year in field goal accuracy gave him the highest percentage of his career (83.3), and his career figures of 99 for 127 give him the highest percentage in team history and one of the best figures all-time (he needs one more field goal to qualify). Last year, he missed three kicks inside 40 yards. He kicked field goals in 11 games, going 4 for 4 against Cleveland. In 1991, his 27 field goals tied the team record, and he kicked at least one in every game except one. However, he missed three field goals in the AFC championship game, when Denver lost to Buffalo by three points. Treadwell is regarded as one of the most consistent kickers in the league. He doesn't have a strong leg — kicking in Denver's high altitude helps him on long ones by about five yards — and he isn't given the opportunity to kick the 50-yarders. He'll be challenged for Jason Elam, the team's third-round draft pick this year, and could lose his job.

SOLID PICKS

NORM JOHNSON / FALCONS

Year	XP	XPA	FG	FGA	Points
1988	39	39	22	28	105
1989	27	27	15	25	72
1990	33	34	23	32	102
1991	38	39	19	23	95
1992	39	39	18	22	93

Distance	1-19	20-29	30-39	40-49	50+
1992	0/0	6/6	4/5	4/7	4/4

Comments: Johnson is rewriting the Falcons' record book with stellar back-to-back seasons after spending most of his career with the Seahawks. In 1991, after joining Atlanta in Game 3, he hit 82.6 percent of his field goal attempts (19 of 23), and last year he missed that mark by .08 (81.8 percent on 18 of 22). Both marks broke Mick Luckhurst's team record. He ranked fourth in the NFL in field goal accuracy last year, behind only Nick Lowery, Morten Andersen and David Treadwell. Better yet, Johnson kicked four field goals of 50-plus yards (on four attempts), which is tied for fourth all-time in the NFL record book, and he's moving up on the all-time list in that category, too. He kicked field goals in 12 games in '92. In '91, Johnson had a personal-best streak of 15 consecutive field goals. All that is not bad for a player cut by Seattle because he missed too many big kicks. Seattle's all-time scoring leader, Johnson can still boom his kickoffs, which won't score points in fantasy football but helps keep him on the Falcons.

CHRIS JACKE / PACKERS

Year	XP	XPA	FG	FGA	Points
1989	42	42	22	28	108
1990	28	29	23	30	97
1991	31	31	18	24	85
1992	30	30	22	29	96

Distance	1-19	20-29	30-39	40-49	50+
1992	0/0	5/7	9/10	6/9	2/3

Comments: Jacke continues to be one of the more consistent kickers in the NFL, averaging 97 points the last four years, which is very good on a team that hasn't contended very often. Now the Packers' seventh all-time leading scorer after leading them in scoring four years, he has kicked 86 consecutive extra points, the longest streak in the NFC. He has also converted on 77 percent of his field goal tries, an excellent mark. The All-Rookie placekicker in 1989, Jacke kicked field goals in 13 games last year, including a season-best four against the Buccaneers. His best game came in 1990 when he kicked five field goals against the Raiders. In his rookie season, Jacke had chances to win five games in the final minutes and five times he came through (which is one reason the Packers won 10 games in 1989). There are a lot of good kickers in the NFL, but Jacke is already one of the best. As long as the Packers keep winning, he's only going to get better.

ROGER RUZEK / EAGLES

Year	XP	XPA	FG	FGA	Points
1988	27	27	12	22	63
1989	28	29	13	22	67
1990	45	45	21	29	108
1991	27	29	28	33	111
1992	40	44	16	25	88

Distance	1-19	20-29	30-39	40-49	50+
1992	2/2	3/3	4/6	6/13	1/1

Comments: After scoring a career-high 111 points in 1991, Ruzek hit on only 64 percent of his field goals (16 of 25) in '92 and slipped to 88 points. He had a streak of 11 straight quarters without an attempt at a field goal and he had more than one attempt in just six games, which contributed to his low totals. Ruzek hit his first seven field goals in 1992 but only five of his last 10. He also had three field goals blocked. Although he missed four extra points, they were all due to bad snaps or bad holds. As long as he holds on to his job, Ruzek should be one of the highest-scoring players in the league because of the team's fine offense. In 1991, he ranked fourth in the NFC and seventh in the NFL. He hit 28 of 33 field goals, the third-best accuracy mark in the NFL that year. Ruzek has never been very accurate on long kicks, but he does lend stability to what had been a trouble spot in Philadelphia for a few years. Still, don't expect him to hit 85 percent of his field goal attempts again like he did two years ago.

FUAD REVEIZ / Vikings

Year	XP	XPA	FG	FGA	Points
1988	31	32	8	12	55
1989	Injured				
1990	26	27	13	19	65
1991	34	35	17	24	85
1992	45	45	19	25	102

Distance	1-19	20-29	30-39	40-49	50+
1992	0/0	4/6	7/7	5/8	3/4

Comments: Reveiz had an excellent season last year for the vastly improved Vikings, and there's no reason he can't do it again in 1993. He scored his most points since he was a rookie in 1985 in Miami, and his 76 percent field goal accuracy ranked fifth in the conference. Reveiz missed the 1989 season with a groin injury. In '90, he lost his job in San Diego after hitting only two of seven field goals. He was signed by the Vikings when Donald Igwebuike was indicted on a heroin-smuggling charge midway through the 1990 season. He played in nine games that year and kicked 11 field goals in 12 attempts. He used to be considered a streak kicker who would either be consistent for an entire season and score a lot of points or just get cut early.

BEST OF THE REST

JASON HANSON / Lions

Year	XP	XPA	FG	FGA	Points
1992	30	30	21	26	93

Distance	1-19	20-29	30-39	40-49	50+
1992	0/0	5/5	10/10	4/6	2/5

Comments: Hanson was named *Pro Football Weekly*'s Offensive Rookie of the Year in 1992 after a fine rookie season. His 21 field goals were the sixth most in a season by a Detroit kicker. He started off a bit slow, hitting only 3 of his first 7 field-goal attempts. But he connected on 18 of his last 19, including a stretch of 12 straight. He was 15 of 15 inside the 45-yard line — the only kicker in the league not to miss from that distance (his misses averaged 51.4 yards). His 80.8 percentage was third in the NFC. Hanson was drafted higher (second round) than any placekicker since Chip Lohmiller in 1988. He quickly proved the team correctly scouted him. If the Detroit offense can improve, Hanson could score 100 points a season. Until then, he would be a good No. 2 kicker on a fantasy team.

KEVIN BUTLER / Bears

Year	XP	XPA	FG	FGA	Points
1988	37	38	15	19	82
1989	43	45	15	19	88
1990	36	37	26	37	114
1991	32	34	19	29	89
1992	34	34	19	26	91

Distance	1-19	20-29	30-39	40-49	50+
1992	1/1	8/8	9/10	0/4	1/3

Comments: Butler became the Bears' all-time leading scorer in 1992, passing Walter Payton. He has scored 813 points in eight seasons, a fine average of 102 points a year. But he has cracked the 100-point barrier only once in the last six years. Once one of the most consistent kickers in the NFL, his 73.1 field goal percentage last season ranked only ninth in the NFC, although it was better than what he had the two previous seasons. In 1988 and '89 he set a league record with 24 consecutive field goals. He has scored in 48 consecutive games, and has nine career 50-yard field goals, a club record. Last year he started off fine, with 13 field goals in the first half of the season. But the Bears' offense slipped and Butler had only 10 attempts the rest of the season. Butler is no longer the clutch kicker he was a few years ago, but he is a good backup kicker in fantasy football.

MATT BAHR / Giants

Year	XP	XPA	FG	FGA	Points
1988	32	33	24	29	104
1989	40	40	16	24	88
1990	29	30	17	23	80
1991	24	25	22	29	90
1992	29	29	16	21	77

Distance	1-19	20-29	30-39	40-49	50+
1992	2/2	1/1	10/11	3/5	0/2

Comments: Bahr played the first 12 games last season, then missed the rest of the year with a knee injury. He was replaced by Ken Willis, with whom he will compete in training camp for the job (as well as rookie Todd Peterson). Bahr hit on 16 of 21 field goal attempts last year, a 76.2 percentage that ranked fourth in the NFC. His 77 points were leading the Giants at the time he was injured and had him on pace to score over 100 points. In 1991, Bahr missed three games with a leg injury, but he still scored 90 points to rank eighth among kickers in the NFC. He also ranked fifth in accuracy with a 75.8 percentage. At 37, Bahr is still amazingly consistent, and he has made 77 percent of his field goals over the last nine seasons (178 of 231), which would rank him among the best kickers all-time if he hadn't started off his career so slowly. He's not as accurate outside 40 yards, but he did kick a 42-yard game-winning field goal in the NFC championship game to send the Giants to the Super Bowl two years ago.

JIM BREECH / BENGALS

YEAR	XP	XPA	FG	FGA	POINTS
1988	56	59	11	16	89
1989	37	38	12	14	73
1990	41	44	17	21	92
1991	27	27	23	29	96
1992	31	31	19	27	88

Distance	1-19	20-29	30-39	40-49	50+
1992	0/0	8/8	7/7	4/11	0/1

Comments: Breech consistently scores about 90 points a season, although, at 37, he doesn't have a great leg and won't be around very much longer. Last season he was perfect (15 of 15) inside the 40-yard line but only 4 of 12 beyond it. His 88 points ranked eighth in the AFC in scoring. In 1991, Breech had his best season in four years, with 23 field goals in 29 attempts (a fine 79 percent), and he was five for six in the 40s. From 1988 to '90, Breech slipped considerably; his range did, too. The Bengals too often are forced to punt from field positions where many other teams will try long field goals. Breech had scored in an NFL-record 186 straight games until the Bengals were shut out by Pittsburgh in Game 6 last season.

1992 SURPRISE

JOHN CARNEY / CHARGERS

YEAR	XP	XPA	FG	FGA	POINTS
1988	6	6	2	5	12
1989	None				
1990	27	28	19	21	84
1991	31	31	19	29	88
1992	35	35	26	32	113

Distance	1-19	20-29	30-39	40-49	50+
1992	0/0	13/14	5/7	7/8	1/3

Comments: Under pressure to display more consistency, Carney seems to have found a home in San Diego after an outstanding performance in 1992. He set four team records — five field goals in one game, 26 for the season, 16 straight at one point and 113 points scored. After a slow start (6 of 10) he hit 20 of his last 22 field goal attempts. His 81.3 percentage ranked third in the AFC and fifth in the NFL, and he kicked five in Game 15 against the Raiders. In 1991, Carney set a team record with a 54-yard field goal, and he also had a 53-yarder. In 1990, he set a club record for accuracy by hitting 19 of his 21 field goal attempts (90.5 percent). That year he was cut in training camp before being brought back for the last 12 games. If you think the Chargers are going to have another good season in '93, Carney might be a very high pick in fantasy football. But he has to prove his consistency for a few more years before he can be considered among the better kickers in the

league. He didn't show a strong leg before the last two years.

SLIPPED IN 1992

JEFF JAEGER / RAIDERS

YEAR	XP	XPA	FG	FGA	POINTS
1988	Injured				
1989	34	34	23	34	103
1990	40	42	15	20	85
1991	29	30	29	34	116
1992	28	29	15	26	73

Distance	1-19	20-29	30-39	40-49	50+
1992	0/0	3/5	4/6	5/9	3/6

Comments: Jaeger had a miserable season in 1992. In his first three games, he missed as many field goals (five) as he did in all of 1991. Things didn't get much better the rest of the season, as he ranked third from the bottom in field goal accuracy for the entire league. In 1991, he was the best kicker in the NFL. He kicked a team-record 29 field goals in 34 attempts for an 85.3 percent accuracy that ranked second in the league. He almost single-handedly kept the Raiders in the playoff race all season, bailing them out on many occasions when they couldn't score a touchdown. The 1991 season was a direct contrast to '90, when he didn't get a lot of opportunities at field goals and thus didn't score as many points as you would expect of a kicker for a division champion. Jaeger is usually reliable inside the 40, hitting 52 of 63 the last three years. He had never kicked a field goal longer than 50 yards until 1991, and he has now done it five times. Jaeger needs to bounce back in '93.

GREG DAVIS / CARDINALS

YEAR	XP	XPA	FG	FGA	POINTS
1988	25	27	19	30	82
1989	25	28	23	34	94
1990	40	40	22	33	106
1991	19	19	21	30	82
1992	28	28	13	26	67

Distance	1-19	20-29	30-39	40-49	50+
1992	0/0	6/10	3/4	4/9	0/3

Comments: Davis suffered through a miserable year for a placekicker in 1992, missing half of his 26 field goal attempts and ranking last in the league in accuracy. His season was epitomized in the final game when he and Tampa Bay's Eddie Murray missed six consecutive field goals (three each) on a bad field in a 7-3 game. His 67 points led the team in scoring but was the lowest total for a full season in his career. He missed his first field goal from inside 40 yards as a Cardinal after 14 successes. He was also only 4 of 12 outside the 40-yard line. He suffered a pulled hamstring in Game 5 and, when punter Rich Camarillo missed an extra point, he returned to the field (after showering) to kick three conversions. For the season, Davis didn't have any field goals in six games, and he kicked more than one on only three occasions. He has been considered one of the better kickers in the NFL, and he should have a chance to score more points this year because the Cardinals improved their offense drastically during the offseason. In 1991, Davis was one of only six kickers who didn't miss a field goal attempt from 40 yards or less (he was 13 for 13), and he also kicked three from 50 yards or longer. Davis scored 106 points for Atlanta in 1990, but he had trouble on the long kicks, hitting only 8-of-18 outside the 40. Over his career, Davis has kicked only 64 percent of his field goals (101 of 157).

JOHN KASAY / Seahawks

Year	XP	XPA	FG	FGA	Points
1991	27	28	25	31	102
1992	14	14	14	22	56

Distance	1-19	20-29	30-39	40-49	50+
1992	0/0	4/5	8/11	2/6	0/0

Comments: Kasay scored the second-fewest points of any kicker who played in all 16 games last year and barely half of the 102 points he had in 1991. The Seattle offense was the most inept in the NFL, but Kasay also didn't play very well, especially late in the season. He connected on only 14 of his 22 field goal attempts, a 63.6 percentage that was fifth worst in the league. He was also only 2 of 6 from beyond the 40-yard line. An unheralded fourth-round draft pick from Georgia, he beat out Norm Johnson during training camp in 1991 and went on to set a team record with 25 field goals in 31 attempts. His 80.6 percent success ratio was third best in team history. He also tied the team record of 13 consecutive field goals, and he had at least one in 14 games. His total of 102 points was the most by a rookie and ranked seventh in the AFC. That year, Kasay was an excellent long-range kicker. This season should give an indication which season was a fluke (unless he's somewhere in between).

ROOKIES

See Chapter 13, The Rookie Report.

OTHERS

TONY ZENDEJAS / Rams

Year	XP	XPA	FG	FGA	Points
1988	48	50	22	34	114
1989	40	40	25	37	115
1990	20	21	7	12	41
1991	25	26	17	17	76
1992	38	38	15	20	83

Distance	1-19	20-29	30-39	40-49	50+
1992	2/2	3/4	7/9	3/5	0/0

Comments: Zendejas followed up an excellent 1991 season with a solid one last year. After being successful on all 17 of his field goal attempts in '91, he missed three tries in the second game of the season (his first attempts) but missed only two more the rest of the year. His 83 points led the team but ranked 11th in the NFC among full-time kickers. In 1991, he wasn't the best kicker in the NFL, but he was the only one who didn't miss a field goal, setting an NFL record for accuracy (he's the only kicker in NFL history not to miss a minimum of 15 field goal attempts needed to qualify in a season). He had a streak of 23 consecutive field goals dating back to his last six attempts in 1990 that was ended in '92. Until 1991, he was not considered to be among the league's most accurate kickers, hitting only 65 percent of his field goal attempts from 1988 to '90. But he seems to be showing some consistency lately and could score 100 points this year if the Rams' offense continues to improve.

MATT STOVER / Browns

Year	XP	XPA	FG	FGA	Points
1990	Injured				
1991	33	34	16	22	81
1992	29	30	21	29	92

Distance	1-19	20-29	30-39	40-49	50+
1992	1/1	11/11	6/8	2/6	1/3

Comments: Stover had a pretty good season in 1992 and should solidly hold the Browns' placekicking job. He hit on 72.4 percent of his 29 field goals to rank ninth in the AFC. However, only three of his kicks were over 40 yards (from where he was just 3 of 9). Stover was shaky going into 1992 after missing clutch field-goal attempts in two 1991 games (a 19-yarder with four seconds left and a 34-yard, last-second attempt that was blocked). He had the longest field goal of the year in the AFC (55 yards) and the second longest in the league. That year he had streaks of 10 and five straight field goals, meaning he missed six of the other seven tries. But he's fine on kickoffs, which could keep him kicking in Cleveland for a while.

CARY BLANCHARD / Jets

Year	XP	XPA	FG	FGA	Points
1992	17	17	16	22	65

Distance	1-19	20-29	30-39	40-49	50+
1992	2/2	2/3	5/7	7/9	0/1

Comments: Blanchard was the backup to Morten Andersen in New Orleans (who had tendonitis) for the first two weeks of the 1992 season, although he did not play. He was signed by the Jets before Game 5, and he kicked three field goals in his first game. He led the Jets in scoring, and had a respectable 73 percent field goal accuracy mark. By the end of the season, he looked like the long-term answer as the placekicker to replace Pat Leahy. Blanchard's 65 points in 12 games translates to 87 over a full season, so he could score close to 100 points this year.

DEAN BIASUCCI / Colts

Year	XP	XPA	FG	FGA	Points
1988	39	40	25	32	114
1989	31	32	21	27	94
1990	32	33	17	24	83
1991	14	14	15	26	59
1992	24	24	16	29	72

Distance	1-19	20-29	30-39	40-49	50+
1992	0/0	3/3	6/11	6/12	1/3

Comments: Biasucci was one of the most accurate kickers from 1987 to '89, hitting on 70 of 86 field goal attempts (81 percent). But he has slipped the last three years because the Colts' offense hasn't been very strong. In 1991, he scored only 59 points because of the team's anemic offense, but an early-season slump didn't help, either. Last year he hit only 55 percent of his field goals, one of the lowest marks in the league. He started off the season making only eight of 19 before hitting eight of 10 at the end. He was only six of 11 from 30 to 39 yards, a distance where a kicker shouldn't miss more than one or two attempts. Now the Colts' all-time field goal leader with 134, Biasucci has a 69 percent career percentage. He has 15 field goals from the 50-plus range (on 37 attempts), which is the fifth most in league history behind Nick Lowery, Morten Andersen, Jan Stenerud and Eddie Murray. He is the NFL's record holder with six 50-yarders in 1988. He has been good on only 21 of his last 51 tries from 40 yards or longer the last four seasons. He set a league record with six 50-plus field goals in '88. With 54 points in 1992, he'll move into second place on the Colts' scoring list. One of these days he is going to be pushed for his job, and he'll probably lose it.

CHARLIE BAUMANN / Patriots

Year	XP	XPA	FG	FGA	Points
1991	15	16	9	12	42
1992	22	24	11	17	55

Distance	1-19	20-29	30-39	40-49	50+
1992	2/2	4/4	3/7	2/4	0/0

Comments: Baumann was handed the Patriots' kicking job in the offseason a year ago and held on to it last year with a so-so performance. He scored the fewest points of any kicker in the league who played all 16 games. The Patriots' 17 field goal attempts tied for the third-lowest total in team history, which obviously didn't give Baumann too many chances to score. He proved to be dependable on short kicks, but he might not have the leg strength for the long ones (although he was 4 for 4 from 40-49 yards in 1991). In 1991, Baumann kicked for Miami the first two games of the season, then was cut when Pete Stoyanovich reported. He signed with New England when Jason Staurovsky was injured in the ninth game. Don't be surprised if Bill Parcells keeps an eye out for somebody to challenge Baumann for the job.

EDDIE MURRAY / Buccaneers

Year	XP	XPA	FG	FGA	Points
1988	22	23	20	21	82
1989	36	36	20	21	96
1990	34	34	13	19	73
1991	40	40	19	28	97
1992	13	13	5	9	28

Distance	1-19	20-29	30-39	40-49	50+
1992	0/0	0/0	2/4	2/4	1/1

Comments: After getting cut by the Lions, Murray played one game for the Chiefs last season when Nick Lowery was injured, hitting a 52-yard field goal. Next, he ended up in Tampa Bay, where he played in Games 10-16, replacing Ken Willis, who was cut after missing too many field goals. Murray hit only 4 of 8 field goals for the Buccaneers, and was not expected to be invited back for this year's training camp. He was the best field goal kicker in the NFL in 1988 and '89, hitting on 20 of 21 attempts in both seasons. But, in the two years since then, he has missed one-third of his field goals. He stands in 14th place on the NFL's all-time scoring list.

KEN WILLIS / Giants

Year	XP	XPA	FG	FGA	Points
1990	26	26	18	25	80
1991	37	37	27	39	118
1992	27	27	10	16	57

Distance	1-19	20-29	30-39	40-49	50+
1992	0/0	4/4	1/4	5/8	0/0

Comments: Willis started last season with the Buccaneers and ended it with the Giants. He scored 44 points in Tampa Bay and 13 in New York. He was cut by the Bucs after nine games because he had hit only 8 of 14 field goal attempts. He was 2 for 2 in New York. Willis will compete with Matt Bahr for the Giants' job this season. He had his best two years in Dallas in 1990 and '91. In '91, he finished second in the NFC and third in the NFL in scoring with 118 points. He tied the Dallas mark for most field goals and broke the record for attempts. He also had four 50-yard field goals, the most in the league and tied for the third most in NFL history. Willis has never missed an extra point. But he is in jeopardy of being without a job again if he loses out to Bahr. He would be wearing a Super Bowl ring now if he hadn't left for bigger money in Tampa Bay.

Other Kickers on Rosters

Brad Daluiso, Broncos
Phillip Doyle, Buccaneers
Ian Howfield, Buccaneers
Carlos Huerta, Oilers

Chapter 9
Defenses

Just as defense can win games in football, it can also win games in fantasy football. That's why many fantasy leagues like to incorporate some form of defense into their game.

There are several commonly used methods for using defensive players.

The most common is to add an eighth "player" to each team in the form of a team defense (rather than individual defensive players). If you draft individual players, it adds a lot of bookkeeping and score-tabulating chores for the commissioner. If an entire defense is drafted, any score by any member of that defense counts. Points are awarded every time a player on a team's defense scores a touchdown on a fumble return or an interception or when a player scores a safety (even a team safety, such as when an opposing punter steps out of the end zone). Most leagues also include touchdowns scored on blocked punts and field goals, as they are basically defensive scores, too. Leagues can also draft special teams and award points for scores on punts and kickoff returns.

Some leagues award points for other defensive categories, such as sacks and interceptions. A common scoring method is one point for a sack or two points for an interception (that is not returned for a score).

But fantasy leagues can also draft individual players. For example, every team can draft one defensive lineman, one linebacker and one defensive back (or more of each). The ways you can score points depend on your league and how detailed you want to get. But remember, as your league's scoring method gets more complicated, so does the work involved in determining the scores.

Believe it or not, there are some leagues that even count tackles. That's really getting complicated, perhaps overly complicated. The biggest problem with counting tackles is that they are unofficial statistics, and the quality of team statisticians ranges from conservative to liberal — for example, some teams' leading tacklers have 200 tackles, while other teams' top tacklers have only 100 or so. Papers such as *USA Today* include tackles and assists in their game summaries, but team coaches change those figures drastically every Monday when they view game film.

So, if you want to include defense the easiest way, allow every team to draft a team defense and just count defensive scores — fumbles and interceptions returned for touchdowns, blocked kicks returned for touchdowns and safeties. This is the category that is most often pure luck. While you are looking to your quarterbacks, running backs and wide receivers for big scores, a defensive score is always a nice — and unexpected — bonus.

The average defensive team scored just about 19 points last season, which is almost the equivalent of three touchdowns and a safety. That's not very many, but you will think six points is a lot when it happens to your team.

It's almost impossible to predict which defenses will score the most points in any given season. Teams that have perennially good defenses — such as the Giants, 49ers, Raiders and Bears — should still have strong defenses in 1993, although they might not score very many defensive points, which is what happened in 1991 and '92.

Since defensive scores are most often a result of luck, you can never figure which teams will improve. For example, the Miami Dolphins' defense scored only one safety and no touchdowns from 1987 to '89, but in 1990, it scored 32 points on defense. Two years ago, the Dolphins were back to six points and last year they scored 18. You just never know.

One thing you can count on is that defenses won't score as many points this year as they did in 1992. That was the year of big defensive plays. In 1991, 22 interceptions were returned for touchdowns. In 1992, 47 interceptions were brought back for scores — six each by the Chiefs and Vikings. That was the most since 1984. Thirty-two fumbles were also returned for touchdowns, the most since 1983. The strategy has changed in pro football these days — once you get the ball, go for the end zone. But don't expect Kansas City and Minnesota to match those numbers again. Remember, luck is the biggest factor in scoring by defenses.

In drafting defenses, there are a lot of factors to take into consideration, such as which teams are most likely to make defensive scores (touchdowns on the returns of fumbles, interceptions or blocked kicks and safeties).

If your league drafts individual defensive players, you will want to know which players get the most sacks and interceptions.

Also in this chapter, because an important factor in determining which offensive players you will play each week is the defenses your players will face in real NFL games, some defensive statistics are also included (rushing touchdowns and yards allowed, passing touchdowns and yards allowed, total points allowed, sacks and takeaways).

And, also in this chapter, special-teams scores from 1992 (kickoffs and punts returned for touchdowns) are also detailed.

Draft Tips In Choosing Defenses
■ Don't spend too much time analyzing the teams to decide which defense you want to draft. Defensive scores

are so rare that they really should be considered a bonus, rather than points that you should expect.

■ Don't waste a pick drafting a defense high in your draft; wait until the last round or two. While a defensive score could mean the difference between winning and losing any given week, it's too chancy, and you are better off drafting players who have a better chance of getting a score.

■ Draft a team with a strong defense. Those who force the most turnovers have the best chance of converting them into scores.

■ Look for opportunistic teams that convert turnovers into touchdowns, such as Kansas City, Minnesota, Dallas, Philadelphia and Houston. Three teams that would be good picks to score more defensive points in 1993 than they did in '92 are Atlanta, Chicago and Seattle.

1992 DEFENSIVE SCORES

Team	Fumble /TD	Int /TD	Blk Kick /TD	Saf	Pts
1. Kansas City	2	6	1	0	54
2. Minnesota	2	6	0	1	50
3. New Orleans	3	3	0	0	36
4. New England	2	3	0	0	30
5. Dallas	1	1	2	1	26
Houston	3	1	0	1	26
Philadelphia	1	2	1	1	26
8. Cleveland	3	1	0	0	24
Tampa Bay	3	1	0	0	24
10. Buffalo	1	2	0	1	20
N.Y. Jets	0	3	0	1	20
Phoenix	0	3	0	1	20
13. Cincinnati	2	1	0	0	18
Detroit	1	0	2	0	18
Miami	0	3	0	0	18
Washington	1	2	0	0	18
17. L.A. Raiders	0	1	1	1	14
18. Denver	1	1	0	0	12
Green Bay	1	1	0	0	12
Pittsburgh	1	1	0	0	12
San Diego	0	1	0	3	12
San Francisco	1	1	0	0	12
23. L.A. Rams	0	0	1	1	8
24. Atlanta	1	0	0	0	6
Chicago	1	0	0	0	6
Indianapolis	0	1	0	0	6
N.Y. Giants	0	1	0	0	6
Seattle	1	0	0	0	6

For an in-depth look at each team's defense, see Chapter 11, "Team Evaluations."

TEAM DEFENSES

One of the hardest — but most enjoyable — aspects of fantasy football is trying to decide whom to start each week.

For example, should you start Emmitt Smith against the tough Eagles defense, or do you go with Mark Higgs against the weak Colts run defense? Or do you go with Willie Anderson against the excellent Saints defensive backs or Wendell Davis vs. the woeful Buccaneers?

The defensive charts that follow should help you decide. But, remember, they are from the 1992 season, and the performance of each team's defense can change drastically from year to year (especially in this era of free agency with so many players changing teams).

1992 Rushing Touchdowns Allowed

Team	Rushing TD's Allowed
1. Philadelphia	4
2. Cleveland	5
San Francisco	5
4. Houston	6
Pittsburgh	6
6. Buffalo	8
New Orleans	8
8. Miami	9
9. Denver	10
San Diego	10
11. Dallas	11
Minnesota	11
Washington	11
14. Green Bay	12
Kansas City	12
16. N.Y. Jets	13
Phoenix	13
18. Chicago	14
Detroit	14
Seattle	14
21. Cincinnati	15
New England	15
Tampa Bay	15
24. Indianapolis	16
25. L.A. Raiders	17
N.Y. Giants	17
27. Atlanta	20
28. L.A. Rams	22

1992 Rushing Yards Allowed

Team	Rushing Yards Allowed	Average Per Game
1. Dallas	1244	77.8
2. Buffalo	1395	87.2
San Diego	1395	87.2
4. San Francisco	1418	88.6
5. Philadelphia	1481	92.6
6. Miami	1600	100.0
7. Cleveland	1605	100.3
New Orleans	1605	100.3
9. Houston	1634	102.1
10. Phoenix	1635	102.2

11.	Tampa Bay	1675	104.7
12.	L.A. Raiders	1683	105.2
13.	Washington	1696	106.0
14.	Minnesota	1733	108.3
15.	Kansas City	1787	111.7
16.	Green Bay	1821	113.8
17.	Detroit	1841	115.1
18.	Pittsburgh	1841	115.1
19.	N.Y. Jets	1919	119.9
20.	Seattle	1922	120.1
21.	Chicago	1948	121.8
22.	New England	1951	121.9
23.	Denver	1963	122.7
24.	Cincinnati	2007	125.4
25.	N.Y. Giants	2012	125.8
26.	Indianapolis	2174	135.9
27.	L.A. Rams	2230	139.4
28.	Atlanta	2294	143.4

1992 Passing Touchdowns Allowed

	Team	Passing TD's Allowed
1.	L.A. Raiders	11
	Seattle	11
3.	Minnesota	12
4.	New Orleans	13
5.	Indianapolis	14
6.	Pittsburgh	15
	Washington	15
8.	Dallas	16
	Green Bay	16
	Miami	16
11.	San Diego	17
12.	L.A. Rams	18
13.	Buffalo	19
	Kansas City	19
	N.Y. Jets	19
16.	Chicago	20
	Detroit	20
	Houston	20
	Philadelphia	20
	San Francisco	20
21.	Denver	21
22.	New England	22
	N.Y. Giants	22
24.	Cleveland	23
25.	Atlanta	24
	Cincinnati	24
	Phoenix	24
28.	Tampa Bay	25

1992 Passing Yards Allowed

	Team	Net Passing Yards Allowed	Net Average Per Game
1.	New Orleans	2470	154.4
2.	Kansas City	2537	158.6
3.	Houston	2577	161.1
4.	Seattle	2661	166.3
5.	Dallas	2687	167.9
6.	Washington	2742	171.4
7.	Minnesota	2782	173.9
8.	Pittsburgh	2817	176.1
9.	San Diego	2832	177.0
10.	L.A. Raiders	2833	177.1
11.	Indianapolis	2900	181.3
12.	Philadelphia	2931	183.2
13.	N.Y. Jets	2961	185.1
14.	Miami	2983	186.4
15.	Chicago	3004	187.8
16.	N.Y. Giants	3031	189.4
17.	New England	3097	193.6
18.	Denver	3120	195.0
19.	Cleveland	3152	197.0
20.	Buffalo	3209	200.6
21.	Detroit	3217	201.1
22.	Atlanta	3255	203.4
23.	Green Bay	3277	204.8
24.	L.A. Rams	3293	205.8
25.	Cincinnati	3326	207.9
26.	San Francisco	3369	210.6
27.	Phoenix	3491	218.2
28.	Tampa Bay	3510	219.4

1992 Total Points Allowed

	Team	Total Points Allowed	Points Per Game
1.	New Orleans	202	12.6
2.	Pittsburgh	225	14.1
3.	San Francisco	236	14.8
4.	San Diego	241	15.1
5.	Dallas	243	15.2
6.	Philadelphia	245	15.3
7.	Minnesota	249	15.6
8.	Washington	255	15.9
9.	Houston	258	16.1
10.	Cleveland	275	17.2
11.	L.A. Raiders	281	17.5
	Miami	281	17.5
13.	Kansas City	282	17.6
14.	Buffalo	283	17.7
15.	Green Bay	296	18.5
16.	Indianapolis	302	18.9
17.	Seattle	312	19.5
18.	N.Y. Jets	315	19.7
19.	Denver	329	20.6
20.	Detroit	332	20.8
	Phoenix	332	20.8

22. Chicago	361	22.6
23. New England	363	22.7
Cincinnati	364	22.7
25. Tampa Bay	365	22.8
26. N.Y. Giants	367	22.9
27. L.A. Rams	383	23.9
28. Atlanta	414	25.6

1992 Sacks

Team	Sacks
1. New Orleans	57
2. Philadelphia	55
3. Minnesota	51
San Diego	51
5. Denver	50
Houston	50
Kansas City	50
8. Cleveland	48
9. L.A. Raiders	46
Seattle	46
11. Cincinnati	45
12. Buffalo	44
Dallas	44
14. Chicago	43
15. San Francisco	41
16. Indianapolis	39
Washington	39
18. Miami	36
N.Y. Jets	36
Pittsburgh	36
Tampa Bay	36
22. Green Bay	34
23. Atlanta	31
L.A. Rams	31
25. Detroit	29
26. Phoenix	27
27. N.Y. Giants	25
28. New England	20

1992 Takeaways

Team	Fumbles	Int.	Total
1. Pittsburgh	21	22	43
2. Minnesota	14	28	42
3. Kansas City	15	24	39
N.Y. Jets	18	21	39
5. New Orleans	20	18	38
6. Philadelphia	13	24	37
7. San Diego	11	25	36
8. Buffalo	12	23	35
Indianapolis	15	20	35
10. Green Bay	19	15	34
Washington	11	23	34
12. Cincinnati	17	16	33
Cleveland	20	13	33

L.A. Rams	15	18	33
Tampa Bay	13	20	33
16. Detroit	11	21	32
Miami	14	18	32
Seattle	12	20	32
19. Dallas	14	17	31
Denver	16	15	31
Houston	11	20	31
22. Chicago	16	14	30
23. New England	15	14	29
San Francisco	12	17	29
25. Phoenix	12	16	28
26. N.Y. Giants	12	14	26
27. Atlanta	12	11	23
28. L.A. Raiders	7	12	19

SPECIAL-TEAMS SCORES

Some leagues like to award points for touchdown returns of kickoffs and punts. Fifteen teams scored touchdowns on kick returns last season (22 total touchdowns in all), so it's a nice bonus if you include them in your scoring. Here are those scores for the 1992 season:

1992 Special-Teams Scores

Team	Punt Ret/TD	Kickoff Ret/TD	Points
1. Atlanta	0	2	12
Dallas	2	0	12
Detroit	1	1	12
Indianapolis	2	0	12
Kansas City	2	0	12
L.A. Rams	2	0	12
Washington	2	0	12
8. Chicago	0	1	6
Cincinnati	1	0	6
Cleveland	1	0	6
Green Bay	1	0	6
N.Y. Giants	0	1	6
Philadelphia	1	0	6
Pittsburgh	1	0	6
San Francisco	1	0	6
16. Buffalo	0	0	0
Denver	0	0	0
Houston	0	0	0
L.A. Raiders	0	0	0
Miami	0	0	0
Minnesota	0	0	0
New England	0	0	0
New Orleans	0	0	0
N.Y. Jets	0	0	0
Phoenix	0	0	0
San Diego	0	0	0
Seattle	0	0	0
Tampa Bay	0	0	0

Chapter 10
Team Evaluations

1992 NFL Standings

AFC East	W	L	T	Pct.	PF	PA
Miami	11	5	0	.688	340	281
Buffalo	11	5	0	.688	381	283
Indianapolis	9	7	0	.563	216	302
N.Y. Jets	4	12	0	.250	220	315
New England	2	14	0	.125	205	363

NFC East	W	L	T	Pct.	PF	PA
Dallas	13	3	0	.813	409	243
Philadelphia	11	5	0	.688	354	245
Washington	9	7	0	.563	300	255
N.Y. Giants	6	10	0	.375	306	367
Phoenix	4	12	0	.250	243	332

AFC Central	W	L	T	Pct.	PF	PA
Pittsburgh	11	5	0	.688	299	225
Houston	10	6	0	.625	352	258
Cleveland	7	9	0	.438	272	275
Cincinnati	5	11	0	.313	274	364

NFC Central	W	L	T	Pct.	PF	PA
Minnesota	11	5	0	.688	374	249
Green Bay	9	7	0	.563	276	296
Tampa Bay	5	11	0	.313	267	365
Chicago	5	11	0	.313	295	361
Detroit	5	11	0	.313	273	332

AFC West	W	L	T	Pct.	PF	PA
San Diego	11	5	0	.688	335	241
Kansas City	10	6	0	.625	348	282
Denver	8	8	0	.500	262	281
L.A. Raiders	7	9	0	.438	249	281
Seattle	2	14	0	.125	140	312

NFC West	W	L	T	Pct.	PF	PA
San Francisco	14	2	0	.875	431	236
New Orleans	12	4	0	.750	330	202
Atlanta	6	10	0	.375	327	414
L.A. Rams	6	10	0	.375	313	383

Playoffs
AFC Wild-Card Playoffs
San Diego 17, Kansas City 0
Buffalo 41, Houston 38 (OT)
NFC Wild-Card Playoffs
Washington 24, Minnesota 7
Philadelphia 36, New Orleans 20
AFC Divisional Playoffs
Buffalo 24, Pittsburgh 3
Miami 31, San Diego 0
NFC Divisional Playoffs
San Francisco 20, Washington 13
Dallas 34, Philadelphia 10
AFC Championship
Buffalo 29, Miami 10
NFC Championship
Dallas 30, San Francisco 20
Super Bowl XXVII
Dallas 52, Buffalo 17

Atlanta Falcons

Season Review — The team that believed it was too legit looked as if it wanted to quit by the end of a season that became what fans had learned to expect from a Jerry Glanville-coached team: respectable but hardly a Super Bowl contender. Deion Sanders played both baseball and football in the fall, sometimes both on the same day, but the Atlanta defense struggled and ranked last in the conference. The gambling style too often resulted in big scores for the opponents. Quarterback Chris Miller was second in the NFC in passing when he was injured in Week Eight and knocked out for the rest of the year. Ex-Viking Wade Wilson looked fantastic in the final three games. The Falcons didn't have a running game to speak of, but receivers Andre Rison (93 catches, 11 TD's) and Michael Haynes (48 and 10) kept the pressure on opponents.

Offseason Update — Quarterback Bobby Hebert was acquired in free agency and backup Wade Wilson was lost (and Chris Miller was expected to go elsewhere). Only two draft picks were skill-position players, and they were late picks.

Significant 1992 Injuries — Quarterback Chris Miller missed the second half of the season with torn knee ligaments. Running back Tony Smith suffered five different injuries that hampered him throughout the season before a knee finally put him on injured reserve. Wide receiver Tony Jones was on I.R. two different times.

Quarterbacks — Bobby Hebert will most likely be the Falcons' starting quarterback on Opening Day, which means he could move into the elite of fantasy football quarterbacks because of the team's explosive passing game. Although Hebert has never thrown more than 20 touchdowns in a season in the NFL, he averaged 27 TD passes a season in three years in the USFL. Yes, he can throw the long ball. Chris Miller was supposed to be traded, and he will be a good pick, too, no matter where he goes. Backing up up Hebert will be Billy Joe Tolliver, who isn't much.

Running Backs — Steve Broussard and Tony Smith are former No. 1 draft picks who haven't done much in the pros and aren't getting too many opportunities to show what they can do. Smith will get the first shot and will probably start most of the season. Broussard, who led the team with 363 yards in 1992, shows flashes but not on a consistent basis. He's also a fumbler and is injury-prone. The Falcons have had only two 100-yard games from backs in the last two seasons, so if you stop them through the air, they don't do much on the ground. The offensive line lost two good guards during the offseason, but some youngsters have moved into the lineup, so the blocking might be improved this year.

Wide Receivers — Andre Rison and Michael Haynes remain one of the most potent receiving duos in the NFL. Last year they accounted for 21 touchdown passes, and that number won't slip by much with Hebert throwing to them. Mike Pritchard, who came on late last season and finished with 77 catches, is the receiver who will benefit the most if either Rison or Haynes slips. Drew Hill decided to come back for another season but is mostly a possession receiver, and Tony Jones is a dangerous backup.

Tight Ends — Harper LeBel and rookie Mitch Lyons are the only tight ends on the roster. LeBel is just a long snapper.

Kicker — Norm Johnson has scored 188 points the last two seasons (missing two games in 1991), which is a pretty good number for a kicker. He's getting old (33), but it doesn't seem as if he has lost much distance as the Seahawks had thought when they released him in '91. He was 4 of 4 from 50-yards-plus last season. He has hit 37 of 45 field-goal attempts (82 percent) in Atlanta.

Defense — The Falcons easily allowed the most points in the league last year, an average of almost 26 a game. But the defense should be vastly improved this year, with the signing of Pierce Holt, Jumpy Geathers and Melvin Jenkins. A blitz-happy group of players, the Falcons usually score a lot of points on defense, though in 1992 they got just one touchdown. Eleven interceptions was also quite a few under their average. The defense was hit for 20 rushing touchdowns and allowed opposing backs almost five yards per carry.

What to Expect in 1993 — The Falcons will probably be out of the playoff hunt in 1993 because the NFC West is a solid division. But the offense will remain explosive, and several players should be considered for fantasy rosters. The catch this year is that Bobby Hebert will be at quarterback, but at least you can count on him to stay healthy (Chris Miller never could last an entire season).

Best Players to Draft — Quarterback Bobby Hebert, wide receivers Andre Rison, Michael Haynes and Mike Pritchard, and kicker Norm Johnson.

1992 GAME-BY-GAME STATISTICS

	NYJ	WAS.	N.O.	CHI.	G.B.	MIA.	S.F.	RAMS	S.F.	PHX.	BUF.	N.E.	N.O.	T.B.	DAL.	RAMS	
QUARTERBACKS																	
Chris Miller	21-29 196 2	11-25 242 1	21-35 204 1	30-48 351 4	16-26 171 3	26-41 254 2	14-27 174 1	13-22 147 1									Att/Cmp Yards TD
Billy Joe Tolliver							5-10 60	6-11 86 1	16-25 178	16-24 209 2	8-23 47	9-18 107 2	6-11 55	3-4 15	4-5 30		Att/Cmp Yards TD
Wade Wilson							4-6 35 1		9-16 88	3-3 31	9-13 89 1	1-1 14	5-10 71 1	19-26 324 5	30-41 342 2	31-47 374 3	Att/Cmp Yards TD
RUNNING BACKS																	
Steve Broussard		5-10 1-11	9-25 1-12	5-21	2-1	2-9		2-17 1-3	4-22	16-87 1-24	4-8 1-3	8-18 1 1-18 1	8-63 2-9	9-39	4-17 2-12	6-26 1-4	Att/Yards TD Rec/Yards TD
Tony Smith	3-40		7-25 1-8	2-(-2)	3-10		8-20	19-58 1	9-36	7-9	2-5	10-81 1	5-13	10-25 1-6	2-9		Att/Yards TD Rec/Yards
Keith Jones	11-41 3-22	4-12	7-20		17-87	12-55 1-12	1-0	1-3	2-20	10-23	7-18 2-14		1-3 1-6	2-3	6-13 1-(-1)		Att/Yards TD Rec/Yards
RECEIVERS																	
Andre Rison		2-22	3-31	10-177 3	6-78 2	7-101 1	8-94	8-99	11-99	7-87 2	6-52	3-26	4-63	5-59 1	6-45 1	7-88 1	Rec/Yards TD
Michael Haynes	4-45 2	1-89 1		2-20	3-29	3-58 1	5-86 2	6-83	5-61	1-12	1-11	1-13 1	5-113 2	5-100	6-88 1		Rec/Yards TD
Mike Pritchard	8-89	3-66	7-85 1	8-52	5-44 1	7-46 1	4-31	2-21	3-27	4-46	3-26	1-16	3-25	3-66 1	9-105	7-82 1	Rec/Yards TD
Drew Hill	3-23		6-45	8-83	1-8	7-57		2-26	3-37	2-22	5-35 1	2-36 1	1-16	3-44	9-84 1	8-107	Rec/Yards TD
Tony Jones	3-17	2-32	3-23	3-41 1	2-21									1-4	2-21		Rec/Yards TD
KICKERS																	
Norm Johnson	2-2	1-1	0-1	1-1	1-1	1-1	1-2	3-3	1-1	2-2	0-1	2-3		1-1	2-2		FG/FGA

1992 SEASON STATISTICS

PLAYERS	PASSING				RUSHING				RECEIVING				KICKING			
	TD 1-9	TD 10-39	TD 40+	Yards 300+	TD 1-9	TD 10-39	TD 40+	Yards 100+	TD 1-9	TD 10-39	TD 40+	Yards 100+	FG 18-39	FG 40-49	FG 50+	PAT
Chris Miller	2	10	3	1												
Billy Joe Tolliver	1	4														
Wade Wilson	4	8	1	3												
Steve Broussard					1				1							
Tony Smith					1	1										
Keith Jones																
Andre Rison									2	8	1	2				
Michael Haynes									1	6	3	2				
Mike Pritchard									1	4		1				
Drew Hill									2	1		1				
Tony Jones										1						
Norm Johnson													10	4	4	39

TEAM EVALUATIONS

Buffalo Bills

Season Review — Three years, three Super Bowls and three super losses. The Bills joined the Broncos and Vikings as kings of the Super Bowl losers, after being demolished by Dallas in Pasadena 52-17. They even failed to win the AFC East crown in 1992, losing out to Miami to a tiebreaker. But it was still a very successful season in Buffalo. The defense, led by league interception leader Henry Jones, improved, and Thurman Thomas led the league in total yards for the fourth straight year, breaking Jim Brown's record. Quarterback Jim Kelly was red-hot for half a season, but he threw a league-high 19 interceptions before getting injured. Backup quarterback Frank Reich will always be remembered for leading the Bills to a victory over Houston in the playoffs after trailing by 32 points in the third quarter.

Offseason Update — The only free-agent acquisition was wide receiver Bill Brooks, who might be a key member in 1993. The draft didn't help much, and even fourth-round pick Russell Copeland, a wide receiver, will have trouble making the team.

Significant 1992 Injuries — Quarterback Jim Kelly missed the first two playoff games with a sprained right knee, and tight end Keith McKeller missed five games with a knee injury and never regained his No. 1 job. There were a lot of other injuries to backup players on offense.

Quarterbacks — Hey, who cares if the Bills can't win a Super Bowl? Jim Kelly remains one of the NFL's best quarterbacks and the coaching staff isn't going to listen to some of the Bills fans who want Frank Reich to take over. Kelly passed for 23 touchdowns last year and ran for another. All he needs is to regain some of the confidence he seems to have lost. Reich is one of the best backups in the league. If Kelly were to get injured, Reich would do a great job as the No. 1 QB.

Running Backs — Thurman Thomas' situation is just like that of Kelly. He's probably the third-best running back in the NFL and certainly the best running-receiving threat in the league. Last year he accumulated over 2,000 total yards and scored 12 touchdowns. Kenneth Davis is definitely the best No. 2 back in the league. Even with Thomas carrying the load in 1992, Davis managed to rush for 613 yards and score six TD's. Fullback Carwell Gardner doesn't play much, but he is one of the top goal-line runners. With more playing time, he could be one of the best short-yardage backs around.

Wide Receivers — Andre Reed had a subpar season for him in 1992. He caught 65 passes but scored only three touchdowns. In the playoffs against Houston, he scored three in one game. He should be back to old form in '93. James Lofton was released in late April, and the Bills lack the speed he possessed. Bill Brooks will move into the starting lineup, and he should put up some excellent numbers. He is a very good possession receiver who is tough over the middle. Don Beebe will most likely remain the No. 3 wideout. He's inconsistent but is always a threat because of his speed. Horace Copeland was acquired in the fourth round of the draft and should stick.

Tight Ends — The Bills weren't pleased with the disappearance of Keith McKeller from the offense last season. Injuries knocked him out for too many games, but he still caught only 14 passes all season. They still like Pete Metzelaars' blocking and knack for making clutch receptions. Last year, he caught 30 passes and scored six touchdowns, but that won't happen again. He lacks speed but is a threat at the goal line.

Kicker — A change in teams from Tampa Bay to Buffalo immediately turned Steve Christie into one of the highest-scoring kickers for fantasy football. Last year he hit 24 of 30 field goals (80 percent), including 10 of 13 beyond the 40-yard line. Look for him to be among the top five scorers again this year.

Defense — If the Bills had an aggressive, turnover-causing defense, they might have won one or two of the last three Super Bowls. It was solid vs. the run last year but very weak against the pass, and this year they have lost linebackers Shane Conlan and Carlton Bailey to free agency. Safety Henry Jones returned two interceptions for touchdowns and two other players added eight points on defense. The team intercepted 23 passes in 1992, and Bruce Smith had 14 sacks, and it didn't allow a 100-yard rusher all season until the Super Bowl.

What to Expect in 1993 — Buffalo will again contend for the AFC East title and might even get to the Super Bowl again. The offense will look the same except for the release of James Lofton at wide receiver. He was considered old at 37, but the rest of the team is still relatively young.

Best Players to Draft — Quarterback Jim Kelly, running backs Thurman Thomas and Kenneth Davis, wide receivers Andre Reed and Bill Brooks, and kicker Steve Christie.

1992 GAME-BY-GAME STATISTICS

Player	RAMS	S.F.	IND.	N.E.	MIA.	RAID.	NYJ	N.E.	PIT.	MIA.	ATL.	IND.	NYJ	DEN.	N.O.	HOU.	Stat
QUARTERBACKS																	
Jim Kelly	13-19	22-33	17-27	15-20	25-48	26-45	15-29	22-33	26-33	19-32	7-15	11-33	20-35	13-23	13-28	5-9	Att/Cmp
	106	403	211	308	306	302	226	205	290	212	93	184	216	213	135	47	Yards
	2	3	2	3	1		2	2	3		2	1	1	1			TD
Frank Reich	6-11				6-10						1-2		0-1			11-23	Att/Cmp
	59				59						4					99	Yards
																	TD
RUNNING BACKS																	
Thurman Thomas	22-103	19-85	14-42	18-120	11-33	16-52	21-142	11-29	37-155	22-73	13-103	21-102	18-116	26-120	24-115	18-97	Att/Yards
	3	1		1					1					1	2		TD
	3-33	4-94	2-29	2-27	9-83	3-27	3-22	5-45	4-30	6-66		3-37	2-24	3-39	6-62	3-8	Rec/Yards
	1	1					1										TD
Carwell Gardner	5-36	1-0	5-19	5-17	2-5	1-0	1-3	2-10		2-4	8-34	1-1	1-(-2)		5-34	1-5	Att/Yards
			1								1						TD
	2-13						1-16			1-8	1-17		1-13			1-0	Rec/Yards
Kenneth Davis	5-44	5-11	12-64	10-39	6-19	9-30	4-22	16-41	4-16	9-27	20-181	6-28	9-19	6-9	8-26	10-37	Att/Yards
							1			2	2		1				TD
	2-13		1-15			2-(-4)		6-44	1-4		1-4		2-3				Rec/Yards
																	TD
RECEIVERS																	
Andre Reed	2-29	10-144	5-77	9-168	6-94	6-85	3-55	2-22	2-2	3-38	4-70	2-21	3-40	1-6	2-19	5-43	Rec/Yards
				1	1						1						TD
James Lofton	6-56	3-39		4-113	6-84	5-72	2-27	4-51	3-79	3-37		1-14	5-83	2-45	1-11	6-75	Rec/Yards
				2			1	1	2								TD
Don Beebe	1-6	1-13				6-106	2-26	8-101	3-37			4-110	1-13	4-104	3-38		Rec/Yards
												1		1			TD
Bill Brooks		5-61	2-20	3-27	7-65	4-45	2-11	1-14	3-21	3-47	5-40		3-23	1-10	3-42	2-32	Rec/Yards
																1	TD
Pete Metzelaars	1-5	4-113	6-53		2-14	6-41		3-17	1-6	1-15	1-3		4-26	1-5			Rec/Yards
		2	1					1					1				TD
KICKERS																	
Steve Christie	2-2	2-2	1-2	2-2	1-1	1-3	1-1			4-5	2-2	2-2	1-1	2-2	2-3	1-2	FG/FGA

1992 SEASON STATISTICS

PLAYERS	PASSING				RUSHING				RECEIVING				KICKING			
	TD 1-9	TD 10-39	TD 40+	Yards 300+	TD 1-9	TD 10-39	TD 40+	Yards 100+	TD 1-9	TD 10-39	TD 40+	Yards 100+	FG 18-39	FG 40-49	FG 50+	PAT
Jim Kelly	7	11	5	4	1											
Frank Reich																
Thurman Thomas					6	3		9	3							
Carwell Gardner					5		1	1								
Kenneth Davis					2											
Andre Reed										2	1	2				
James Lofton										5	1	1				
Don Beebe											2	4				
Bill Brooks										1						
Pete Metzelaars									4	1	1	1				
Steve Christie													14	7	3	43

Chicago Bears

Season Review — Da Bears hit Da Skids with one of the biggest collapses in the team's 73-year history, losing seven of their last eight games. Coach Mike Ditka provided a steady supply of controversy all season and was fired after it ended. The biggest problems were an aging defense and an offense that had trouble generating points. Paramount to all the Bears' troubles was the lack of players on either side of the ball who could make things happen. Jim Harbaugh entered the season as the division's best quarterback, but he slumped to a point where backups Peter Tom Willis and Will Furrer got opportunities to show what they could do (and it wasn't much). Neal Anderson had another subpar year at halfback, even losing his starting job for a time to Darren Lewis.

Offseason Update — Dave Wannstedt came over from the Super Bowl champion Cowboys to replace Mike Ditka as head coach. Free agency amounted to a swap of fullback Brad Muster to the Saints for Craig Heyward, and tight end Jim Thornton signed with the Jets. Speed was obtained in the draft in wide receiver Curtis Conway, and tight end Chris Gedney will be a keeper, too. Undrafted rookie quarterback Shane Matthews could stick, too.

Significant 1992 Injuries — Wide receiver Ron Morris played in just four games and Tom Waddle missed the last four games. Tight end James Thornton missed all of 1992 with a foot injury.

Quarterbacks — The Bears and coach Dave Wannstedt will live or die with Jim Harbaugh at quarterback, but watch for him to flourish in the offense that has been installed. It is better suited for his skills. Harbaugh threw 13 touchdown passes in 1992 when he was replaced for four games, and he always scores a few times himself. More speed in the receiving ranks will help, too. Backups Peter Tom Willis and Will Furrer have ability but don't do much when they get playing time.

Running Backs — Will Neal Anderson be rejuvenated after two subpar seasons? He was named the starter in the offseason and will get the ball enough to be back rushing for 1,000 yards. He always scores 10-plus touchdowns, so he remains a top fantasy pick at the position. He's a fine receiver out of the backfield (last year he scored six of his 11 TD's on passes). The question is at fullback, where Craig Heyward takes over. He could be the goal-line runner the team has lacked for quite a while. If so, he might

score half a dozen times. Darren Lewis, who looked good as a backup last year but not very good as the starter, is back but won't play much unless Anderson slips.

Wide Receivers — Curtis Conway, the No. 1 draft choice, adds speed to a team badly in need of it. He might not play a lot this season, but he'll be a threat whenever he's in a game. As a kick returner, he will be one of the league's best. Wendell Davis is a solid starter, and the new offense will showcase his skills, too. It's an intermediate passing system, and that's the kind of receiver Davis is because he lacks deep speed. He should catch about six TD passes this year. Last season he led the team with 54 catches. Tom Waddle will be the third-down possession receiver if Conway can move into the starting lineup quickly enough. He's one of the best in the league when it comes to getting first downs. Anthony Morgan is a speedster who might be hurt by the addition of Conway. Ron Morris remains a question mark after two injury-riddled seasons.

Tight Ends — Rookie third-round pick Chris Gedney is a receiver first and blocker second. He might end up being the Bears' starter. Keith Jennings is a decent receiver. Last year he caught 23 passes. Both of them were wide receivers at one time.

Kickers — Kevin Butler is a good backup kicker in fantasy football, although he has missed a few clutch kicks the last few years for the Bears. He has averaged 102 points per season since joining the Bears in 1985, but he cracked the 100-point barrier only once in the last six years. He also hasn't hit better than 73 percent of his field goals since 1989.

Defense — The "D" should be back in defense this year with Dave Wannstedt in charge, and he'll be freely substituting up to 18 players depending on down and distance. Last year, Chicago allowed 124 fourth-quarter points, and that won't happen again. The team needs to improve on its 14 interceptions last season.

What to Expect in 1993 — The Bears aren't the most talented team in the division, but the enthusiasm generated by the new coaching staff could be enough to help them win the NFC Central title — just like the Steelers and Chargers of 1992. The Bears aren't as good as they have been in the past, but they aren't as bad as they seemed to be in 1992. Dave Wannstedt will get the most out of every player.

Best Player to Draft — Running back Neal Anderson.

1992 GAME-BY-GAME STATISTICS

Player	Stat	DET.	N.O.	NYG	ATL.	MIN.	T.B.	G.B.	MIN.	CIN.	T.B.	G.B.	CLE.	HOU.	PIT.	DET.	DAL.
QUARTERBACKS																	
Jim Harbaugh	Att/Cmp	19-30	25-45	17-28	18-24	20-34	13-26	16-23	16-24	11-28	17-33	8-18			11-21	11-24	
	Yards	227	260	183	280	201	304	194	149	168	225	97			90	108	
	TD	2		2	2	1	2	1		1	1				1		
Peter Tom Willis	Att/Cmp					4-8				16-23	19-26	11-24				4-11	
	Yards					40				160	285	185				46	
	TD					1					2	1					
RUNNING BACKS																	
Neal Anderson	Att/Yards	13-52	10-36	11-56	15-74	16-46	15-42	11-33	8-23	12-35	6-22	7-25	8-34	5-10	11-56	5-21	3-17
	TD	1		2							1				1		
	Rec/Yards	3-32	3-13	4-24	6-80	6-48	1-4	2-15	1-20		3-23	3-30	4-49	3-27	1-15	2-19	
	TD	1		1							1		1	1	1		
Craig Heyward	Att/Yards	1-3	3-9	2-10	3-12	9-34	7-19	6-30	7-33	8-19	2-7	7-26	12-58	11-53	11-50	9-19	6-34
	TD							1							1		1
	Rec/Yards	1-2	1-(-1)	1-21	1-3			2-13	1-15		2-26	1-4	1-5	1-7	4-36	3-28	
	TD																
Darren Lewis	Att/Yards	4-23	3-22		3-2	1-0	2-9	5-31	3-24	4-72	13-64	2-9	4-6	9-35	16-47	8-43	7-(-5)
	TD						1	1		1					1		
	Rec/Yards	1-24	1-8		1-9					4-31		4-23	1-10	1-30	1-0	2-21	1-6
RECEIVERS																	
Wendell Davis	Rec/Yards	4-66	6-66	4-35	1-11	3-46	1-14	3-60	8-81	2-30	4-88	8-106	2-26	2-21	3-41	2-30	1-13
	TD				1				1								
Tom Waddle	Rec/Yards	2-9	5-53		3-62	5-64	3-114	6-65	2-17	7-78	4-50	5-62	4-100				
	TD	1			1	1							1				
Anthony Morgan	Rec/Yards						2-90			1-46		1-16		3-94		2-24	5-53
	TD						1			1							
Dennis Gentry	Rec/Yards		2-22	2-24		1-4	1-9		1-9	1-14		2-18			1-5	1-9	
	TD																
Keith Jennings	Rec/Yards	3-43	2-9	3-34	2-25	1-9	1-9	2-23	1-10		2-41		1-22		2-15	1-7	2-17
	TD							1									
KICKERS																	
Kevin Butler	FG/FGA	2-3	2-3		2-2	2-2	1-2	3-3	1-1	0-2	1-3	1-1			3-3	1-1	

1992 SEASON STATISTICS

PLAYERS	PASSING				RUSHING				RECEIVING				KICKING			
	TD 1-9	TD 10-39	TD 40+	Yards 300+	TD 1-9	TD 10-39	TD 40+	Yards 100+	TD 1-9	TD 10-39	TD 40+	Yards 100+	FG 18-39	FG 40-49	FG 50+	PAT
Jim Harbaugh	4	5	4	1	1											
Peter Tom Willis		3	1													
Neal Anderson					2	2	1		1	5						
Craig Heyward					3											
Darren Lewis					2	2										
Wendell Davis										2	1					
Tom Waddle									1	1	2	2				
Anthony Morgan										2						
Dennis Gentry																
Keith Jennings									1							
Kevin Butler													18	0	1	34

Cincinnati Bengals

Season Review — Dave Shula took over as the youngest head coach in the league, and, even though a 2-0 start had everybody thinking he was as good as his father Don, the team finished with back-to-back 10-loss seasons for the first time in over a decade. Two five-game losing streaks were the main culprit. Boomer Esiason finished the season as the backup to rookie David Klingler, who became the team's quarterback of the present when he was surprisingly drafted early in the first round during the offseason. Another era ended when tackle Anthony Munoz announced his retirement following 13 seasons of dominating line play (though he was injured much of the season). Among the positives were running back Harold Green (who had 1,170 yards) and nose tackle Tim Krumrie, who led the defense with 97 tackles. Rookies Carl Pickens, Darryl Williams and Ricardo McDonald were impressive.

Offseason Update — Wide receiver Tim McGee was lost in free agency, and tight end Rodney Holman was cut. But the big news of the offseason was the trade of quarterback Boomer Esiason to the Jets for a draft pick. Obtained in the draft were tight end Tony McGee and kicker Doug Pelfrey.

Significant 1992 Injuries — The biggest was the season-long loss of wide receiver Eddie Brown with a preseason knee injury. After taking over the starting quarterback job late in the season, David Klingler was knocked out for the final game, and Don Hollas, who replaced him, was then injured. And Klingler's top receiver, Jeff Query, missed the last two games.

Quarterbacks — David Klingler is on the hotseat now, but he has a lot to learn before he can start putting up the kinds of statistics he did in college. In limited playing time last year, Klingler threw three touchdown passes in 98 attempts. He has great raw tools but is very inexperienced and needs time, although new quarterback coach Ken Anderson, the ex-Bengal, is helping a lot. Klingler will also be at a disadvantage because of a suspect line and inexperienced wide receivers, and the Bengals rarely complete long passes these days. The backups are Donald Hollas and Erik Wilhelm.

Running Backs — The Bengals were the only NFL team in 1992 with more yards rushing than passing. With James Brooks gone, they went to a power running game in 1992. Harold Green is the prime ball carrier in what is basically a one-back offense. Last year he rushed for 1,170 yards but scored only two TD's. In short-yardage situations, Cincinnati goes with Derrick Fenner and Eric Ball, and Green goes out. Fenner scored seven touchdowns last year while rushing for 500 yards. Ball added two TD's both rushing and receiving.

Wide Receivers — The return of Eddie Brown from a neck injury would help, but there was a question about whether or not he would return to the team (he filed a grievance asking to be declared a free agent). From 1988 to '91 he scored 26 touchdowns. After Brown, there's Jeff Query, Carl Pickens and Reggie Rembert, all of whom possess good potential that has yet to be tapped. Query seemed to be Klingler's favorite receiver late last season (which is when he caught all three of his TD passes). Pickens was a second-round draft pick in 1992 who had some big catches but tailed off late. He caught only 26 passes as a rookie. Rembert is one of coach Dave Shula's favorites. He caught 19 passes.

Tight Ends — Tony McGee was the team's second-round draft pick, and he should emerge as the starter sometime in 1992. Second-year pro Craig Thompson, who caught 19 passes for two TD's in 1992, has the speed to stretch a defense.

Kicker — The Bengals might not score a lot of points these days, but Jim Breech consistently scores around 90 points a year. He's reliable inside the 40-yard line, but last year he hit only 4 of 12 field-goal attempts from beyond the 40. In a large league of 10 or more fantasy teams, he's a good backup kicker. Rookie Doug Pelfrey will push Breech in training camp and could win the job.

Defense — The Bengals have been pushed around on defense for years, and that will happen again this year, although No. 1 draft pick John Copeland, a defensive tackle, will help. In 1992, the Bengals ranked 24th against the run, 25th against the pass and 26th overall. They did score three times off turnovers last year. The Bengals lost their best defensive back, Eric Thomas, in free agency to the Jets.

What to Expect in 1993 — Another fourth-place finish. The Bengals are easily the least-talented team in the division, and an unproven quarterback and too many inexperienced players will make 1992 a long rebuilding year. Still, there is quite a bit of talent, so if a few players come through, Cincinnati could surprise.

Best Player to Draft — Running back Harold Green.

1992 GAME-BY-GAME STATISTICS

	SEA.	RAID.	G.B.	MIN.	HOU.	PIT.	HOU.	CLE.	CHI.	NYJ	DET.	PIT.	CLE.	S.D.	N.E.	IND.	
QUARTERBACKS																	
David Klingler											16-34 40	12-25 134 2	13-26 195 1	6-13 61			Att/Cmp Yards TD
Donald Hollas			1-1 9	1-4 4	8-12 68 1	0-2		1-2 3				5-8 64 1			7-12 84	12-17 103	Att/Cmp Yards TD
RUNNING BACKS																	
Harold Green	21-123 5-18	19-97 1 2-10	21-101 1-4	13-41 3-24	10-16 4-28	12-45 3-8	11-38 7-35	17-58 3-37	25-117 2-(-1)	16-52	14-26 6-26	16-116	14-38 3-13	16-73 1-8	31-190 1	9-39 1-4	Att/Yards TD Rec/Yards
Derrick Fenner	9-32 1-(-1)	17-70 1-9 1	14-52 1-6	7-29 1	3-39	6-4	4-20 1-15	9-31	5-11 1	8-92 2 2-12	4-15		3-23	1-(-6)	5-8 1	17-79 2 1-0	Att/Yards TD Rec/Yards TD
Eric Ball	1-1 1	2-3 1 1-17 1	1-(-1)	1-1	2-6		4-30	2-16	2-4 2-41 1		1-2 1-2	1-0				1-(-1)	Att/Yards TD Rec/Yards TD
Tim McGee	3-19	3-43	3-43	5-45	4-56 2	3-33	1-10	3-70 1	3-30		1-6		2-22	1-9	1-7	2-15	Rec/Yards TD
Carl Pickens	1-5	2-27		1-13	1-38	2-25	2-47	2-34	2-29 1	2-24		4-34	2-20	2-12	3-18		Rec/Yards TD
Jeff Query								1-11	3-37			5-49	6-85 2	1-83 1			Rec/Yards TD
Reggie Rembert	5-47	2-30								1-17			4-50	3-35	4-40		Rec/Yards TD
Craig Thompson				1-4		1-6		1-1 1	2-33 1		2-18	5-40	2-24		5-68		Rec/Yards TD
KICKERS																	
Jim Breech	0-2	1-1	3-3		1-2	0-1	1-1	3-3	1-1	0-1	2-3	3-3		1-1	2-4	1-1	FG/FGA

1992 SEASON STATISTICS

PLAYERS	PASSING				RUSHING				RECEIVING				KICKING			
	TD 1-9	TD 10-39	TD 40+	Yards 300+	TD 1-9	TD 10-39	TD 40+	Yards 100+	TD 1-9	TD 10-39	TD 40+	Yards 100+	FG 18-39	FG 40-49	FG 50+	PAT
David Klingler		2	1													
Donald Hollas		2														
Harold Green					1	1		5								
Derrick Fenner					4	2	1		1							
Eric Ball					2					2						
Tim McGee										3						
Carl Pickens										1						
Jeff Query										2	1					
Reggie Rembert																
Craig Thompson									2							
Jim Breech													15	4	0	31

TEAM EVALUATIONS

Cleveland Browns

Season Review — With a playoff berth at stake entering Game 14, the Browns promptly lost three straight games for their third consecutive losing season. They lacked any real explosiveness on offense, especially after quarterback Bernie Kosar went down with a broken ankle in the second game (and then again in the season finale). Todd Philcox was injured next, and then Mike Tomczak was signed for most of the rest of the season. No Cleveland players finished among the conference leaders in any major offensive category, especially the running backs who rotated all year long. Wide receiver Michael Jackson did catch seven touchdown passes. Linebacker Clay Matthews, the NFL's oldest defensive player, continued to set team marks for longevity and career sacks.

Offseason Update — The Browns have a new backup quarterback in Vinny Testaverde, rather than Mike Tomczak, and wide receiver Mark Carrier came over from Tampa Bay and will win a starting job. Tight end Mark Bavaro left for Philadelphia. The draft was a washout for fantasy players.

Significant 1992 Injuries — Quarterback Bernie Kosar missed nine weeks with a broken ankle, and then re-broke it in the final game. His first replacement, Todd Philcox, suffered a broken thumb in his first start and missed the rest of the year. Running back Kevin Mack missed the first month of the season, and rookie Tommy Vardell was out the last two games. Lawyer Tillman returned and was a pleasant surprise at wide receiver, but then he broke his ankle in the last game.

Quarterbacks — Bernie Kosar is one of the league's better quarterbacks when he's healthy, but that seems to be only every other year. An improved offensive line will give him more time to throw and should keep him from getting hit so often after he throws the ball (the Browns were sacked only 34 times in 1992, but that's a misleading figure because the quarterbacks were creamed often). Kosar has an improved receiving corps to work with this year. A change of scenery should help Vinny Testaverde, an offseason free-agent signee. He'll back up Kosar, his former college teammate.

Running Backs — The Browns are deep in the backfield, but it prevents one player from dominating the statistics. Kevin Mack remains the primary ball carrier. Last year he missed a month but still gained 543 yards and scored six touchdowns. Tommy Vardell will play more in 1993. He carried the ball only 28 times in the final eight

games of his rookie season in '92. Mack and Vardell give the team two big backs to wear down defenses. Eric Metcalf is the biggest threat. He scored four touchdowns in one game against the Raiders last season and tied for the team lead with 47 receptions. He'd be a real star if he could get the ball more often. Leroy Hoard, who scored 11 touchdowns in 1991, is the swingback. He scored just once in '92.

Wide Receivers — The Browns addressed one of their needs at the position during the offseason, picking up veteran Mark Carrier from Tampa Bay. He caught 56 passes and scored four times in 1992. Michael Jackson is one of the most underrated wideouts in the NFL. He caught 47 passes with seven TD's last season and is a deep threat. Lawyer Tillman finally emerged last season after missing most of 1991 and '92, but he was hobbling again during the offseason. Patrick Rowe, the No. 2 pick in 1992 who suffered a knee injury in training camp and missed the season, has rehabbed and will push for a spot.

Tight Ends — Pete Holohan is a pretty good receiver but nothing close to as good as he was a few years ago with the Rams. He missed several games in '92 but finished with 20 catches. Scott Galbraith had only four receptions. Neither one is starting material.

Kicker — Matt Stover very quietly scored 92 points last season, more than quite a few other kickers who were on fantasy rosters in 1992. He hit 21 of 29 field goals but was only 3 of 9 from 40 yards and beyond. He had been very shaky after a 1991 season in which he missed a few clutch field goals. The jury is still out on Stover.

Defense — At one point last season, the Browns went 14 quarters without allowing a touchdown, and gave up an average of just 17.2 points per game. They also recorded a team-record 48 sacks and didn't allow a 100-yard rusher until the final game. Three fumbles and an interception were returned for touchdowns, so coach Bill Belichick, one of the best defensive coaches in the league, is doing his job. Overall, the defense ranked 14th.

What to Expect in 1993 — The Browns could compete for the AFC Central title with a bit of luck, but Bill Belichick and his troops are still in a rebuilding mode. The team has a lot of talent on offense, but it's mostly blue-collar with no superstars. The defense is good enough to keep Cleveland in most of the games.

Best Players to Draft — Running back Kevin Mack and wide receiver Michael Jackson.

1992 GAME-BY-GAME STATISTICS

Opponents: IND. MIA. RAID. DEN. PIT. G.B. N.E. CIN. HOU. S.D. MIN. CHI. CIN. DET. HOU. PIT.

QUARTERBACKS

Player	IND	MIA	RAID	DEN	PIT	G.B.	N.E.	CIN	HOU	S.D.	MIN	CHI	CIN	DET	HOU	PIT	
Bernie Kosar	15-26	19-28									8-17	19-23	20-28	17-26	5-7		Att/Cmp
	175	230									59	239	276	140	41		Yards
	0	2										2	2	2			TD
Vinny Testaverde	14-25	22-25	3-8	17-30	23-47	16-32	5-11			12-21	19-31	12-22	12-22	11-14	16-31	24-41	Att/Cmp
	167	363	25	248	286	171	26			182	187	172	177	121	201	228	Yards
	1	2		1	1	1				1	1	2	2		1	1	TD

RUNNING BACKS

Player	IND	MIA	RAID	DEN	PIT	G.B.	N.E.	CIN	HOU	S.D.	MIN	CHI	CIN	DET	HOU	PIT	
Kevin Mack					12-32	19-75	16-38	11-30	13-39	17-35	14-47	20-53	10-40	6-27	21-95	10-32	Att/Yards
						2					1	1	1		1	1	TD
					1-9		1-4	2-22	2-10			1-3	1-3	1-23	3-14	1-(-7)	Rec/Yards
Eric Metcalf	1-(-1)	2-16	4-10	8-21	7-49	4-21	1-3	5-(-1)	7-23	6-21	1-(-1)	5-45	9-53	4-13	2-4	7-25	Att/Yards
			1														TD
	1-11	4-59	5-177	3-11	3-48	3-42	3-29	2-23	3-25	3-33	5-36	1-3	6-73	1-5	3-35	1-4	Rec/Yards
			3										1	1			TD
Leroy Hoard	5-15	2-0	6-(-4)	10-71		2-7		3-12			3-8	1-2	1-4	4-20	10-46	7-55	Att/Yards
																	TD
	1-16	1-2	2-10	4-54			1-11	3-20	2-68	1-25	3-31		1-7	4-40	2-15	1-11	Rec/Yards
									1								TD
Tommy Vardell	9-26	16-84	6-8	6-14	3-7	9-38	17-80	5-11	5-31	1-(-1)	11-29	6-15	4-27	1-0			Att/Yards
																	TD
	3-36	2-29							1-11				4-37	3-15			Rec/Yards

RECEIVERS

Player	IND	MIA	RAID	DEN	PIT	G.B.	N.E.	CIN	HOU	S.D.	MIN	CHI	CIN	DET	HOU	PIT	
Michael Jackson	3-49	5-98			2-62	4-43	3-30	6-96	3-19	4-84	4-25	3-15	3-64	2-80	1-5	4-85	Rec/Yards
		1			1			1		1			1	1		1	TD
Lawyer Tillman						1-18	2-71	2-65	2-29	8-148	3-71	2-29	2-17	1-30	2-20		Rec/Yards
																	TD
Mark Carrier		7-115	5-74	2-20	5-51				4-33	1-22	7-76	5-87	6-65	3-32	3-28	7-88	Rec/Yards
		1										1	1			1	TD
Pete Holohan	4-30	1-6	3-13	2-10								1-9		6-69	3-33		Rec/Yards
																	TD

KICKERS

Player	IND	MIA	RAID	DEN	PIT	G.B.	N.E.	CIN	HOU	S.D.	MIN	CHI	CIN	DET	HOU	PIT	
Matt Stover	1-2	1-1	0-1		1-1	1-1	4-7	1-1	1-2	2-2	2-2	2-3	3-3		0-1	2-2	FG/FGA

1992 SEASON STATISTICS

PLAYERS	PASSING				RUSHING				RECEIVING				KICKING			
	TD 1-9	TD 10-39	TD 40+	Yards 300+	TD 1-9	TD 10-39	TD 40+	Yards 100+	TD 1-9	TD 10-39	TD 40+	Yards 100+	FG 18-39	FG 40-49	FG 50+	PAT
Bernie Kosar	4	1	2													
Vinny Testaverde	2	10	2	1	2											
Kevin Mack					6											
Eric Metcalf					1				2	1	2	1				
Leroy Hoard										1						
Tommy Vardell																
Michael Jackson									1	3	3					
Lawyer Tillman												1				
Mark Carrier									1	3		1				
Pete Holohan																
Matt Stover													18	2	1	29

Dallas Cowboys

Season Review — The Cowboys culminated one of the most remarkable comebacks in NFL history, going from 1-15 in 1989 to 13-3 and the Super Bowl championship in 1992. Dallas had several of the biggest impact players in the NFL. Troy Aikman passed for 23 TD's and was the Super Bowl MVP, Emmitt Smith led the NFL in rushing with 1,713 yards and touchdowns with 19, Michael Irvin caught 78 passes for 1,396 yards and seven scores and Jay Novacek led the league's tight ends with 68 catches. Nearly 20 players were rotated in and out of the lineup on one of the league's best defenses, although none of them made the Pro Bowl. Charles Haley and Thomas Everett, who were obtained in preseason trades, were the impact players on defense. In the end, coach Jimmy Johnson was getting doused with ice water and Jerry Jones was enjoying every second as owner of the finest team in the land.

Offseason Update — Backup quarterback Steve Beuerlein signed with Phoenix as a free agent, but Hugh Millen was picked up from New England in a trade to replace him. Wide receiver Kelvin Martin left for Seattle, but he'll be missed more as a kick returner. Obtained in the draft were wide receiver-return specialist Kevin Williams and running back Derric Lassic, who will back up Emmitt Smith.

Significant 1992 Injuries — None among the offensive stars, or else Dallas would never have won the Super Bowl. Rookie Jimmy Smith was supposed to help at wide receiver but he was sidelined all season. Backup tight end Alfredo Roberts, a key to the running game, was injured in the final game and missed the playoffs.

Quarterbacks — Troy Aikman silenced his critics with his 1992 performance. During the regular season, he threw 23 touchdown passes, the second-best figure in the NFC. Twenty of those TD passes came in the final nine games (and he added eight more in the playoffs). Backup Steve Beuerlein left as a free agent, so Dallas traded for New England's Hugh Millen. Millen is reunited with Norv Turner, his QB coach with the Rams a few years ago, but he's just average. If Aikman goes down, so do the team's Super Bowl hopes. And it's the same thing with the ...

Running Backs — If Emmitt Smith gets injured, like with Aikman, the team will slide right out of the playoff picture. Smith was the best back in the league last year. He led all rushers with 1,713 yards and 19 touchdowns. That was the most TD's in a season since Jerry Rice had 23 in 1987. The Cowboys have won 16 games in a row when Smith has rushed for 100 yards or more. Behind him, however, there isn't much. Fullbacks Daryl Johnston and Tommie Agee are just blockers and receivers. Rookie

Derrick Lassic, the fourth-round pick, will back up Smith. He has talent but obviously is inexperienced. Michael Beasley, a free agent, might also get some playing time.

Wide Receivers — Michael Irvin is the most productive receiver in the league as far as total yards. In the last two years he has caught 171 passes for 2,919 yards and 17 touchdowns. Alvin Harper, the other starter, came on late last season after dropping a lot of passes early. He loosens up secondaries that used to concentrate solely on Irvin. Harper had 35 receptions and four TD's in '92. Jimmy Smith, a 1992 draft pick, didn't catch a pass after breaking a leg during the first scrimmage. A sideline burner, he will compete for the No. 3 role with Kevin Williams, this year's second-round pick. Williams is a gamebreaker who was recruited at Miami (Fla.) by Johnson. Smith and Williams have the most speed of the receiving corps.

Tight Ends — Jay Novacek was the All-Pro tight end last season after catching 68 passes for 630 yards and six touchdowns. He's not spectacular but is certainly one of the league's best. The problem is that the Cowboys often use two tight ends, and backup Alfredo Roberts will be racing to prepare his reconstructed knee in time for the season. Roberts is a very good blocker.

Kicker — Anybody who kicked for the Cowboys in 1992 was going to score a lot of points, but after a slow start, Lin Elliott actually did a very good job. He scored 119 points on 24 of 35 kicking. He started the season hitting only 8 of his first 16 field-goal attempts and was just a game away from getting cut. Then, he hit 13 straight (a team record) and 18 of his last 21 kicks, including two 53-yarders.

Defense — The Cowboys don't have the most talented defense in the league, but it is one of the most opportunistic. You remember the Super Bowl when the Cowboys defense almost outscored the Buffalo offense, but during the regular season, the Dallas "D" scored 14 points, too. The defense ranked first against the run, fifth vs. the pass and first overall.

What to Expect in 1993 — The youngest team in the NFL last year, the Cowboys will be the Super Bowl favorite this season — and perhaps for a few more to come. However, if either Troy Aikman or Emmitt Smith were to get injured, the team would slip to third place in the division.

Best Players to Draft — Quarterback Troy Aikman, running back Emmitt Smith, wide receiver Michael Irvin, tight end Jay Novacek and kicker Lin Elliott.

1992 GAME-BY-GAME STATISTICS

WAS. NYG PHX. PHI. SEA. K.C. RAID. PHIL. DET. RAMS PHX. NYG DEN. WAS. ATL. CHI.

QUARTERBACKS

Player	WAS	NYG	PHX	PHI	SEA	K.C.	RAID	PHIL	DET	RAMS	PHX	NYG	DEN	WAS	ATL	CHI	
Troy Aikman	18-31	22-35	14-21	19-38	15-23	21-29	16-25	19-33	16-25	22-37	25-36	19-29	25-35	23-35	18-21	10-20	Att/Cmp
	216	238	263	256	173	192	234	214	214	272	237	143	231	245	239	78	Yards
	1	2	3	1		1		2	1		2	2	3	2	3		TD
Steve Beuerlein					2-5				2-2							8-11	Att/Cmp
					27				26							99	Yards
																	TD

RUNNING BACKS

Player	WAS	NYG	PHX	PHI	SEA	K.C.	RAID	PHIL	DET	RAMS	PHX	NYG	DEN	WAS	ATL	CHI	
Emmitt Smith	26-139	23-89	26-112	19-67	22-78	24-95	29-152	30-163	19-67	19-80	23-84	17-120	26-62	25-99	24-174	20-131	Att/Yards
	1	1	1		2	1	3		3	1		1	1		2	1	TD
	3-13	8-55		2-5		4-35	3-15	1-9	3-13	2-8	12-67	6-41	6-45	5-16	2-5	2-8	Rec/Yards
											1						TD
Daryl Johnston	1-14	1-1	3-7	1-2	4-9		1-4	1-1			2-6	1-1		2-16			Att/Yards
																	TD
	4-39	1-7				5-29	2-11	4-46	3-9	2-13	1-8	3-30	3-18	1-15		3-24	Rec/Yards
						1		1									TD
Tommie Agee				2-11	3-10				1-1						1-2	9-30	Att/Yards
																	TD
				1-4	1-8											1-6	Rec/Yards

RECEIVERS

Player	WAS	NYG	PHX	PHI	SEA	K.C.	RAID	PHIL	DET	RAMS	PHX	NYG	DEN	WAS	ATL	CHI	
Michael Irvin	5-89	4-73	8-210	4-105	6-113	6-84	3-54	2-29	5-114	8-108	1-18	4-37	6-62	5-105	6-89	5-46	Rec/Yards
		1	3						1				2				TD
Alvin Harper	3-59	1-11	1-14	1-42	2-20		4-79	1-9	3-61	1-5	5-88	2-15	2-17	4-51	3-53	2-38	Rec/Yards
	1										1			1			TD
Jimmy Smith																	Rec/Yards
																	TD
Jay Novacek	1-4	5-33	3-28	6-61	5-22	5-36	3-60	4-38	3-29	5-27	5-50	3-22	7-87	5-25	5-69	3-39	Rec/Yards
		1									1		1	2	1		TD
Alfredo Roberts		1-18		1-4					1-14								Rec/Yards
																	TD

KICKERS

Player	WAS	NYG	PHX	PHI	SEA	K.C.	RAID	PHIL	DET	RAMS	PHX	NYG	DEN	WAS	ATL	CHI	
Lin Elliott	0-1	2-2	1-2	0-1	2-3	1-2	0-1	2-4	3-3	3-3	1-1	3-3	1-2	1-1	2-3	2-3	FG/FGA

1992 SEASON STATISTICS

PLAYERS	PASSING				RUSHING				RECEIVING				KICKING			
	TD 1-9	TD 10-39	TD 40+	Yards 300+	TD 1-9	TD 10-39	TD 40+	Yards 100+	TD 1-9	TD 10-39	TD 40+	Yards 100+	FG 18-39	FG 40-49	FG 50+	PAT
Troy Aikman	11	10	2		1											
Steve Beuerlein																
Emmitt Smith					13	4	1	7		1						
Daryl Johnston									1	1						
Tommie Agee																
Michael Irvin									3	2	2	6				
Alvin Harper									1	3						
Jimmy Smith																
Jay Novacek									5	1						
Alfredo Roberts																
Lin Elliott													16	5	3	47

Denver Broncos

Season Review — Dan Reeves was fired following an 8-8 season in which quarterback John Elway was injured and replaced by rotating quarterbacks in rookie Tommy Maddox and Shawn Moore. After a 7-3 start, Elway missed four starts, all losses, which killed any chances Denver had of making the playoffs. Without Elway, the offense fell apart, and the Broncos were outscored by 67 points in the 16 games. The running game, led by Gaston Green, failed to take some pressure off the passers, who were under siege when they dropped back, being sacked 52 times. Wideout Mark Jackson scored a team-high eight touchdowns, and linebacker Simon Fletcher had a team-record 16 sacks, making it 10 or more for him in four consecutive seasons. After the season, defensive coordinator Wade Phillips was promoted to head coach.

Offseason Update — Wade Phillips was promoted to head coach after Dan Reeves was fired. Several new offensive linemen were signed to block for John Elway, and running backs Rod Bernstine and Robert Delpino were acquired as free agents, too, though wideout Mark Jackson, the leading receiver in 1992, was lost to the Giants. Running back Gaston Green was traded to the Raiders. In the draft, Denver acquired running backs Glyn Milburn and Kevin Williams and kicker Jason Elam, who might displace David Treadwell.

Significant 1992 Injuries — Quarterback John Elway was out for four games with a bruised right shoulder, and that's when the Broncos fell apart and were knocked out of the playoff race. Third-down back Steve Sewell missed all year with a broken ankle, and Sammie Smith played in just four games because of various ailments after coming over from Miami. Wide receiver Derek Russell was out the last four games.

Quarterbacks — John Elway should be able to stay healthy this year after the revamping of the offensive line. Last year he missed four games with a shoulder injury, and the Broncos lost all four of those games. They were 8-4 with Elway in the lineup, although he threw only 10 touchdown passes vs. 17 interceptions. He'll be throwing more to the backs this season in a new offense patterned after the 49ers. Backup Tommy Maddox is too raw to be counted upon if something happens to Elway. The Broncos have thrown the third-fewest touchdowns passes over the last three seasons.

Running Backs — Rod Bernstine came over from San Diego and will be the feature back as long as he is healthy enough to play. He has missed 32 games in six years due to injuries. Last year he gained only 499 yards on the ground. A former tight end, he might catch 75 passes this year if he plays all 16 games. Robert Delpino left the Rams for Denver. He's a solid goal-line runner but is not an every-down back if something happens to Bernstine. Fullback Reggie Rivers (45 catches in 1992) will start in the Tom Rathman role in the two-back offense, and Greg Lewis is a situational guy who is best at the goal line. The status of Sammie Smith and Steve Sewell is up in the air.

Wide Receivers — Vance Johnson is the old veteran on the weakest position on the team. Johnson is steady, but last year he caught just 24 passes for two touchdowns. There are three promising youngsters on the roster in Arthur Marshall, Derek Russell and Cedric Tillman. They will compete for the other starting job. Marshall is a speedster, Tillman came on late last season and Russell had a good 1991 rookie season.

Tight Ends — The Broncos put a greater emphasis on tight ends in 1992. Shannon Sharpe proved that he is more than just Sterling Sharpe's younger brother. He led the Broncos in receiving with 53 catches for 640 yards and two TD's. Sharpe isn't exactly a tight end since he plays a lot of wide receiver and H-back.

Kicker — In 1992, David Treadwell failed to score 100 points for the first time in his four-year career because of the Broncos' sporadic offense. Still, he averages 107 points a season and should be back over 100 in '93 if he remains the kicker. Treadwell hit 20 of his 24 field-goal attempts (83 percent) and seemed to show a little more range than in past years (he was 4 of 5 from beyond the 40). Jason Elam was drafted in the third round and will compete for the kicking job. He was the best collegiate kicker last year.

Defense — The Broncos' defense slipped to 22nd in the league and allowed 329 points. But coordinator Wade Phillips has been promoted to head coach and he spent his top draft picks on defensive players. If the offense can control the ball longer, the defense will be improved. It scored two touchdowns on turnovers and made 50 sacks last year.

What to Expect in 1993 — The Broncos will be back in the hunt for the AFC West title this year as long as John Elway stays in the lineup. If he goes down, 1993 will be a repeat of '92. The offense will have several new faces and should be better.

Best Players to Draft — Running back Rod Bernstine, tight end Shannon Sharpe and kicker David Treadwell.

1992 GAME-BY-GAME STATISTICS

Player	RAID.	S.D.	PHI.	CLE.	K.C.	WAS.	HOU.	S.D.	NYJ	NYG	RAID.	SEA.	DAL.	BUF.	SEA.	K.C.	
QUARTERBACKS																	
John Elway	10-24	14-24	8-18	10-17	23-38	15-32	13-21	21-39	18-33	6-9					19-28	16-32	Att/Cmp
	171	186	59	157	311	128	192	260	261	96					213	211	Yards
		2			2		1	2	1	1						1	TD
Tommy Maddox						2-8					9-11	18-26	11-26	10-17	13-28	3-3	Att/Cmp
						10					134	207	127	104	122	53	Yards
													1	3	1		TD
RUNNING BACKS																	
Rod Bernstine	1	12-83	11-65	9-22	18-74	23-150							11-33	3-11	9-16		Att/Yards
	1					2							1				TD
			1-7	3-14	3-17	2-23								1-14	2-11		Rec/Yards
Reggie Rivers	1-1	4-21	2-0	8-66	6-34	4-5	1-20	3-12	7-27	5-6	5-8	9-12	3-8	8-21	5-14	3-27	Att/Yards
	1						1			1							TD
	1-24			1-17	2-14	1-7	2-17	9-76	3-13	5-70	5-46	1-16	4-38	2-22	6-54	3-35	Rec/Yards
													1				TD
Gaston Green	12-30	11-21	4-12	18-57	9-23	8-21	8-98	6-18	9-50	18-92	13-83	20-63			13-50	12-30	Att/Yards
							1								1		TD
	1-1	1-13		1-8		1-3			1-14	1-2		1-4			1-33	2-1	Rec/Yards
																	TD
Greg Lewis	1-0	3-5	6-22	3-44	1-3	4-(-2)		1-3	4-10	7-29		2-5	10-59	16-47	6-22	9-21	Att/Yards
									1	1				1		1	TD
										1-6			2-25			1-(-1)	Rec/Yards
RECEIVERS																	
Vance Johnson					1-12		3-29	4-48	4-43		3-30	2-45	4-71	3-16			Rec/Yards
					1								1				TD
Arthur Marshall	3-72		2-33	1-12	4-49		1-14	5-134	1-10	4-48			1-19	2-33	1-7	1-62	Rec/Yards
								1									TD
Derek Russell	2-38	3-28	1-5	1-15	1-11	3-32		1-11									Rec/Yards
																	TD
Shannon Sharpe		3-61	2-2	2-61	9-118	9-71	3-37	2-12	1-9	4-34		3-16	7-109	3-23	5-87		Rec/Yards
		1											1				TD
KICKERS																	
David Treadwell	1-1		0-2	4-4	2-3	1-1	2-2		2-2	2-2	0-1	2-2		1-1	1-1	2-2	FG/FGA

1992 SEASON STATISTICS

PLAYERS	PASSING TD 1-9	PASSING TD 10-39	PASSING TD 40+	PASSING Yards 300+	RUSHING TD 1-9	RUSHING TD 10-39	RUSHING TD 40+	RUSHING Yards 100+	RECEIVING TD 1-9	RECEIVING TD 10-39	RECEIVING TD 40+	RECEIVING Yards 100+	KICKING FG 18-39	KICKING FG 40-49	KICKING FG 50+	PAT
John Elway		7	3	1	2											
Tommy Maddox	2	3														
Rod Bernstine					3	1		1								
Reggie Rivers					2	1				1						
Gaston Green					1		1									
Greg Lewis					4											
Vance Johnson										2						
Arthur Marshall										1	1					
Derek Russell																
Shannon Sharpe									1	1		2				
David Treadwell													16	4	0	28

Detroit Lions

Season Review — The Lions slumped from division champs to the cellar with tragedies, injuries and quarterback controversies all year long. The offensive line was the No. 1 headache, especially for the quarterbacks, who were batted around like a beach ball. On top of Mike Utley's injury that left him paralyzed in 1991, guard Eric Andolsek was killed before the '92 season began, and two other starters were lost by midseason. Thus, running back Barry Sanders was a marked man all season, although he did overcome a slow start to become only the third player to rush for 1,000 yards in each of his first four seasons. Receivers Herman Moore and Brett Perriman and kicker Jason Hanson were solid performers, but quarterbacks Rodney Peete, Erik Kramer and Andre Ware were mostly ineffective.

Offseason Update — The biggest acquisitions were three free-agent offensive linemen to block for Barry Sanders and linebacker Pat Swilling to help the defense. Tight end Rodney Holman might be a nice addition. The draft didn't help much.

Significant 1992 Injuries — The injuries that had the biggest impact were those on the offensive line. In 1991, guard Mike Utley was paralyzed and before the '92 season started, guard Eric Andolsek was killed in an accident. Thus, running back Barry Sanders couldn't find much running room. The top receiver, Herman Moore, missed a month early because of a quadriceps injury.

Quarterbacks — For the first time, Andre Ware will seriously challenge Rodney Peete for the starting job. In the final three games of last year, Ware looked pretty good and showed more promise than he had in his first two seasons, and he ran well. His mobility provides options in the passing game. Peete has never been able to stay healthy for an entire season, although he does move the team when he's in the lineup. He threw nine TD passes last year (Ware tossed three).

Running Backs — Look for Barry Sanders to have a tremendous season in 1993 after the additions of three free-agent offensive linemen. Sanders slipped to 1,352 yards and 10 touchdowns last year when the Detroit line couldn't open holes for him. Still, that was more yards than in 1990 when he led the league in rushing. The Lions are desperate

for a backup. If Sanders were to get injured, the Lions' season would end immediately.

Wide Receivers — The Lions have a very underrated but quality group of wideouts, starting with Herman Moore. In 1992, Moore averaged 18.9 yards — tops in the NFC — on 51 catches, and he rarely dropped a ball. Brett Perriman led the team in receiving and ranked sixth in the conference. Perriman, a clutch third-down receiver, and Moore each scored four times. Willie Green is the third wideout. He caught five TD passes in 33 receptions in '92 but isn't consistent. Reggie Barrett has yet to show the consistency or durability to take over a starting role. He caught only four passes last year. Mike Farr, Jeff Campbell and Aubrey Matthews provide solid depth.

Tight Ends — The Lions want to incorporate a tight end into the offense more this season, so they signed Rodney Holman after he had been cut by Cincinnati. He is 33 and has slowed, but he might have a season or two left. Neither ex-Redskin Jimmie Johnson nor rookie Thomas McLemore did much in 1992.

Kicker — Jason Hanson had a tremendous season as a rookie in 1992, hitting 21 of 26 field-goal attempts and scoring 93 points. Like Dallas' Lin Elliott, he started a little slow (3 of 7) before getting hot — 18 of his last 19, including 12 straight at one point. He should be the kicker in Detroit for years to come, and, with Barry Sanders finally having a line to run behind, should score 100 points with ease.

Defense — In 1992, the Detroit defense specialized in blowing leads while letting up 133 fourth-quarter points. Overall, it ranked 20th, but new defensive coordinator Hank Bullough should help. The Lions returned two blocked kicks for touchdowns last year and added a score on a fumble.

What to Expect in 1993 — If Sanders is able to run wild, the Lions will be a formidable foe in the up-for-grabs NFC Central. But, if he gets injured or can't find daylight, the Lions will finish back in the pack. Detroit needs more consistency from its quarterback, but the defense should be better this season.

Best Player to Draft — Running back Barry Sanders.

1992 GAME-BY-GAME STATISTICS

	CHI.	MIN.	WAS.	T.B.	N.O.	MIN.	T.B.	G.B.	DAL.	PIT.	CIN.	HOU.	G.B.	CLE.	CHI.	S.F.	
QUARTERBACKS																	
Rodney Peete	18-26 / 273 / 2	10-15 / 105 / 1	14-26 / 181 / 1	20-31 / 323 / 1	15-30 / 173 / 1	13-23 / 171	11-19 / 208 / 3	14-28 / 148	6-10 / 69				2-5 / 51				Att/Cmp Yards TD
Erik Kramer						5-6 / 81 / 1	3-5 / 28	3-5 / 33	3-7 / 21	20-37 / 304 / 1	12-25 / 141	12-21 / 163 / 2					Att/Cmp Yards TD
Andre Ware													13-23 / 133 / 1	10-14 / 138 / 2	12-20 / 290	15-29 / 116	Att/Cmp Yards TD
RUNNING BACKS																	
Barry Sanders	19-109 / 1	26-66 / 2-14	14-34 / 4-23	20-70 / 1-4	9-36	16-52 / 1 / 2-18	21-122 / 2 / 1-5	12-38 / 5-30	18-108 / 1-3	21-94 / 1 / 3-23	29-151 / 1 / 1-3	22-54 / 1 / 2-12 / 1	16-114 / 3-20	30-87 / 1 / 2-18	20-113 / 1 / 1-48	19-104 / 1-4	Att/Yards TD Rec/Yards TD
Troy Stradford	3-12						8-28 / 1-3	1-12	1-1								Att/Yards TD Rec/Yards
RECEIVERS																	
Herman Moore	6-82					3-76 / 1	3-108 / 1	3-43	4-57	5-71	5-86	2-88 / 1	8-114 / 1	2-52	3-108	7-81	Rec/Yards TD
Brett Perriman	7-70 / 1	1-4	2-14	9-117	4-26 / 1	8-124	3-41 / 1	5-67	1-6	5-89	3-24	5-46	3-26	3-34 / 1	4-87	6-28	Rec/Yards TD
Willie Green	5-114 / 1	3-34 / 1	1-67 / 1	5-66	6-84	1-13	2-45 / 1		6-115 / 1		1-7				3-41		Rec/Yards TD
Mike Farr				1-13	2-15	4-21		2-14			3-28	1-9		2-15			Rec/Yards TD
Rodney Holman	2-21	3-18	229				1-15	2-12 / 1	3-26	1-10	1-5	2-17	2-34 / 1	1-6	2-29	4-44	Rec/Yards TD
KICKERS																	
Jason Hanson	1-1	1-2	1-3	3-4			1-1	2-2	1-1		4-4		1-1	1-2	3-3	2-2	FG/FGA

1992 SEASON STATISTICS

PLAYERS	PASSING				RUSHING				RECEIVING				KICKING			
	TD 1-9	TD 10-39	TD 40+	Yards 300+	TD 1-9	TD 10-39	TD 40+	Yards 100+	TD 1-9	TD 10-39	TD 40+	Yards 100+	FG 18-39	FG 40-49	FG 50+	PAT
Rodney Peete	1	4	4	1												
Erik Kramer	1		3	1												
Andre Ware		3														
Barry Sanders					5	2	2	7	1							
Troy Stradford																
Herman Moore										1	3	3				
Brett Perriman									1	2	1	2				
Willie Green										3	2	2				
Mike Farr																
Rodney Holman									1	1						
Jason Hanson													15	4	2	30

Green Bay Packers

Season Review — Brett Favre and Sterling Sharpe were the big stories in Green Bay, as the Packers contended for a playoff spot until the final weekend of the season. In his second season after being obtained in an offseason trade with Atlanta, Favre mastered the ball-control passing game of new coach Mike Holmgren and threw for 3,227 yards and 18 touchdowns after replacing Don Majkowski. Sharpe was on the receiving end of many of Favre's passes, as he set an NFL single-season record with 108 receptions. He also led the league with 1,461 receiving yards and 13 touchdowns. Other than tight end Jackie Harris (55 catches), the Packers were devoid of stars. The Green Bay defense wasn't dominant but certainly respectable, led by safety Chuck Cecil and linebacker Tony Bennett, who had 12.5 sacks.

Offseason Update — Green Bay has been the busiest team since the end of last season, greatly upgrading itself through trades, free-agent signings and the draft. The Packers acquired running back John Stephens and backup quarterback Ken O'Brien in trades. Defensive end Reggie White was the biggest free-agent signing, but new offensive linemen Harry Galbreath and Tunch Ilken will help the running game. Running back Vince Workman left for Tampa Bay. They also added tight end Jesse Anderson and fullback Robert Wilson. Quarterback Mark Brunell, a draft choice, will compete for the third-string job.

Significant 1992 Injuries — Quarterback Don Majkowski was injured in Game Two, but that turned out to be a blessing in disguise because it thrust Brett Favre into the starting lineup. Running back Darrell Thompson was sidelined early, and then after he came back, Vince Workman went down. They played together for just five weeks, and thus the Green Bay running game wasn't much of a threat.

Quarterbacks — Brett Favre immediately turned into the NFL's best young quarterback in 1992 when he took over the starting job and became the youngest quarterback ever to play in the Pro Bowl. Favre looked like a seasoned veteran when he passed for 18 touchdowns and 3,227 yards in less than a full season. The Packers have a new backup in former Jet Ken O'Brien. Fifth-round pick Mark Brunell will battle Ty Detmer for the No. 3 job.

Running Backs — This is the Packers' weakness. They haven't had a 1,000-yard rusher since 1978 and just last year got their first 500-yard rusher since '89. They even went 40 games without a 100-yard rusher until the now-departed Vince Workman hit that mark in Game 8 of last year. Former Patriot Rookie of the Year John Stephens will compete for the job with second-year pro Edgar Bennett and disappointing Darrell Thompson. But none of them is a threat to gain 1,000 yards. Fullback will be solid with Harry Sydney, Buford McGee, Dexter McNabb and Robert Wilson.

Wide Receivers — Sterling Sharpe had one of the greatest seasons ever for a receiver in NFL history in 1992. He caught a league-record 108 passes for 1,461 yards and 13 touchdowns and could approach those numbers again with Favre and without a decent threat at the other WR spot. Vying for that job will be Robert Brooks, a disappointment as a rookie last year; Ron Lewis, who was cut by San Francisco before earning the starting job late last season; and Sanjay Beach, who started the year. After Sharpe's 108 catches, the next leading wideout, Beach, had only 17 receptions.

Tight Ends — Jackie Harris emerged as a Pro Bowl-caliber tight end last season when he hauled in 55 catches, second on the team. He is only going to get better playing for Mike Holmgren and will be the next Brent Jones. Ed West has been phased out of the offense, and ex-Buccaneer Jesse Anderson might replace him.

Kicker — Chris Jacke has always been one of the most underrated kickers in the NFL. Last year, he connected on 22 of 29 field goals, although he did miss three chip shots from 32 yards and closer. In four years, Jacke averages 97 points a season. The improved Packers offense will give him more opportunities to score.

Defense — The Green Bay defense isn't nearly as good as people in Packerland think it is, but free-agent acquisitions Reggie White and Bill Maas will help on the line and the loss of safety Chuck Cecil was negated by the signing of Mike Prior. Rookie linebacker Wayne Simmons will help with the pass rush and take some double-teaming off White. Cornerback Terrell Buckley is a touchdown waiting to happen on defense (and special teams).

What to Expect in 1993 — It didn't take long for Ron Wolf and Mike Holmgren to turn the Packers around, so they will be competing for the NFC Central title this year. The most improved team during the offseason, Green Bay lacks a threat at running back, needs another wide receiver and perhaps a few more solid defenders. But in the weak NFC Central, the Pack could be back on top.

Best Players to Draft — Quarterback Brett Favre, wide receiver Sterling Sharpe, tight end Jackie Harris and kicker Chris Jacke.

1992 GAME-BY-GAME STATISTICS

	MIN.	T.B.	CIN.	PIT.	ATL.	CLE.	CHI.	DET.	NYG	PHI.	CHI.	T.B.	DET.	HOU.	RAMS	MIN.	
QUARTERBACKS																	
Brett Favre		8-14 73	22-39 289 2	14-19 210 2	33-43 276 1	20-33 223	20-37 214 1	22-37 212 2	27-44 279	23-33 275 2	16-24 209 1	26-41 223 1	15-19 214 3	19-30 155 1	14-23 188 2	23-35 187	Att/Cmp Yards TD
Ken O'Brien		1-4 17	23-41 264 2			3-5 37	21-29 240 3	2-5 34			4-9 38	1-3 13					Att/Cmp Yards TD
RUNNING BACKS																	
Vince Workman	25-89 12-50	7-36 2-12	14-50 5-56	26-85 4-20	17-70 8-37	10-30 8-84	11-40	23-101 1 4-21	19-67 1 3-5	7-63 1 1-5							Att/Yards TD Rec/Yards TD
John Stephens	2-4	2-1	1-(-3) 1-9	2-23	16-49 2-5	1-6 4-18	5-29	2-9 2-16	1-5	9-34 4-13	14-51 2 1-14	2-14 1-6	1-8	9-37 2-42	5-2 1-7	6-39	Att/Yards TD Rec/Yards
Harry Sydney	1-2 1-1	4-18 4-40	3-23	1-3 1-10	4-29	3-6 1-7	5-30	6-16 1 4-43	1-3 4-27	1-8 4-44	4-18 3-30	7-13 6-55	8-41 3-22 1	4-2 1-6	7-29 1-(-1)	4-4 1 4-18	Att/Yards TD Rec/Yards TD
Edgar Bennett		6-22	3-4	2-5				2-7			29-107	13-38	4-13			2-18	Att/Yards TD
RECEIVERS																	
Sterling Sharpe	8-99 1	5-62	7-109 1	2-93 1	9-107 1	4-48	9-144 1	6-84 1	11-160	7-116 1	5-79 1	9-52	6-107 2	6-46 1	8-110 2	6-45	Rec/Yards TD
Ron Lewis											2-21	4-57	1-13	4-39		2-22	Rec/Yards TD
Sanjay Beach	2-7 1	3-17	1-11		5-32	2-22		2-6					1-20			1-7	Rec/Yards TD
Robert Brooks	1-6	1-15		1-8 1		1-8	3-31	1-8		1-4	1-12	1-8	1-18	1-16			Rec/Yards TD
Jackie Harris	2-17	1-7	1-16	2-23	6-63	4-54	2-6	5-50 1	9-87	8-98	2-43	2-16 1	2-20	2-14	2-22	5-59	Rec/Yards TD
KICKERS																	
Chris Jacke	2-2	1-1	1-3	1-2	1-2	2-2	1-2	2-2	0-1	2-2	1-1	4-5	1-1	3-3			FG/FGA

1992 SEASON STATISTICS

	PASSING				RUSHING				RECEIVING				KICKING			
PLAYERS	TD 1-9	TD 10-39	TD 40+	Yards 300+	TD 1-9	TD 10-39	TD 40+	Yards 100+	TD 1-9	TD 10-39	TD 40+	Yards 100+	FG 18-39	FG 40-49	FG 50+	PAT
Brett Favre	8	7	3													
Ken O'Brien	2	2	1													
Vince Workman					2			1								
John Stephens					1	1										
Harry Sydney					2				1							
Edgar Bennett								1								
Sterling Sharpe									4	6	3	7				
Ron Lewis																
Sanjay Beach									1							
Robert Brooks									1							
Jackie Harris									1	1						
Chris Jacke													14	6	2	30

Houston Oilers

Season Review — Houston earned its NFL-best sixth straight postseason appearance during an up-and-down season. Like the Steelers, the Oilers operated down the stretch without their starting quarterback, with Cody Carlson taking over for the injured Warren Moon until the playoffs. Lorenzo White, who rushed for 1,226 yards, emerged as a star in a backfield that was far less crowded than in past years. With 90 catches, Haywood Jeffires led the AFC in receptions for the third straight year, and Ernest Givins led the AFC with 10 TD receptions. The Houston defense was again strong, ranking No. 1 in the AFC and No. 3 in the NFL. With an offense that finished second in the AFC, no other conference team could claim that kind of balance. But the season ended after Houston blew a 32-point lead against Buffalo in the playoffs.

Offseason Update — Travis Hannah, a wide receiver drafted in the fourth round, adds speed to a position that needed both speed and some depth. John Henry Mills, a fifth-rounder, becomes the team's only tight end.

Significant 1992 Injuries — Quarterback Warren Moon missed Games 11-15 with a separated shoulder before returning in time for the playoffs, although Cody Carlson was more than an adequate replacement. The receiving corps was healthy once again.

Quarterbacks — Warren Moon and Cody Carlson combined for 27 touchdown passes last season, so if Moon stays healthy this year he should easily approach that number again. With the best starting four wideouts in the league, it really doesn't matter who is throwing the ball. Moon is 36, but he still runs well and can throw the deep ball. Carlson proved last year he can take over without a dropoff.

Running Backs — Lorenzo White carried the ball 265 times last year, while the other backs combined for only 20 carries. White gained 1,226 yards and caught 57 passes, although he reached the end zone only eight times. One of the top multipurpose backs in the league, he averaged 4.6 yards per carry with teams keying on him. Gary Brown is a solid backup who should get the ball more.

Wide Receivers — Ernest Givins, Haywood Jeffires, Webster Slaughter and Curtis Duncan will catch about 300 passes between them this season if all remain healthy. Last year, Jeffires caught 90 passes, third in the league, for nine touchdowns, although he averaged only 10.1 yards per reception. Givins was the biggest threat, scoring 10 times, although he, too, had a low average (11.7). Slaughter was a key addition when he signed with Houston after being declared a free agent. He caught four TD passes in roughly half the season. Curtis Duncan had only one TD reception in 82 catches and is the team's possession receiver. Leonard Harris, who took over in the starting lineup for Drew Hill a year ago but was later replaced by Slaughter, is the only decent backup. Rookie Travis Hannah will provide some much-needed speed to the position if he makes the final cut.

Tight Ends — The Oilers play four wide receivers, although they drafted John Henry Mills in the fifth round. He is a semi-wide receiver who will have a hard time making the team.

Kickers — Al Del Greco scored 104 points in his first full season with the Oilers last year, but they signed ex-Miami (Fla.) kicker Carlos Huerta to give him competition this year. Del Greco hit 21 of 27 field-goal attempts for 78 percent, but he had only a 66 percent career average heading into the season. He missed two of three pressure kicks, which is why the Oilers are hoping to replace him. Huerta was cut by the Chargers in training camp a year ago.

Defense — Any defense that blows a 32-point lead has some problems, but the Oilers are actually pretty good. The defense ranked third in the league last year (third against the pass and ninth vs. the run). Buddy Ryan was hired as the new defensive coordinator and, unless he creates a lot of turmoil, could be what the team needs to get to the Super Bowl. The defense scored four touchdowns (three fumbles and an interception) and got one safety last year.

What to Expect in 1993 — Houston will be favored over Pittsburgh in the division, but if new defensive coordinator Buddy Ryan causes problems, the whole season could go up in turmoil. However, if Ryan works his magic with the defense, the Oilers might also win the Super Bowl, because there is that much talent on the team. The offense is set.

Best Players to Draft — Quarterback Warren Moon, running back Lorenzo White, wide receivers Haywood Jeffires and Ernest Givins and kicker Al Del Greco.

1992 GAME-BY-GAME STATISTICS

Player / Stat	PIT.	IND.	K.C.	S.D.	CIN.	DEN.	CIN.	PIT.	CLE.	MIN.	MIA.	DET.	CHI.	G.B.	CLE.	BUF.	
QUARTERBACKS																	
Warren Moon	29-45	29-39	19-28	17-28	21-32	23-39	27-40	13-19	12-25	28-38					6-13		Att/Cmp
	330	361	279	175	216	321	342	104	70	243					80		Yards
	2	2	2	1	5	2	1			1					1		TD
Cody Carlson				3-7				15-23	9-11	2-2	22-35	24-33	18-27	25-36	19-34	12-19	Att/Cmp
				22				137	111	13	228	338	178	330	248	105	Yards
								1	2		1	1	1		2	1	TD
RUNNING BACKS																	
Lorenzo White	13-100	17-69	17-72	15-63	25-149	15-70	17-59	12-44	14-76	18-81	18-69	15-68	20-116	15-54	16-70	17-66	Att/Yards
				1		1	1			1		1	1	1			TD
	3-24	4-106	2-39	1-18	1-4	1-1		6-32	3-17	9-58	5-64	6-69	2-4	6-28	6-105	2-22	Rec/Yards
		1															TD
Gary Brown		1-1		6-31	4-34				1-5						8-21		Att/Yards
															1		TD
																	Rec/Yards
RECEIVERS																	
Haywood Jeffires	7-117	6-59	6-84	10-77	9-82	7-83	4-20	9-68	1-5	6-49	5-42	4-54	3-59	5-48	2-20	6-46	Rec/Yards
		1		1	3	1					1	1				1	TD
Ernest Givins	4-42	5-44	2-34	2-23	5-45	8-79	8-100	5-47	4-50	8-91	2-16	4-100	1-12	3-30	4-38	2-36	Rec/Yards
	2		1		2	1	1		1	1					1		TD
Curtis Duncan	8-98	8-94	5-64	4-51	2-40	5-133	9-84	3-23	5-45	4-24	5-39	3-31	8-64	6-100	4-41	3-23	Rec/Yards
															1		TD
Webster Slaughter						1-22	4-68	5-71	5-31		1-8	7-84	4-39	5-74	3-44	4-45	Rec/Yards
							1	1	1				1				TD
Leonard Harris	7-49	6-58	4-58	2-24	3-39	1-3	2-70		2-28	3-34	4-59				1-13		Rec/Yards
			1												1		TD
Pat Coleman				1-4	1-6												Rec/Yards
																	TD
KICKERS																	
Al Del Greco	1-1	2-3	3-3	2-2	1-1	0-1	1-2	2-3		1-1	3-4	1-2	1-1		1-1	2-2	FG/FGA

1992 SEASON STATISTICS

PLAYERS	PASSING				RUSHING				RECEIVING				KICKING			
	TD 1-9	TD 10-39	TD 40+	Yards 300+	TD 1-9	TD 10-39	TD 40+	Yards 100+	TD 1-9	TD 10-39	TD 40+	Yards 100+	FG 18-39	FG 40-49	FG 50+	PAT
Warren Moon	11	6	1	4	1											
Cody Carlson	5	4		2	1											
Lorenzo White					7			3		1		2				
Gary Brown					1											
Haywood Jeffires									7	2		1				
Ernest Givins									6	4		2				
Curtis Duncan									1			2				
Webster Slaughter									1	3						
Leonard Harris									1	1						
Pat Coleman																
Al Del Greco													15	5	1	41

Indianapolis Colts

Season Review — The Colts completed one of the best turnarounds in NFL history, going from 1-15 to 9-7 under new head coach Ted Marchibroda. They won their last five games by a total of only 20 points. It was a remarkable comeback, considering quarterback Jeff George struggled and the running game was weak. Even Steve Emtman and Quentin Coryatt, whom the Colts drafted with the first two overall picks in the draft, were injured and missed the last two months of the season. Both of them, however, proved to be impact players, as did rookie halfback Rodney Culver, who scored nine touchdowns. Backup quarterback Jack Trudeau was calm in the storm when George was injured for six games.

Offseason Update — Indianapolis signed two top offensive linemen in Kirk Lowdermilk and Will Wolford, and they will give quarterback Jeff George the best protection of his career. There will be changes at wide receiver, where Bill Brooks left for Buffalo, Aaron Cox came in from the Rams and Sean Dawkins, the second-rated rookie, was picked up in the draft. The Colts hope running back Roosevelt Potts, a second-round draft pick, can help a very weak position.

Significant 1992 Injuries — The biggest injuries were on defense, where the top two draft picks, Steve Emtman and Quentin Coryatt, were forced onto injured reserve. On offense, quarterback Jeff George missed three games early and then three after midseason with injuries.

Quarterbacks — Jeff George looked like a phenom as a rookie in 1990, but he hasn't done much since then. Last year, he threw only seven touchdown passes against 15 interceptions, and by the end of the season, fans were calling for Jack Trudeau. George has everything he needs to be a great quarterback, but he seems to throw into coverages too much. Trudeau had a bad 4-8 TD-to-interception ratio last year, but he moved the team and won some games down the stretch. If George falters this year, look for Trudeau to get the call.

Running Backs — The Colts have finished dead last in the NFL in rushing the last two years, and their 2.9-yard rushing average in '92 was the worst in the league. Rodney Culver was the only back to score in 1992 — he had nine touchdowns — but he isn't going to be the team's feature back. Anthony Johnson rushed for 592 yards and caught 49 passes, but he shouldn't be an every-down back. Ken Clark is just average. So who will be No.1 this year? How about Roosevelt Potts, the team's second-round draft pick? He might be the real thing.

Wide Receivers — The addition of first-round draft pick Sean Dawkins gives Indianapolis the big over-the-middle receiver it has lacked. George needed someone with speed to throw to, so they signed Aaron Cox, who has been injury-prone. Add to the mix starters Reggie Langhorne (team-leading 65 receptions for 811 yards in 1992) and Jessie Hester (52 for 792 yards) and you have a deep and talented receiving corps. Now it's up to George. Last year, the Colts went 11 games without a TD reception by a wide receiver and got only three all season.

Tight Ends — The Colts don't have a big blocking tight end, but Kerry Cash and Charles Arbuckle are fine receivers. Cash has been injury-prone, but last year he caught 43 passes — the most by a Colts tight end since 1979 — for 521 yards and three touchdowns. Arbuckle added 13 receptions late in the season.

Kicker — Dean Biasucci is literally on his last legs as the Colts' kicker. Last season he connected on just 16 of 29 field-goal attempts and is only 31 of 55 the last two years. He was only 8 of 19 at one point in 1992 before hitting 8 of 10. The Colts justify his kicking by saying his misses weren't off by much. That's their problem. If you have Biasucci on your fantasy team, he'll be your problem.

Defense — The addition of top draft picks Steve Emtman and Quentin Coryatt helped drastically in 1992, but, after they were lost to injuries for half of the season, the defense allowed only 36 points in the final four games. The Colts ranked 11th vs. the pass but were vulnerable against the run. Emtman scored the defense's only touchdown on the return of an interception. Chip Banks and Duane Bickett are the team's sack artists.

What to Expect in 1993 — It comes down to George and how he performs. If he plays well, Indianapolis could contend for a wild-card playoff spot. If not, the team will be fighting to stay out of the cellar. The Colts are not nearly as good as the 7-9 record of 1992 might indicate, but there is a lot of young talent, especially on defense.

Best Player to Draft — Running back Rodney Culver.

1992 GAME-BY-GAME STATISTICS

	CLE.	HOU.	BUF.	T.B.	NYJ	S.D.	MIA.	S.D.	MIA.	N.E.	PIT.	BUF.	N.E.	NYJ	PHX.	CIN.	
QUARTERBACKS																	
Jeff George				15-33 234 2	19-39 194	27-39 318 2	18-33 179	7-18 53	15-26 113	18-35 330 2				16-30 168	25-41 328 1	7-12 46	Att/Cmp Yards TD
Jack Trudeau		4-5 36	6-14 78		1-1 11	1-2 1		5-11 61	1-4 8		19-41 266 1	26-41 337	23-35 209	4-8 81 1		15-19 183 2	Att/Cmp Yards TD
RUNNING BACKS																	
Rodney Culver	19-52 1 7-78	17-25 2-17	14-14 2-12	1-2 1	3-2	1-(-1) 1-1	2-7 1		3-4	4-10 1 1-1 1	2-3 1 1-4 1	5-10 1	28-53 5-46	3-21	5-7	14-92 1 7-51	Att/Yards TD Rec/Yards TD
Anthony Johnson	6-15 3-21 1	1-11 3-31	5-13 4-34	20-67 3-23	15-75 4-42 1	9-6 4-28	16-55 4-22	11-28 4-17	11-37 7-163	20-77 2-4	19-68 3-34	13-50 1-6		17-43 3-13	14-41 5-85 1		Att/Yards TD Rec/Yards TD
Ken Clark	2-3			4-8	6-28 4-38	11-48		2-1	1-1		14-45 1-8						Att/Yards TD Rec/Yards
RECEIVERS																	
Reggie Langhorne	2-39 1	1-10		4-77	5-57	4-30	3-37	2-13	4-47	4-79	8-98	5-67	4-39	5-71	6-76	8-71	Rec/Yards TD
Jessie Hester	4-55	2-16	3-42	3-82 1	3-36	8-105	3-37	3-34	1-12	1-11	2-88	6-80	1-13	2-27	8-97	2-57	Rec/Yards TD
Aaron Cox	2-25	1-16		1-8	1-26		5-73	1-13	5-74	2-26							Rec/Yards TD
Kerry Cash		1-3	3-37	1-14 1	2-24	2-55	6-66	1-10	4-24	1-23 1	1-22	2-42	7-65	1-104	2-14	3-18 1	Rec/Yards TD
Charles Arbuckle												9-106	3-23	1-23 1			Rec/Yards TD
KICKERS																	
Dean Biasucci		1-1	0-1	1-1	2-5	0-1	1-3			2-4		3-5	2-3	1-1	3-4		FG/FGA

1992 SEASON STATISTICS

PLAYERS	PASSING				RUSHING				RECEIVING				KICKING			
	TD 1-9	TD 10-39	TD 40+	Yards 300+	TD 1-9	TD 10-39	TD 40+	Yards 100+	TD 1-9	TD 10-39	TD 40+	Yards 100+	FG 18-39	FG 40-49	FG 50+	PAT
Jeff George	3	3	1	3	1											
Jack Trudeau	2	2		1												
Rodney Culver					6	1			2							
Anthony Johnson									2	1	1					
Ken Clark																
Reggie Langhorne										1						
Jessie Hester										1		1				
Aaron Cox																
Kerry Cash									1	2		1				
Charles Arbuckle										1		1				
Dean Biasucci													9	6	1	24

Kansas City Chiefs

Season Review — Quarterback Dave Krieg was supposed to be the missing piece to a Super Bowl puzzle. Instead, the Chiefs needed three defensive touchdowns in their last game to even make the playoffs. An 8-4 start evaporated into a struggle for the playoffs, and, even though they qualified for postseason play for the third straight year, the season was a disappointment. The offense was inconsistent at best, even with three solid runners in Barry Word, Christian Okoye and Harvey Williams. Each was capable of 1,000 yards, but they totaled only 1,317 yards between them. Neil Smith and Derrick Thomas, each of whom had 14.5 sacks, continued to be the center of attention on defense.

Offseason Update — Quarterback Joe Montana was acquired in a trade with the 49ers, and he is already being expected to get the team to the Super Bowl. Wide receiver Danan Hughes (seventh round) might be a sleeper in the draft. Alonzo Highsmith, a former No. 1 draft pick, was signed as a free agent.

Significant 1992 Injuries — Running back Barry Word was sidelined for two games at two different points in the second half of the season, and wide receiver Tim Barnett missed a month early on.

Quarterbacks — The Chiefs have finally found the quarterback they think will get them to the Super Bowl in Joe Montana, and he might just do that as long as he stays healthy. Montana has played just two quarters in the last two years and he has always been injury prone. But he may prove this year that he is still the best quarterback in the league. Dave Krieg is now the best backup in the NFL.

Running Backs — Like last year, who is going to be the running back? Last year Barry Word, Christian Okoye and Harvey Williams split time and coach Marty Schottenheimer admitted after the season had ended he had made a mistake in not choosing a top back. He'll do that this year, but in the offseason it was still unknown as to which one it would be (and one of them might be traded). Williams has the most long-range potential and is the favorite to win the job, Okoye is the best runner at the goal line and might be the starting fullback and Word is the best combination of the two. The Chiefs have gone away from their power running game to a two-back set. Here's a hint: Okoye is best against 3-4 defenses and Word the best vs. four-man odd fronts. Alonzo Highsmith is trying to make his final comeback, and Todd McNair is one of the finest third-down backs in the game.

Wide Receivers — One of Montana's biggest problems is trying to figure out who are his top receivers, and, with the shift in offensive philosophy, this position becomes more of a focal point. Tim Barnett and speed receivers Willie Davis and J.J. Birden will battle for starting assignments. Davis averaged a league-high 21.0 yards per reception last year and should win one spot. Barnett scored four touchdowns last year, and Birden was the leading receiver among the wideouts with 42 catches. He might be used as the third-down specialist. Fred Jones and Tony Hargain also figure in the picture, and rookie Danan Hughes could surprise if he doesn't play baseball.

Tight Ends — Jonathan Hayes is strictly an in-line blocker, so the Chiefs are looking for a receiver to use in the new offense. A former wideout, Keith Cash should win the position. Last year he caught 12 passes and scored twice. He can really fly after catching the ball.

Kicker — Nick Lowery has hit an amazing 89 percent of his field goals the last three seasons, so he obviously isn't getting old yet. In 1992 he scored 105 points, passing the 100-point barrier for the fifth straight season and ninth in the last 10. He was 22 of 24 on field goals and 4 of 5 from 40 yards and beyond. Believe it or not, he did miss a 20-yarder. That won't happen again.

Defense — The Chiefs scored nine touchdowns on defense in 1992 and set up 112 points to help a very conservative offense. It also made 50 sacks, forced 39 turnovers and allowed only 270 yards per game while ranking fifth in the league. For fantasy football, it's the one to draft first. Derrick Thomas and Neil Smith are among the league's best sackers.

What to Expect in 1993 — If Montana doesn't get injured this year, the Chiefs will be one of the favorites to go to the Super Bowl; otherwise they are merely contending for the division title with Krieg. Montana is a good gamble, but the offensive personnel doesn't come close to resembling what is needed in the new scheme. That could cause problems.

Best Players to Draft — Quarterback Joe Montana, whichever of the running backs wins the starting job, and kicker Nick Lowery.

1992 GAME-BY-GAME STATISTICS

	S.D.	SEA.	HOU.	RAID.	DEN.	PHI.	DAL.	PIT.	S.D.	WAS.	SEA.	NYJ	RAID.	N.E.	NYJ	DEN.	
QUARTERBACKS																	
Dave Krieg	15-25	13-19	17-30	9-18	22-31	12-26	16-31	9-27	10-28	19-29	11-15	17-21	18-33	10-21	18-34	14-25	Att/Cmp
	154	231	177	80	301	272	170	82	114	302	103	222	276	196	259	176	Yards
		1	1		1	3				2		2	1	1	1	2	TD
RUNNING BACKS																	
Barry Word	18-37	13-46	22-114	27-125	21-84		13-46	8-32		19-85		13-30	4-4			5-4	Att/Yards
	1	1					1			1							TD
	1-22	2-18			3-19		1-5					1-9				1-7	Rec/Yards
																	TD
Harvey Williams	5-9	2-1			1-(-4)		6-28	3-12	6-24	19-88	3-11	15-42	1-(-1)	27-86	11-36	1-8	Att/Yards
										1							TD
	1-8					1-0					1-2				1-2	1-2	Rec/Yards
																	TD
Christian Okoye		18-63	8-17	8-35	4-4	16-48	5-17	11-73	19-38	8-7	3-7	4-10	1-(-1)	27-86	11-36	1-8	Att/Yards
									1	2				1	1	1	TD
Todd McNair	1-3		4-29		1-6	1-12		2-14	3-34		3-13	2-(-3)	4-16				Att/Yards
			1														TD
	3-20	3-42	5-31	5-28	3-30	1-6	3-16	4-27	2-18	1-36	3-9	2-21	3-57	1-10	4-21	1-8	Rec/Yards
																	TD
RECEIVERS																	
J.J. Birden	3-30	1-72	6-77		3-46	3-79	1-10	4-46	1-15	7-60	1-28	3-41	5-88	1-24	1-15	2-13	Rec/Yards
		1				2											TD
Willie Davis	1-6	2-42	1-5	1-10	5-127	5-167	6-100	1-9	2-36	1-8	2-20	3-79	1-24	1-43	3-35	1-45	Rec/Yards
					1	1								1			TD
Tim Barnett	2-29	1-12	1-14	1-26				3-30	6-148	2-30	2-19	2-17	1-14	1-77	2-26		Rec/Yards
									2		1			1			TD
Fred Jones	1-10	1-32	4-50	1-7	3-31	1-7	2-24			2-19		1-9	1-20	1-56			Rec/Yards
																	TD
Keith Cash	1-15	2-10			2-26							1-2	3-35	2-20	1-5		Rec/Yards
												1	1				TD
KICKERS																	
Nick Lowery	1-1	2-2	2-3	2-2	4-5	1-1	1-1		3-3		1-1	3-3		2-2			FG/FGA

1992 SEASON STATISTICS

PLAYERS	PASSING				RUSHING				RECEIVING				KICKING			
	TD 1-9	TD 10-39	TD 40+	Yards 300+	TD 1-9	TD 10-39	TD 40+	Yards 100+	TD 1-9	TD 10-39	TD 40+	Yards 100+	FG 18-39	FG 40-49	FG 50+	PAT
Dave Krieg	5	3	7	2	2											
Barry Word					3		1	2								
Harvey Williams					1											
Christian Okoye					6											
Todd McNair					1				1							
J.J. Birden										1	2					
Willie Davis										3	3					
Tim Barnett									1	1	2	1				
Fred Jones																
Keith Cash									2							
Nick Lowery													18	3	1	39

Los Angeles Raiders

Season Review — The Raiders finished 7-9 while juggling three quarterbacks and three halfbacks, and their minus-19 turnover ratio was the worst in the league. Jay Schroeder and Todd Marinovich played most of the season, then longtime veteran Vince Evans took over in the last game. Eric Dickerson was acquired in a Draft Day trade, but he played like his best days were behind him, rushing for only 729 yards. And Marcus Allen, the wily veteran, was in Al Davis' doghouse and asked to be traded at the end of the year. The best player on offense was wide receiver Tim Brown, who led the team with 49 receptions and seven touchdowns. Veteran defensive lineman Howie Long continued to amaze, as he turned in another solid performance.

Offseason Update — The new quarterback is Jeff Hostetler, who was let go by the Giants and signed as a free agent. Jay Schroeder was then let go by the Raiders. And the drafting of quarterback Billy Joe Hobert in the third round might signal the end of the experiment with Todd Marinovich. Marcus Allen was expected to leave via free agency, but Gaston Green was picked up in a trade with Denver. Wide receiver Mervyn Fernandez was traded to San Francisco.

Significant 1992 Injuries — Backup wide receiver Sam Graddy, who missed nine games because of a broken right arm, was the only casualty of the skill-position players.

Quarterbacks — Jeff Hostetler is the new quarterback. Although he doesn't seem to fit the Raiders' vertical passing game, he should be more consistent than Jay Schroeder was the last few years. Hostetler threw eight touchdowns and only three interceptions in '92 and will be working with the best group of wide receivers he has ever had. The Todd Marinovich experiment seems to have failed, because the Raiders drafted Washington's Billy Joe Hobert in the third round.

Running Backs — One of these years the Raiders are just going to hand the ball to Nick Bell and keep giving it to him, and it might be this year. However, the Raiders acquired Gaston Green in the offseason, and he might turn into the top back. Green has tremendous speed but not much in the way of moves. Eric Dickerson, the team's leading rusher with 729 yards last year, figures in the picture somewhere. But, with three halfbacks on the roster, one of them isn't going to get much playing time. Last year, the team struggled to find a way to use three halfbacks (Marcus Allen instead of Green) before finally settling on a rotation of Dickerson and Bell for the second half of the season. Steve Smith is an effective inside runner and dependable receiver.

Wide Receivers — Tim Brown has turned into one of the most productive wide receivers in the league. Last year, he led the Raiders with 49 receptions and seven touchdowns. There are a lot of possibilities at the other position. Willie Gault started every game last year but caught only 27 passes, although he averaged 18.8 yards per reception. Too often he just didn't make anything happen. Alexander Wright showed some potential after being acquired in a trade from Dallas midway through last season, and Sam Graddy even showed some progress. In May, the Raiders were negotiating with Raghib "Rocket" Ismail, so he might wind up starting and showcasing his talents. Olanda Truitt was drafted in the fifth round. Mervyn Fernandez, a solid starter just a year ago, was traded to the 49ers.

Tight Ends — Ethan Horton dropped too many passes last year and slipped to 33 catches and only two scores. He could be one of the best tight ends in the NFL with more consistency. Andrew Glover looked impressive with 15 catches, and second-year man David Jones has lots of potential.

Kicker — Which is the real Jeff Jaeger? In 1991, he was the best placekicker in the NFL, hitting 29 of 34 field goals and scoring 116 points, but last year he connected on only 15 of 26 and slipped to 73 points. In fact, he missed as many field goals in the first three games as he did in all of '91. He should be able to bounce back, although he might not score 100 points this year.

Defense — The Raiders ranked ninth in total defense in 1992 (12th vs. the run and 10th vs. the pass). But the team recovered only seven fumbles and made just 12 interceptions. Thus, it scored only eight points (blocked punt for touchdown and a safety) on defense. Defensive end Anthony Smith had a team-high 13 sacks, and Howie Long added nine.

What to Expect in 1993 — Another season out of the playoff picture. The Raiders have some solid talent but too many questions and too many weaknesses. Jeff Hostetler has yet to prove he can lead a team for an entire season. But, in the AFC West, which is really up for grabs, a surprise could be in order. Just don't bet on it.

Best Player to Draft — Wide receiver Tim Brown.

1992 GAME-BY-GAME STATISTICS

	S.F.	DAL.	CHI.	RAID.	PHX.	RAMS	SEA.	WAS.	G.B.	DEN.	PHI.	DAL.	WAS.	PHX.	K.C.	PHI.	
QUARTERBACKS																	
Jeff Hostetler				9-17		5-9	15-29	9-16	6-12	11-28				10-16	20-33		Att/Cmp
				142		94	161	133	59	154				131	202		Yards
				1		1	2			1				2	1		TD
Jay Schroeder	7-24	25-40		1-2		9-19	0-3	11-27	10-23	16-30	14-19	12-18	10-24	4-13	4-11		Att/Cmp
	181	380		18		84		127	108	160	166	93	93	25	41		Yards
		2				1		1	1	3		3					TD
Todd Marinovich			33-59	12-26	14-23	11-21	0-3	8-23	3-10								Att/Cmp
			395	161	216	188		117	25								Yards
			1		1	2		1									TD
RUNNING BACKS																	
Eric Dickerson	22-58	10-28	6-22	12-69	12-52	16-52	9-24	8-42	9-28	10-31	16-107	17-103	23-77	11-25	6-11		Att/Yards
			1	1						1							TD
		2-14		1-4	2-11	2-9			1-5		2-12			1-14	3-16		Rec/Yards
					1												TD
Nick Bell	9-42	2-5	2-5	3-17	2-2		10-97	2-4	3-21	13-35	7-38	2-6	5-19		21-75		Att/Yards
	1						1								1		TD
Steve Smith	8-25	3-10	3-20	2-7	5-21	3-4	4-7	3-8	3-7	2-2	2-13		1-2	1-	(-4)		Att/Yards
																	TD
	5-44	3-28	1-4	3-26	2-15		1-4	2-13		3-34	2-6		4-39	2-4			Rec/Yards
Marcus Allen	1-4	4-22	8-52	6-(-3)		10-37	10-38	3-9	6-23	1-3	1-5	4-20	5-37	1-2	2-12	5-40	Att/Yards
		1						1									TD
		3-49	8-57	1-10		1-11			1-14		2-21	3-34	1-8	3-23	1-13	4-37	Rec/Yards
											1						TD
RECEIVERS																	
Tim Brown	2-45	6-104	2-29		2-80	1-52	1-22	2-28	4-41	3-17	6-79	6-60		3-33	3-15	8-88	Rec/Yards
		1			1	1			1		1				1	1	TD
Willie Gault	2-72	3-39	3-45	3-37	3-63	2-47	2-13	1-31	1-8	2-33		1-29	1-17	2-24		1-50	Rec/Yards
			1					1					1				TD
Ethan Horton	1-28	5-88	3-22	3-48	3-33	1-22	1-26	1-13	1-9	3-41	3-28	5-18	1-6			2-17	Rec/Yards
									1			1					TD
Andrew Glover		1-11	1-14		3-28	1-9	2-32	1-10	2-35	1-15	1-1				1-22	1-1	Rec/Yards
											1						TD
KICKERS																	
Jeff Jaeger	2-2	0-3	3-5	0-1	2-4	2-2	1-1		1-1	2-2	1-2	1-2		0-1			FG/FGA

1992 SEASON STATISTICS

PLAYERS	PASSING				RUSHING				RECEIVING				KICKING			
	TD 1-9	TD 10-39	TD 40+	Yards 300+	TD 1-9	TD 10-39	TD 40+	Yards 100+	TD 1-9	TD 10-39	TD 40+	Yards 100+	FG 18-39	FG 40-49	FG 50+	PAT
Jeff Hostetler	2	6			2	1										
Jay Schroeder	5	6		1												
Todd Marinovich	1	2	2	1												
Eric Dickerson					1		1	2	1							
Nick Bell					2		1									
Steve Smith										1						
Marcus Allen					2					1						
Tim Brown									3	2	2	1				
Willie Gault									1	3						
Ethan Horton									2							
Andrew Glover									1							
Jeff Jaeger													7	5	3	28

Los Angeles Rams

Season Review — Jim Everett began to break out of his two-year-long doldrums, throwing for 3,323 yards and 22 touchdowns. As expected, Chuck Knox bolstered what had been an anemic running game. Cleveland Gary returned to form and rushed for 1,125 yards and topped the team with 52 receptions. Flipper Anderson scored seven touchdowns, and Henry Ellard caught 47 passes to lead the wideouts. Another Ram who rebounded in 1992 was Kevin Greene, who led the team in tackles and sacks after switching back to linebacker. For the most part, the Rams' defensive woes, which saw them rank next to last in the NFC, were a product of their inexperience. Two rookies, Sean Gilbert and Marc Boutte, started up front. The last game saw running back David Lang score three TD's and Todd Kinchen return two punts for scores.

Offseason Update — Jerome Bettis, the tenth player chosen overall in the April draft, will compete with Cleveland Gary for the starting job. Also picked up in the draft were tight end Troy Drayton, running back Russell White and wide receiver Sean LaChapelle, all of whom will make the team. Fullback Robert Delpino and wide receiver Aaron Cox were lost in free agency.

Significant 1992 Injuries — Running back Robert Delpino was sidelined for six games in the middle of the year with a knee injury. Wide receiver Aaron Cox was once again shelved for a lengthy period, this time with a hamstring injury. And tight end Damone Johnson was out the last 12 games because of a left shoulder injury.

Quarterbacks — In 1992, Jim Everett had his best season since 1989 and moved back among the top fantasy quarterbacks with 23 touchdown passes. He doesn't throw long as much as he used to because the offense calls for a lot of underneath passes. But he's solid and could even improve upon his 1992 numbers. Mike Pagel could be ousted as the primary backup by promising youngster T.J. Rubley.

Running Backs — Chuck Knox finally has his every-down feature back in fullback Jerome Bettis, his first-round draft pick from Notre Dame. Bettis is a combination halfback-fullback who can run inside and out. In the third round of the draft, the Rams chose Russell White, another

back with lots of promise. That could leave Cleveland Gary out of the picture, even though he rushed for 1,125 yards, led the team in receiving and scored 10 touchdowns last year. If he stays on the team — Knox doesn't like the way he fumbles the ball — then neither he nor Bettis will be the dominant back. David Lang will also push for more playing time after looking impressive at the end of 1992. The Rams want to use a two-back power scheme this season.

Wide Receivers — Henry Ellard slipped noticeably last season with 47 catches and only three touchdowns, but Willie "Flipper" Anderson had his best year with seven scores. Ellard is no longer a feared receiver, and Anderson has never developed into the deep threat he was thought to be. However, they do provide a good tandem for Everett to throw to. Jeff Chadwick and Todd Kinchen are good reserves.

Tight Ends — The Rams were deep at the position but still drafted Troy Drayton in the second round. A former wide receiver, he adds a new dimension to the offense because of his speed. Jim Price, Damone Johnson, Pat Carter and Travis McNeal add lots of depth, but at least two of them will be gone.

Kicker — Tony Zendejas continues to kick for the Rams, although he'll never match his 1991 season when he hit on all 17 of his field-goal attempts to set a league record. In 1992, he scored 93 points on 15 of 20 kicking. He's OK but nothing special.

Defense — In 1992, the Rams ranked 27th vs. the run while allowing 2,231 yards and 22 touchdowns. Opposing offenses also converted on 45 percent of their third-downs. They did force 33 turnovers, but got only one touchdown off them (as well as a safety). In free agency, the Rams lost Kevin Greene but signed Fred Stokes and Shane Conlan.

What to Expect in 1993 — Knox has the Rams on the comeback, though they are still a year or two away from contending again in the division. The offense should be strong, but the team's defense is the weak point. Last year, Los Angeles allowed an average of nearly 24 points a game, and the draft brought in mostly offensive players.

Best Players to Draft — Quarterback Jim Everett and running back Jerome Bettis.

1992 GAME-BY-GAME STATISTICS

	BUF.	N.E.	MIA.	NYJ	S.F.	N.O.	NYG	ATL.	PHX.	DAL.	S.F.	MIN.	T.B.	N.O.	G.B.	ATL.	
QUARTERBACKS																	
Jim Everett	18-35 / 160 / 1	10-22 / 130	17-32 / 229 / 1	13-25 / 151 / 1	20-24 / 232 / 2	11-20 / 165	18-21 / 242 / 2	22-33 / 253 / 4	21-32 / 248 / 1	22-37 / 251 / 2	13-29 / 158 / 1	12-23 / 174 / 1	25-38 / 342 / 3	24-42 / 226 / 2	24-44 / 222 / 1	11-18 / 140	Att/Cmp, Yards, TD
Mike Pagel	1-3 / 10											7-17 / 89 / 1					Att/Cmp, Yards, TD
RUNNING BACKS																	
Cleveland Gary	9-24 / 3-28	19-71 / 2 / 1-0	17-76 / 3-11	19-74 / 2-11	18-110 / 3-10	19-38 / 1	31-126 / 2 / 4-27	18-144 / 7-39 / 2	17-55 / 1 / 7-60	29-110 / 1 / 7-44 / 1	11-35 / 1-8	8-13 / 2-11	15-47 / 3-7	13-58 / 3-28	16-48 / 4-4	20-96 / 2-5	Att/Yards, TD, Rec/Yards, TD
Robert Delpino	9-30 / 5-46 / 1	8-50 / 2-19		2-10 / 4-27	5-7								4-8 / 2-12	1-(-1) / 3-17	1-3 / 1-8	2-8 / 1-10	Att/Yards, TD, Rec/Yards, TD
David Lang				1-(-1)		2-4	1-1 / 1 / 2-38	1-(-2) / 2-84 / 1	1-24	1-7		11-62 / 1-19	4-13 / 2-26	1-1 / 1 / 3-17	4-72 / 3 / 4-36	8-53 / 2-32	Att/Yards, TD, Rec/Yards, TD
RECEIVERS																	
Henry Ellard	2-8		4-73	3-50	3-33	5-89		2-35	3-54 / 1	2-23	3-59 / 1	5-83	2-43	4-70 / 1	8-94	1-13	Rec/Yards, TD
Willie Anderson	3-30	2-57	3-57 / 1	1-31 / 1	3-33 / 1	1-44	1-31		1-7	3-77	2-20	5-73 / 1	4-63 / 1	2-23 / 1	5-54 / 1	2-57	Rec/Yards, TD
Jeff Chadwick	1-7	1-8	5-67		1-15		2-26 / 1	6-58		4-38 / 1	2-30	2-32	3-59 / 1	1-7	1-15		Rec/Yards, TD
Jim Price	3-26				5-57	3-23	1-6	2-10 / 1	2-10	1-10	5-41	2-31 / 1	4-45	4-47	1-11	1-7	Rec/Yards, TD
Pat Carter		2-29	2-21	1-16	3-42 / 1	1-3	3-41 / 1	1-7	1-8	2-26		1-15	1-8 / 1			2-16	Rec/Yards, TD
KICKERS																	
Tony Zendejas		0-3	1-1	3-4	1-1	1-1	1-1			2-2	1-1	1-1	1-2		2-2	1-1	FG/FGA

1992 SEASON STATISTICS

PLAYERS	PASSING				RUSHING				RECEIVING				KICKING			
	TD 1-9	TD 10-39	TD 40+	Yards 300+	TD 1-9	TD 10-39	TD 40+	Yards 100+	TD 1-9	TD 10-39	TD 40+	Yards 100+	FG 18-39	FG 40-49	FG 50+	PAT
Jim Everett	8	12	2	1												
Mike Pagel																
Cleveland Gary					7			4	3							
Robert Delpino										1						
David Lang					4	1				1						
Henry Ellard										3						
Willie Anderson									1	5	1					
Jeff Chadwick									1	2						
Jim Price									1	1						
Pat Carter									3							
Tony Zendejas													12	3	0	38

Miami Dolphins

Season Review — The Dolphins won their first division title since 1985. With a 6-0 start, they brought back memories of the 1972 unbeaten team. Then reality struck, as they lost five of seven games before ending with three consecutive victories. The October acquisition of free-agent Keith Jackson was a big lift for the team and gave quarterback Dan Marino another weapon in his arsenal. However, the Dolphins offense struggled late in the season, scoring only six touchdowns in the last five and a half games. The Dolphins found a defense in 1992, with new stars such as Troy Vincent, Marco Coleman and Bryan Cox. They won their first playoff game in seven years, shutting out San Diego before losing to the eventual AFC champion Bills. Head coach Don Shula got his 300th NFL victory in Week 16, and was less than a full season away from catching George Halas on the career victories list.

Offseason Update — Miami went big for wide receivers, obtaining Irving Fryar from New England in a trade, Mark Ingram from the Giants in free agency and O.J. McDuffie in the draft. Running back Bobby Humphrey had offseason troubles and his status was up in the air, so the Dolphins drafted Terry Kirby, a big halfback-fullback. Backup quarterback Scott Secules and tight end Ferrell Edmunds were sent packing in free agency (and wide receiver Mark Clayton was expected to follow suit).

Significant 1992 Injuries — Running back Mark Higgs was placed on injured reserve for the playoffs because of torn cartilage in his right knee. Wide receiver Mark Clayton missed the first three games because of a neck injury, and tight end Ferrell Edmunds was out for six contests at midseason, but both will be with other teams.

Quarterbacks — Dan Marino remains the most prolific passer in the NFL, and he is assured of throwing for more than 20 touchdowns every season. With three new receivers, Marino might have a tremendous season, although it won't come close to 1984 when he threw 48 TD's. Scott Mitchell is the backup, and he looked pretty good in limited action last season. With Miami's offense, anybody would look good.

Running Backs — The problem on offense is at running back, where Mark Higgs is coming off a knee injury, Bobby Humphrey is questionable because of personal troubles and Aaron Craver has never panned out. Miami drafted Terry Kirby in the third round, and he might be the starter on opening day. Kirby is a big back who might be the steal of the draft. Higgs should be back 100 percent, but he isn't very dangerous, even though he does rush for 900 yards a season. As for Humphrey, who knows? Tony Paige is the fullback, though he's just a blocker and receiver out of the backfield. Don Shula knows he needs a balanced offense if he is to get back to a Super Bowl.

Wide Receivers — The addition of Irving Fryar, Mark Ingram and No. 1 pick O.J. McDuffie, plus the return of Mark Duper, make this the strength of the team. Fryar might have the best season of his career, Ingram will finally have a great quarterback throwing to him, and McDuffie is the youngster speedster Shula wanted. And don't forget about Duper, who scored seven times last year. There's even a lot of quality depth in Tony Martin and Fred Banks.

Tight Ends — The signing of Keith Jackson last year gave Marino his first threat at the position, and he will be another primary threat. He's already the top tight end in the NFL, and with Marino throwing to him, Jackson's statistics could be awesome. However, Miami needs a good backup.

Kicker — Pete Stoyanovich led the NFL in scoring last year with 124 points, although he did miss two clutch extra points, one of which helped lose a game. He has surpassed 100 points three of his four seasons while averaging 110 points. Stoyanovich has kicked 61 field goals the last two seasons and 101 in four years. His 80.8 percent field-goal accuracy mark is tops in NFL history. For fantasy football, he should be one of the top three picks among kickers.

Defense — The Miami defense was greatly improved in 1992, which is why the team was back in the playoffs and the Super Bowl hunt. It ranked 10th overall and forced 32 turnovers, returning three interceptions for touchdowns. Top rookies Marco Coleman, who had a team-high 14 sacks, and Troy Vincent looked like future stars.

What to Expect in 1993 — The Dolphins will contend for the AFC East title again with Buffalo, but to make a Super Bowl run they'll need one of the running backs to come through and the defense to play at least as good as it did in 1992. Shula didn't go after defense in the draft or free agency, and that could come back to haunt him if somebody gets injured or slips.

Best Players to Draft — Quarterback Dan Marino, wide receiver Irving Fryar, tight end Keith Jackson and kicker Pete Stoyanovich.

1992 GAME-BY-GAME STATISTICS

	CLE.	RAMS	SEA.	BUF.	ATL.	N.E.	IND.	NYJ	IND.	BUF.	HOU.	MIA.	S.F.	RAID.	NYJ	N.E.	
QUARTERBACKS																	
Dan Marino	25-35 322 1	21-37 223 2	24-39 260 1	21-33 282 3	20-40 250	21-30 294 4	25-45 355 2	14-26 225 2	22-28 245 2	22-33 321 2	19-40 237 1	26-42 259 1	19-31 192	16-26 234 1	15-30 206 2	21-39 217	Att/Cmp Yards TD
Scott Mitchell			1-1 18										1-5 14				Att/Cmp Yards TD
RUNNING BACKS																	
Mark Higgs	25-90 2 1-6	23-1111	21-54 1-11	15-37	13-58 2 2-11	18-63 1 2-15	18-50 1 1-11	8-22 1-7	20-107 1 4-41	12-34 1-21	10-35	15-46 1-12	6-11	26-94 1-6	17-80 1-1	9-23	Att/Yards TD Rec/Yards TD
Bobby Humphrey	2-11 4-24	7-46 2-5	4-7 2-13	4-22 6-72 1	7-42 2-33	2-7 5-57	1-5 3-33	8-46 1-9	10-56 4-45	7-30 3-43	6-33 4-36	2-13 6-40	8-21 4-42	8-33	6-11 1-4	20-88 1 7-51	Att/Yards TD Rec/Yards TD
Tony Paige	3-20	3-7 3-26	8-71	3-35 1	3-27	2-4 4-42	6-35		1-1 1 3-20	2-22		1-(-1) 2-16	2-8	2-16	4-31	3-30	Att/Yards TD Rec/Yards TD
RECEIVERS																	
Mark Duper	4-70 1	4-66 1	3-47	1-2	3-27	3-55 1	1-48 1	4-74 1	1-42	5-100		7-75 1	2-39	1-62 1	1-17	4-38	Rec/Yards TD
Irving Fryar	7-71	6-101 1	3-29	8-165 2	2-31	5-87 1		2-37	4-39	5-65	1-12	2-17	5-50	2-48	1-5	2-34	Rec/Yards TD
Mark Ingram	4-62	1-21		4-65	2-40	5-62	1-22	1-20					2-17	1-15	1-21 1	5-63	Rec/Yards TD
Tony Martin	4-74	1-11	5-72	2-47	2-54		5-90 1	1-12			2-28	3-39	3-32	3-28	1-55 1	1-11	Rec/Yards TD
Keith Jackson				4-64 1	3-43	4-70 2	3-26	4-74 1	6-69 1	5-36	4-44		7-63	2-38	3-24	3-43	Rec/Yards TD
KICKERS																	
Pete Stoyanovich	2-2	4-5	4-4	3-3	0-2	1-1			0-1	2-3	4-4	2-3	1-1	2-3	2-2	3-3	FG/FGA

1992 SEASON STATISTICS

PLAYERS	PASSING				RUSHING				RECEIVING				KICKING			
	TD 1-9	TD 10-39	TD 40+	Yards 300+	TD 1-9	TD 10-39	TD 40+	Yards 100+	TD 1-9	TD 10-39	TD 40+	Yards 100+	FG 18-39	FG 40-49	FG 50+	PAT
Dan Marino	9	10	5	3												
Scott Mitchell																
Mark Higgs					6	1		2								
Bobby Humphrey					1				1							
Tony Paige					1				1							
Mark Duper									1	3	3	1				
Irving Fryar										3	1	2				
Mark Ingram										1						
Tony Martin										1	1					
Keith Jackson									3	2						
Pete Stoyanovich													23	4	3	34

Minnesota Vikings

Season Review — New head coach Dennis Green turned whiners into winners and captured the division title by providing tough, prove-it-or-lose-it leadership that was desperately needed. He shipped out Herschel Walker, Joey Browner, Keith Millard and Wade Wilson, but Green couldn't decide on a quarterback, flip-flopping between Rich Gannon and journeyman Sean Salisbury late in the season when the playoffs were on the line. The Vikings' defense was a force all year, and it provided the team with a couple of victories with some of the eight turnovers that were returned for touchdowns. Defensive end Chris Doleman had a resurgence, and Audray McMillian and Todd Scott provided fireworks from the secondary. Terry Allen rushed for a club-record 1,102 yards and scored 15 touchdowns.

Offseason Update — The Vikings were hit hard in free agency on both sides of the line. They did sign quarterback Jim McMahon, who is expected to take over the starting job (Rich Gannon was being shopped in a trade). The top draft picks were running back-wide receiver Robert Smith and wideout Quadry Ismail. Heisman Trophy-winning quarterback Gino Torretta was drafted in the seventh round. Wide receiver Stephone Paige, who last played for Kansas City in 1991, was signed, too.

Significant 1992 Injuries — Cris Carter, the top wide receiver, missed the last four games with a broken collarbone but returned for the playoffs. No. 3 wideout Hassan Jones was sidelined twice with a back injury, missing seven games. Tight end Steve Jordan missed two games, and backup Mike Tice was out for a month.

Quarterbacks — Jim McMahon will be the starter on opening day unless he gets injured during the preseason, but don't expect him to last the entire year. He may be in the best shape of his career, or so the team says, but he is too fragile and will be working behind a line that lost two starters to free agency. The backup is Sean Salisbury, who looked pretty good last year, though he threw only five TD passes in 175 attempts. Rich Gannon fell out of favor with the coaching staff and was expected to be elsewhere.

Running Backs — Terry Allen was one of the top backs in the NFL in 1992 with a team-record 1,201 yards, an impressive 4.6-yard average and 15 touchdowns. He added 49 receptions, second on the team. Roger Craig is the main backup, and although he's getting old, he can still run well

and catch passes. Robert Smith was somewhat of a surprise as the Vikings' first-round draft pick. He is a breakaway back who will play on third downs and return kicks. He could also play wide receiver, but coach Dennis Green was planning on using him primarily at running back.

Wide Receivers — Cris Carter, Anthony Carter and Hassan Jones are all considered possession receivers with limited deep-threat potential. Minnesota needed a game-breaker and might have gotten him in the draft in Robert Smith, although he probably won't play much as a wide-out. Cris Carter has caught 25 TD passes the last four years and is the top receiver. Anthony Carter aged quickly and has lost some quickness, although he'll probably retain his starting position. Jones scored four times on his 22 receptions and is one of the league's better backups. Second-round draft pick Quadry Ismail will be counted on to add speed and could move into the starting lineup. Don't be surprised if Jake Reed comes on.

Tight Ends — Steve Jordan has also gotten old in a hurry, and he doesn't fit into the new offense very well. Last year he dropped to 28 receptions and two touchdowns. There's little behind him.

Kicker — Fuad Reveiz seems to have solidified his position as the Vikings' kicker after hitting 19 of 25 field-goal attempts last year for 102 points, his best season since 1985. His accuracy on long-range kicks was impressive, hitting on 3 of 4 from 50-plus yards. Assuming the Vikings' offense doesn't falter, Reveiz makes for a good No. 2 kicker on a fantasy team.

Defense — The Minnesota defense scored eight touchdowns and a safety in 1992, the second-most points in the league. The defense ranked eighth overall and allowed only 249 points. Defensive lineman Al Noga left in free agency, which won't help, but the overall defense is still very good. It made 51 sacks and forced 42 turnovers last year.

What to Expect in 1993 — Minnesota lost a lot in free agency and didn't replace those losses. But, if Jim McMahon can stay in the lineup, the Vikings are still the best overall team in the division. They might make it to the playoffs, but they are definitely a notch below teams like Dallas and San Francisco.

Best Players to Draft — Running back Terry Allen and wide receiver Cris Carter.

1992 GAME-BY-GAME STATISTICS

	G.B.	DET.	T.B.	CIN.	CHI.	DET.	WAS.	CHI.	T.B.	HOU.	CLE.	RAMS	PHI.	S.F.	PIT.	G.B.	
QUARTERBACKS																	
Jim McMahon							10-19 122	12-24 157 1									Att/Cmp Yards TD
Rich Gannon	21-44 266 2	20-36 190 1	3-6 57 1	25-32 318 4	20-25 187 1	8-10 146 2	16-29 177	7-15 157 1	16-21 168	9-28 111	5-12 26		9-21 102				Att/Cmp Yards TD
Sean Salisbury			12-22 162 1	3-6 32	13-24 149 1		1-1 8	2-3 39		4-12 30 1	23-34 238	12-23 122		7-17 131	20-33 292 2		Att/Cmp Yards TD
RUNNING BACKS																	
Terry Allen	12-140 5-53	12-33 1 4-32	26-87 1	11-40 2 5-64 1	11-72 5-69	13-50 1 2-24	14-51 1 2-6	20-74 1 1-4	14-84 2-15	13-44 1-6	17-75 1 1-1	23-88 10-110 1	18-82 2 4-31	9-39 1 2-12	33-172	20-100 1 2-22	Att/Yards TD Rec/Yards TD
Roger Craig	9-31 3-22	8-24 2-13	10-33	6-24	7-17 1 3-40	6-21 2-(-2)	5-12 3-25	8-26 1	3-12 2 3-37	6-26 1-22	6-36 1-10)		5-41 2-9	4-32 1-3	5-27	17-54 1-5	Att/Yards TD Rec/Yards
Keith Henderson		2-6		4-11		3-11 1-13	7-33	2-2 1-23		3-9 1-19	10-47 1 1-5			2-(-1)	3-1		Att/Yards TD Rec/Yards
RECEIVERS																	
Cris Carter	2-27	2-27	4-84	11-124 2	8-67 1	6-83 1	3-67	3-49	7-76	3-38	2-12	2-27					Rec/Yards TD
Anthony Carter	2-30	5-45 1		3-39	2-15	5-109 1	3-33	2-15	1-10	1-8	4-36	2-47	2-68	4-64	2-21		Rec/Yards TD
Hassan Jones	5-57 2	4-47		2-65 1	2-10	1-43 1					1-11	2-13	1-4				Rec/Yards TD
Joe Johnson				2-20			4-41	1-37	1-8	2-34	2-8 1	2-14	1-5	2-9		4-35	Rec/Yards TD
Steve Jordan	4-77	3-26		3-19					1-60 1	1-4	2-26	4-71	1-17	1-6	1-11	6-69 1	Rec/Yards TD
KICKERS																	
Fuad Reveiz	3-3	1-3	1-1			1-2	2-2	1-1		2-2	1-1	1-1	1-2	1-2	2-2	2-3	FG/FGA

1992 SEASON STATISTICS

PLAYERS	PASSING				RUSHING				RECEIVING				KICKING			
	TD 1-9	TD 10-39	TD 40+	Yards 300+	TD 1-9	TD 10-39	TD 40+	Yards 100+	TD 1-9	TD 10-39	TD 40+	Yards 100+	FG 18-39	FG 40-49	FG 50+	PAT
Jim McMahon			1													
Rich Gannon	1	8	3	1												
Sean Salisbury	1	4														
Terry Allen					12	1		3		2		1				
Roger Craig					4											
Keith Henderson		1			1											
Cris Carter										6		1				
Anthony Carter						1				1	1	1				
Hassan Jones									1	2	1					
Joe Johnson									1							
Steve Jordan										1	1					
Fuad Reveiz													11	5	3	45

TEAM EVALUATIONS

New England Patriots

Season Review — The Patriots were 1992's version of Team Turmoil. Too much was expected of them from the start, and they didn't have the talent to match their 6-10 mark in 1991. Coach Dick MacPherson was hospitalized with diverticulitis and missed the next seven games. The team was shut out three games and was forced to start four quarterbacks (Hugh Millen, Tommy Hodson, Scott Zolak and Jeff Carlson). The running game — especially second-year back Leonard Russell — was abysmal, with only 1,550 yards and six TD's. Receivers Irving Fryar and Marv Cook were consistent. Chief executive officer Sam Jankovich fired MacPherson after the season ended, then quit himself a day later. Bill Parcells, who led the Giants to two Super Bowl titles, was hired as the next coach, and hopes were raised immediately.

Offseason Update — Bill Parcells returned to football after two years in the announcer's booth and is the Patriots' new head coach. The only free agent who would factor in fantasy football is quarterback Scott Secules, the former Dolphin and Cowboy. New England lost three of its best offensive players when it traded wide receiver Irving Fryar to Miami, running back John Stephens to Green Bay and quarterback Hugh Millen to Dallas. The draft saw the arrival of quarterback Drew Bledsoe, the overall No. 1 pick, wide receiver Vincent Brisby and kicker Scott Sisson.

Significant 1992 Injuries — Quarterback was a merry-go-round all season because of injuries. First, Hugh Millen suffered a third-degree shoulder separation and missed nine games. Then Tommy Hodson took over before suffering a broken thumb. Next, rookie Scott Zolak moved into the position, but he suffered an ankle injury. (You can also throw in current quarterback Scott Secules, who spent 1992 on Miami's injured reserve list with a shoulder injury.) Running back Leonard Russell missed games at three different points in the season with injuries and never did play very well, and Ivy Joe Hunter was on I.R. all year with a knee injury. Wide receiver Hart Lee Dykes missed his second consecutive season with a broken kneecap.

Quarterbacks — Because of injuries, four quarterbacks started games in 1992, and the Patriots ranked 26th in passing. Experience will be a factor in choosing the new quarterback, and the contenders are Tommy Hodson, Scott Zolak and Scott Secules, though either Hodson or Zolak will be gone in September. Look for Secules to win the job, although he has thrown only 70 passes in four years as a pro. No. 1 pick Drew Bledsoe will get a chance, too, and he might be one quarterback who can do well as a rookie.

Running Backs — Leonard Russell is being counted on to be the top running back, but he needs to get back to his form of 1991 when he rushed for 959 yards and garnered Rookie of the Year honors. Last year he slipped to 390 yards. Jon Vaughn led the team with 451 yards rushing, but coach Bill Parcells doesn't like Vaughn's fumbling. Second-year pros Scott Lockwood, Kevin Turner and Sam Gash might get their chances. Parcells likes to pound away at defenses, and none of these guys are heavy-duty backs.

Wide Receivers — No matter who the quarterback is, he doesn't have much to throw to. Greg McMurtry and Michael Timpson should be No. 3 receivers, not starters. Last year they totaled only 51 receptions and two touchdowns between them. Second-round draft pick Vincent Brisby might have been a reach, but he has all the tools and just needs to develop them.

Tight Ends — Marv Cook and Ben Coates are the best receivers on the team. Cook caught 52 passes in 1992, far off his total of 82 the year before, but that was due to the team's quarterbacking problems. Coates is a good complement to Cook. He caught 20 passes and scored three times in '92. The two attack defenses differently. Cook is steady in the short areas, while Coates has the speed and ability to provide a dimension teams like from their tight ends.

Kicker — Charlie Baumann struggled last year and will be challenged in training camp by Scott Sisson, their fifth-round draft pick. Baumann was only 11 of 17 on field goals last year, when he scored the fewest points of any kicker who played in all 16 games. Sisson was a clutch kicker at Georgia Tech.

Defense — Bill Parcells is back in football and should eventually turn the New England defense into one of the league's sturdiest. But this year that won't be the case as it has too many holes. Because opposing quarterbacks were sacked only 20 times in 1992, the Patriots hoped they filled a need for pass rushers in free agency in linemen Leon Seals and Aaron Jones. The defense ranked 19th overall last year but allowed an average of 22.7 points per game. Bad defense or not, New England scored six touchdowns off turnovers last season, an excellent figure.

What to Expect in 1993 — The Patriots aren't a horrible team, but they will be lucky to leave the AFC East cellar. A lack of talent on offense will keep the defense on the field too long. Bill Parcells has to develop a running back to control the clock while Drew Bledsoe matures as a quarterback.

Best Player to Draft — Tight end Marv Cook.

1992 GAME-BY-GAME STATISTICS

	RAMS	SEA.	BUF.	NYJ	S.F.	MIA.	CLE.	BUF.	N.O.	IND.	NYJ	ATL.	IND.	K.C.	CIN.	MIA.	
QUARTERBACKS																	
Hugh Millen	18-32 145	17-27 185 1	24-33 202 1	23-33 259 3	20-34 181 1		17-33 194 2					5-11 37					Att/Cmp Yards TD
Tommy Hodson						25-43 267 2		17-26 171	8-22 58								Att/Cmp Yards TD
Scott Zolak									5-9 20	20-29 261 2	7-16 102	9-15 58	6-20 55	5-10 65			Att/Cmp Yards TD
RUNNING BACKS																	
Leonard Russell	18-71 / 4-9	18-81 / 3-5	18-59 / 1-(-3)	9-15 / 2-6		6-10	8-9	15-40	10-31 1 / 1-7			11-39	10-35 1				Att/Yards TD Rec/Yards TD
Jon Vaughn	1-3 / 1-(-1)	1-6	1-0	2-15	9-11 / 3-2	7-7 / 1-2	3-34	5-15	2-8 / 1-7	16-88 / 2-32	20-110 1 / 1-28	16-70 / 2-5	6-3	9-23	14-58 / 2-9	1-0	Att/Yards TD Rec/Yards TD
Scott Lockwood															5-39	30-123	Att/Yards TD
RECEIVERS																	
Greg McMurtry		2-31	7-69	1-6	7-84	3-35		4-36	3-12	1-65 1	2-17	1-16	2-12		1-8	1-33	Rec/Yards TD
Michael Timpson	4-51	2-23	1-7		1-14	6-74 1	3-41	2-18		3-54				1-11		3-22	Rec/Yards TD
Walter Stanley						1-15	2-48										Rec/Yards TD
Marv Cook	2-15	2-17	7-60 1	6-35 1		2-23	7-39	6-57	4-13	3-31	2-31	3-14	3-22	2-14	2-31	1-11	Rec/Yards TD
Ben Coates		1-6	4-31	3-23	5-45 1	1-6	3-35 1		1-7	1-2 1						1-16	Rec/Yards TD
KICKERS																	
Charlie Baumann	0-1			0-1	2-2	1-2	1-1			3-3	1-1	0-1	0-1	0-1	1-1	2-2	FG/FGA

1992 SEASON STATISTICS

PLAYERS	PASSING				RUSHING				RECEIVING				KICKING			
	TD 1-9	TD 10-39	TD 40+	Yards 300+	TD 1-9	TD 10-39	TD 40+	Yards 100+	TD 1-9	TD 10-39	TD 40+	Yards 100+	FG 18-39	FG 40-49	FG 50+	PAT
Hugh Millen	2	6														
Tommy Hodson		1	1													
Scott Zolak	1		1													
Leonard Russell					2											
Jon Vaughn					1			1								
Scott Lockwood								1								
Greg McMurtry										1						
Michael Timpson										1						
Walter Stanley																
Marv Cook									2							
Ben Coates									1	2						
Charlie Baumann													9	2	0	22

New Orleans Saints

Season Review — The Saints would have won the division title, but they couldn't defeat the 49ers, dropping both games, as well as contests with the Eagles and Bills, by a total of 13 points. New Orleans sent an unprecedented four linebackers to the Pro Bowl — Rickey Jackson, Vaughan Johnson, Sam Mills and Pat Swilling — and end Wayne Martin emerged as a pass-rushing force. But the offense remained average at best. When hot, quarterback Bobby Hebert formed a dangerous combination with Eric Martin (68 catches, five touchdowns). But for the most part, coach Jim Mora's troops relied on a ground game that was anything but spectacular. Rookie Vaughn Dunbar led the team with 565 yards rushing, but he lost his starting job by midseason. Morten Andersen tied for the NFC lead with 120 points.

Offseason Update — New Orleans will have a new quarterback in 1993, after Wade Wilson was signed as a free agent and Bobby Hebert was let go. The Saints also had what came out to be a free-agent swap of fullbacks with Chicago in Craig Heyward for Brad Muster. Fullback Buford Jordan retired. The draft brought in Irv Smith, the top tight end available, and running back Lorenzo Neal.

Significant 1992 Injuries — Before the preseason games even started, running back Allen Pinkett tore ligaments in a knee and was lost for the year. Wide receiver Floyd Turner suffered a broken thigh in Game 2 and missed the rest of the season. And running back Fred McAfee, after taking over the starting job in Game 14, immediately suffered a shoulder injury and was placed on injured reserve.

Quarterbacks — There's a battle at quarterback in the Crescent City, with Mike Buck, Wade Wilson and Steve Walsh in the hunt. Buck seems to be the favorite, although he has thrown only six passes as a pro. He has a great arm and looks good in practice, but he hasn't really grasped the system. Wilson looked fantastic in the final three games of last year when he passed for over 1,000 yards and 10 touchdowns. But that was with a bevy of outstanding receivers, and besides, Wilson's best years are behind him. Walsh has what Buck lacks and lacks what Buck has.

Running Backs — The Saints ranked only 17th in rushing last year, even through their backfield is deep and talented. Rookie Vaughn Dunbar led the team with 565 yards but seemed to lack confidence instead of relying on his instincts. Dalton Hilliard scored seven touchdowns (three rushing and four receiving) but is strictly a third-down back. Brad Muster wants to be the feature back, but

he's not as good as he thinks he is. However, he is a fine receiver and good runner who fits into a role and might do well in New Orleans. Fred McAfee is a very good backup, and Allen Pinkett will vie for playing time if he returns at 100 percent. Lorenzo Neal and Derek Brown were drafted in the fourth round. New Orleans didn't get its first rushing touchdown until the fifth game of last year and had only 10 all season.

Wide Receivers — Eric Martin is one of the most underrated receivers in the league. In 1992, he caught 68 passes for 1,041 yards in a ball-control offense. The receiver who plays opposite him always does well. In 1991 it was Floyd Turner (eight TD's but injured most of '92), and last year Quinn Early scored five times on 30 receptions. Torrance Small and Wesley Carroll are excellent backups who scare defenses.

Tight Ends — The Saints drafted Irv Smith in the first round, and he is the best tight end on the team in years. He is a good blocker who catches well and runs after the catch. Hoby Brenner, John Tice and Frank Wainright will fight for backup roles.

Kicker — Morten Andersen remains the best placekicker in the NFL and one of the top picks in fantasy football. In 1992, he scored 120 points with a conservative offense, the seventh time in the last eight years he has hit the century mark. He hit on 29 of 34 field goals, including his last 20 attempts, but he might not get as many opportunities this year if the team's quarterbacking is weak. Still, he's good for 100 points.

Defense — The New Orleans defense ranked second in total defense in 1992 and first against the pass. It allowed the fewest points in the league, only 202 (but 81 in the fourth quarter), and recorded 57 sacks. The loss of linebacker Pat Swilling in a trade to Detroit will hurt some, but defensive end Wayne Martin has turned into an All-Pro. The defense is getting old, however, with five starters in their 30s. New Orleans scored six touchdowns off turnovers in 1992, three each on fumbles and interceptions.

What to Expect in 1993 — Quarterback could be a problem in 1993 because nobody looks like the starter on a playoff-caliber team. If somebody comes through, the Saints will contend for the division title again, but they'll have to learn how to beat the 49ers. The defense will again be one of the NFL's best.

Best Players to Draft — Running back Brad Muster, wide receiver Eric Martin and kicker Morten Andersen.

1992 GAME-BY-GAME STATISTICS

	PHI.	CHI.	ATL.	S.F.	DET.	RAMS	PHX.	T.B.	N.E.	S.F.	WAS.	MIA.	ATL.	RAMS	BUF.	NYJ	
QUARTERBACKS																	
Bobby Hebert	12-30	13-25	9-19	25-40	15-19	15-24	19-26	14-27	14-26	22-35	-18	11-22	20-29	15-25	17-32	14-25	Att/Cmp
	156	264	119	267	155	166	355	173	198	301	142	135	244	238	189	185	Yards
	1	2	1	1		1	3	1	3	2	1			2	1		TD
Mike Buck					1-2									1-2			Att/Cmp
					10									0			Yards
																	TD
RUNNING BACKS																	
Vaughn Dunbar	11-27	13-47	16-85	12-47	22-70	14-68	11-15	8-25	17-52	1-2			1-2	13-91	5-10	10-24	Att/Yards
					1				1					1			TD
				1-(-1)	2-20	1-0		1-7	2-16	1-13					1-7		Rec/Yards
																	TD
Dalton Hilliard	2-20	7-39	4-20	3-3	7-29	7-44	4-8	14-55	11-42	12-34	13-53	5-15	8-28		4-16	14-38	Att/Yards
								1			1	1					TD
	1-10	3-29		3-19	2-16	3-26	3-60	5-60	4-51	6-88	5-20	3-16	2-16	1-11	2-16	5-27	Rec/Yards
							1	1	1	1							TD
Fred McAfee	1-0		1-(-1)	1-2			1-2			2-1	10-43	17-43	6-24				Att/Yards
												1	1				TD
												1-16					Rec/Yards
																	TD
RECEIVERS																	
Eric Martin	2-30	2-58	4-48	8-92	5-67	6-103	8-151	3-20	3-54	5-56	1-45	4-52	5-82	3-46	4-43	5-94	Rec/Yards
		1		1		1	1							1			TD
Quinn Early	2-53	1-44	1-11	3-75	1-13	2-16	2-85	1-11	3-62	1-10	2-10	1-32	4-48	2-44	1-5	3-47	Rec/Yards
			1				2		1		1						TD
Wesley Carroll	1-10	1-72	2-31	3-32	1-7	2-16		1-5		2-33	2-38	1-11		1-22	1-15		Rec/Yards
	1	1															TD
Torrance Small				4-29	2-21		1-10	2-55	1-9	5-55	1-8		1-9	2-24	4-58		Rec/Yards
										1				1	1		TD
Hoby Brenner	1-19	2-38			1-18	1-5			1-6			1-19	3-18	2-38			Rec/Yards
																	TD
KICKERS																	
Morten Andersen	2-3	0-1	1-1	1-2	2-3	2-2	1-1	3-4	1-1	2-2	2-2	1-1	5-5	1-1	3-3	2-2	FG/FGA

1992 SEASON STATISTICS

PLAYERS	PASSING				RUSHING				RECEIVING				KICKING			
	TD 1-9	TD 10-39	TD 40+	Yards 300+	TD 1-9	TD 10-39	TD 40+	Yards 100+	TD 1-9	TD 10-39	TD 40+	Yards 100+	FG 18-39	FG 40-49	FG 50+	PAT
Bobby Hebert	4	12	3	2												
Mike Buck																
Vaughn Dunbar					3											
Dalton Hilliard					1	2			1	3						
Fred McAfee					1											
Eric Martin									1	3	1	2				
Quinn Early									2	2	1					
Wesley Carroll										1	1					
Torrance Small										3						
Hoby Brenner																
Morten Andersen													18	8	3	33

New York Giants

Season Review — Maybe the highlight of the Ray Handley era was that he wasn't the first coach fired after the season. The shortest reign of any coach in New York history — 19 months — spelled the end of Handley, and some time later Dan Reeves moved east from Denver to take over. Future Hall of Famer Lawrence Taylor was planning to retire, but then he suffered a season-ending injury which caused him to rethink his plans. There was a merry-go-round at quarterback with three different starters because of injuries and a defense that aged quickly. Half-back Rodney Hampton proved to be one of the league's top runners with 1,141 yards and 14 touchdowns. Six losses in the final seven games and a season full of turmoil meant changes in New York as 1993 approached.

Offseason Update — Dan Reeves was fired in Denver and took over a month later in New York. Phil Simms was named the starting quarterback, prompting the departure of Jeff Hostetler. Wide receiver Mark Ingram left in free agency, but Mark Jackson and Mike Sherrard were signed, more than making up for that loss. The draft didn't help much, although Todd Peterson will vie for the placekicking job.

Significant 1992 Injuries — Quarterback Phil Simms didn't play the last 12 games because of an elbow injury, although he could have returned, Jeff Hostetler missed three games late after suffering a concussion, and even rookie Dave Brown was sidelined with a broken thumb. Wide receiver Mark Ingram missed November with a knee injury, and kicker Matt Bahr missed the last four games with a knee injury.

Quarterbacks — The Giants will throw the ball more in 1993; they ranked 25th in passing a year ago. Phil Simms is the unquestioned starter, and although he's getting old, he still can do a capable job. More than anything, Simms will be the the mentor for Dave Brown, who was chosen in last year's supplemental draft, costing them a first-round pick this year. The jury is still out on Brown, although the Giants love him. Time will tell.

Running Backs — Rodney Hampton has quickly made Giants fans forget about Joe Morris and Ottis Anderson. Last year he rushed for 1,141 yards and 14 touchdowns, but new head coach Dan Reeves is going to alter the offense some and that could affect Hampton's numbers. Still, he should be among the top half-dozen backs in the NFL.

Fullback Jarrod Bunch improved a lot last year, finishing with 501 yards and three scores. Dave Meggett is one of the best multipurpose backs, so Reeves certainly has a better backfield than he ever had in Denver.

Wide Receivers — The signings of Mark Jackson and Mike Sherrard shored up the receiving corps with ability and experience. They will compete with Stephen Baker and Ed McCaffrey for starting roles. Jackson will probably start, because he's one of Reeves' favorites from Denver. Neither Sherrard nor Baker has ever turned potential into production, and McCaffrey is best used as a possession receiver.

Tight Ends — Look for Derek Brown to be utilized more this year, and he certainly has the ability to be one of the game's best tight ends. He caught only four passes last year, with only 12 being thrown his way all season. Aaron Pierce didn't catch any, although he's a highly touted second-year pro. Howard Cross might be on the bubble, even though he caught 27 balls in '92.

Kickers — Matt Bahr and Ken Willis will compete for the job in training camp. Last year, Bahr did a capable job, connecting on 16 of 21 field goals in the first 12 games before being injured. He might have scored over 100 points if he had played all 16 games. Willis was cut by Tampa Bay after nine games but was just 10 of 16 for the season. Bahr has the edge, although he is getting up in age. Todd Peterson, the seventh-round draft pick from Georgia, will also compete.

Defense — The Giants' defense is no longer anywhere near as good as it was just a few years ago. In 1992, it ranked 18th overall and 25th vs. the run, and it produced only one defensive score and forced just 26 turnovers. Worse yet, the Giants allowed 367 points — an average of 23 points per game. Lawrence Taylor will be back following reconstructive knee surgery, but the outlook isn't good for his defensive mates.

What to Expect in 1993 — Reeves has proven he can take a team to the Super Bowl, but this team isn't going to get there. He will correct problems of the last two years under Ray Handley and have the Giants back to respectability, but that's about all you can ask of a team that grew old too quickly.

Best Player to Draft — Running back Rodney Hampton.

1992 GAME-BY-GAME STATISTICS

Player	S.F.	DAL.	CHI.	RAID.	PHX.	RAMS	SEA.	WAS.	G.B.	DEN.	PHI.	DAL.	WAS.	PHX.	K.C.	PHI.	
QUARTERBACKS																	
Phil Simms	20-37	25-42	19-30	19-29		18-32											Att/Cmp
	223	273	220	196		149											Yards
		3	2														TD
Kent Graham						2-4			2-2	11-26	12-28	8-16	7-21				Att/Cmp
						39			12	141	151	73	54				Yards
										1							TD
RUNNING BACKS																	
Rodney Hampton	16-77	17-64	22-94	18-49	21-167	11-38	20-69	23-138	15-44	20-87	10-47	10-33	13-64	12-51	18-84	12-35	Att/Yards
	2	1	1		1	2			2		1		1		3		TD
	2-22	5-36	1-3	6-29	1-31	1-7		3-13		1-0	2-15	2-13	1-8		2-32	1-6	Rec/Yards
																	TD
Jarrod Bunch	4-47		11-39	9-48	9-50	5-29	12-77	11-27	3-7	6-17	4-7	6-20	5-18	4-19	10-84	5-12	Att/Yards
				1	1			1									TD
	1-4	2-7	1-2			2-5			1-7		1-13					3-12	Rec/Yards
		1															TD
Dave Meggett	2-(-5)		2-16	2-4	1-3	1-15	1-5	3-39	1-4	2-11	5-25	3-22	3-6	2-2	2-2	2-18	Att/Yards
																	TD
	4-30	2-(-1)	1-9	2-16	1-(-1)	7-70	1-9	2-11	2-12	3-19	4-37	2-13		4-8	1-1	2-(-4)	Rec/Yards
								1			1						TD
RECEIVERS																	
Mark Jackson	1-15	4-59	1-6	2-26	5-59	2-21	3-90	5-113	2-32	3-108	5-76	3-20	3-39	4-38	3-33	2-10	Rec/Yards
		1			1		1	2		1		1	1				TD
Mike Sherrard	1-10	6-159	5-66	3-50	3-39		1-33	5-82	1-12	2-12		1-15	2-25	1-24	3-64	4-16	Rec/Yards
																	TD
Ed McCaffrey	5-56	5-82	4-40	4-33	3-37	2-12	1-7	4-45	1-26	3-27	5-73	6-105	3-33		3-34		Rec/Yards
					1		1	1			1				1		TD
Chris Calloway	2-19	2-23	2-22	1-12	1-20	2-27	1-10			1-25	1-14	2-15	1-5	3-33	4-54	4-56	Rec/Yards
															1		TD
Howard Cross	2-30	6-77	3-35				3-58	3-42		3-31	2-11	1-10	1-13	1-15		2-35	Rec/Yards
		1	1														TD
KICKERS																	
Matt Bahr			2-3	1-1	1-2	1-2	3-3	1-1	2-2	2-2	2-2	1-3					FG/FGA
Ken Willis	3-4	1-1	2-2	2-3	0-1		0-1		0-2				1-1		1-1		FG/FGA

1992 SEASON STATISTICS

PLAYERS	PASSING				RUSHING				RECEIVING				KICKING			
	TD 1-9	TD 10-39	TD 40+	Yards 300+	TD 1-9	TD 10-39	TD 40+	Yards 100+	TD 1-9	TD 10-39	TD 40+	Yards 100+	FG 18-39	FG 40-49	FG 50+	PAT
Phil Simms	3	2														
Kent Graham		1														
Rodney Hampton					10	3	1	2								
Jarrod Bunch					3				1							
Dave Meggett									1	1						
Mark Jackson									1	5	2	2				
Mike Sherrard												1				
Ed McCaffrey									1	4		1				
Chris Calloway										1						
Howard Cross									1	1						
Matt Bahr													13	3	0	27
Ken Willis													5	5	0	27

New York Jets

Season Review — The Jets' rebuilding took a step backward in 1992. Overconfidence after a 5-0 preseason played a major role, and they lacked an impact player on either side of the ball. But other factors were out of their control. Wide receiver Al Toon retired after suffering too many concussions, and defensive end Dennis Byrd was paralyzed in a November game after colliding with teammate Scott Mersereau. Quarterback Browning Nagle was given the starting job in training camp but failed to excite. He passed for 366 yards in the season opener, then struggled mightily the rest of the year. Defensive end Jeff Lageman was lost in Week Two with a knee injury, and running back Blair Thomas was again disappointing, even before missing half of the year.

Offseason Update — The Jets were one of the most active teams during the offseason. They acquired running back Johnny Johnson in a draft-day trade, and tight end James Thornton in free agency. Quarterback Ken O'Brien was shipped off to Green Bay and running back Freeman McNeil retired. Some middle-rounders were acquired in the draft — tight end Fred Baxter, running backs Adrian Murrell and Richie Anderson, and wide receiver Kenny Shedd.

Significant 1992 Injuries — Running back Blair Thomas was once again ineffective, and he missed seven games because of a groin injury and a sprained knee. Wide receiver Al Toon was forced to retire in November after recurring concussions.

Quarterbacks — The Jets fooled themselves into believing they could make the playoffs with a first-year starter at quarterback in 1992, so an 0-4 start was a slap of reality. Browning Nagle still thinks the starting job is his to lose. In reality, he lost it the day the Jets traded for Boomer Esiason. The team isn't going to pay Esiason $3 million to sit on the bench, which means Nagle goes back to his "quarterback of the future" role. Esiason is only 32 and just needs to repair his mechanics and start making right reads again.

Running Backs — When are the Jets going to admit that Blair Thomas has been a bust? Thomas might have his last chance to show what he can do, but he'll have to beat out draft-day acquisition Johnny Johnson to earn a starting

role. Johnson has too many personal troubles, but he's a great talent who could be a Pro Bowler with his head on right. Fullback Brad Baxter is one of the best goal-line runners around, and he showed late last season he could be a pretty good feature back, too.

Wide Receivers — With Al Toon gone, it's time for Rob Moore to take over and turn into a top-flight receiver. Last year, he caught 50 passes and scored four TD's, but he has yet to really reach his potential. Chris Burkett replaced Toon in the starting lineup and led the Jets with 57 catches, but he's more ideally suited as a No. 3 wideout. Terrance Mathis is a burner who scored three times in '92.

Tight Ends — Johnny Mitchell will take over the starting job this year. He has the potential to be one of the premier threats at the position in the NFL, but it might take a while for his raw talent to be developed. James Thornton will be the blocker, and fifth-round pick Fred Baxter will figure in somewhere.

Kickers — The Jets had the same kicker for 18 seasons (Pat Leahy), then used two in 1992. Cary Blanchard played the last 12 games, turning into an excellent acquisition off the waiver wire from New Orleans after replacing Jason Staurovsky. Blanchard hit on 16 of 22 field-goal attempts and scored 65 points for an anemic offense. He has both a strong leg and the range on shorter kicks. He will not be challenged by rookie Craig Hentrich for the job (Hentrich will compete as a punter).

Defense — The addition of free agents Ronnie Lott, Leonard Marshall and Eric Thomas and No. 1 draft pick Marvin Jones will tremendously help a defense that allowed almost 20 points a game last year and ranked 16th in the league. It returned three interceptions (of 39 turnovers) and forced a safety, but the losses of Jeff Lageman and Dennis Byrd to injuries hurt.

What to Expect in 1993 — The Jets are certainly not a playoff-caliber team, but they could surprise and walk off with another wild-card spot this year. Boomer Esiason wants to show people he can still play football, and there is talent on the offense. The defense was revamped during the offseason and will determine the fate of the team.

Best Player to Draft — Wide receiver Rob Moore.

1992 GAME-BY-GAME STATISTICS

	SEA.	RAID.	G.B.	MIN.	HOU.	PIT.	HOU.	CLE.	CHI.	NYJ	DET.	PIT.	CLE.	S.D.	N.E.	IND.	
QUARTERBACKS																	
Boomer Esiason	18-29	16-27	11-23	11-21	12-25	11-22	13-19	13-24	16-29	11-33	12-25				0-1		Att/Cmp
	115	154	128	97	151	86	139	192	172	109	64						Yards
		1	1		2		1	3	3								TD
Browning Nagle	21-37	9-29		19-39	20-33	6-16	19-32		14-25	8-24	9-24	13-27	14-22	13-33	12-18	15-28	Att/Cmp
	366	117		200	195	102	167		163	98	77	146	176	158	176	139	Yards
	2				2				1			1			1		TD
RUNNING BACKS																	
Blair Thomas	9-17	10-49	9-41	12-69	13-71	15-49	20-88		7-51		2-5						Att/Yards
																	TD
			2-12	2-14	1-8		2-15										Rec/Yards
																	TD
Brad Baxter	5-28	6-43	3-8	6-43	10-20	2-5	9-24	20-103	12-96	22-72	6-26	15-57	19-98	13-60	4-15		Att/Yards
				1	1		1			1			2				TD
	1-12				1-8		1-8	1-4									Rec/Yards
Freeman McNeil	3-23	4-28	2-0	4-19	6-23	4-7		11-37		9-33							Att/Yards
																	TD
		2-21	2-17		1-12	1-2		4-28	1-10	1-8	2-13				2-43		Rec/Yards
																	TD
Pat Chaffey			3-13	1-7			2-30	2-15			7-64	5-26	5-25	2-6			Att/Yards
							1										TD
RECEIVERS																	
Rob Moore	5-99	3-50	1-10	4-71	6-58		7-80	2-25	2-35	4-67	1-6	2-25	4-68	1-5	2-67	6-60	Rec/Yards
					1			1	1						1		TD
Chris Burkett	3-57	3-32	3-38	4-35	3-34	2-38	1-6	3-55	6-91		5-39	5-65	5-64	6-110	3-18	4-41	Rec/Yards
	1																TD
Terance Mathis	2-32		4-111		2-30		1-17	1-12	1-9	2-22		3-31	2-22	2-17		2-13	Rec/Yards
			1		1							1					TD
Rob Carpenter	6-109		2-16						2-17			1-12	2-8				Rec/Yards
			1														TD
Johnny Mitchell	1-23						1-18	4-78	2-22			3-41		1-1	2-20	2-7	Rec/Yards
								1									TD
KICKERS																	
Cary Blanchard					3-3	1-1	2-2	1-1	3-5	1-3	1-1		1-2	2-3	1-1		FG/FGA

1992 SEASON STATISTICS

PLAYERS	PASSING				RUSHING				RECEIVING				KICKING			
	TD 1-9	TD 10-39	TD 40+	Yards 300+	TD 1-9	TD 10-39	TD 40+	Yards 100+	TD 1-9	TD 10-39	TD 40+	Yards 100+	FG 18-39	FG 40-49	FG 50+	PAT
Boomer Esiason	4	7														
Browning Nagle	1	5	1	1												
Blair Thomas																
Brad Baxter					6			1								
Freeman McNeil																
Pat Chaffey					1											
Rob Moore										3	1					
Chris Burkett										1		1				
Terance Mathis									1	1	1	1				
Rob Carpenter									1			1				
Johnny Mitchell										1						
Cary Blanchard													9	7	0	17

Philadelphia Eagles

Season Review — Keith Jackson held out and was awarded free agency, eventually signing with Miami, and by the end of the year, Reggie White, Seth Joyner and Clyde Simmons had already been declared free agents. Quarterback Randall Cunningham experienced a splendid comeback from the knee injury that caused him to miss the 1991 season, throwing 19 TD passes. Philadelphia obtained Herschel Walker in a June trade, and he responded with over 1,000 yards rushing and 10 touchdowns. The defense was again one of the league's best, but it missed tackle Jerome Brown, who was killed in a car accident before training camp began. So a season that began so promising with the Super Bowl as the goal ended with free agency destined to destroy continuity.

Offseason Update — The Eagles lost their top two backup quarterbacks in Jim McMahon (who went to the Vikings) and David Archer (to the CFL). Tight end Mark Bavaro was signed as a free agent, and wide receiver Victor Bailey was drafted in the second round. Keith Byars was expected to leave as a free agent.

Significant 1992 Injuries — None; the key players in 1992 all played the entire season.

Quarterbacks — Randall Cunningham is still one of the most dangerous quarterbacks in the NFL because he can hurt defenses with both his passing and his running. He had a great September last year, then slipped and was mediocre the rest of the season. Still, his passing statistics were pretty good, and he did run for 549 yards and five touchdowns. The Eagles need a backup badly.

Running Backs — Herschel Walker and Heath Sherman form a solid one-two punch in the backfield. They split time much of last year and the Eagles want one of them to emerge as the go-to back. Walker, strictly a straight-ahead runner these days, gained 1,070 yards and scored 10 TD's last year. Sherman, meanwhile, rushed for 583 yards and had six scores. Tony Brooks and Siran Stacy are 1992 rookies who didn't carry the ball but should be good backups.

Wide Receivers — Fred Barnett is one of the league's premier wideouts. Last year, he caught 67 passes for 1,083 yards and six touchdowns. Calvin Williams, the other starter, knows how to get open in the end zone. He scored seven TD's in 1992. They provide plenty of weapons for Cunningham. Philadelphia drafted Victor Bailey in the second round to take over the first-off-the-bench role. Backups Jeff Sydner and Roy Green won't see the ball much.

Tight Ends — Keith Jackson hasn't been replaced very well. The Eagles think free-agent acquisition Mark Bavaro still has it, but it isn't much. Last year in Cleveland, Bavaro caught 25 passes and scored twice. Behind him is Pat Beach. Running back James Joseph bulked up in the offseason and might be moved to tight end. Keith Byars was unhappy at being forced to play tight end last season, and he was looking to sign with another team late in the off-season.

Kicker — Roger Ruzek slipped badly in 1992, as he was successful on only 16 of 25 field-goal attempts while scoring just 88 points. He had three field goals blocked. Still, he had scored over 100 points the previous two seasons and should continue to score quite a few points for a team that has a pretty good offense. Consider him for a backup kicker.

Defense — Reggie White left Philadelphia during the offseason for Green Bay, and it won't be long before Seth Joyner and Clyde Simmons take off, too. With the tragic death of Jerome Brown a year ago, that means the Eagles' defense will be nearly decimated. The team ranked sixth in total defense last year but 12th vs. the pass, quite a bit off 1991 when it was first in all three major categories. The Eagles' defense scored 26 points in '92. Philadelphia acquired Tim Harris and Erik McMillan during the 1993 offseason.

What to Expect in 1993 — The Eagles haven't given up on winning the NFC Eastern Division and going to the Super Bowl, but this will be their last shot because free agency has cost them dearly. Randall Cunningham has to rebound from a subpar second half of the season, but there's a lot of talent to complement him. The defense remains one of the league's best and will keep the Eagles in most games.

Best Players to Draft — Quarterback Randall Cunningham and wide receivers Fred Barnett and Calvin Williams.

1992 GAME-BY-GAME STATISTICS

	N.O.	PHX.	DEN.	DAL.	K.C.	WAS.	PHX.	DAL.	RAID.	G.B.	NYG.	S.F.	MIN.	SEA.	WAS.	NYG	
QUARTERBACKS																	
R. Cunningham	18-25 167 2	17-22 267 3	18-25 270 3	11-19 126	16-27 168 2	22-40 207 1	9-20 121 1	3-8 13		14-23 169 1	10-21 209 2	28-42 257 2	16-23 164	27-44 365	13-24 149 1	11-21 125 1	Att/Cmp Yards TD
Casey Weldon																	Att/Cmp Yards TD
RUNNING BACKS																	
Herschel Walker	26-112 4-28 1	28-115 2-2	22-53 1-8	19-84 2 3-14	19-89 2-11	7-8 2-13	20-112 2-9	16-44 1 2-5	20-47 2	12-47 1 2-7	10-61 1 4-79 1	3-2 7-38	13-44 2-20	23-111 1 3-11	13-35	16-104 2-31	Att/Yards TD Rec/Yards TD
Heath Sherman	8-50	1-8		2-6			5-30		9-81 1 2-18 1	6-31 1 1-75 1	17-109 1	10-31 4-33	17-53 1 -50	8-35 3-22	18-96 1 2-11	12-61 1-2	Att/Yards TD Rec/Yards TD
RECEIVERS																	
Fred Barnett	4-50 1	8-193 2	5-102 1	5-76	6-86	6-51	1-16	1-15	3-63 1	2-15	2-62	6-70 1	5-49	9-161	3-59	1-15	Rec/Yards TD
Calvin Williams	3-23	1-10 1	5-108 2	1-13		7-76 1	3-65 1	2-54	4-49	1-7	1-8	5-56	1-13	4-35 1	2-38	2-43 1	Rec/Yards TD
Roy Green								1-13	1-10	2-31	1-9	1-7	1-20			1-15	Rec/Yards TD
Keith Byars	6-60	1-5	6-36	1-14	4-28	6-57		6-37	1-(-5)	1-4	2-51 1	5-47 1	3-25	5-93	6-41	3-9	Rec/Yards TD
Mark Bavaro	1-6	4-37 1			1-23	1-9	1-15		4-57 1	2-32	3-23		2-38	2-14		4-61	Rec/Yards TD
Pat Beach		1-11	1-16	1-7	3-24 2	1-10				1-7							Rec/Yards TD
KICKERS																	
Roger Ruzek	1-1	1-1	3-3	1-1	1-3	1-1	0-2	1-1	1-1	1-1			0-1	2-3	1-3	2-3	FG/FGA

1992 SEASON STATISTICS

PLAYERS	PASSING				RUSHING				RECEIVING				KICKING			
	TD 1-9	TD 10-39	TD 40+	Yards 300+	TD 1-9	TD 10-39	TD 40+	Yards 100+	TD 1-9	TD 10-39	TD 40+	Yards 100+	FG 18-39	FG 40-49	FG 50+	PAT
R. Cunningham	3	12	4	1	4	1		1								
Casey Weldon																
Herschel Walker					6	2		5	1	1						
Heath Sherman					1	4		1			1					
Fred Barnett										4	2	3				
Calvin Williams									1	4	2	1				
Roy Green																
Keith Byars						1				2						
Mark Bavaro									1	1						
Pat Beach									1	1						
Roger Ruzek													9	6	1	40

Phoenix Cardinals

Season Review — The Cardinals were once again probably the best last-place team in the NFL. Playing hard, stopping enemy running games and strong special-teams play were components of every Cardinals game. Phoenix defeated playoff teams Washington and San Francisco for two of its four wins. Quarterback Timm Rosenbach was injured again, and Chris Chandler took over and showed that he deserved the starting job. The defense had a couple of stars in Tim McDonald (who led the team in tackles for the fourth time in five years), Eric Swann and Freddie Joe Nunn. But with six losses in the last seven games, when the season ended coach Joe Bugel and general manager Larry Wilson were given one more year to turn things around.

Offseason Update — Here's a team that has been completely revamped for fantasy football. Quarterback Steve Beuerlein and wide receiver Gary Clark were signed as free agents and running back Garrison Hearst was taken with the third pick of the draft (in a trade that included Johnny Johnson). Fourth-round pick Ronald Moore might stick as a backup running back.

Significant 1992 Injuries — Quarterback Timm Rosenbach was knocked out of the starting lineup again, this time with a separated shoulder. Running back Johnny Johnson missed several starts with a shoulder injury, but it was his attitude problem that caused him to be shipped off to the Jets. Backup back Johnny Bailey missed the last two games with an ankle injury, and wide receiver Ernie Jones missed a month with an injury.

Quarterbacks — Steve Beuerlein will take over at quarterback, assuming he can win the starting job from Chris Chandler. Beuerlein has never started for a complete season and has a career high of only 13 TD passes in one year. But he has been considered one of the top backup quarterbacks ever since he went 6-0 and led the Cowboys to the playoffs in 1991. Some people think he was a product of the Dallas system, so this will be his opportunity to show what he can do. Chandler passed for 15 touchdowns in 1992 and thinks he can retain the starting job. Timm Rosenbach was considering retirement, leaving Tony Sacca as No. 3. The Cardinals have thrown the second-fewest TD passes in the NFL the last three seasons.

Running Backs — The Cardinals ranked 26th in rushing a year ago, and Garrison Hearst has already been handed the No. 1 job and is the early favorite for Rookie of the Year. He could be another Emmitt Smith or Barry Sanders. Johnny Bailey and Larry Centers are backups who shine on third downs, and Ivory Lee Brown has shown promise but not much productivity. Ronald Moore, a fourth-rounder, will probably back up Hearst.

Wide Receivers — Gary Clark might not put up the kind of numbers he did in Washington the last few years, but he is still one of the game's best wide receivers. Randal Hill is still developing as a big-play threat who will benefit from better quarterbacking. Ricky Proehl is a sure-handed possession receiver who led the team with 60 catches last year. The future of Ernie Jones is in question after his offseason arrest on cocaine charges.

Tight Ends — The Cardinals utilize a two-tight-end set, with Walter Reeves and Butch Rolle as the starters. They combined for only 19 catches last year. Second-year man Derek Ware is the receiver of the trio, and he occasionally shows some flashes.

Kicker — Greg Davis had the lowest percentage for any field-goal kicker in the league last year — 50 percent on 13 of 26 kicking. He was only 4 of 12 from 40 yards and beyond and even missed four chip shots within 30 yards, costing the team the opportunity to win several games. He has one of the stronger legs in the NFL, but he'll have to revert back to his form of previous years (although he has never hit a high percentage of his kicks).

Defense — Before switching to a 4-2-5 defense in the sixth game of 1992, the Cardinals were getting clobbered. After that game, however, the defense allowed 20 or more points just three times, even after injuries to linebackers Ken Harvey and Freddie Joe Nunn. Phoenix lost safety Tim McDonald in free agency but then signed Chuck Cecil from Green Bay. Cornerback Robert Massey returned three inteceptions for touchdowns to lead the league, but the defense ranked only 24th overall and 27th vs. the pass.

What to Expect in 1993 — Because of a multitude of changes, the Cardinals might contend for a playoff spot this season if Steve Beuerlein comes through at quarterback. Hearst is guaranteed of being a superstar as long as his knee doesn't bother him, and the rest of the offense could be explosive.

Best Players to Draft — Running back Garrison Hearst and wide receiver Gary Clark.

1992 GAME-BY-GAME STATISTICS

	T.B.	PHI.	DAL.	WAS.	NYG	N.O.	PHI.	S.F.	RAMS	ATL.	DAL.	WAS.	S.D.	NYG	IND.	T.B.	
QUARTERBACKS																	
Chris Chandler	6-9	17-29	28-43	21-31	16-30	19-30	8-16	19-33	21-30	19-34	5-7		20-35	12-18	11-25	23-43	Att/Cmp
	31	211	383	196	209	218	118	197	224	261	38		251	130	131	234	Yards
		2	1	1	2	2		3		1	1		2				TD
Timm Rosenbach	12-22	2-5				6-13					10-17	19-34				0-1	Att/Cmp
	77	19				45					80	262					Yards
																	TD
RUNNING BACKS																	
Johnny Johnson				4-20	1-2			26-102	24-91	12-33	12-45		15-48	36-156	28-146	20-91	Att/Yards
									2				1	2	1		TD
			1-13	1-7				1-1	1-0	1-26	2-12		1-9	3-13		3-22	Rec/Yards
																	TD
Johnny Bailey	6-35	3-2	2-22	4-26	6-32	9-42	14-55	1-2	3-11	2-5	2-1						Att/Yards
						1											TD
	3-5	4-15	3-53	2-10	1-7	5-50	3-53	3-28	1-8	5-68	3-34						Rec/Yards
					1												TD
Larry Centers	1-(-4)	1-28	1-2		1-10	4-17	14-30	1-4		1-(-2)		3-3	6-30	2-3		2-18	Att/Yards
																	TD
	3-15	1-0	7-64	5-36	3-27	1-3	2-12	2-5	1-7	1-2	5-28	7-63	4-58		1-10	7-87	Rec/Yards
				1							1						TD
RECEIVERS																	
Gary Clark	8-97	6-73	4-58	4-106	2-71	5-66	3-19	2-27	4-56	4-43	2-43	4-65	3-47	4-50	4-27	5-64	Rec/Yards
	1	1			1	1						1					TD
Randal Hill	7-58	5-109	2-74	3-41	3-30	4-60	5-76	6-92	4-33	4-91	1-18	1-45	2-6	4-63	1-6	6-56	Rec/Yards
			1					2									TD
Ricky Proehl	4-37	3-29	4-51	1-21	3-20	4-45	1-9	4-51	9-126	5-52		7-104	6-112		3-40	6-47	Rec/Yards
		1						1					1				TD
Ernie Jones	2-14	2-53	5-78	5-52	6-125	2-21					4-50	5-51	1-23	5-70	1-22		Rec/Yards
		1			1	1						1					TD
Butch Rolle	1-1	2-17	4-19	1-4		1-4	1-6	1-11		1-2		1-0					Rec/Yards
																	TD
KICKERS																	
Greg Davis		0-1	2-2			1-2	1-2	2-4	1-4	1-1	1-2	0-1	1-1	2-2	1-4		FG/FGA

1992 SEASON STATISTICS

PLAYERS	PASSING				RUSHING				RECEIVING				KICKING			
	TD 1-9	TD 10-39	TD 40+	Yards 300+	TD 1-9	TD 10-39	TD 40+	Yards 100+	TD 1-9	TD 10-39	TD 40+	Yards 100+	FG 18-39	FG 40-49	FG 50+	PAT
Chris Chandler	7	5	3	1	1											
Timm Rosenbach																
Johnny Johnson					3	2	1	3								
Johnny Bailey					1				1							
Larry Centers					2											
Gary Clark										4	1	1				
Randal Hill									1	2		1				
Ricky Proehl										2	1	3				
Ernie Jones									2		2	1				
Butch Rolle																
Greg Davis													9	4	0	28

Pittsburgh Steelers

Season Review — New head coach Bill Cowher, only 35 years old, infused the team with new enthusiasm, and the Steelers won their first division title since 1984. It was also the Steelers' first 11-win season since 1979, when they last won a Super Bowl. But Barry Foster was the story of the year. He led the conference in rushing with 1,690 yards and 11 touchdowns. Besides breaking many of Franco Harris' team records, he tied Eric Dickerson's league record with 12 100-yard games in a season. Quarterback Neil O'Donnell was 9-3 as the starter before going out with a broken leg. Cornerback Rod Woodson was his usual All-Pro self, and solid showings were turned in by wide receiver Jeff Graham and rookie safety Darren Perry. Tight end Eric Green had his troubles and was suspended by the league for substance abuse.

Offseason Update — Mike Tomczak was signed as the backup quarterback (and Bubby Brister was expected to go elsewhere). A new old face was brought back when the Steelers signed wide receiver Louis Lipps. Wide receiver Andre Hastings might have been a steal in the third round of the draft.

Significant 1992 Injuries — Quarterback Neil O'Donnell missed the last three regular-season games because of a fractured right leg before returning for the playoffs. But the biggest loss was that of tight end Eric Green, who missed the first month because of a bruised shoulder. He was later suspended by the NFL for six weeks for substance abuse.

Quarterbacks — The Steelers twice had to hold off the Buccaneers, who badly wanted to acquire Neil O'Donnell. O'Donnell fits the team's ball-control offense well because he limits mistakes and is accurate on short to intermediate passes. Last season, his first as the full-time starter, he threw 13 TD passes, although the team ranked only 21st in the league in passing offense. Mike Tomczak is with his fourth team in four years and will back up O'Donnell. Bubby Brister will either be traded or released.

Running Backs — The entire offense revolves around Barry Foster, who gained 1,690 yards and scored 11 touchdowns in 1992. He'll carry the load again this year, and he is built sturdily enough so that he doesn't get nicked much. Tim Worley was working out regularly, had successfully undergone rehabilitation and seemed to have turned his life around. If he returns, the Steelers may pair him with Foster in the backfield. Merril Hoge is now just a lead blocker and pass receiver.

Wide Receivers — Pittsburgh needs one of its receivers to come through in a big way. Jeff Graham started off 1992 in a flurry but then did little as the season progressed. He finished with a team-leading 49 receptions but only one touchdown. Dwight Stone is a one-dimensional home-run threat who lacks consistency but always seems to catch three TD's a season. Ernie Mills is an accomplished receiver with good hands, but he seems to disappear at times. The player to watch this season is Charles Davenport, who caught only nine passes as a rookie in '92. Andre Hastings might have been a steal in the third round of the draft.

Tight Ends — Eric Green has the best talent of any tight end in the NFL, but he has been held back by a contract holdout, injuries, a suspension and excess weight. If he ever becomes serious about playing football, he would be awesome. Adrian Cooper is a tremendous blocker who found the end zone three times last year on 16 receptions.

Kicker — Gary Anderson continues to kick well. He had the sixth 100-point season of his career in 1992, and he hit on 28 of 36 field-goal attempts, although four of the misses were inside the 39-yard line. He lacks the leg he once had, but he should be considered either as a No. 1 kicker in fantasy football or as a high backup man.

Defense — Because of a bad defensive line, Pittsburgh got only 12 sacks all of 1992 from its front line but 28 from the other players. The defense still forced 43 turnovers and gave up the fewest points (225) in the AFC, despite ranking only 13th in the league. In the offseason, the loss of linebacker Hardy Nickerson was negated by the signing of Kevin Greene, a very good sack specialist.

What to Expect in 1993 — The Steelers might be better than they were in 1992 but still not win the division. The team lacks a solid quarterback and top receivers, but coach Bill Cowher manages to get 100 percent from all of his players. A playoff berth is certainly in reach, however, unless the injury bug hits.

Best Players to Draft — Running back Barry Foster, tight end Eric Green and kicker Gary Anderson.

1992 GAME-BY-GAME STATISTICS

	HOU.	NYJ	S.D.	G.B.	CLE.	CIN.	K.C.	HOU.	BUF.	DET.	IND.	CIN.	SEA.	CHI.	MIN.	CLE.	
QUARTERBACKS																	
Neil O'Donnell	14-23 / 223 / 2	11-22 / 185	17-24 / 215 / 2	16-41 / 224	25-32 / 241	23-37 / 287 / 2	13-22 / 114 / 1	14-22 / 201 / 2	15-24 / 159 / 2	17-31 / 181 / 1		10-18 / 149	10-17 / 104 / 1				Att/Cmp Yards TD
Mike Tomczak				9-19 / 75	10-17 / 171 / 1	13-21 / 158	14-29 / 186 / 1	16-28 / 252 / 1	17-26 / 219 / 2	18-32 / 322 / 1	15-24 / 169				8-15 / 141 / 1		Att/Cmp Yards TD
Bubby Brister										2-4 / 15 / 1	10-22 / 109		6-12 / 69	14-31 / 143	13-22 / 160	18-25 / 223 / 1	Att/Cmp Yards TD
RUNNING BACKS																	
Barry Foster	26-107 / 1 / 2-26	33-190 / 2 / 1-0	21-36 / 1-(-1)	12-117	24-84 / 6-47	24-108 / 1 / 1-21	24-105 / 1 / 1-12	31-118 / 1 / 2-15	22-77 / 4-36	25-107 / 5-52	28-168 / 2 / 1-42	25-102 / 2 / 1-16	33-125 / 1 / 5-29	12-25 / 2-10	24-118 / 2-8	26-103 / 1 / 2-29	Att/Yards TD Rec/Yards
Merril Hoge	3-8 / 2-19	8-29 / 2-13	8-34 / 3-23	3-18 / 3-29	3-12 / 2-9	1-7 / 2-8	3-6 / 1-5	1-3 / 1-20	1-1 / 2-18 / 1	1-5 / 1-7	3-14 / 2-6	3-8 / 1-9	2-10	1-7	2-3 / 1-18	1-2 / 2-31	Att/Yards TD Rec/Yards TD
Leroy Thompson		1-1	1-7	1-0		8-33 / 2-25	6-32 / 4-47	1-(-4) / 1-20	2-8 / 1-8	1-13 / 1-15	8-52 / 1 / 2-16	2-(-7)	3-41	1-0 / 2-10	3-30 / 3-56	1-(-1) / 2-23	Att/Yards TD Rec/Yards
RECEIVERS																	
Jeff Graham	7-89 / 1	6-146	3-67	3-32	8-87	7-115		1-11				5-60	2-30	3-30	1-20	3-24	Rec/Yards TD
Dwight Stone	2-80			5-69 / 1	5-101	3-31	6-58 / 2	1-20				2-33	3-44	1-2	1-2	5-61	Rec/Yards TD
Ernie Mills		1-12	1-14	2-24	2-21	3-52	1-2	4-61	1-12 / 1	4-43 / 1	4-36		1-19 / 1	1-20	2-24	3-43	Rec/Yards TD
Eric Green					3-36	1-2	3-21 / 1	3-52 / 1	4-41								Rec/Yards TD
Adrian Cooper	1-9 / 1	1-14	3-36 / 1	1-17	1-8		3-27	1-2 / 1		1-6				3-58	1-20		Rec/Yards TD
KICKERS																	
Gary Anderson	3-3	2-3	1-1	1-2	3-4	2-3	2-2		2-2	1-3	3-3	0-1	2-2	2-2	1-2	3-3	FG/FGA

1992 SEASON STATISTICS

PLAYERS	PASSING				RUSHING				RECEIVING				KICKING			
	TD 1-9	TD 10-39	TD 40+	Yards 300+	TD 1-9	TD 10-39	TD 40+	Yards 100+	TD 1-9	TD 10-39	TD 40+	Yards 100+	FG 18-39	FG 40-49	FG 50+	PAT
Neil O'Donnell	6	7			1											
Mike Tomczak	1	4	2	1												
Bubby Brister	2															
Barry Foster					7	3	1	12								
Merril Hoge										1						
Leroy Thompson					1											
Jeff Graham										1	2					
Dwight Stone									2	1	1					
Ernie Mills										3						
Eric Green									2							
Adrian Cooper									2	1						
Gary Anderson													24	4	0	29

TEAM EVALUATIONS

San Diego Chargers

Season Review — The Chargers became the first team ever to go from 0-4 to the playoffs, and they won their first division title since 1981. After losing quarterback John Friesz in the preseason, San Diego acquired Stan Humphries in a trade with Washington. He took over as the starter in two games, and although the offense scored just 29 points in the first four games, the turnaround and eventual 11-1 finish under new head coach Bobby Ross was remarkable. Linebacker Junior Seau started to be recognized as one of the best defensive players in the game, but Leslie O'Neal, Chris Mims, Stanley Richard and others also spurred the comeback. Ronnie Harmon led NFL running backs with 79 receptions, and wide receiver Anthony Miller caught 72 passes for 1,060 yards and seven touchdowns.

Offseason Update — Running back Rod Bernstine signed with Denver in free agency, but San Diego seemed to have filled the void by drafting Natrone Means in the second round.

Significant 1992 Injuries — Quarterback John Friesz lost his starting job in the preseason when he suffered torn knee ligaments and was lost for the entire year. His eventual replacement, Stan Humphries, suffered a separated shoulder in the final regular-season game but played with a sling in the playoffs. Running back Rod Bernstine, now with Denver, missed seven starts with a separated shoulder.

Quarterbacks — Stan Humphries should be able to stave off a challenge from John Friesz in the 1993 training camp. Last year, Humphries led the Chargers to their first playoff berth since 1982 with a quick-strike offense and a solid ground game. He threw 16 TD passes in '92, although 18 interceptions were too much. Friesz will be a good backup.

Running Backs — Marion Butts becomes the every-down back again, and he could be back at the 1,000-yard plateau unless somebody else comes through. Butts ran for 809 yards and four touchdowns last season. Eric Bieniemy might emerge as the goal-line runner, and Ronnie Harmon is such a threat that opposing defenses have yet to figure out how to stop his all-around skills. But general manager Bobby Beathard wanted more, so he traded up to draft Natrone Means in the second round this year. Don't be surprised if Means is the starter in December in the Chargers' one-back offense.

Wide Receivers — Anthony Miller is one of the best wide receivers in the NFL when he gets consistent quarterbacking, as was the case in 1992 when he caught 72 passes for 1,060 yards and seven touchdowns. He was the only receiver in the conference to hit the 1,000-yard mark. Nate Lewis and Shawn Jefferson drop too many passes at the other slot but aren't bad. In the fifth round, San Diego picked Walter Dunson, who is too raw to help immediately.

Tight Ends — San Diego is solid here, with Derrick Walker operating as the pass-catching threat and Duane Young as the blocking tight end. Walker had solid numbers again in 1992, with 34 receptions for 393 yards and two touchdowns in 1992.

Kicker — John Carney enjoyed an outstanding year in 1992, hitting on 16 straight field goals to set a club record. Overall he hit on 26 of 32 field goals and scored 113 points. Since the Chargers will receive more competition for the division title this year and won't have the benefit of a fifth-place schedule, don't expect Carney to score so many points this time around. A year ago he was considered shaky as the team's kicker, but he should be pretty solid this year.

Defense — Bill Arnsparger returned to the NFL and coordinated one of the league's best defenses in 1992. San Diego ranked fourth in total defense (second vs. the run and ninth against the pass) — which was its highest since the 1970 merger — while forcing 36 turnovers. Opposing quarterbacks were sacked 51 times, led by Leslie O'Neal's league-high 17. Burt Grossman added eight sacks, three that were for safeties.

What to Expect in 1993 — San Diego was one of the NFL's surprise teams in 1992, and the schedule doesn't favor the team this year. Still, with no clear favorite in the AFC West, the Chargers will be in the hunt and could be back on top.

Best Players to Draft — Running back Marion Butts and wide receiver Anthony Miller.

1992 GAME-BY-GAME STATISTICS

	K.C.	DEN.	PIT.	HOU.	SEA.	IND.	DEN.	IND.	K.C.	CLE.	T.B.	RAID.	PHX.	CIN.	RAID.	SEA.	
QUARTERBACKS																	
Stan Humphries	7-10	23-45	13-29	22-38	15-28	12-17	20-27	22-33	20-35	19-32	13-28	13-26	20-32	19-28	17-32	8-14	Att/Cmp
	62	231	151	219	200	205	349	256	294	234	126	164	275	209	237	138	Yards
		1			2		2	2	1	2	1	1	1	1	2		TD
Bob Gagliano	7-20		3-7													9-15	Att/Cmp
	55		78													125	Yards
																	TD
RUNNING BACKS																	
Marion Butts	11-37	16-78	9-23	11-20	6-18		21-73	27-120	17-37	19-61	22-104	16-71	9-5	6-47	16-52	13-64	Att/Yards
								1	1			1				1	TD
				1-4				2-20	1-6	1-12			1-22	1-7	1-0	1-2	Rec/Yards
																	TD
Ronnie Harmon	2-7	1-0	3-17	3-10	5-4	3-13	4-12	3-18	6-14	3-19	4-25	4-41	1-1	5-30	6-20	2-8	Att/Yards
											1		1			1	TD
	6-44	7-91	3-77	4-78	1-8	1-4	7-66	6-62	7-96	8-60	4-43	4-74	6-52	8-80	4-46	3-27	Rec/Yards
											1						TD
Eric Bieniemy					1-4	10-48	4-14	4-13		3-9	5-23	10-49	9-24	12-41	11-29	5-10	Att/Yards
						1							1		1		TD
				1-3			1-9	1-3				1-9	1-25				Rec/Yards
																	TD
RECEIVERS																	
Anthony Miller	2-26	4-41	2-49	4-42	9-142	3-47	6-129	6-105	5-76	7-110	5-34	3-18	4-68	4-46	3-31	6-96	Rec/Yards
					2		1			1			1	1	1		TD
Nate Lewis	1-9	6-50	3-36		1-19	3-94	2-41	2-26	2-13	1-10	2-25	2-22	4-77	1-8	2-70	2-80	Rec/Yards
		1						2							1		TD
Shawn Jefferson	1-13	3-25	4-45	5-39				1-7	1-51	1-26	2-24	2-30	2-20	2-38	3-29	2-30	Rec/Yards
										1		1					TD
Derrick Walker	4-25	3-24	3-15	2-11	1-14	2-48	4-104	2-10	4-52	1-16		1-7	1-5	2-18	3-47	1-17	Rec/Yards
							1		1								TD
Duane Young				1-13			1-9	2-34									Rec/Yards
																	TD
KICKERS																	
John Carney	1-1	2-3	2-3		1-3	2-2	1-2	1-1		0-1	2-2	2-2	2-2	2-2	5-5	3-3	FG/FGA

1992 SEASON STATISTICS

PLAYERS	PASSING				RUSHING				RECEIVING				KICKING			
	TD 1-9	TD 10-39	TD 40+	Yards 300+	TD 1-9	TD 10-39	TD 40+	Yards 100+	TD 1-9	TD 10-39	TD 40+	Yards 100+	FG 18-39	FG 40-49	FG 50+	PAT
Stan Humphries	4	9	3	1	4											
Bob Gagliano																
Marion Butts					4			2								
Ronnie Harmon					3				1							
Eric Bieniemy					3											
Anthony Miller									1	4	2	4				
Nate Lewis									2	1	1					
Shawn Jefferson										2						
Derrick Walker										2		1				
Duane Young																
John Carney													18	7	1	35

San Francisco 49ers

Season Review — Joe Montana played only 30 minutes of the season, and it was a much-celebrated event in the season finale. But Steve Young is the quarterback of the present in San Francisco, and all he did was lead the NFL in passing with 25 touchdowns and only seven interceptions and run for 537 yards and four scores. Jerry Rice was his usual fantastic self (84 catches, 11 TD's), and the 49ers found a new star at running back in Ricky Watters, who rushed for 1,013 yards. The defense, particularly a young secondary, was ravaged in a 34-31 loss to Buffalo in Week Two, but it improved as the season progressed. In the end, Young failed to win the Super Bowl, which left many 49ers fans wondering what Montana might have done.

Offseason Update — Quarterback Joe Montana is now a Kansas City Chief, but he hadn't played in two years, so the loss isn't big. Mike Sherrard, the third wideout, left for the Giants, but Mervyn Fernandez was acquired from the Raiders to balance the loss.

Significant 1992 Injuries — Quarterback Joe Montana didn't play until the second half of the last game because of his elbow injury. Running back Ricky Watters missed what amounted to five games with various injuries, and Dexter Carter was out for 10 games with a shoulder injury. Wide receiver John Taylor missed seven games with a broken leg. Tight end Wesley Walls spent the season on injured reserve with a shoulder injury.

Quarterbacks — There's no longer any question about who should be starting in San Francisco. Steve Young was the league's Most Valuable Player in 1992, but he had better get the team to the Super Bowl soon, because 49ers fans won't accept less. Young leads a versatile offense and an explosive passing attack. Last year, he passed for 3,465 yards and 25 touchdowns while running for 537 yards and four more scores. Backup Steve Bono has played very well in limited time.

Running Backs — Ricky Watters emerged as one of the best all-purpose backs in the league last season. Despite missing about five full games, he rushed for 1,013 yards, caught 43 passes and scored 11 touchdowns. In the 49ers' high-scoring offense, he would compile tremendous stats if he played all 16 games. When Watters was out of the lineup last year, Amp Lee played very well, including rushing for 134 yards in one game. Fullback Tom Rathman

is too often unnoticed, but he scored nine touchdowns last year. He's a rugged lead blocker, gets the tough yards and is used extensively in the passing offense.

Wide Receivers — Jerry Rice remains the unparalleled premier receiver in pro football. He doesn't put up the kind of numbers with Young as he did with Joe Montana, but he's the only receiver in the NFL who is a threat to score every time he touches the ball. Last year, he caught 84 passes for 1,201 yards and 10 scores. John Taylor caught only 25 passes for three TD's in half a season but should bounce back strongly. Odessa Turner and ex-Raider Mervyn Fernandez are the only experienced backups.

Tight Ends — Sure-handed Brent Jones caught 45 passes for four touchdowns last season. He fits the system well and is an integral part of the passing game. When Jamie Williams is in the game, you know the 49ers are going to run.

Kicker — Mike Cofer is the worst kicker in the NFL, and it's a surprise he's still around. He was on the verge of losing his job in 1992 before hanging on. For the season he hit only 18 of 27 field-goal tries, although that figure was better than the 14 of 28 he did in '91. But, as long as Cofer kicks for the 49ers, he'll remain one of the highest-scoring kickers in the NFL. He's a starter in fantasy football, but he'll frustrate you by missing easy field goals in games you lose by two points.

Defense — San Francisco ranked fourth in the NFL vs. the run in 1992 but only 26th vs. the pass and 15th overall. Still, the team allowed only 236 points, an average of just 14.8 per game, the third-lowest total in the league. Pierce Holt and Tim Harris, two of the best defensive players, were lost in free agency, but safety Tim McDonald was brought in.

What to Expect in 1993 — The 49ers are the biggest threat to the Cowboys in the run for the Super Bowl. The defense lost some players in free agency, but there is enough depth to make up for it. With Steve Young, Jerry Rice and others on a talented offense, San Francisco will roll up the points on many opponents.

Best Players to Draft — Quarterback Steve Young, running back Ricky Watters, wide receivers Jerry Rice and John Taylor, tight end Brent Jones and placekicker Mike Cofer.

1992 GAME-BY-GAME STATISTICS

Opponents: NYG BUF. NYJ N.O. RAMS N.E. ATL. PHX. ATL. N.O. RAMS PHI. MIA. MIN. T.B. DET.

QUARTERBACKS

Player	NYG	BUF.	NYJ	N.O.	RAMS	N.E.	ATL.	PHX.	ATL.	N.O.	RAMS	PHI.	MIA.	MIN.	T.B.	DET.	
Steve Young	4-6	26-37	15-23	17-26	20-29	19-27	18-28	6-8	12-18	24-37	14-26	24-35	19-27	20-26	18-31	12-18	Att/Cmp
	27	449	163	187	247	234	399	76	143	205	167	342	220	183	270	153	Yards
	1	3	2			2	3		3	2	1	2	2	1	3		TD
Steve Bono	15-22		3-5				0-3	17-24	1-1				0-1				Att/Cmp
	187		41					222	13								Yards
	2																TD
Joe Montana															15-21		Att/Cmp
															126		Yards
															2		TD

RUNNING BACKS

Player	NYG	BUF.	NYJ	N.O.	RAMS	N.E.	ATL.	PHX.	ATL.	N.O.	RAMS	PHI.	MIA.	MIN.	T.B.	DET.	
Ricky Watters	13-100	16-83	17-55	18-76	20-83	19-104	15-75	7-36	19-75	21-115	26-163	5-20			7-13	3-15	Att/Yards
			1		1	1	3	1			2						TD
	5-50	4-22	1-4	7-52	2-26	8-84	3-57	3-48	3-25	3-11	3-16					1-10	Rec/Yards
						1			1							1	TD
Tom Rathman	4-11	5-20	2-5	5-18	4-31		3-3	4-19	4-11	1-3	7-28	6-25	5-14	3-0	4-6		Att/Yards
				1			1		1				1				TD
	5-34	5-37	2-10	2-17	6-36	5-37	1-11	3-23	1-15	5-33	2-6	3-29	1-27	2-17	1-11		Rec/Yards
	3												1				TD
Amp Lee	3-4		2-5				9-35	1-6	6-26		11-25	16-58	23-134	10-25	10-44		Att/Yards
												1	1				TD
			1-4								3-8	4-22	4-7	1-5	7-56		Rec/Yards
												1	1		1		TD

RECEIVERS

Player	NYG	BUF.	NYJ	N.O.	RAMS	N.E.	ATL.	PHX.	ATL.	N.O.	RAMS	PHI.	MIA.	MIN.	T.B.	DET.	
Jerry Rice	5-56	3-26	5-73	2-5	5-57	3-60	7-183	6-87	4-45	8-68	4-93	8-133	7-79	5-56	7-118	5-62	Rec/Yards
			1			1	2		1		1	1	1		2		TD
John Taylor	2-60	5-112	1-19								3-25	4-82	2-32	4-39	4-57		Rec/Yards
		2													1		TD
Odessa Turner		2-80	1-14	1-19		1-19	1-29		1-12						2-27		Rec/Yards
		1							1								TD
Brent Jones				2-44	4-89	2-34	5-86	6-58	2-34	4-54	2-27	4-32	2-26	4-40	2-13	6-91	Rec/Yards
							1			2						1	TD

KICKERS

Player	NYG	BUF.	NYJ	N.O.	RAMS	N.E.	ATL.	PHX.	ATL.	N.O.	RAMS	PHI.	MIA.	MIN.	T.B.	DET.	
Mike Cofer	1-2	1-3	1-2	3-3	2-2	1-2			2-2	0-1	2-2	2-3	0-1	2-2		1-2	FG/FGA

1992 SEASON STATISTICS

PLAYERS	PASSING				RUSHING				RECEIVING				KICKING			
	TD 1-9	TD 10-39	TD 40+	Yards 300+	TD 1-9	TD 10-39	TD 40+	Yards 100+	TD 1-9	TD 10-39	TD 40+	Yards 100+	FG 18-39	FG 40-49	FG 50+	PAT
Steve Young	8	12	5	3	1	2										
Steve Bono	1	1														
Joe Montana	2															
Ricky Watters					9			4	1	1						
Tom Rathman					5				2	2						
Amp Lee					2			1	2							
Jerry Rice									1	6	3	3				
John Taylor									2		1	1				
Odessa Turner										2						
Brent Jones									2	2						
Mike Cofer													12	6	0	18

Seattle Seahawks

Season Review — The Seahawks were clearly the worst team in the National Football League, with a horrible offense but a very good defense. The defensive players didn't mutiny against an offense that left them on the field too long, didn't take advantage of turnovers they created and yielded almost as many touchdowns (seven, plus two safeties) as it scored (13). Seattle scored only 140 points, the fewest by any team since the NFL went to a 16-game schedule in 1978. The Seahawks lost their top quarterbacks, Kelly Stouffer and Dan McGwire, to season-ending injuries. Stan Gelbaugh finished the year. A nice surprise on offense was halfback Chris Warren, who rushed for 1,017 yards. On defense, tackle Cortez Kennedy had 14 sacks and was named the league's Defensive Player of the Year.

Offseason Update — Seattle had the second pick in the 1993 draft and went for quarterback Rick Mirer, although he might not play much this season. Kelly Stouffer, who started 1992 as the starter, was released. Two new receivers were picked up in Kelvin Martin and tight end Ferrell Edmunds.

Significant 1992 Injuries — Quarterback was the troublespot in 1992. Kelly Stouffer suffered a dislocated left shoulder in Game 5, and a week later, Dan McGwire fractured his left hip, leaving the job to journeyman Stan Gelbaugh. Wide receiver Brian Blades was out for 10 games after separating a shoulder on the first play of his season in Game 2, and tight end Paul Green missed the last 12 games with a shoulder injury.

Quarterbacks — Rick Mirer is the quarterback of the future, but if he plays much in 1993, the Seahawks will be in for a season as bad as that of 1992. Stan Gelbaugh is just a journeyman, but he might wind up the starter because he's somewhat consistent (he was 0-11 as the starter). Dan McGwire hasn't shown anything in two years, and has started just two games. Last year, the Seahawks went from Kelly Stouffer to McGwire to Gelbaugh to Stouffer and to Gelbaugh. It could be more of the same this year. Seattle has thrown the fewest TD passes in the league the last three years.

Running Backs — Chris Warren would be a well-publicized back on a better team. Last year he came out of nowhere to rush for 1,017 yards, though he scored only three times. Warren aggressively hits holes and can make tacklers miss. He should figure more into the passing attack this year. John L. Williams had an injury-plagued 1992 and finished with less than 1,000 rushing and receiving yards for the first time in four years. He averaged only three yards per carry but did lead the team with 74 receptions. Better backups are needed.

Wide Receivers — With bad quarterbacking, receivers get bad statistics. Brian Blades missed most of the year but showed he's still a good one when he returned. Tommy Kane has the best speed on the team, but he's too inconsistent. Kelvin Martin, the ex-Cowboy, will be a good third-down specialist and will put pressure on Robb Thomas, David Daniels and Doug Thomas to even make the team. The Seahawks don't have any quick-strike ability to speak of.

Tight Ends — Ferrell Edmunds has been given the starting job and would be a good one if he got his act together. In Seattle's offense, the tight end should catch 50 passes because the underneath areas are cleared out, and Edmunds could be a vital contributor. Paul Green, Ron Heller and Mike Jones are decent backups, but they won't scare anyone.

Kicker — John Kasay suffered through a terrible year in 1992, connecting on just 14 of 22 field goals and scoring only 56 points. He was only 2 of 6 beyond the 40-yard line. Based on his 25 of 31 kicking as a rookie in '91, he will probably bounce back. But, kicking for a bad offense in Seattle, he won't score close to the 102 points he had that year.

Defense — While the Seattle offense was the league's worst last year, the defense was one of its best. It ranked 10th overall and fourth vs. the pass, with 20 interceptions and 46 sacks. The Seahawks' offense gave up 112 points by itself, and the defense let in only 194. It figures to be even more improved this year if the offense can sustain a few drives.

What to Expect in 1993 — The Seahawks will be lucky to win four games, as they are clearly the worst team in the AFC — and that's considering they have a very good defense. There are just too many holes on offense, starting at quarterback.

Best Player to Draft — Running back Chris Warren.

1992 GAME-BY-GAME STATISTICS

	CIN.	K.C.	N.E.	MIA.	S.D.	DAL.	RAID.	NYG	WAS.	RAID.	K.C.	DEN.	PIT.	PHI.	DEN.	S.D.	
QUARTERBACKS																	
Stan Gelbaugh						3-10 33	17-41 238	22-32 130 1	9-24 75	6-12 65		12-21 164 1	13-28 179 2	9-31 66 1	13-24 135	17-32 222 1	Att/Cmp Yards TD
Dan McGwire				12-21 70	5-9 46												Att/Cmp Yards TD
RUNNING BACKS																	
Chris Warren	14-49 1-33	12-53 1-1	24-122 1 1-7	13-47 4-49	13-76 3-1	7-14	6-18 1-13	10-29 1-(-1)	19-103 1-4	15-63 1-7	20-154 1	16-34 2-20	14-43	19-49	16-97	5-66 1	Att/Yards TD Rec/Yards TD
John L. Williams	10-48 2-6	9-37 3-21	8-18 6-39	7-13 1 2-11	3-8 7-51	8-10 3-24	7-10 6-61	11-44 11-45	6-17 1-8	12-43 5-33	4-9 2-19	10-40 6-33	4-3 8-98 1	4-10 1-11 1	9-17 6-41	2-12 5-55	Att/Yards TD Rec/Yards TD
RECEIVERS																	
Brian Blades											6-66 1	2-40	4-36	1-11	6-103		Rec/Yards TD
Tommy Kane		1-18	2-48					1-13 1	2-6		5-65 1	5-79	2-40 1	2-15	5-66	2-19	Rec/Yards TD
Kelvin Martin	2-12	2-41	1-7	3-31 1	4-45		1-15	7-83 1		4-51	1-6		1-2	3-33	2-23 1	1-10	Rec/Yards TD
Louis Clark	5-69	1-8		4-61 1	4-43		4-72	1-15		1-22							Rec/Yards TD
Robb Thomas						3-28	2-17	2-13	2-27		1-20	1-31					Rec/Yards TD
Ferrell Edmunds	3-24	4-32 1	3-35														Rec/Yards TD
KICKERS																	
John Kasay	1-1		1-2	1-1	2-2	0-1		1-1	1-2	1-2		3-4	0-3	1-1	2-2		FG/FGA

1992 SEASON STATISTICS

PLAYERS	PASSING				RUSHING				RECEIVING				KICKING			
	TD 1-9	TD 10-39	TD 40+	Yards 300+	TD 1-9	TD 10-39	TD 40+	Yards 100+	TD 1-9	TD 10-39	TD 40+	Yards 100+	FG 18-39	FG 40-49	FG 50+	PAT
Stan Gelbaugh	3	3														
Dan McGwire																
Chris Warren					1	1		3								
John L. Williams					1				1	1						
Brian Blades									1		1					
Tommy Kane										3						
Kelvin Martin									1	2						
Louis Clark										1						
Robb Thomas																
Ferrell Edmunds									1							
John Kasay													12	2	0	14

Tampa Bay Buccaneers

Season Review — New head coach Sam Wyche had high hopes after the Buccaneers started out 3-1. But then they were subjected to a slow death, as they lost 10 of their last 12 games. Following a strong start, Vinny Testaverde's interception problems returned, and he did little to convince Wyche that he should be brought back for another season. Offensive bright spots were running back Reggie Cobb (1,058 yards rushing and nine touchdowns) and receiver Lawrence Dawsey (58 catches). Defensively, the Bucs had their usual problems. They finished 21st in team defense and were especially vulnerable against the pass, although cornerback Ricky Reynolds was one of the league's best. Two top rookies were defensive linemen Santana Dotson and Mark Wheeler, while veterans Broderick Thomas and Keith McCants were again disappointments.

Offseason Update — Quarterback Vinny Testaverde left for Cleveland in free agency and nobody had been brought in as of mid-May to replace him. Wide receiver Mark Carrier also joined Testaverde in Cleveland, but running back Vince Workman was signed. Selected in the draft were wide receivers Lamar Thomas and Horace Copeland and running back Rudy Harris.

Significant 1992 Injuries — Tight end Ron Hall missed the last three games of last season with a sprained knee, and several other players missed time with various minor ailments.

Quarterbacks — If Sam Wyche thinks Steve DeBerg can start at quarterback this year, the coach is kidding nobody but himself. The oldest player in the NFL, DeBerg doesn't have much left. Wyche does think highly of second-year pro Craig Erickson, but Erickson is too inexperienced to take over this year (although that might be exactly what happens). Mike Pawlawski, like Erickson a second-year pro, might have the best long-term potential on the team.

Running Backs — Reggie Cobb is one of the premier backs in the league. He rushed for 1,171 yards last year, scored nine touchdowns and was the team's only threat on offense. Late-round steal Anthony McDowell developed into a solid complement at fullback late in the season. He is a superb pass receiver who can go deep. Gary Anderson is the third-down back, although he will be pushed by ex-Packer Vince Workman, who was picked up during the offseason.

Wide Receivers — Lawrence Dawsey and Courtney Hawkins would benefit from better quarterbacking, but they won't have it this year. Dawsey suffered from sophomore jinx last season, though he still led the team with 60 receptions (only one touchdown). Hawkins caught only 20 passes but will take over for Mark Carrier. Lamar Thomas and Horace Copeland were third- and fourth-round draft picks.

Tight Ends — Ron Hall is an underrated tight end who caught 39 passes and scored four touchdowns in 1992. Second-year pro Tyji Armstrong adds a deep-threat dimension.

Kicker — Eddie Murray finished the 1992 season as Tampa Bay's placekicker, but he will most likely be knocked off the roster this year by Daron Alcorn, the eighth-round draft pick from Akron. Murray was only 4 of 8 on field goals for the Bucs (and 1 of 1 for Kansas City earlier in the year).

Defense — Tampa Bay ranked only 25th in the league in 1992 and last vs. the pass thanks to a secondary that couldn't cover opposing receivers and allowed 25 passing touchdowns. The defense did score four touchdowns of its own. Offseason acquisitions included free-agent cornerback Martin Mayhew and No. 1 draft pick defensive end Eric Curry, both of whom will immensely help a defense that has talent but hasn't played like it does.

What to Expect in 1993 — Without a decent quarterback, the Buccaneers are looking at another fifth-place finish in 1993. The defense is improved and there is talent at the other skill positions. But everything starts with the man behind center, and Tampa Bay doesn't have a very good one.

Best Player to Draft — Running back Reggie Cobb.

1992 GAME-BY-GAME STATISTICS

Player	K.C.	DEN.	PIT.	HOU.	SEA.	IND.	DEN.	IND.	K.C.	CLE.	T.B.	RAID.	PHX.	CIN.	RAID.	SEA.	
QUARTERBACKS																	
Steve DeBerg		0-1	19-29				11-20	13-25	28-42				5-8				Att/Cmp
			213				135	94	239				29				Yards
			2					1									TD
Craig Erickson					2-3	1-3		5-6			3-6		4-8				Att/Cmp
					17	6		51			20		27				Yards
																TD
RUNNING BACKS																	
Reggie Cobb	18-70	10-30	15-41	26-107	23-76	24-109	18-66	19-72	19-64	28-114	17-73	20-94	26-100	15-54	21-90	11-11	Att/Yards
	1			1	1	1	1	1		1				1	1		TD
		2-37				2-11		1-4	4-20	2-34	1-3	1-0		4-36	2-14	2-(3)	Rec/Yards
																	TD
Anthony McDowell						2-18	1-5		1-1			1-3	3-9	3-36	1-2	2-7	Att/Yards
																	TD
				1-11		2-25	1-9		4-36	2-1	4-24	1-15	3-10	4-30	2-55	3-42	Rec/Yards
										1					1		TD
Gary Anderson	8-41	6-0	7-61	6-22		5-10	3-4	2-3	4-10		4-12	2-4		2-0	4-24	2-3	Att/Yards
									1								TD
	2-31	2-8	7-60	1-8		1-7	2-(-2)	2-16	7-61		2-16			1-3	4-64	3-12	Rec/Yards
																	TD
RECEIVERS																	
Lawrence Dawsey	6-76	5-107	1-14	6-99	5-61	5-41	4-38		5-40	3-56	3-44	2-51	1-15	4-40	3-23	7-71	Rec/Yards
			1														TD
Courtney Hawkins	1-9	2-57	2-50		2-20	5-102	3-52	2-11	1-16		1-6					1-13	Rec/Yards
			1			1											TD
Willie Drewrey	1-21	2-23		2-38	3-61	1-13		3-22	4-59								Rec/Yards
		1						1									TD
Ron Hall	2-16		4-35	6-83	3-16	1-11	5-45	4-32	4-25	3-37	3-26	3-19	1-6				Rec/Yards
	1			1						1	1						TD
Tyji Armstrong		1-17											1-81	3-28	1-7	1-5	Rec/Yards
													1				TD
KICKERS																	
Eddie Murray								1-1	2-2			0-1	2-2			0-3	FG/FGA

1992 SEASON STATISTICS

PLAYERS	PASSING				RUSHING				RECEIVING				KICKING			
	TD 1-9	TD 10-39	TD 40+	Yards 300+	TD 1-9	TD 10-39	TD 40+	Yards 100+	TD 1-9	TD 10-39	TD 40+	Yards 100+	FG 18-39	FG 40-49	FG 50+	PAT
Steve DeBerg	1	2														
Craig Erickson																
Reggie Cobb					9			4								
Anthony McDowell									1	1						
Gary Anderson					1											
Lawrence Dawsey										1		1				
Courtney Hawkins										2		1				
Willie Drewrey									1	1						
Ron Hall									1	3						
Tyji Armstrong											1					
Eddie Murray													2	2	1	13

Washington Redskins

Season Review — The Redskins followed up their Super Bowl season in 1991 by slipping into the playoffs, but the talk in the nation's capital was about what happened to Mark Rypien. After a long training camp holdout, the quarterback finished as the lowest-rated passer in the NFC. Art Monk became pro football's all-time leading receiver, but he had a mediocre season. Gary Clark led the team in receptions but also dropped more balls than an amateur juggler. Want more? Earnest Byner gained 1,000 yards rushing, then lost a few yards and was injured, ending with 998. The offense scored 185 fewer points than in '91, but positions on both sides of the ball were riddled with injuries. Two months after the season ended, coach Joe Gibbs surprised everyone with his retirement. Defensive coordinator Richie Petitbon was quickly promoted to head coach.

Offseason Update — Joe Gibbs is gone and Richie Petitbon is the new head coach. Free agency saw the loss of wide receiver Gary Clark to Phoenix and the signing of Tim McGee from Cincinnati. Running back Reggie Brooks was a very good pick in the second round of the draft.

Significant 1992 Injuries — After playing the entire regular season, wide receiver Desmond Howard was lost for the playoffs with an injury, and tight end Don Warren was out the last five games.

Quarterbacks — Mark Rypien might receive a strong challenge from Cary Conklin during the 1993 training camp and might lose his job. Rypien couldn't find his rhythm last year after a training camp holdout. He ranked last in the NFC in passing and threw only 13 TD passes even though the Washington receivers are excellent. Too often he missed wide-open targets downfield. Conklin has all the intangibles you want in a quarterback, but he's very green.

Running Backs — Earnest Byner just missed another 1,000-yard season and isn't showing much age yet. Ricky Ervins was a perfect example of the sophomore jinx, as he slipped to 495 yards rushing on an average of 3.3 yards per carry. Notre Dame's Reggie Brooks was drafted in the second round, but he's another Ervins — a short fireplug of a back with shifty moves. There's talk Washington might go with some two-back offense this year, which would give more playing time to all three running backs. Brian Mitchell might also get an opportunity to show what he can do after looking really good in one of last year's playoff games.

Wide Receivers — Change is in store for the Redskins, and the starters this year will most likely be Ricky Sanders and Desmond Howard, with Tim McGee as the No. 3 wide receiver and Art Monk demoted to No. 4. Sanders will benefit from being the go-to receiver and could score a dozen touchdowns like he did in 1988. He hasn't done a lot since then. Howard will probably be a big factor, especially near the goal line, because that is where he excels. McGee is looking for a fresh start, and Monk will be used as the possession receiver.

Tight Ends — Ron Middleton is the key to the running game, and Terry Orr is the receiver. Last year, Orr caught 22 passes and scored three touchdowns with a 16.2-yard average.

Kicker — Chip Lohmiller continues to be the highest-scoring kicker in the NFL over the last five seasons. He has averaged 125 points and 30 field goals a season and should score 130 points or more this year if the Washington offense bounces back. Lohmiller was somewhat up and down in 1992, missing six field goals from the 30-to-39-yard range, but he was 10 of 14 from 40 and beyond, which is very good.

Defense — The Redskins allowed only 255 points in 1992 and would have progressed further in the playoffs if the offense had been consistent. The defense ranked seventh overall and sixth against the pass, and its 23 interceptions ranked third in the NFC. Free agency saw the loss of linemen Jumpy Geathers and Fred Stokes and cornerback Martin Mayhew, and the signing of defensive end Al Noga.

What to Expect in 1993 — The Cowboys will be the favorites, but there's no reason Washington can't win the division title again. The biggest factors will be how well the team responds to the change in coaches from Joe Gibbs to Richie Petitbon and whether or not Mark Rypien can bounce back.

Best Players to Draft — Quarterback Mark Rypien, running back Earnest Byner, wide receiver Ricky Sanders and kicker Chip Lohmiller.

1992 GAME-BY-GAME STATISTICS

QUARTERBACKS

Player	Stat	DAL.	ATL.	DET.	PHX.	DEN.	PHI.	MIN.	NYG	SEA.	K.C.	N.O.	PHX.	PHI.	DAL.	PHI.	RAID.
Mark Rypien	Att/Cmp	20-38	18-28	14-24	12-28	16-26	14-24	18-32	14-31	21-30	23-40	21-38	14-25	15-18	12-29	22-38	15-29
	Yards	208	181	136	254	245	240	148	187	248	217	207	175	216	144	272	204
	TD	1	2		1	1	1			1			2	2		1	1
Cary Conklin	Att/Cmp												2-2				
	Yards												16				
	TD												1				

RUNNING BACKS

Player	Stat	DAL.	ATL.	DET.	PHX.	DEN.	PHI.	MIN.	NYG	SEA.	K.C.	N.O.	PHX.	PHI.	DAL.	PHI.	RAID.
Earnest Byner	Att/Yards	13-56	22-91	30-120	20-73	16-46	18-45	17-79	9-32	13-47	6-21	13-29	16-62	20-100	19-69	16-93	14-35
	TD			1	2								1	2			
	Rec/Yards	4-31	4-26	3-20	2-48	2-7		5-37	1-12	7-61		4-10		2-15	2-19	2-33	1-19
	TD		1														
Ricky Ervins	Att/Yards	6-16	16-71	9-10	13-29	11-52	18-55	10-26	8-29	10-17	10-17	3-6	11-52	13-68	2-0	1-1	10-46
	TD										1						1
	Rec/Yards	2-12		1-7	1-2	2-22		3-28		3-27	10-66	2-23	1-5	2-18	1-8	2-34	2-4
	TD																
Brian Mitchell	Att/Yards										1-33	2-25			3-12		
	TD																
	Rec/Yards														3-30		
	TD																

RECEIVERS

Player	Stat	DAL.	ATL.	DET.	PHX.	DEN.	PHI.	MIN.	NYG	SEA.	K.C.	N.O.	PHX.	PHI.	DAL.	PHI.	RAID.
Ricky Sanders	Rec/Yards	3-20	2-38	4-38	1-19	2-18	2-62	3-13	4-72	2-12	5-71	4-54	4-54	5-69	3-53	7-114	
	TD				1								1			1	
Tim McGee	Rec/Yards	3-19	3-43	3-43	5-45	4-56	3-33	1-10	3-70	3-30		1-6		2-22	1-9	1-7	2-15
	TD					2			1								
Art Monk	Rec/Yards	2-43	6-44	1-12	3-59	7-69	6-96	2-25	5-61	1-9	2-19	3-27	2-21	1-42	1-9	1-11	3-97
	TD												1	1			1
Desmond Howard	Rec/Yards											1-8	1-5				1-7
	TD																
Terry Orr	Rec/Yards				1-24	1-58	1-16	2-76	2-15	3-82	1-13	3-23	3-2	2-25	2-46		1-3
	TD									1				1			

KICKERS

Player	Stat	DAL.	ATL.	DET.	PHX.	DEN.	PHI.	MIN.	NYG	SEA.	K.C.	N.O.	PHX.	PHI.	DAL.	PHI.	RAID.
Chip Lohmiller	FG/FGA	1-1	1-3	2-3	1-2	2-3	3-4	5-5	0-1	3-4	3-3	1-1	2-2		2-2	2-2	2-4

1992 SEASON STATISTICS

PLAYERS	PASSING				RUSHING				RECEIVING				KICKING			
	TD 1-9	TD 10-39	TD 40+	Yards 300+	TD 1-9	TD 10-39	TD 40+	Yards 100+	TD 1-9	TD 10-39	TD 40+	Yards 100+	FG 18-39	FG 40-49	FG 50+	PAT
Mark Rypien	1	8	4		2											
Cary Conklin																
Earnest Byner			1		5	1		2	1							
Ricky Ervins					2											
Brian Mitchell																
Ricky Sanders										2	1	1				
Tim McGee										3						
Art Monk										1	2					
Desmond Howard																
Terry Orr										2	1					
Chip Lohmiller													20	8	2	30

Chapter 11
Rick's Picks

Every year, strategy plays a key role in drafting. And every year that strategy changes. Last year, wide receiver was the deepest position; this year it is running back. Last year there were seven good quarterbacks before it dropped off; this year there are nine to 11.

Here's a look at the five positions, with a quick synopsis on each. These are intended for a league that uses a basic scoring system with some bonus points included for game performance and long scoring plays, but the overall suggestions will be helpful in any league.

Quarterbacks — Quarterback is stronger than it has been the last few years, about 10 players deep and solid through about the 15th player. There are seven or eight quarterbacks that are sure picks to have very good seasons (unless, of course, they get injured). In an eight-team league, don't be the last person to draft a quarterback. If you do, wait a while longer and stock up on other players before picking a quarterback, and then take two right away. Remember, because of the two byes this year, you will have to play your backup quarterback at least twice. Don't start the run on backup quarterbacks, but be sure to jump in it as soon as it does begin. The iffy quarterbacks this year are Joe Montana and Mark Rypien, both of whom could have good years or do nothing at all. The best passers to have as your backups are John Elway, Stan Humphries, Bernie Kosar and Jeff George.

Running Backs — This is a very deep position this year, much more so than in 1992. And there are a lot of players who could come on and have excellent seasons. Try to get one of the top three running backs — Barry Sanders, Emmitt Smith or Thurman Thomas — at all costs, or else get two of the players in the next tier of running backs. If you get two solid runners, you might want to draft one of the top backs who could come on in 1993 (such as Harvey Williams or Leonard Russell). If you don't have two solid backs, take a good one for your third back, and then gamble with your last pick. Remember to consider two rookies who might have excellent seasons — Garrison Hearst and Jerome Bettis. And, in leagues that use a performance scoring method, pick players like Harold Green and Chris Warren higher than you would in a league that uses a basic scoring system.

Wide Receivers — Wide receiver is not very deep this year, and is the thinnest position of the five. The top six wide receivers are very good, and the next three or four players should be solid performers. But after that, it's a real crapshoot. The dropoff is immediate, as the next 10 or 20 wideouts are all possible of having either very good years or else seasons that are nothing special. Thus, your second wide receiver is probably going to be a gamble, and certainly so are your third and fourth picks at the position. Make sure you get one of the top 10. Jerry Rice is clearly the best wide receiver, and everybody should be happy to have him. After him, however, it's a lot different. Consider rookies for your late picks, especially Sean Dawkins and O.J. McDuffie. This year, more than any other position, wide receiver is where fantasy football games are going to be won or lost. If you pick the surprises — and you won't know who they are when you're drafting — you'll win your league.

Tight Ends — This position is deeper than in the past few years. Keith Jackson is clearly the No. 1 draft pick and should be picked no later than the fourth round, and Eric Green might be a top pick, too, depending on his status during the preseason. When drafting tight ends, unless you get Jackson, wait until the run starts or else wait until the end of your draft before picking one. That's because the difference between the best tight end and the 10th best tight end is only a couple of touchdowns. On the backups, roll the dice.

Kickers — Nearly all of the kickers in the NFL are good, and the position is solid for at least the top 15 picks. For a change, practically all of the highest-scoring kickers are assured of keeping their jobs when September rolls around (Denver's David Treadwell might be the only one who gets replaced). Don't be the first person to draft a kicker, but once the run starts, either jump in early or else wait. If you do wait, grab the eighth- or 10th-best kicker, and then draft another again a round or two later before everybody else gets their backup. That way you can start your kickers according to the weekly matchups, which might be more beneficial than having one of the top kickers and only using your backup twice (because of the byes). If you get a top kicker, such as Chip Lohmiller or Pete Stoyanovich, don't draft your second kicker until your last pick or two.

Overall — Try to draft one of the following in the first round — Steve Young, Emmitt Smith, Barry Sanders, Thurman Thomas or Jerry Rice. After that, load up on running backs because wide receivers are such a gamble. For example, get your second running back before your second wide receiver, and try to draft tight end Eric Green before your second wideout, because Green has more potential (and one of the second tier of wide receivers could score anywhere from two to eight touchdowns; Green will certainly do better than two). Since everyone is assured of getting a good quarterback and kicker and most likely a decent tight end, focus most on running backs and wide receivers.

Quarterbacks

1. Steve Young, 49ers
2. Dan Marino, Dolphins
3. Warren Moon, Oilers
4. Randall Cunningham, Eagles
5. Jim Kelly, Bills
6. Troy Aikman, Cowboys
7. Bobby Hebert/Chris Miller, Falcons
8. Brett Favre, Packers
9. Jim Everett, Rams
10. Joe Montana, Chiefs
11. Mark Rypien, Redskins
12. John Elway, Broncos
13. Stan Humphries, Chargers
14. Bernie Kosar, Browns
15. Jeff George, Colts
16. Jim Harbaugh, Bears
17. Neil O'Donnell, Steelers
18. Phil Simms, Giants
19. Boomer Esiason, Jets
20. Steve Beuerlein, Cardinals
21. Jim McMahon, Vikings
22. Jeff Hostetler, Raiders
23. Rodney Peete, Lions
24. David Klingler, Bengals
25. Wade Wilson, Saints
26. Steve DeBerg, Buccaneers
27. Dan McGwire, Seahawks
28. Scott Secules, Patriots

Running Backs

1. Barry Sanders, Lions
2. Emmitt Smith, Cowboys
3. Thurman Thomas, Bills
4. Rodney Hampton, Giants
5. Barry Foster, Steelers
6. Ricky Watters, 49ers
7. Terry Allen, Vikings
8. Lorenzo White, Oilers
9. Neal Anderson, Bears
10. Jerome Bettis, Rams
11. Marion Butts, Chargers
12. Garrison Hearst, Cardinals
13. Reggie Cobb, Buccaneers
14. Brad Baxter, Jets
15. Harold Green, Bengals
16. Herschel Walker, Eagles
17. Christian Okoye, Chiefs
18. Earnest Byner, Redskins
19. Kevin Mack, Browns
20. Tom Rathman, 49ers
21. Rod Bernstine, Broncos
22. Mark Higgs, Dolphins
23. Brad Muster, Saints
24. Barry Word, Chiefs
25. Derrick Fenner, Bengals
26. Leonard Russell, Patriots
27. Craig Heyward, Bears
28. Chris Warren, Seahawks
29. Harvey Williams, Chiefs
30. Rodney Culver, Colts
31. Kenneth Davis, Bills
32. Heath Sherman, Eagles
33. Johnny Johnson, Jets
34. Vaughn Dunbar, Saints
35. Tony Smith, Falcons
36. Eric Metcalf, Browns
37. Gaston Green, Rams
38. Jarrod Bunch, Giants
39. Dalton Hilliard, Saints
40. Terry Kirby, Dolphins
41. Bobby Humphrey, Dolphins
42. Cleveland Gary, Rams
43. Tommy Vardell, Browns
44. Blair Thomas, Jets
45. Eric Dickerson, Colts
46. Eric Bieniemy, Chargers
47. Nick Bell, Raiders
48. Ricky Ervins, Redskins
49. John L. Williams, Seahawks
50. Marcus Allen, Raiders

Wide Receivers

1. Jerry Rice, 49ers
2. Andre Rison, Falcons
3. Sterling Sharpe, Packers
4. Haywood Jeffires, Oilers
5. Michael Irvin, Cowboys
6. Michael Haynes, Falcons
7. Ernest Givins, Oilers
8. Fred Barnett, Eagles
9. John Taylor, 49ers
10. Andre Reed, Bills
11. Anthony Miller, Chargers
12. Irving Fryar, Dolphins
13. Cris Carter, Vikings
14. Ricky Sanders, Redskins
15. Calvin Williams, Eagles
16. Bill Brooks, Bills
17. Gary Clark, Cardinals
18. Rob Moore, Jets
19. Webster Slaughter, Browns
20. Tim Brown, Raiders
21. Mike Pritchard, Falcons
22. Eric Martin, Saints
23. Herman Moore, Lions
24. Willie Anderson, Rams
25. Desmond Howard, Redskins
26. Mark Duper, Dolphins
27. Michael Jackson, Browns
28. Henry Ellard, Rams
29. Willie Green, Lions
30. Mark Jackson, Giants
31. Wendell Davis, Bears
32. Curtis Duncan, Oilers
33. Tim McGee, Redskins
34. Alvin Harper, Cowboys
35. James Lofton, Raiders
36. Eddie Brown, Bengals
37. Mark Ingram, Dolphins
38. Quinn Early, Saints
39. Brian Blades, Seahawks
40. Randal Hill, Cardinals
41. Mark Carrier, Browns
42. Vance Johnson, Broncos
43. Reggie Langhorne, Colts
44. Jessie Hester, Colts
45. Brett Perriman, Lions
46. Nate Lewis, Chargers
47. O.J. McDuffie, Dolphins
48. Anthony Carter, Vikings
49. Willie Davis, Chiefs
50. Sean Dawkins, Colts

Tight Ends

1. Keith Jackson, Dolphins
2. Eric Green, Steelers
3. Jay Novacek, Cowboys
4. Brent Jones, 49ers
5. Jackie Harris, Packers
6. Marv Cook, Patriots
7. Shannon Sharpe, Broncos
8. Keith McKeller, Bills
9. Keith Byars, Eagles
10. Johnny Mitchell, Jets
11. Ethan Horton, Raiders
12. Ron Hall, Buccaneers
13. Terry Orr, Redskins
14. Derek Brown, Giants
15. Pete Metzelaars, Bills
16. Ferrell Edmunds, Seahawks
17. Adrian Cooper, Steelers
18. Kerry Cash, Colts
19. Ben Coates, Patriots
20. Rodney Holman, Lions
21. Chris Gedney, Bears
22. Irv Smith, Saints
23. Pete Holohan, Browns
24. Troy Drayton, Rams
25. Derrick Walker, Chargers

Kickers

1. Chip Lohmiller, Redskins
2. Pete Stoyanovich, Dolphins
3. Steve Christie, Bills
4. Morten Andersen, Saints
5. Nick Lowery, Chiefs
6. Lin Elliott, Cowboys
7. Mike Cofer, 49ers
8. Al Del Greco, Oilers
9. Gary Anderson, Steelers
10. David Treadwell, Broncos
11. Norm Johnson, Falcons
12. Chris Jacke, Packers
13. Roger Ruzek, Eagles
14. Fuad Reveiz, Vikings
15. Jason Hanson, Lions
16. John Carney, Chargers
17. Kevin Butler, Bears
18. Matt Bahr, Giants
19. Jim Breech, Bengals
20. Greg Davis, Cardinals
21. Jeff Jaeger, Raiders
22. Matt Stover, Browns
23. Tony Zendejas, Rams
24. Cary Blanchard, Jets
25. Dean Biasucci, Colts
26. Daron Alcorn, Buccaneers
27. Charlie Baumann, Patriots
28. John Kasay, Seahawks

Top 100 Picks

1. Barry Sanders, Lions
2. Emmitt Smith, Cowboys
3. Jerry Rice, 49ers
4. Steve Young, 49ers
5. Thurman Thomas, Bills
6. Rodney Hampton, Giants
7. Ricky Watters, 49ers
8. Andre Rison, Falcons
9. Sterling Sharpe, Packers
10. Dan Marino, Dolphins
11. Terry Allen, Vikings
12. Barry Foster, Steelers
13. Warren Moon, Oilers
14. Haywood Jeffires, Oilers
15. Michael Irvin, Cowboys
16. Lorenzo White, Oilers
17. Randall Cunningham, Eagles
18. Neal Anderson, Bears
19. Jim Kelly, Bills
20. Michael Haynes, Falcons
21. Keith Jackson, Dolphins
22. Ernest Givins, Oilers
23. Troy Aikman, Cowboys
24. Bobby Hebert/Chris Miller, Falcons
25. Brett Favre, Packers
26. Jim Everett, Rams
27. Fred Barnett, Eagles
28. John Taylor, 49ers
29. Chip Lohmiller, Redskins
30. Pete Stoyanovich, Dolphins
31. Jerome Bettis, Rams
32. Andre Reed, Bills
33. Jerome Bettis, Rams
34. Steve Christie, Bills
35. Anthony Miller, Chargers
36. Joe Montana, Chiefs
37. Irving Fryar, Dolphins
38. Mark Rypien, Redskins
39. Morten Andersen, Saints
40. Marion Butts, Chargers
41. Nick Lowery, Chiefs
42. Lin Elliott, Cowboys
43. Garrison Hearst, Cardinals
44. Cris Carter, Vikings
45. Ricky Sanders, Redskins
46. Reggie Cobb, Buccaneers
47. Brad Baxter, Jets
48. Herschel Walker, Eagles
49. Mike Cofer, 49ers
50. Harold Green, Bengals
51. Calvin Williams, Eagles
52. Christian Okoye, Chiefs
53. Jay Novacek, Cowboys
54. Gary Clark, Cardinals
55. Rob Moore, Jets
56. Webster Slaughter, Oilers
57. Al Del Greco, Oilers
58. Earnest Byner, Redskins
59. Kevin Mack, Browns
60. John Elway, Broncos
61. Tom Rathman, 49ers
62. Gary Anderson, Steelers
63. Rod Bernstine, Broncos
64. Tim Brown, Raiders
65. Mike Pritchard, Falcons
66. Brent Jones, 49ers
67. David Treadwell/Jason Elam, Broncos
68. Chris Miller, Falcons
69. Mark Higgs, Dolphins
70. Brad Muster, Saints
71. Stan Humphries, Chargers
72. Bernie Kosar, Browns
73. Bill Brooks, Bills
74. Eric Martin, Saints
75. Herman Moore, Lions
76. Jackie Harris, Packers
77. Willie Anderson, Rams
78. Norm Johnson, Falcons
79. Barry Word, Chiefs
80. Derrick Fenner, Bengals
81. Jeff George, Colts
82. Marv Cook, Patriots
83. Leonard Russell, Patriots
84. Craig Heyward, Bears
85. Chris Warren, Seahawks
86. Harvey Williams, Chiefs
87. Jim Harbaugh, Bears
88. Shannon Sharpe, Broncos
89. Chris Jacke, Packers
90. Roger Ruzek, Eagles
91. Johnny Johnson, Jets
92. Rodney Culver, Colts
93. Kenneth Davis, Bills
94. Mark Duper, Dolphins
95. Michael Jackson, Browns
96. Fuad Reveiz, Vikings
97. Jason Hanson, Lions
98. Johnny Mitchell, Jets
99. Desmond Howard, Redskins
100. Cleveland Gary, Rams

Defenses

1. Kansas City Chiefs
2. Minnesota Vikings
3. Dallas Cowboys
4. Atlanta Falcons
5. New Orleans Saints
6. Houston Oilers
7. Philadelphia Eagles
8. Miami Dolphins
9. Green Bay Packers
10. Chicago Bears

Possible Busts

1. Pete Metzelaars, Bills
2. Cleveland Gary, Rams
3. Rodney Culver, Colts
4. Chris Miller, Falcons
5. Mark Jackson, Giants
6. Gary Clark, Cardinals
7. John Carney, Chargers
8. Michael Haynes, Falcons
9. Michael Jackson, Browns
10. Mark Clayton, Dolphins

Sleepers

1. Bobby Hebert, Falcons
2. Irving Fryar, Dolphins
3. Harvey Williams, Chiefs
4. Leonard Russell, Patriots
5. Johnny Mitchell, Jets
6. Terry Kirby, Dolphins
7. Bill Brooks, Bills
8. Jackie Harris, Packers
9. Desmond Howard, Redskins
10. Jeff George, Colts

Chapter 12
Offseason Update

THE INJURY REPORT

You cannot rely strictly on last year's statistics when you choose your team. A lot of players suffered injuries in 1992 that either lowered their stats considerably or hampered them enough to the point where they didn't have typical seasons.

Here's a look at the players who were injured last season, as well as a report on their recovery as of mid-May.

Quarterbacks

DAVE BROWN, Giants — Rushed into action last year because of the Giants' injuries at quarterback, Brown played in two games before suffering a broken thumb. He has recovered and will be Phil Simms' backup this year.

JOHN ELWAY, Broncos — Elway missed four games late last season because of a bruised right shoulder, but returned for the last two. He will be 100 percent heading into 1993.

JOHN FRIESZ, Chargers — Friesz missed the entire 1992 season after he suffered torn ligaments in his left knee in the first preseason game. He should be ready to go in July, and he'll either compete with Stan Humphries for the starting job or take over as the backup.

TOM HODSON, Patriots — Hodson suffered a broken thumb midway through last season and was sidelined for the remainder of it. Like the rest of the New England quarterbacks, he's healthy now, but it's anybody's guess as to who'll be the starter in September.

DONALD HOLLAS, Bengals — Hollas started the final game of 1992 but tore ligaments in his knee. He may not be ready to go by the start of training camp, so the Bengals re-signed Erik Wilhelm to back up David Klingler if Hollas can't go.

STAN HUMPHRIES, Chargers — Humphries suffered a dislocated right shoulder in Game 16 last year and played with special padding for the two playoff games. With a lot of rest, he was expected to be fully recovered for the start of the '93 season.

JIM KELLY, Bills — After missing two playoff games with a sprained right knee last season, Kelly returned in time for the AFC championship game and Super Bowl XXVII. However, he was knocked out of action again in the Super Bowl when he reinjured the knee. It didn't take him long to recover, and he's all set for the start of the new season.

DAVID KLINGLER, Bengals — After taking over the starting job in Cincinnati late last season, Klingler suffered a hip pointer and slight concussion and missed the last game of the year. He has recovered completely.

BERNIE KOSAR, Browns — Kosar seems to alternate injured seasons with healthy ones, and last year was one in which he was oft-injured. He broke his right ankle in Game 2 and didn't return for nine weeks. Then, after playing in five games, he rebroke the same ankle in the season finale. The Browns don't expect any problems with his rehab.

DON MAJKOWSKI, Packers — Majkowski has lost his starting job in Green Bay with no hope of getting it back as long as Brett Favre is healthy. Last year he started the first two games, then went out with strained ankle ligaments. He's not healthy yet, though he's also looking for a new team.

DAN McGWIRE, Seahawks — After taking over the starting job in the sixth week of 1992, McGwire promptly fractured his left hip and missed the rest of the season. His return to action shouldn't be slowed at all.

JIM McMAHON, Vikings — McMahon is in the best shape of his career after playing very little in 1992. So why is he on this list? Because he'll be injured before the 1993 season is half over.

HUGH MILLEN, Cowboys — After starting the first five games for New England in 1992, Millen played in only two games the rest of the season because of a third-degree shoulder separation from which he never recovered fully. He has by now, but he's also lost his starting job.

CHRIS MILLER, Falcons — Miller should be one of the best fantasy quarterbacks in the league, but he can't stay healthy for an entire season. Last year he suffered torn knee ligaments in Game 8 and missed the rest of the year. The Falcons say his recovery is on schedule, but there are some questions because the team did go out and sign Bobby Hebert from the Saints in the offseason. It's Hebert, not Miller, who will be the starter in 1993.

WARREN MOON, Oilers — Moon missed Games 11-15 last year with a shoulder injury before returning for the season finale and the playoffs. He has recovered completely, but he has been getting injured in recent years. If he goes down, make sure you pick up Cody Carlson immediately.

KEN O'BRIEN, Packers — O'Brien missed the last month of 1992 because of a fractured right arm. He has recovered fully, was traded to Green Bay in the offseason, and will serve as Brett Favre's backup.

NEIL O'DONNELL, Steelers — O'Donnell missed the last three regular-season games of 1992 with a broken right leg before returning in time for the playoffs. He has recovered fully.

TODD PHILCOX, Bengals — Philcox replaced an

injured Bernie Kosar in Game 3 but suffered a broken thumb and missed the remainder of the season. He's healthy again and re-signed with Cincinnati.

TIMM ROSENBACH, Cardinals — Rosenbach was on the Cardinals' roster at the end of last season after recovering from a separated shoulder. Now, after missing most of the last two seasons, even he has admitted he has lost a lot of confidence and might not want to play football again. That's not a good sign for a quarterback if he decides to return.

MARK RYPIEN, Redskins — Rypien played all 16 games in 1992 but was complaining of soreness in his right shoulder in the playoffs. He underwent minor arthroscopic surgery in February and should be 100 percent recovered for the start of training camp.

SCOTT SECULES, Patriots — With Miami in 1992, Secules spent the entire season on injured reserve with a torn muscle in his right shoulder (although he was activated in time for the AFC championship game). He has recovered fully and might compete for a starting job in New England this year.

PHIL SIMMS, Giants — Simms heads into 1993 as the unquestioned starter in New York. He missed the last 12 games of last season because of an elbow injury, although he could have played by December. He's getting old, but he'll start the season healthy.

SCOTT ZOLAK, Patriots — Zolak started four games last year before suffering an ankle injury. He'll be fine for the start of training camp, but he most likely won't be competing for a starting job.

Running Backs

JOHNNY BAILEY, Cardinals — Bailey missed the final two games of last season with an ankle injury but was healthy in time for his first appearance in the Pro Bowl.

BRAD BAXTER, Jets — Baxter missed the final game of last season with a hamstring injury but has already recovered.

ROD BERNSTINE, Broncos — Bernstine has rarely been able to stay healthy for an entire season. Last year, after missing seven games with a separated shoulder, he returned only to injure his right ankle, though he continued to play. He is healthy again, but for how long?

TONY BROOKS, Eagles — Brooks went on injured reserve last October with a knee injury. The Eagles said he was expected to be ready for training camp.

DEXTER CARTER, 49ers — Carter missed 10 games last season with a shoulder injury, returned for three and was then lost with a knee injury. He has recovered but will probably be traded.

PAT CHAFFEY, Jets — Chaffey missed the last two games last year with a rib injury but has recovered.

MARK HIGGS, Dolphins — Higgs suffered torn cartilage in his right knee in the final regular-season game of 1992 and missed the playoffs. His recovery is going well, although the Dolphins were looking for a more durable and better halfback.

BOBBY HUMPHREY, Dolphins — Humphrey was healthy all of 1992. But when the offseason began he got into several troubles with the law, including an argument with a friend in which he was shot by a gun in his right thigh. As of mid-May, the Dolphins had had little contact with Humphrey and it was not known if he would play football in the fall.

DARYL JOHNSTON, Cowboys — Johnston should have had surgery before the start of the 1992 season to repair bone spurs in his right shoulder, but he delayed it until it was too late. He finally underwent surgery in March and should be ready for training camp.

FRED McAFEE, Saints — After taking over a starting role in Week 14 of last season, McAfee suffered a shoulder injury and was lost for the rest of the season. He's OK now.

ALLEN PINKETT, cut by Saints — Pinkett suffered torn knee ligaments during a July scrimmage last year when he was with the Saints and missed the entire season. His rehabilitation was progressing well, but the team didn't offer him a contract for this season.

LEONARD RUSSELL, Patriots — Russell missed five games last year with a sprained ankle and a hip pointer but was expected to be 100 percent for the start of training camp.

JOHN SETTLE, Redskins — Settle has missed the last two seasons with a knee injury. He had recovered by January, when he was placed on the team's practice squad.

STEVE SEWELL, Broncos — Sewell missed the entire 1992 season because of an ankle that was broken in five places. He participated in the May minicamp, but was still rehabbing and was going to have a hard time making the team.

SAMMIE SMITH, cut by Broncos — Smith played in only four games last year because of injuries. A torn stomach muscle sidelined him for the last half of the season. He wasn't offered a contract by Denver for this season.

TONY SMITH, Falcons — Five different injuries hampered Smith throughout his 1992 rookie season, including a knee injury that put him on injured reserve at the end of the year. He should be 100 percent going into 1993, but he's going to have to prove he can stay in the lineup.

BLAIR THOMAS, Jets — Thomas missed seven of the last nine games of 1992 with a groin injury and a sprained left knee. He is expected to be in good shape heading into '93, but the Jets would like to replace him in the starting lineup. His durability has always been in question.

TOMMY VARDELL, Browns — Vardell missed the last two games of 1992 with a calf injury, but it isn't expected to hamper him this year.

JOHN L. WILLIAMS, Seahawks — Williams was bothered by a sore ankle some of last season and was planning to have bone spurs removed from it in the offseason. He should be fine for the start of training camp.

VINCE WORKMAN, Buccaneers — Workman suffered a separated shoulder in the 10th game of last season but will be fully recovered by the start of his first training camp in Tampa Bay.

Wide Receivers

MIKE BARBER, Buccaneers — A shoulder injury put

Barber on injured reserve for the end of the 1992 season. He'll be fine.

EDDIE BROWN, Bengals — A neck injury suffered early in last year's preseason shelved Brown for all of 1992. His recovery was progressing well during the offseason, but he was trying to get out of his contract with the team and get declared a free agent.

CRIS CARTER, Vikings — Carter missed the final four games of 1992 with a broken collarbone but returned in time for the playoffs. He has recovered 100 percent.

LOUIS CLARK, Seahawks — Clark missed the final six games of 1992 with a rib injury. He has recovered.

SHAWN COLLINS, Browns — Collins finished 1992 on injured reserve with a rib injury. He'll be ready to go by the start of training camp.

AARON COX, Colts — Cox can't go an entire season without some kind of an injury. Last year he missed the final six games with a hamstring injury. He has recovered and the Colts are optimistic he can stay healthy.

HART LEE DYKES, Patriots — Dykes has missed the last two years because of a broken kneecap. It is questionable whether or not he will be ready by this year's training camp.

AL EDWARDS, Bills — Edwards was placed on injured reserve during the playoffs with a thigh injury but is OK now.

STEPHEN HOBBS, Redskins — Hobbs missed the final 14 games of last season after suffering a knee injury. He has recovered.

DESMOND HOWARD, Redskins — Howard was placed on injured reserve with a shoulder injury before the start of the playoffs but will be 100 percent for the start of training camp.

FRED JONES, Chiefs — Jones was out of action for the last two games of '92 with a knee injury. He's fine.

HASSAN JONES, Vikings — A back injury sidelined Jones twice during the 1992 season, but he is OK by now.

TONY JONES, Falcons — Jones spent time on injured reserve at two different points of the 1992 season, a sore ankle sidelining him for the final game. He should be ready to go for training camp.

BRAD LAMB, Bills — Lamb missed the final nine games of 1992 because of a knee injury. He recovered in time for the playoffs and was activated off injured reserve.

RON MORRIS, Bears — Morris has played in just seven games the last two years because of a knee injury that hasn't come around yet. His prognosis for 1993 is questionable, and he isn't being counted on by the new coaching staff.

JEFF QUERY, Bengals — An ankle injury put Query on injured reserve for the final two games of last season. He has recovered completely during the offseason.

DEREK RUSSELL, Broncos — Because of a thumb injury, Russell missed the final four games of 1992. He has recovered and shouldn't be bothered by it this year.

LAWYER TILLMAN, Browns — Finally returning in the middle of 1992 after missing two-plus seasons, Tillman broke his right ankle in the final game of the year. It was healing OK in the offseason, but he has developed some pain in his left ankle, where he had the stress fractures. Whether or not he'll be 100 percent by July was questionable.

FLOYD TURNER, Saints — Turner suffered a broken left thighbone in the second game of 1992 and missed the remainder of the season. He did not participate in the May minicamp because he was still rehabilitating, but the team expected him to be recovered in time for this year's training camp.

TOM WADDLE, Bears — Waddle missed the last four games of 1992 with an injured hip. He has completely recovered.

Tight Ends

ERIC GREEN, Steelers — In 1992, Green missed three games with a bruised shoulder and then, after returning, was suspended for six games by the league. He returned by the playoffs.

PAUL GREEN, Seahawks — Green broke his left shoulder blade in practice before the fifth game of last season and was sidelined the rest of the year. He should be fine.

RON HALL, Buccaneers — Hall was sidelined for the final three games of 1992 because of a sprained knee but has recovered and will be 100 percent for the start of training camp.

DAMONE JOHNSON, Rams — Johnson missed the last 12 games of 1992 with a partial tear of the rotator cuff in his left shoulder. He should recover in time, but the Rams aren't keeping him in their plans for 1993.

TERRY ORR, Redskins — Orr underwent minor knee surgery in January but will be ready to go in September.

JIM RIGGS, Bengals — Riggs missed the last four games of last year with a sprained ankle but has recovered.

ALFREDO ROBERTS, Cowboys — Roberts suffered a severe knee injury in the final regular-season game of 1992 and missed the playoffs and Super Bowl. He had reconstructive surgery in January and is projected to begin contact work the first week of August, so he should miss only the first two weeks of training camp.

JIM THORNTON, Jets — With Chicago in 1992, Thornton spent the season on injured reserve with an arch injury. He had surgery again in January, but the Jets don't think it will bother him this season.

WESLEY WALLS, 49ers — Walls missed all of the 1992 regular season because of a shoulder injury but was activated for the NFC championship game. He's 100 percent now.

DON WARREN, Redskins — A shoulder injury put Warren on injured reserve for the last five games of 1992. He has been injury-prone the last few years but will head into 1993 in good condition.

Kickers

MATT BAHR, Giants — Bahr missed the last four games of last season with a knee injury and was replaced by Ken Willis, with whom he will compete for the job this year in training camp.

ROSTER CHANGES

Like it or not, free agency is now a fact of life in pro football. It was also a very difficult factor in the writing of this book, because players were changing teams practically every day until this book went to press in mid-May. The free agency period ran all the way to July 15, so there will undoubtedly be many changes that obviously could not be included in this book.

The teams that had improved the most as of mid-May were the Packers, Falcons, Jets and Broncos, while the Vikings, Eagles, Bills, 49ers and Redskins all lost quite a few good players.

From a fantasy football standpoint, the best players who changed teams were: quarterbacks Bobby Hebert (from Saints to Falcons); running backs Brad Muster (from Bears to Saints) and Rod Bernstine (from Chargers to Broncos); wide receivers Gary Clark (from Redskins to Cardinals), Mark Jackson (from Broncos to Giants), Mark Ingram (from Giants to Dolphins) and Tim McGee (from Bengals to Redskins); and tight end Ferrell Edmunds (from Dolphins to Seahawks). No kickers changed teams.

Among free agents who were still expected to change teams were Marcus Allen, Keith Byars and Mark Clayton.

Here's a list of the players who changed teams during the offseason.

SIGNED		LOST	
Atlanta Falcons			
WR	Bobby Hebert	QB	Wade Wilson
Buffalo Bills			
WR	Bill Brooks		
Chicago Bears			
RB	Craig Heyward	TE	Jim Thornton
		RB	Brad Muster
Cincinnati Bengals			
QB	Jay Schroeder	WR	Tim McGee
Cleveland Browns			
QB	Vinny Testaverde	QB	Mike Tomczak
WR	Mark Carrier	TE	Mark Bavaro
Dallas Cowboys			
		WR	Kelvin Martin
		QB	Steve Beuerlein
Denver Broncos			
RB	Rod Bernstine	WR	Mark Jackson
RB	Robert Delpino		
WR	Emile Harry		
Detroit Lions			
RB	James Jones	WR	Mike Farr
Green Bay Packers			
		RB	Vince Workman

Houston Oilers
No transactions involving skill-position players.

Indianapolis Colts			
WR	Aaron Cox	WR	Bill Brooks
Kansas City Chiefs			
		QB	Mark Vlasic
Los Angeles Raiders			
QB	Jeff Hostetler	QB	Jay Schroeder
Los Angeles Rams			
		RB	Robert Delpino
		WR	Aaron Cox
		WR	Emile Harry
Miami Dolphins			
WR	Mark Ingram	TE	Ferrell Edmunds
		QB	Scott Secules
Minnesota Vikings			
QB	Jim McMahon		
New England Patriots			
QB	Scott Secules		
WR	Mike Farr		
New Orleans Saints			
QB	Wade Wilson	QB	Bobby Hebert
RB	Brad Muster	RB	Craig Heyward
New York Giants			
WR	Mark Jackson	WR	Mark Ingram
WR	Mike Sherrard	QB	Jeff Hostetler
New York Jets			
TE	Jim Thornton		
Philadelphia Eagles			
TE	Mark Bavaro	QB	Jim McMahon
Phoenix Cardinals			
QB	Steve Beuerlein		
WR	Gary Clark		
Pittsburgh Steelers			
QB	Mike Tomczak		
San Diego Chargers			
		RB	Rod Bernstine
San Francisco 49ers			
		WR	Mike Sherrard
Seattle Seahawks			
WR	Kelvin Martin	RB	James Jones
TE	Ferrell Edmunds		

Tampa Bay Buccaneers

RB	Vince Workman	QB	Vinny Testaverde
QB	Mark Vlasic	WR	Mark Carrier

Washington Redskins

WR	Tim McGee	WR	Gary Clark

FREE AGENTS RE-SIGNED

The following players could have changed teams during the offseason but decided to re-sign with the teams they played for in 1992.

Player	Position	Team
Steve Bono	Quarterback	San Francisco
Mike Buck	Quarterback	New Orleans
Vince Evans	Quarterback	L.A. Raiders
Jim Harbaugh	Quarterback	Chicago
Sean Salisbury	Quarterback	Minnesota
Phil Simms	Quarterback	N.Y. Giants
Steve Smith	Running Back	L.A. Raiders
J.J. Birden	Wide Receiver	Kansas City
Chris Burkett	Wide Receiver	N.Y. Jets
Drew Hill	Wide Receiver	Atlanta
Odessa Turner	Wide Receiver	San Francisco
Clarence Verdin	Wide Receiver	Indianapolis
Trey Junkin	Tight End	Seattle

FREE AGENTS' OFFERS MATCHED

The following players could have changed teams, but the contract sheets they signed with other teams were matched by the team they played for in 1992.

Player	Offer Made By	Matched By
QB Neil O'Donnell	Tampa Bay	Pittsburgh
QB T.J. Rubley	Cleveland	L.A. Rams
RB Chris Warren	N.Y. Jets	Seattle
RB Derrick Fenner	N.Y. Jets	Cincinnati
WR Pat Newman	Tampa Bay	New Orleans
WR Ricky Proehl	New England	Phoenix

TRADES

There were quite a few big offseason trades involving skill-position players between the end of the 1992 season and mid-May. Most of these will have big impacts on their teams in 1993, and players such as Joe Montana and Irving Fryar could have very big seasons for fantasy football players.

Here's a list of those trades.

Player	1992 Team	1993 Team
QB Boomer Esiason	Cincinnati	N.Y. Jets
QB Hugh Millen	New England	Dallas
QB Joe Montana	San Francisco	Kansas City
QB Ken O'Brien	N.Y. Jets	Green Bay

RB Gaston Green	Denver	L.A. Raiders
RB Johnny Johnson	Phoenix	N.Y. Jets
RB John Stephens	New England	Green Bay
WR M. Fernandez	L.A. Raiders	San Francisco
WR Irving Fryar	New England	Miami

RETIREMENTS

The following players announced their retirement:

Player	Position	Team
Dennis Gentry	Wide Receiver	Chicago
Buford Jordan	Running Back	New Orleans
Freeman McNeil	Running Back	N.Y. Jets

SUSPENSIONS

Steelers running back Tim Worley was suspended for the entire 1992 season because he missed two mandatory urine tests and was awaiting a decision by the NFL to reinstate him.

CUTS

The following veteran players were cut during the offseason and had not been re-signed by another team:

Player	Position	Team
David Archer	Quarterback	Philadelphia
Kelly Stouffer	Quarterback	Seattle
Maurice Carthon	Running Back	Indianapolis
Johnny Hector	Running Back	N.Y. Jets
Ivy Joe Hunter	Running Back	New England
Sammie Smith	Running Back	Denver
Willie Culpepper	Wide Receiver	Tampa Bay
Millard Hamilton	Wide Receiver	N.Y. Giants
Hassan Jones	Wide Receiver	Minnesota
James Lofton	Wide Receiver	Buffalo
Walter Stanley	Wide Receiver	New England
Clarence Kay	Tight End	Denver
John Tice	Tight End	New Orleans

ROSTER ADDITIONS

Here is a list of players who signed contracts during the offseason. Most of them did not play in the NFL in 1992 (list does not include practice squad players).

Player	Last Team	1993 Team
QB Brad Goebel	Philadelphia	Cleveland
QB Troy Taylor	N.Y. Jets	Miami
RB Latin Berry	Cleveland	Green Bay
RB Terrence Flagler	San Francisco	Miami
RB Derek Loville	Seattle	San Francisco
RB Craig Taylor	Cincinnati	New Orleans
RB Robert Wilson	Tampa Bay	Green Bay
RB Alonzo Highsmith	Tampa Bay	Kansas City

WR Michael Bates	Unsigned in '92	Seattle
WR Robert Claiborne	San Diego	Tampa Bay
WR Floyd Dixon	Philadelphia	Washington
WR Willie Drewrey	Tampa Bay	Houston
WR Derrick Faison	San Diego	San Francisco
WR Troy Kyles	San Francisco	Green Bay
WR Louis Lipps	New Orleans	Pittsburgh
WR Sammy Martin	Indianapolis	New Orleans
WR Stephone Paige	Kansas City	Minnesota
WR Kitrick Taylor	Green Bay	Denver
WR Walter Wilson	San Diego	Tampa Bay
WR Michael Young	Denver	Kansas City
TE Jesse Anderson	Pittsburgh	Green Bay
TE Rodney Holman	Cincinnati	Detroit
TE Orson Mobley	Denver	Miami
TE Derek Tennell	Dallas	Minnesota
TE Danta Whitaker	Minnesota	Miami
K Phillip Doyle	Phoenix	Tampa Bay
K Ian Howfield	Houston	Tampa Bay
K Carlos Huerta	San Diego	Houston

A LOOK AT THE NEW COACHES

Because a new head coach often means a team's philosophy will change considerably, you should be aware of that when drafting players from those teams. There will be five new head coaches in the NFL in 1993. Here's a look at them and what kind of changes to expect.

BILL PARCELLS, Patriots — Parcells assumes control of a team that isn't all that bad but lacks star talent at practically every position. The drafting of quarterback Drew Bledsoe addresses the biggest problem, but Bledsoe will not play much this year. Parcells will run his offense like he did with the Giants. He says it has been proven that teams have to be able to run effectively week in and week out in order to win, and he wants a 2-1 ratio of runs to passes. First he'll have to find an every-down back, and Leonard Russell will get the first opportunity. The starting quarterback is in question, and that obviously will affect the entire offense. However, Parcells won Super Bowls with two different styles of offenses in New York, so he will gear his offense around the personnel. The best thing Parcells did was hire almost his entire Giants coaching staff.

RICHIE PETITBON, Redskins — The surprise retirement of Joe Gibbs elevated Petitbon to head coach, although the team will pretty much look the same as it did under Gibbs. The biggest changes will be that Petitbon will be more inclined to make changes. If quarterback Mark Rypien struggles again, Pettibon will not hesitate to give Cary Conklin a chance (the two, in fact, will most likely compete in training camp for the starting job). He has also talked about going to a two-back offense, with Earnest Byner and Ricky Ervins as the starters, but there's little depth after them. Petitbon has already announced some changes at wide receiver. The departure of Gary Clark in free agency means Petitbon will go with Ricky Sanders and

Desmond Howard as the starters and ex-Bengal Tim McGee as the much-used third wideout. That leaves Art Monk as an unhappy backup. However, when the games start, no matter who is playing, the offense will look the same because Petitbon will concern himself mostly with the defense. But it'll be up to coordinator Rod Dowhower to take over for Gibbs when it comes to the offense.

WADE PHILLIPS, Broncos — Phillips is the most low-key of the five new head coaches this year, but he has made a lot of moves since taking over from Dan Reeves. He says his philosophy will be to pass to set up the run, and his No. 1 weapon will be quarterback John Elway, who will use more of the 49ers' offense. The passing game will incorporate running backs and tight ends as persistent threats and will attack defenses aggressively to take advantage of Elway's big-play abilities. Newly acquired running back Rod Bernstine will be used both as a runner and receiver if he can stay healthy. There's a lot of depth in the backfield, too. Among the problems is a lack of veteran talent at wide receiver, but Phillips did address the biggest problem by signing several free agents for the offensive line to protect Elway.

DAN REEVES, Giants — The biggest change Giants fans will notice in 1993 will be a bigger emphasis on the passing game. Reeves ended any possibility of a quarterback controversy shortly after taking over by naming Phil Simms as the starter and releasing Jeff Hostetler. Simms may be old, but he'll be a great tutor for Dave Brown, a second-year pro who will take over in about 1995. Reeves also upgraded the receivers with the addition of ex-Bronco Mark Jackson and Mike Sherrard. Reeves never had a great tight end in Denver, but he has a super talent to work with in Derek Brown, last year's No. 1 draft pick, who should get more playing time in '93. There will be less of an emphasis on the running game, but Rodney Hampton should still get his share of yards and touchdowns. Don't be surprised if Jarrod Bunch and Dave Meggett get more involved in the offense.

DAVE WANNSTEDT, Bears — Mike Ditka is gone and Wannstedt takes over a Bears team that isn't as bad as it appeared in 1992 and isn't as good as the division winner of '91. Wannstedt will pattern the offense after that of Dallas and San Francisco with a controlled passing attack. He hired Ron Turner as the offensive coordinator. Turner is the former head coach of San Jose State and the brother of Norv Turner, the Cowboys' offensive coordinator. Shortly after being hired, Wannstedt named Neal Anderson as the starting halfback, and he should be able to get something out of new fullback Craig Heyward (who, incidentally, was recruited and coached in college by Ron Turner). Wannstedt knew he needed to get more speed on the Bears, especially at wide receiver, where the Bears are one of the slowest teams in the league (he drafted Curtis Conway No. 1). Jim Harbaugh is the unquestioned starter at quarterback. Defensively, Wannstedt will readily substitute 16 or 17 players depending on down and distance, just as he did in Dallas last year.

Chapter 13
The Rookie Report

FORECASTING THE 1993 ROOKIES

In most years, rookies are bad performers in fantasy football. But that could be different this year because the rookie salary cap will entice rookies to sign earlier and a deadline on when rookies can sign before being forced to miss the entire season has been set. Look for very few holdouts this year as well as more impact from rookies.

Most years, there are a number of rookies who make impacts in the NFL. In 1990, the first-year stars (among the skill-position players) included Emmitt Smith, Jeff George, Johnny Johnson, Rob Moore and Steve Christie.

But the last two years it was a different story. The Offensive Rookie of the Year in 1991 was New England running back Leonard Russell, who gained 959 yards but averaged only 3.6 yards per carry and scored only four touchdowns. In 1992, Detroit kicker Jason Hanson was voted the top offensive rookie, which didn't say much for the quarterbacks, running backs and receivers in that rookie class.

Last season, several rookie quarterbacks started games, but none of them was very good. Running back was almost a total washout, as neither Tony Smith, Vaughn Dunbar nor Tommy Vardell was worthy of first-round status and Rodney Culver wasn't much of a runner other than at the goal line. Some of the receivers were pretty good, but Desmond Howard, Carl Pickens, and Courtney Hall didn't excite people much at all. And the two top tight ends, Derek Brown and Johnny Mitchell, did little. The best rookies were the kickers — Hanson and Lin Elliott, a free agent.

But 1993 is another year. And, even though the draft was weak, there are quite a few fine prospects, players who are capable of rushing for 1,000 yards or catching six or eight touchdown passes this season.

The top two players drafted were quarterbacks, although they went to the two worst teams in the league and will take several years before they start producing big numbers.

Running backs usually have the best chance to break into a team's starting lineup, with receivers next, and this year will be no different. Garrison Hearst and Jerome Bettis will start for the Cardinals and Rams, respectively, and both should have solid or even spectacular years. There are also several game-breaking wideouts who are capable of starring for their teams and in fantasy football. The tight ends are pretty good, with four of them expected to play a lot. And at least two or three rookie placekickers will make rosters and displace some aging veterans.

In preparing for your draft, you need to know who are the best rookies and which have the best chances of starting and contributing. A successful rookie is one who is in training camp, filling a hole, or on a good team. How much one played during the preseason is also an indication of a team's plans.

Rookies in this chapter are evaluated and then ranked according to the impact they might have this season, based on their expected playing time.

TEAM-BY-TEAM DRAFT ANALYSIS

The 1993 draft was considered one of the worst in recent years. The first round was fairly good, but then it dropped off quickly and was weak by the middle of Round 2.

A record number of trades occurred on Draft Day this year, with teams moving up a few spots to draft players they thought would be able to help right away.

Some teams drafted specifically to fill holes lost by defecting free agents, while others were looking for help right away from untested rookies.

ATLANTA FALCONS

Rd.	Player	Pos.	College	Pick
6	Lyons, Mitch	TE	Michigan State	151
8	Baker, Shannon	WR	Florida State	205

The Falcons concentrated on defense during the offseason and picked up two late-round receivers in the draft. Lyons joins Harper LeBel as the only tight ends on the roster, but he's just a blocker. Baker is a long shot to make the team, although he does have the kind of deep speed the Falcons are looking for because most of their receivers are possession guys.

BUFFALO BILLS

Rd.	Player	Pos.	College	Pick
4	Copeland, Russell	WR	Memphis State	111
7	Harris, Willie	WR	Mississippi State	195

The Bills are loaded on offense, so their draft focused on other positions. The two wide receivers selected will have a hard time making the team unless they quickly show something. Copeland's chances improved after the team released James Lofton, and he's also a good kick returner. He could display big-play abilities the team needs.

CHICAGO BEARS

Rd.	Player	Pos.	College	Pick
1	Conway, Curtis	WR	Southern Cal	7
3	Gedney, Chris	TE	Syracuse	61

The Bears finally got the speed — and perhaps the impact player — they needed on offense. Curtis Conway might not play a real lot at wide receiver this season, but he is expected to contribute right away on kickoff and punt returns. In time, he could be a gamebreaker. Tight end Chris Gedney helps at a position at which the Bears haven't had a decent receiver since Mike Ditka was playing. He might start and could be the next Jay Novacek if the Bears throw to him enough.

CINCINNATI BENGALS

Rd.	Player	Pos.	College	Pick
2	McGee, Tony	TE	Michigan	37
8	Pelfrey, Doug	PK	Kentucky	202

Tony McGee should immediately move into the starting lineup because Rodney Holman is no longer around. He's an all-around tight end who does everything well, and he can get deep as Holman used to be able to do. Pelfrey will battle Jim Breech for the kicking job and might win it. He can kick the long ones as well as handle the kickoffs, something Breech hasn't done for years. If he shows some promise, he'll replace Breech, who is kicking well but is certainly getting old.

CLEVELAND BROWNS

The Browns didn't draft any players at the skill positions.

DALLAS COWBOYS

Rd.	Player	Pos.	College	Pick
2	Williams, Kevin	WR	Miami (Fla.)	46
4	Lassic, Derrick	RB	Alabama	94

Sure, the Cowboys are loaded on offense, but Williams gives them another gamebreaker who can score every time he touches the ball. He came out of college a little early, but he can play both wide receiver and halfback, as well as return kicks. Look for Jimmy Johnson to utilize Williams in a lot of ways. Lassic will back up Emmitt Smith at halfback and should give him the rest he has needed but hasn't received the last three years. And that will help Smith in the long run.

DENVER BRONCOS

Rd.	Player	Pos.	College	Pick
2	Milburn, Glyn	RB	Stanford	43
3	Elam, Jason	P-PK	Hawaii	70
5	Williams, Kevin	RB	UCLA	126
6	Bonner, Melvin	WR	Baylor	154
7	Williams, Clarence	TE	Washington State	169
7	Kimbrough, Antonius	WR	Jackson State	182
8	Stablein, Brian	WR	Ohio State	210

The Broncos loaded up on offensive players and might even have found a new kicker. Milburn gives them an exciting scatback who can run, catch the ball and return kicks — the likes of which Broncos fans haven't seen in years. Elam was a bit of a surprise pick, but since he can also kick off deep, he might beat out David Treadwell, who can't. Williams is very inconsistent and joins a deep backfield, but he can provide excellent play at times.

Bonner, Kimbrough and Stablein will vie for jobs at a position at which the Broncos are deep but not overly talented. Williams joins a position that might already be set.

DETROIT LIONS

The Lions didn't draft any players at the skill positions. They did trade their first-round pick, the eighth overall, to New Orleans for linebacker Pat Swilling, who will fortify the defense. Detroit had already improved its needs on the offensive line by signing three free agents, so it didn't have to use the draft for that position.

GREEN BAY PACKERS

Rd.	Player	Pos.	College	Pick
5	Brunell, Mark	QB	Washington	118

The Packers didn't get the receiver they were looking for to complement Sterling Sharpe, so they still have a big hole on the offense. Brunell will compete for the No. 3 job at quarterback with Ty Detmer and could be a real sleeper.

HOUSTON OILERS

Rd.	Player	Pos.	College	Pick
4	Hannah, Travis	WR	Southern Cal	102
5	Mills, John Henry	TE	Wake Forest	131
7	Robinson, Patrick	WR	Tennessee State	187

The Oilers are already loaded at the skill positions, so they fortified their lines and defense in the draft. Hannah is the kind of speed receiver the team lacks, and he adds youth to the position. Mills is basically a big wideout, though he will probably play H-back (there isn't another tight end on the roster). Robinson will compete for a job as an inside receiver.

INDIANAPOLIS COLTS

Rd.	Player	Pos.	College	Pick
1	Dawkins, Sean	WR	California	16
2	Potts, Roosevelt	RB	Northeast Louisiana	49
6	Etheredge, Carlos	TE	Miami (Fla.)	157
7	Lewis, Lance	RB	Nebraska	184

The Colts didn't have a big need at wide receiver, but Dawkins is the kind of pass-catcher they have lacked. Jeff George has an improved line blocking for him, and Dawkins might quickly turn into his most-used receiver and should turn a few short passes into big plays. Potts will be given the first opportunity to start in the one-back offense. He is a huge runner who can move the pile and even catch the ball. Etheredge and Lewis will have a hard time making the team.

KANSAS CITY CHIEFS

Rd.	Player	Pos.	College	Pick
6	Turner, Darius	RB	Washington	159
7	Hughes, Danan	WR	Iowa	186

Kansas City added quarterback Joe Montana in a trade for draft picks. Turner could fill a need at fullback in the new two-back offense that has been installed. Hughes is the player to watch. If he decides to play football rather than baseball, he might be the best wide receiver on the team. And Montana certainly needs a few top players to throw to. He would have gone in the second round if he wasn't playing baseball.

LOS ANGELES RAIDERS

Rd.	Player	Pos.	College	Pick
3	Hobert, Billy Joe	QB	Washington	58
5	Truitt, Olanda	WR	Mississippi State	125
8	Robinson, Greg	RB	Northeast Louisiana	208

The Raiders again surprised everyone, this time by taking quarterback Billy Joe Hobert in the third round. Hobert never lost a game as the starter at Washington, and the pick means the team has lost its pateince with Todd Marinovich, the No. 1 pick just two years ago. Truitt could be a steal in the fifth round. He's not overly impressive, but he always seems to find a hole in a defense.

LOS ANGELES RAMS

Rd.	Player	Pos.	College	Pick
1	Bettis, Jerome	RB	Notre Dame	10
2	Drayton, Troy	TE	Penn State	39
3	White, Russell	RB	California	73
5	LaChapelle, Sean	WR	UCLA	122

Bettis will be given the ball immediately by Chuck Knox and then over and over again. He can play both halfback and fullback and fits the bill in a one-back offense. But he can also catch the ball, and he doesn't fumble, which is the problem with Cleveland Gary, the incumbent. He might be utilized the way the Redskins used to use John Riggins. Drayton might start immediately, too. He adds a new dimension to the offense in the form of a tight end who can go deep. White slipped his last two years in college but flashes big-time ability at times. LaChapelle is a possession receiver who will help on third downs.

MIAMI DOLPHINS

Rd.	Player	Pos.	College	Pick
1	McDuffie, O.J.	WR	Penn State	25
3	Kirby, Terry	RB	Virginia	78

McDuffie will be used in a lot of ways by Miami — as the third receiver, as a third-down running back and on kick returns. He isn't overly fast, but he is an impact player (though he does fumble too much, which Don Shula won't like). Kirby was a steal in the third round and will split time with Mark Higgs or even start. He's a big back who is a slashing runner, good blocker and excellent receiver. The Miami offense has reloaded and the team is looking to get back to the Super Bowl.

MINNESOTA VIKINGS

Rd.	Player	Pos.	College	Pick
1	Smith, Robert	RB	Ohio State	21
2	Ismail, Qadry	WR	Syracuse	52
7	Torretta, Gino	QB	Miami (Fla.)	192

Minnesota needed linemen on both sides of the ball but instead drafted at positions it really didn't need desperately. Smith is a scoring machine who will be used in the backfield to spell Terry Allen, as a receiver and on kickoffs. As long as he has his head in order, he could be a nice surprise. Ismail adds speed and youth to a position that needed both. He is a big-play receiver-returner who is sometimes inconsistent. With both of them returning kicks, the Vikings should usually start in great field position.

NEW ENGLAND PATRIOTS

Rd.	Player	Pos.	College	Pick
1	Bledsoe, Drew	QB	Washington State	1
2	Brisby, Vincent	WR	Northeast Louisiana	56
5	Sisson, Scott	PK	Georgia Tech	113
5	Griffith, Richard	TE	Arizona	138
8	Brown, Troy	KR	Marshall	198

Bledsoe was the No. 1 overall pick in the draft and should develop into a franchise quarterback in time. But since the Patriots don't have anybody good enough to hold down the job this year, Bledsoe might be starting by the time December rolls around. He has everything it takes to be a great quarterback except a good supporting cast. Brisby could be a steal in the second round. He's raw, but he can do it all. Sisson will challenge Charlie Baumann for the placekicking job and should be able to win it. He handles pressure well and can kick the long ones. Griffith joins a position that is set. Brown is strictly a kick returner, though he's a good one.

NEW ORLEANS SAINTS

Rd.	Player	Pos.	College	Pick
1	Smith, Irv	TE	Notre Dame	20
4	Neal, Lorenzo	RB	Fresno State	89
4	Brown, Derek	RB	Nebraska	109

The Saints got the top players at two positions — offensive lineman (Willie Roaf) and tight end (Irv Smith). Smith should win the starting job from the start. He is a good blocker who catches well and can run after the catch. He didn't get the ball much in college, so he needs some refinement. But in time he should be a good one. Neal is a bowling ball type of fullback who will back up Brad Muster. He was known for his hard-nosed blocking and running. Brown is a third-down, pass-catching scatback who can also return kicks.

NEW YORK GIANTS

Rd.	Player	Pos.	College	Pick
7	Peterson, Todd	PK	Georgia	177

The Giants had already used this year's first-round pick in 1992 for quarterback Dave Brown, who is Phil Simms' understudy. He is at least two years away from being the starter. Peterson will be given a chance to win the placekicking job from Matt Bahr and Ken Willis, though he certainly isn't favored. His long kickoffs will help him.

NEW YORK JETS

Rd.	Player	Pos.	College	Pick
5	Baxter, Fred	TE	Auburn	115
5	Murrell, Adrian	RB	West Virginia	120
5	Shedd, Kenny	WR	Northern Iowa	129
6	Anderson, Richie	RB	Penn State	144
8	Hentrich, Craig	PK-P	Notre Dame	200

Running backs Richie Anderson and Adrian Murrell will compete for roster spots. Anderson, a big slasher who scored 18 touchdowns last year at Penn State, could surprise. Murrell is an excellent receiver who can turn the corner on runs. Toss in running back Johnny Johnson as a draft-day acquisition, too. He will push Blair Thomas in the backfield. Tight end Fred Baxter will compete for the No. 3 job, and wideout Kenny Shedd could find a spot, too. Shedd is a big-play specialist and kick returner. Craig Hentrich should push for a punting job — not as a kicker.

PHILADELPHIA EAGLES

Rd.	Player	Pos.	College	Pick
2	Bailey, Victor	WR	Missouri	50
7	Mickey, Joey	TE	Oklahoma	190

The Eagles had a lot of picks early but seemed to draft more for quantity than quality. Bailey is a top-notch receiver who will wind up as the No. 3 wideout behind Fred Barnett and Calvin Williams. Bailey is an acrobatic pass catcher who isn't afraid to go over the middle. He might challenge Williams for a starting role in time.

PHOENIX CARDINALS

Rd.	Player	Pos.	College	Pick
1	Hearst, Garrison	RB	Georgia	3
4	Moore, Ronald	RB	Pittsburg (Kan.) State	87
8	Anderson, Steve	WR	Grambling	215

Phoenix had three picks in the top 32, picking up running back Garrison Hearst and two offensive tackles. The Cardinals might have given away too much when they dealt running back Johnny Johnson to the Jets to move up one pick to take Hearst. But, if Hearst is another Emmitt Smith, the deal will be well worth it. And he might well be. Moore dominated Division II last year and will spell Hearst. Anderson is a long shot.

PITTSBURGH STEELERS

Rd.	Player	Pos.	College	Pick
3	Hastings, Andre	WR	Georgia	76
7	Keith, Craig	TE	Lenoir-Rhyne (N.C.)	189
8	Van Pelt, Alex	QB	Pittsburgh	216

Hastings is considered a possession receiver, but he's better than most because he can occasionally break one for a score. He is a natural receiver who can make the difficult catches, and he can also return kickoffs. Keith is a blocker who will challenge for the No. 3 spot at tight end. And Van Pelt, the local quarterback, might make it in the No. 3 spot.

SAN DIEGO CHARGERS

Rd.	Player	Pos.	College	Pick
2	Means, Natrone	RB	North Carolina	41
5	Dunson, Walter	WR	Middle Tennessee St.	134
8	Green, Trent	QB	Indiana	222

Bobby Beathard traded away next year's No. 1 pick to get Means, a big back in the mold of Marion Butts. If Means keeps his weight down, he will be worth it, because he is ideally suited for a one-back offense. He is a strong runner who can elude tacklers in the open field. Dunson will be tried at both wideout and cornerback. As a receiver, he has great quickness, and he can also return kicks. Green has some good abilities and might surprise.

SAN FRANCISCO 49ERS

Rd.	Player	Pos.	College	Pick
8	Grbac, Elvis	QB	Michigan	219

Grbac isn't going to be a very good pro quarterback, but the 49ers' system fits him better than anything else. He will battle Bill Musgrave for the No. 3 role.

SEATTLE SEAHAWKS

Rd.	Player	Pos.	College	Pick
1	Mirer, Rick	QB	Notre Dame	2
5	Warren, Terrence	WR	Hampton (Va.) Inst.	114

Mirer is a great talent, but a lot of people have mixed opinions about what kind of pro quarterback he is going to be. The Seahawks preferred Drew Bledsoe, who went to New England on the first pick of the draft, and they might have reached with Mirer, who will need some time to develop. He has great intangibles and is a leader with a strong arm. But if he's forced to play too soon — and he might be in Seattle — his progress will be hindered. Warren is a super prospect with size, speed and breakaway abilities. He needs a lot of development, but he might be the big-play maker the team needs.

TAMPA BAY BUCCANEERS

Rd.	Player	Pos.	College	Pick
3	Thomas, Lamar	WR	Miami (Fla.)	60
4	Harris, Rudy	RB	Clemson	91
4	Copeland, Horace	WR	Miami (Fla.)	104
7	Davis, Tyree	WR	Central Arkansas	176
8	Branch, Darrick	WR	Hawaii	220
8	Alcorn, Daron	PK	Akron	224

The Buccaneers needed a quarterback but instead went for wide receivers with nobody to throw to them. Thomas and Copeland were teammates at Miami. Thomas may have been the most developed receiver in the draft, and he might move right into the lineup. Copeland has great abilities but is raw around the edges. Harris is the big blocking back the Bucs have needed, and he will complement Reggie Cobb well. Branch and Davis will have a hard time making the team; both are excellent kick returners (Davis is the brother of the Chiefs' Willie Davis). And Alcorn will probably inherit the placekicking job with a decent preseason. He has a very strong leg and handles pressure well.

WASHINGTON REDSKINS

Rd.	Player	Pos.	College	Pick
2	Brooks, Reggie	RB	Notre Dame	45
6	Wycheck, Frank	TE	Maryland	160

The acquisition of Brooks could spell trouble for either the aging Earnest Byner or Ricky Ervins, who slumped badly in his second season in 1992. Brooks runs like former Giant Joe Morris, except he's quicker and has better moves (though he's not as durable). But he can break tackles. The Redskins like tight ends, and Wycheck joins a position that is deep. He's more of a receiver than a blocker.

ROOKIES BY POSITION

Players are ranked according to how well they might do in fantasy football this year.

Quarterbacks

DREW BLEDSOE, Patriots — The No. 1 pick in the draft, Bledsoe has "franchise player" written all over him, but he is not going to move right into the starting lineup. He has great size, a quick release and the arm strength to make the most difficult throws, and great footwork like John Elway. He possesses great pocket presence and knows how to find a receiver, and has a fiery attitude. He's a leader, but coach Bill Parcells quickly said Bledsoe will not play until he is ready. Because of the Patriots' problems at quarterback, he will certainly see game time this year, and he might be forced to start before Parcells would like.

RICK MIRER, Seahawks — The No. 2 pick in this year's draft, Mirer joins a team that badly needs a quarterback, but he isn't ready to play yet. He is an exceptional runner who stays in the pocket and can handle the pressure. He has good footwork and a quick, compact release and can throw upfield. But he lacks experience in a pro-style offense and would get killed if he's forced to play too quickly.

BILLY JOE HOBERT, Raiders — The third quarterback drafted this year, Hobert has an accurate arm and can find the soft spots in a zone. He's a tough quarterback who can run and hit receivers in stride. But he's going to be the No. 3 man on the Raiders' roster, and that won't get him into many games.

MARK BRUNELL, Packers — The second quarterback drafted from the University of Washington, Brunell will challenge Ty Detmer for the No. 3 job in Green Bay. Brunell is a short lefty who can spark a team and could be the sleeper of the 1993 quarterback crop.

ELVIS GRBAC, 49ers — The former Michigan star will battle it out with Bill Musgrave for the 49ers' No. 3 job. Grbac is the type of quarterback who fits into the San Francisco offense, because he is an efficient passer. But he gets flustered under pressure and lacks a strong arm and mobility.

GINO TORRETTA, Vikings — The 1992 Heisman Trophy winner never did project to be a top quarterback in the pros. He will compete with Brad Johnson for Minnesota's No. 3 role. Torretta won 26 of 28 games in college but doesn't have the mechanics, arm strength or mobility required of a pro quarterback.

Running Backs

GARRISON HEARST, Cardinals — Hearst might have been the best player in this year's draft. He is the total package, with terrific speed, acceleration and vision, and he has been called a combination of Barry Sanders and Emmitt Smith. The only question is the strength of his left knee, which has a partially torn ligament. But scouts and doctors determined that the tear occurred years ago and shouldn't bother him (much like what Buffalo's Thurman Thomas overcame). Hearst is the early favorite for Rookie of the Year. He knows how to set up defenders, and he can outrun the fastest defensive backs and catch passes. He rushed for 1,547 yards and scored 21 touchdowns last season while leading the nation in scoring. He was third in the Heisman balloting.

JEROME BETTIS, Rams — Chuck Knox has always had one featured back throughout his coaching career, and Bettis is going to be the one in the coach's second stint with the Rams. Bettis was chosen with the 10th pick in the draft. The Notre Damer can play as a well-rounded fullback or as the single runner in the Rams' one-back offense. He has the power to run over tacklers or the speed to scoot in the open field, and it takes more than one tackler to bring him down. Bettis, who averaged 5.4 yards per carry at Notre Dame, also catches the ball well and doesn't fumble.

TERRY KIRBY, Dolphins — Kirby might have been the steal of the draft in the third round. He might be able to share time with Mark Higgs at halfback and could also play fullback. A fine inside power runner and excellent receiver, his quickness is a question. He ran for 1,130 yards last year at Virginia despite missing three games.

REGGIE BROOKS, Redskins — A second-round pick, Brooks is a slashing runner with excellent moves and outside speed. He has been compared to former Giant Joe Morris. Brooks lacks height (he's 5-foot-7), but his size can fool tacklers because his strong legs make him hard to bring down. The Redskins think he can carry the ball 15 times a game in a change-of-pace role. He averaged eight yards per carry last season at Notre Dame.

NATRONE MEANS, Chargers — Chargers general manager Bobby Beathard wanted Means so much he traded next year's first-round pick to get him in the second round. A powerful runner, Means is hard to bring down and doesn't fumble, and he can catch the ball. He is well-suited for a one-back offense in the mold of Marion Butts and Rod Bernstine. Means ran for 1,195 yards last year at North Carolina.

ROBERT SMITH, Vikings — Somewhat of a surprise pick for Minnesota in the first round, Smith had troubles in college that caused him to sit out his sophomore season at Ohio State. He plays both halfback and wide receiver, though the Vikings plan on playing him in the backfield and returning kicks. He has great acceleration, tremendous speed and good size and can find the end zone. He will be the team's third-down back and occasionally line up in the slot as a receiver.

GLYN MILBURN, Broncos — A surprise pick for Denver, which had signed Rod Bernstine and Robert Delpino in the offseason, Milburn is a multipurpose threat who runs, catches and returns kickoffs and punts. He has great body control and makes tacklers miss in the open field, but the Broncos are deep and he won't get too many chances except on third downs and kicks.

RUSSELL WHITE, Rams — A third-round choice from California, White has great versatility in running, receiving and returning kicks. He has a low center of gravity and good balance and can break tackles. Consistency has always been a question, and he actually played better as a sophomore than as a senior.

ROOSEVELT POTTS, Colts — A second-rounder from Northeast Louisiana, Potts is a big back at 258 pounds, but he has the ability to run outside and catch passes. He might be the starter on opening day if he picks up the offense quickly enough, which means he might have a very good rookie year.

DERRICK LASSIC, Cowboys — A legitimate backup for Emmitt Smith who can also catch the ball, Lassic gained 905 yards (5.1-yard average) last season for national champion Alabama. He lacks size and isn't a breakaway threat, but he seemed to be coming on at the end of his college career, which is a good sign.

RONALD MOORE, Cardinals — A fourth-rounder from Pittsburg State, Moore is a very productive small fullback who needs to hone his skills. He is a great athlete and tough workhorse who can handle punishment. Blocking is a question, and he'll have a hard time finding playing time with Garrison Hearst in the lineup.

RICHIE ANDERSON, Jets — Anderson has a nose for the end zone. He scored 18 touchdowns last season at Penn State. He's a big slashing runner but often goes down when hit. He was drafted one round later than Adrian Murrell, another back, but might have more upside potential.

LORENZO NEAL, Saints — A strong competitor who has power and balance, Neal can break tackles and also catch the ball. A fourth-rounder from Fresno State, he will line up in power formations.

RUDY HARRIS, Buccaneers — Harris was drafted in the fourth round out of Clemson and may be the big blocking back the Bucs have been looking for. He is a 260-pound battering ram who should be a superb blocker for Reggie Cobb.

DEREK BROWN, Saints — The second running back chosen in the fourth round by the Saints, Brown rushed for over 1,000 yards last year at Nebraska. He is a third-down, pass-catching scatback who can also return kicks.

KEVIN WILLIAMS, Broncos — A superb athlete who will be tried first at wide receiver, Williams was chosen in the fifth round out of UCLA. He has great speed but either has tremendous games or is invisible.

ADRIAN MURRELL, Jets — Murrell was very productive in college at West Virginia as both a runner and receiver. He rushed for over 1,000 yards as a senior. He will give the Jets more depth and will be tried first as the third-down receiver.

Wide Receivers

CURTIS CONWAY, Bears — The best combination of speed and talent in the draft, Conway gives the Bears what they have lacked for years — deep speed. The seventh pick in the draft from Southern Cal, Conway is a breakaway threat who will help immediately as a kick returner while fine-tuning his receiving skills. Conway can hurt opposing teams in a variety of ways, and he has never been caught from behind on a football field. He was eighth in the country in all-purpose yardage in 1992. From now on, teams won't be able to just shut down the Bears' running game to win. He has great upside potential.

SEAN DAWKINS, Colts — Bigger and more polished than Conway, the wideout from a pro offense at the University of California is a big-play receiver who has been compared to Michael Irvin and Sterling Sharpe. He has an explosive separation burst and knows how to use his size, and the Colts have needed somebody who can produce like he does. He was considered a steal on the 16th pick of the draft.

O.J. McDUFFIE, Dolphins — The Dolphins didn't seem to need another receiver, but they couldn't resist taking the versatile Penn State star. McDuffie lacks size and top speed but is an exciting player who is adept at breaking tackles. He will also return kicks. Some people question his hands, but he's aggressive over the middle and knows how to set up routes well. He might not get much action this year unless one of Miami's veteran receivers gets injured.

QUADRY ISMAIL, Vikings — The Rocket's brother, Quadry is a dangerous threat with excellent size to complement his sprinter's speed. He will also make an impact as a kick returner. A second-round pick from Syracuse, he is a shifty, elusive runner who can pull away and separate deep. He gives the Vikings the deep speed they have lacked, and some much-needed youth at the position.

ANDRE HASTINGS, Steelers — A quick possession receiver who is acrobatic and can catch in a crowd, Hastings lacks great speed. But he will find a job in Pittsburgh, a team that has been looking for a top-flight receiver for a few years.

VICTOR BAILEY, Eagles — A third-rounder from Missouri, Bailey has deceptive, gliding speed, fine concentration and ball reactions. He can make tough, acrobatic grabs and should take over as the Eagles' No. 3 receiver almost immediately.

KEVIN WILLIAMS, Cowboys — The former Miami Hurricane can also play halfback and has already been penciled in as the punt returner and one of the kickoff returners. Williams is very fast and has great leaping ability over the middle, and is a threat to score every time he gets his hands on the ball. The Cowboys have been looking for Alvin Harper to become a big-play No. 2 receiver or for somebody to take over the No. 3 role, and Williams will get a shot at both jobs.

LAMAR THOMAS, Buccaneers — The University of Miami's all-time leading receiver with 144 catches, Thomas was Tampa Bay's third-round pick. He has great acceleration and is an effective blocker. He's best on sideline patterns, and was one of the most polished receivers in the draft.

VINCENT BRISBY, Patriots — A second-round pick from Northeast Louisiana, Brisby has everything it takes to excel in the NFL as long as he handles the move up in competition. He could start right away for New England.

HORACE COPELAND, Buccaneers — A fourth-round pick from Miami (Fla.), Copeland might be a better pro in the long run than college and pro teammate Lamar Thomas, who went a round earlier. Copeland possesses rare size, speed and jumping ability and needs to improve his skills, but he has great upside potential.

TRAVIS HANNAH, Oilers — An explosive speedster on sideline routes, something the Oilers lack, Hannah has world-class speed, moves and hand-eye coordination but has trouble getting off the line. He'll stick.

RUSSELL COPELAND, Bills — Copeland, a fourth-rounder from Memphis State, might be the deep threat the Bills need since James Lofton has been released. He is a big, physical receiver who can catch over the middle and is a good blocker.

WALTER DUNSON, Chargers — A fifth-round pick from Middle Tennessee State, Dunson is a small receiver who can also return kicks. He can also play halfback and might excel on third downs.

DANAN HUGHES, Chiefs — Hughes would have been drafted in the second round rather than the seventh if he wanted to play football rather than baseball. Iowa's all-time leading receiver, Hughes is the kind of big, sure-handed pass receiver the Chiefs need.

OLANDA TRUITT, Raiders — Truitt might be a steal in the fourth round. He has good hands and runs fine routes, makes highlight-film catches and always seems to get open.

SEAN LaCHAPELLE, Rams — A fifth-rounder from UCLA, LaChapelle is an excellent possession receiver who will help Jim Everett on third downs. He's not afraid to go over the middle.

KENNY SHEDD, Jets — A fifth-rounder from Northern Iowa, Shedd is very small and doesn't run precise routes, but he has incredible quickness and will also double as a kick returner. He returned four punts for touchdowns last year in college.

TERRENCE WARREN, Seahawks — Drafted in the fifth round from Hampton Institute, Warren is a diamond in the rough. He is big, fast and strong and returns kicks but is very raw.

Tight Ends

IRV SMITH, Saints — A first-round pick, Smith is an excellent blocker who lacks some receiving skills because he was rarely used at Notre Dame. He has great separation off the line and runs precise routes. Smith is reminiscent of Mark Bavaro in that he runs over tacklers. The Saints haven't had a good receiving tight end for years, so they want him to start and contribute right away.

TROY DRAYTON, Rams — A second-round pick from Penn State, Drayton is a former wideout with the speed to stretch defenses down the middle. He's fluid on deep routes and has great leaping ability for high passes. It shouldn't take him long to move into the Rams' starting lineup.

TONY McGEE, Bengals — McGee has a chance to start right away now that Rodney Holman is gone. An excellent blocker who can separate from a defender at the line, he was a key third-down target at Michigan last year. McGee catches the ball well and can run, but he is slightly inexperienced.

CHRIS GEDNEY, Bears — The consensus All-American at Syracuse is a pass-catcher who could also develop into a good blocker. A big, tough, clutch receiver, he has outstanding hands and is often compared to Jay Novacek.

FRED BAXTER, Jets — A fifth-rounder from Auburn, Baxter will compete for the team's third tight end position. He's a good receiver.

JOHN HENRY MILLS, Oilers — A fifth-round pick from Wake Forest, Mills is more of a wide receiver than a tight end. They will use him at H-back and as a kick returner.

Kickers

JASON ELAM, Broncos — The first kicker chosen in the third round, Elam converted on more than 80 percent of his field goals in a record-setting college career at Hawaii. He has an explosive leg. Since he can boom kickoffs into the end zone, the Broncos won't have to keep two kickers on the roster, so his chances of beating out David Treadwell are enhanced. He might have to prove himself kicking in inclement weather, however.

DARON ALCORN, Buccaneers — The last pick in the draft out of Akron, Alcorn has a strong leg and had moments on long field goals in college. He can boom kickoffs into the end zone, which will help him win the job in Tampa Bay.

DOUG PELFREY, Bengals — An eighth-rounder from Kentucky, Pelfrey has more range than the Bengals' Jim Breech and can put his kickoffs into the end zone. He'll win the job if he has a good preseason.

SCOTT SISSON, Patriots — Sisson handles pressure well and was a money kicker in college at Georgia Tech. He will compete with Charlie Baumann for the kicking job and should be able to beat him out. Sisson was drafted in the fifth round.

TODD PETERSON, Giants — Peterson had a good senior year at Georgia and was chosen in the seventh round. He will compete with Matt Bahr and Ken Willis for the Giants' job.

CRAIG HENTRICH, Jets — Hentrich hasn't shown consistency on long field goals, so he will challenge for the team's punting job rather than placekicker.

Chapter 14
Fantasy Lists

(Based on potential; rookies are not included)

QUARTERBACKS

Most Dangerous
Steve Young, 49ers
Randall Cunningham, Eagles
John Elway, Broncos
Troy Aikman, Cowboys
Joe Montana, Chiefs
Warren Moon, Oilers
Jim Kelly, Bills
Dan Marino, Dolphins

Best Two-Minute Quarterbacks
Joe Montana, Chiefs
Dan Marino, Dolphins
John Elway, Broncos
Jim Kelly, Bills

Best Bets to Throw 4 Touchdowns in a Game
Steve Young, 49ers
Warren Moon, Oilers
Jim Kelly, Bills
Troy Aikman, Cowboys
Dan Marino, Dolphins

Best Runners
Steve Young, 49ers
Randall Cunningham, Eagles
John Elway, Broncos
Chris Miller, Falcons
Steve Young, 49ers
Rodney Peete, Lions
Andre Ware, Lions
Jeff Hostetler, Raiders
Jim Harbaugh, Bears
Warren Moon, Oilers
Stan Humphries, Chargers
Vinny Testaverde, Browns

Overlooked
Jim Everett, Rams
Bernie Kosar, Browns
Jim Harbaugh, Bears
Bobby Hebert, Falcons

Comeback Quarterbacks
Joe Montana, Chiefs
John Elway, Broncos
Mark Rypien, Redskins
Boomer Esiason, Jets
Jeff George, Colts

Don't Expect the Same From
Dave Krieg, Chiefs
Cody Carlson, Oilers

Could Be Replaced
Mark Rypien, Redskins
Chris Miller, Falcons
Jeff George, Colts
Rodney Peete, Lions
Chris Chandler, Cardinals

Sleepers
Mike Buck, Saints
Andre Ware, Lions
Steve Beuerlein, Cardinals
Jeff Klingler, Bengals
Cary Conklin, Redskins
Jack Trudeau, Colts
Scott Secules, Patriots
Sean Salisbury, Vikings

Apt to Get Injured
Jim McMahon, Vikings
Joe Montana, Chiefs
Rodney Peete, Lions
Chris Miller, Falcons
Bernie Kosar, Browns

Growing Old
Joe Montana, Chiefs
Warren Moon, Oilers
Phil Simms, Giants
Steve DeBerg, Buccaneers

Best Backups
Cody Carlson, Oilers
Steve Bono, 49ers
Frank Reich, Bills
Vinny Testaverde, Browns
Ken O'Brien, Packers
Chris Chandler, Cowboys
Steve Walsh, Saints

RUNNING BACKS

Best Bets for 1,500 yards
Barry Sanders, Lions
Thurman Thomas, Bills
Emmitt Smith, Cowboys

Best Bets for 12 Touchdowns
Barry Sanders, Lions
Emmitt Smith, Cowboys
Barry Foster, Steelers
Marion Butts, Chargers
Rodney Hampton, Giants
Terry Allen, Vikings
Ricky Watters, Vikings
Thurman Thomas, Bills
Neal Anderson, Bears
Lorenzo White, Oilers

Best Bets for Three Touchdowns in a Game
Barry Sanders, Lions
Thurman Thomas, Bills
Emmitt Smith, Cowboys
Brad Baxter, Jets
Ricky Watters, 49ers

Most Dangerous
Barry Sanders, Lions
Thurman Thomas, Bills
Emmitt Smith, Cowboys
Barry Foster, Steelers
Ricky Watters, 49ers
Neal Anderson, Bears
Eric Metcalf, Browns
Terry Allen, Vikings
Kenneth Davis, Bills

Designated Touchdown Scorers
Rodney Culver, Colts
Brad Baxter, Jets
Derrick Fenner, Bengals
Tom Rathman, 49ers
Kevin Mack, Browns

Best Receivers
Ronnie Harmon, Chargers
Neal Anderson, Bears
Thurman Thomas, Bills
Keith Byars, Eagles
John L. Williams, Seahawks
Leroy Hoard, Browns
Emmitt Smith, Cowboys
Gary Anderson, Buccaneers
Eric Metcalf, Browns
Dave Meggett, Giants
Tom Rathman, 49ers
Anthony Johnson, Colts
Vince Workman, Buccaneers

Terry Allen, Vikings
Ricky Watters, Vikings
Lorenzo White, Oilers
Cleveland Gary, Rams
Bobby Humphrey, Dolphins
Johnny Bailey, Cardinals
Tony Paige, Dolphins
Todd McNair, Chiefs
Anthony McDowell, Buccaneers

Best Moves
Barry Sanders, Lions
Thurman Thomas, Bills
Eric Metcalf, Browns
Dave Meggett, Giants

Comeback Running Backs
Neal Anderson, Bears
Barry Word, Chiefs
Leonard Russell, Patriots
Blair Thomas, Jets
John Stephens, Packers
Marcus Allen, Raiders
Sammie Smith, Dolphins

Overlooked
Brad Muster, Saints
Brad Baxter, Jets
Christian Okoye, Chiefs
Kevin Mack, Browns
Kenneth Davis, Bills
Harold Green, Bengals
Tom Rathman, 49ers
Derrick Fenner, Bengals
Jarrod Bunch, Giants

Sleepers
Harvey Williams, Chiefs
Tony Smith, Falcons
Vaughn Dunbar, Saints
Nick Bell, Raiders
Johnny Johnson, Jets
Heath Sherman, Eagles
Eric Bieniemy, Chargers
Tommy Vardell, Browns
Jon Vaughn, Patriots
Darren Lewis, Bears
David Lang, Rams
Aaron Craver, Dolphins
Amp Lee, 49ers

Don't Expect the Same From
Cleveland Gary, Rams
Rodney Culver, Colts
Earnest Byner, Redskins
Reggie Cobb, Buccaneers
Herschel Walker, Eagles
Dalton Hilliard, Saints

Could Lose Their Jobs
Cleveland Gary, Rams
Christian Okoye, Chiefs
Herschel Walker, Vikings
Eric Dickerson, Raiders
Blair Thomas, Jets

Best Backups
Harvey Williams, Chiefs
Darren Lewis, Bears
Heath Sherman, Eagles
Amp Lee, 49ers
Nick Bell, Raiders
Ricky Ervins, Redskins
Dave Meggett, Giants
Kenneth Davis, Bills
Ronnie Harmon, Chargers
David Lang, Rams
Marcus Allen, Raiders

Apt to Get Injured
Rod Bernstine, Broncos
Kevin Mack, Browns
Nick Bell, Raiders

Growing Old
Roger Craig, Vikings
Eric Dickerson, Raiders
Earnest Byner, Redskins

WIDE RECEIVERS

Most Dangerous
Jerry Rice, 49ers
Andre Rison, Falcons
Michael Haynes, Falcons
Sterling Sharpe, Packers
John Taylor, 49ers
Michael Irvin, Cowboys
Fred Barnett, Eagles
Anthony Miller, Chargers
Gary Clark, Cardinals
Willie Anderson, Rams

Best Bets for 90 Catches
Haywood Jeffires, Oilers
Sterling Sharpe, Packers
Jerry Rice, 49ers
Andre Rison, Falcons
Michael Irvin, Cowboys

Best Bets for 12 Touchdowns
Jerry Rice, 49ers
Andre Rison, Falcons
Haywood Jeffires, Oilers
Sterling Sharpe, Packers
Michael Haynes, Falcons

Best Bets for Three Touchdowns in a Game
Jerry Rice, 49ers
Andre Rison, Falcons
Sterling Sharpe, Packers
John Taylor, 49ers
Michael Irvin, Cowboys
Andre Reed, Bills
Desmond Howard, Redskins

Best Deep Threats
Michael Haynes, Falcons
Willie Anderson, Rams
Michael Irvin, Cowboys
Eddie Brown, Bengals
Anthony Miller, Chargers
Jerry Rice, 49ers
Mark Duper, Dolphins
Willie Davis, Chiefs
Rob Moore, Jets
Willie Gault, Raiders
Fred Barnett, Eagles
Dwight Stone, Steelers
J.J. Birden, Chiefs

Sleepers
Desmond Howard, Redskins
Alvin Harper, Cowboys
Mike Pritchard, Falcons
Tim McGee, Redskins
Lawyer Tillman, Browns
Tim Barnett, Chiefs
Randal Hill, Cardinals
Arthur Marshall, Broncos
Nate Lewis, Chargers
Jeff Query, Bengals
Willie Davis, Chiefs
Jeff Graham, Steelers

Overlooked
Irving Fryar, Dolphins
Tim Brown, Raiders
Michael Jackson, Browns
Rob Moore, Jets
Brett Perriman, Lions
Ricky Sanders, Redskins
Herman Moore, Lions
Mark Carrier, Browns
Wendell Davis, Bears
Eric Martin, Saints
Webster Slaughter, Oilers
Hassan Jones, Vikings

Don't Expect the Same From
Michael Haynes, Falcons
Gary Clark, Redskins
Mark Jackson, Giants
Sterling Sharpe, Packers

Could Lose Their Jobs
Art Monk, Redskins
Mark Duper, Dolphins
Quinn Early, Saints
Anthony Carter, Vikings
Tom Waddle, Bears

Best Backups
Bill Brooks, Bills
Mark Ingram, Dolphins
Art Monk, Redskins
Odessa Turner, 49ers
Mervyn Fernandez, Raiders
Tony Jones, Falcons
Hassan Jones, Vikings
Don Beebe, Bills
Kelvin Martin, Seahawks

Comeback Wide Receivers
Eddie Brown, Bengals
John Taylor, 49ers
Andre Reed, Bills
Ricky Sanders, Redskins
Tim McGee, Redskins
Stephone Paige, Vikings
Vance Johnson, Broncos
Floyd Turner, Saints
Mark Carrier, Browns

Best Possession Receivers
Art Monk, Redskins
Haywood Jeffires, Oilers
Tom Waddle, Bears
Andre Rison, Falcons
Andre Reed, Bills
Bill Brooks, Colts
Ricky Proehl, Cardinals
Curtis Duncan, Oilers
Kelvin Martin, Seahawks

Growing Old
James Lofton, cut by Bills
Art Monk, Redskins
Anthony Carter, Vikings
Henry Ellard, Rams

TIGHT ENDS

Most Dangerous
Keith Jackson, Eagles
Eric Green, Steelers
Terry Orr, Redskins
Shannon Sharpe, Broncos

Best Bets to Catch Eight Touchdowns
Keith Jackson, Eagles
Eric Green, Steelers

Best Bets to Catch 60 Passes
Marv Cook, Patriots
Keith Jackson, Eagles
Brent Jones, 49ers
Jay Novacek, Cowboys
Jackie Harris, Packers
Shannon Sharpe, Broncos

Sleepers
Derek Brown, Giants
Johnny Mitchell, Jets
Adrian Cooper, Steelers
Ben Coates, Patriots
Ferrell Edmunds, Seahawks
Pete Holohan, Browns
Terry Orr, Redskins
Reggie Johnson, Broncos
Kerry Cash, Colts

Overlooked
Jackie Harris, Packers
Shannon Sharpe, Broncos
Ron Hall, Buccaneers
Craig McEwen, Chargers
Jim Price, Rams

Comeback Tight Ends
Eric Green, Steelers
Keith McKeller, Bills
Ethan Horton, Raiders
Ferrell Edmunds, Seahawks
Rodney Holman, Lions
Damone Johnson, Rams

Could Lose Their Jobs
Howard Cross, Giants
Pete Metzelaars, Bills
Mark Boyer, Jets
Keith Jennings, Bears
Hoby Brenner, Saints

Growing Old
Rodney Holman, Lions
Steve Jordan, Vikings
Mark Bavaro, Eagles

Best Backups
Adrian Cooper, Steelers
Pete Metzelaars, Bills
Reggie Johnson, Broncos
Ben Coates, Patriots
Andrew Glover, Raiders
Ed West, Packers
Charles Arbuckle, Colts
Greg Baty, Dolphins

KICKERS

Best Bets to Score 100 Points
Chip Lohmiller, Redskins
Steve Christie, Bills
Nick Lowery, Chiefs
Lin Elliott, Cowboys
Mike Cofer, 49ers
Morten Andersen, Saints
David Treadwell, Broncos
Pete Stoyanovich, Dolphins
Roger Ruzek, Eagles
Gary Anderson, Steelers
Al Del Greco, Oilers
Chris Jacke, Packers

Best Bets to Kick 25 Field Goals
Pete Stoyanovich, Dolphins
Chip Lohmiller, Redskins
Morten Andersen, Saints
Nick Lowery, Chiefs
Steve Christie, Bills
Chris Jacke, Packers
David Treadwell, Broncos

Best Bets to Kick Four Field Goals in a Game
Nick Lowery, Chiefs
Chip Lohmiller, Redskins
Steve Christie, Bills
Pete Stoyanovich, Dolphins
Morten Andersen, Saints

Best Long-Distance Kickers
Nick Lowery, Chiefs
Pete Stoyanovich, Dolphins
Morten Andersen, Saints
Chip Lohmiller, Redskins
Steve Christie, Buccaneers
Lin Elliott, Cowboys
Chris Jacke, Packers
Norm Johnson, Falcons
Jeff Jaeger, Raiders

Best Kickers in the Clutch
Nick Lowery, Chiefs
Chris Jacke, Packers
Morten Andersen, Saints

Most Accurate
Nick Lowery, Chiefs
Morten Andersen, Saints
Gary Anderson, Steelers
Pete Stoyanovich, Dolphins
Chris Jacke, Packers
Chip Lohmiller, Redskins
Steve Christie, Bills
Jason Hanson, Lions
Norm Johnson, Falcons

Overlooked
Chris Jacke, Packers
Roger Ruzek, Eagles
David Treadwell, Broncos
Fuad Reveiz, Vikings
Norm Johnson, Falcons

Sleepers
Jason Hanson, Lions
Cary Blanchard, Jets

Could Lose Their Jobs
Mike Cofer, 49ers
Al Del Greco, Oilers
Matt Bahr, Giants
David Treadwell, Broncos
Eddie Murray, Buccaneers
Dean Biasucci, Colts
Charlie Baumann, Patriots

Growing Old
Norm Johnson, Falcons
Eddie Murray, Buccaneers
Jim Breech, Bengals
Dean Biasucci, Colts

Chapter 15
Statistics

1992 Quarterbacks

Player	Team	GP/GS	PASSING						RUSHING		
			ATT	CMP	YDS	TD	INT	RTG	ATT	YDS	TD
Steve Young	San Francisco	16/16	402	268	3465	25	7	107.0	76	537	4
Chris Miller	Atlanta	8/8	253	152	1739	15	6	90.7	23	89	0
Troy Aikman	Dallas	16/16	473	302	3445	23	14	89.5	37	105	1
Warren Moon	Houston	11/10	346	224	2521	18	12	89.3	27	147	1
R. Cunningham	Philadelphia	15/15	384	233	2775	19	11	87.3	87	549	5
Brett Favre	Green Bay	15/13	471	302	3227	18	13	85.3	47	198	1
Dan Marino	Miami	16/16	554	330	4116	24	16	85.1	20	66	0
Neil O'Donnell	Pittsburgh	12/12	313	185	2285	13	9	83.6	27	5	1
Bobby Hebert	New Orleans	16/16	422	249	3287	19	16	82.9	32	95	0
Jim Kelly	Buffalo	16/16	462	269	3457	23	19	81.2	31	53	1
Cody Carlson	Houston	11/6	227	149	1710	9	11	81.2	27	77	1
Jim Everett	L.A. Rams	16/16	475	281	3323	22	18	80.2	32	133	0
Dave Krieg	Kansas City	16/16	413	230	3115	15	12	79.9	37	74	2
Chris Chandler	Phoenix	15/13	413	245	2832	15	15	77.1	36	149	1
Stan Humphries	San Diego	16/15	454	263	3356	16	18	76.4	28	79	4
Jim Harbaugh	Chicago	16/13	358	202	2486	13	12	76.2	47	272	1
V. Testaverde	Tampa Bay	14/14	358	206	2554	14	16	74.2	36	197	2
Rich Gannon	Minnesota	12/12	279	159	1905	12	13	72.9	45	187	0
Mark Rypien	Washington	16/16	479	269	3282	13	17	71.1	36	50	2
John Elway	Denver	12/12	316	174	2242	10	17	65.7	34	94	2
Jay Schroeder	L.A. Raiders	13/9	253	123	1476	11	11	63.3	28	160	0
Jeff George	Indianapolis	10/10	306	167	1963	7	15	61.5	14	26	1
Boomer Esiason	Cincinnati	12/11	278	144	1407	11	15	57.0	21	66	0
Browning Nagle	N.Y. Jets	14/13	387	192	2280	7	17	55.7	24	57	0
Stan Gelbaugh	Seattle	10/8	255	121	1307	6	11	52.9	16	79	0
Non-qualifiers											
Rodney Peete	Detroit	10/10	213	123	1702	9	9	80.0	21	83	0
Mike Tomczak	Cleveland	12/8	211	120	1693	7	7	80.1	24	39	0
Hugh Millen	New England	7/7	203	124	1203	8	10	70.3	17	108	0
Jeff Hostetler	N.Y. Giants	13/9	192	103	1225	8	3	80.8	35	172	3
Kelly Stouffer	Seattle	9/7	190	92	900	3	9	47.7	9	37	0
Jack Trudeau	Indianapolis	11/5	181	105	1271	4	8	68.6	13	6	0
Sean Salisbury	Minnesota	10/4	175	97	1203	5	2	81.7	11	0	0
Todd Marinovich	L.A. Raiders	7/7	165	81	1102	5	9	58.2	9	30	0
Wade Wilson	Atlanta	9/3	163	111	1366	13	4	110.1	15	62	0
Bernie Kosar	Cleveland	7/7	155	103	1160	8	7	87.0	5	12	0
Phil Simms	N.Y. Giants	4/4	137	83	912	5	3	83.3	6	17	0
Billy J. Tolliver	Atlanta	10/5	131	73	787	5	5	70.4	4	15	0
Steve DeBerg	Tampa Bay	6/2	125	76	710	3	4	71.1	3	3	0
Tommy Maddox	Denver	13/4	121	66	757	5	9	56.4	9	20	0
Bubby Brister	Pittsburgh	6/4	116	63	719	2	5	61.0	10	16	0

Erik Kramer	Detroit	7/3	106	58	771	4	8	59.1	12	34	0
Scott Zolak	New England	6/4	100	52	561	2	4	58.8	18	71	0
Ken O'Brien	N.Y. Jets	10/3	98	55	642	5	6	67.6	8	8	0
David Klingler	Cincinnati	4/4	98	47	530	3	2	66.3	11	53	0
Kent Graham	N.Y. Giants	6/3	97	42	470	1	4	44.6	6	36	0
Peter Tom Willis	Chicago	9/2	92	54	716	4	8	61.7	1	2	0
Timm Rosenbach	Phoenix	8/3	92	49	483	0	6	41.2	9	11	0
Tommy Hodson	New England	9/3	91	50	496	2	2	68.8	5	11	0
Andre Ware	Detroit	4/3	86	50	677	3	4	75.6	20	124	0
Donald Hollas	Cincinnati	10/1	58	35	335	2	0	87.9	20	109	0
Steve Bono	San Francisco	16/0	56	36	463	2	2	87.1	15	23	0
Don Majkowski	Green Bay	14/3	55	38	271	2	2	77.2	8	33	0
Vince Evans	L.A. Raiders	5/0	53	29	372	4	3	78.5	11	79	0
Jeff Carlson	New England	3/2	49	18	232	1	3	33.7	11	32	0
Frank Reich	Buffalo	16/0	47	24	221	0	2	46.5	9	-9	0
Jim McMahon	Philadelphia	4/1	43	22	279	1	2	60.1	6	23	0
Bob Gagliano	San Diego	6/1	42	19	258	0	3	35.6	3	-4	0
Shawn Moore	Denver	3/0	34	17	232	0	3	35.4	8	39	0
Tom Tupa	Indianapolis	3/0	33	17	156	1	2	49.6	3	9	0
Dan McGwire	Seattle	2/1	30	17	116	0	3	25.8	3	13	0
Todd Philcox	Cleveland	2/1	27	13	217	3	1	97.3	0	0	0
Craig Erickson	Tampa Bay	6/0	26	15	121	0	0	69.9	1	-1	0
Will Furrer	Chicago	2/1	25	9	89	0	3	7.3	0	0	0
Mark Herrmann	Indianapolis	1/1	24	15	177	1	1	81.4	3	-2	0
Joe Montana	San Francisco	1/0	21	15	126	2	0	118.4	3	28	0
Mike Pagel	L.A. Rams	16/0	20	8	99	1	2	33.1	1	0	0
Steve Beuerlein	Dallas	16/0	18	12	152	0	1	69.7	4	-7	0
Tony Sacca	Phoenix	4/0	11	4	29	0	2	5.3	0	0	0
Jeff Blake	N.Y. Jets	3/0	9	4	40	0	1	18.1	2	-2	0
Scott Mitchell	Miami	16/0	8	2	32	0	1	4.2	8	10	0
Dave Brown	N.Y. Giants	2/0	7	4	21	0	0	62.2	2	-1	0
Mike Buck	New Orleans	2/0	4	2	10	0	0	56.3	3	-4	0
Brad Goebel	Cleveland	1/0	3	2	32	0	0	102.1	0	0	0
Cary Conklin	Washington	1/0	2	2	16	1	0	139.6	3	-4	0

1992 Running Backs

Player	Team	GP/GS	RUSHING			RECEIVING		
			ATT	YDS	TD	REC	YDS	TD
Emmitt Smith	Dallas	16/16	373	1713	18	59	335	1
Barry Foster	Pittsburgh	16/15	390	1690	11	36	344	0
Thurman Thomas	Buffalo	16/16	312	1487	9	58	626	3
Barry Sanders	Detroit	16/16	312	1352	9	29	225	1
Lorenzo White	Houston	16/16	265	1226	7	57	641	1
Terry Allen	Minnesota	16/16	266	1201	13	49	472	2
Reggie Cobb	Tampa Bay	13/13	310	1171	9	21	156	0
Harold Green	Cincinnati	16/15	265	1170	2	41	214	0
Rodney Hampton	N.Y. Giants	16/16	257	1141	14	28	215	0
Cleveland Gary	L.A. Rams	16/16	279	1125	7	52	293	3
Herschel Walker	Philadelphia	16/16	267	1070	8	38	278	2
Chris Warren	Seattle	16/16	223	1017	3	16	134	0
Ricky Watters	San Francisco	14/13	206	1013	9	43	405	2
Earnest Byner	Washington	16/16	262	998	6	39	338	1
Mark Higgs	Miami	16/15	256	915	7	16	142	0
Marion Butts	San Diego	15/15	218	809	4	9	73	0
Johnny Johnson	Phoenix	12/7	178	734	6	14	103	0
Eric Dickerson	L.A. Raiders	16/15	187	729	2	14	85	1
Brad Baxter	N.Y. Jets	15/15	152	698	6	4	32	0
Gaston Green	Denver	14/13	161	648	2	10	79	0
Vince Workman	Green Bay	10/10	159	631	2	47	290	0
Kenneth Davis	Buffalo	16/0	139	613	6	15	80	0
Barry Word	Kansas City	12/11	163	607	4	9	80	0
Anthony Johnson	Indianapolis	16/13	178	592	0	49	517	3
Heath Sherman	Philadelphia	16/7	112	583	5	18	219	1
Neal Anderson	Chicago	16/11	156	582	5	42	399	6
Vaughn Dunbar	New Orleans	16/8	154	565	3	9	62	0
Kevin Mack	Cleveland	12/6	169	543	6	13	81	0
Jarrod Bunch	N.Y. Giants	16/13	104	501	3	11	50	1
Derrick Fenner	Cincinnati	16/1	112	500	7	7	41	1
Rod Bernstine	San Diego	9/1	106	499	4	12	86	0
Ricky Ervins	Washington	16/0	151	495	2	32	252	0
Bobby Humphrey	Miami	16/1	102	471	1	54	507	1
Jon Vaughn	New England	16/5	113	451	1	13	84	0
Christian Okoye	Kansas City	15/5	144	448	6	1	5	0
Dalton Hilliard	New Orleans	16/4	115	445	3	48	465	4
Blair Thomas	N.Y. Jets	9/7	97	440	0	7	49	0
Roger Craig	Minnesota	15/1	105	416	4	22	164	0
Craig Heyward	New Orleans	16/13	104	416	3	19	159	0
Brad Muster	Chicago	16/16	98	414	3	34	389	2
Leonard Russell	New England	11/10	123	390	2	11	24	0
Tommy Vardell	Cleveland	14/10	99	369	0	13	128	0
Darren Lewis	Chicago	16/15	90	382	4	18	175	0
Nick Bell	L.A. Raiders	16/1	81	366	3	4	40	0
Steve Broussard	Atlanta	15/1	84	363	1	11	96	1
Amp Lee	San Francisco	16/3	91	362	2	20	102	2
John L. Williams	Seattle	16/16	114	339	1	74	556	2
Tony Smith	Atlanta	14/6	87	329	2	2	14	0
Rodney Culver	Indianapolis	16/2	121	321	7	26	210	2
Marcus Allen	L.A. Raider	16/0	67	301	2	28	277	1
Eric Metcalf	Cleveland	16/5	73	301	1	47	614	5

Player	Team	G/S	Att	Yds	TD	Rec	Yds	TD
Reggie Rivers	Denver	16/3	74	282	3	45	449	1
Keith Jones	Atlanta	14/8	79	278	0	12	94	0
John Stephens	New England	16/16	75	277	2	21	161	0
Greg Lewis	Denver	16/2	73	268	4	4	30	0
Eric Bieniemy	San Diego	15/0	74	264	3	5	49	0
Harvey Williams	Kansas City	14/0	78	262	1	5	24	0
Darrell Thompson	Green Bay	7/4	76	254	2	13	129	1
Leroy Hoard	Cleveland	16/9	54	236	0	26	310	1
Ronnie Harmon	San Diego	16/2	55	235	3	79	914	1
Johnny Bailey	Phoenix	14/3	52	233	1	33	331	1
Edgar Bennett	Green Bay	16/2	61	214	0	13	93	0
David Lang	L.A. Rams	16/11	33	203	5	18	281	1
Tom Rathman	San Francisco	15/15	57	194	5	44	343	4
Gary Anderson	Tampa Bay	15/4	55	194	1	34	284	0
Ivory Lee Brown	Phoenix	7/5	68	194	2	7	54	0
Pat Chaffey	N.Y. Jets	14/0	27	186	1	7	56	0
Curvin Richards	Dallas	9/0	49	176	1	3	8	0
Freeman McNeil	N.Y. Jets	12/1	43	170	0	16	154	0
Dave Meggett	N.Y. Giants	16/0	32	167	0	38	229	2
Carwell Gardner	Buffalo	16/7	40	166	2	7	67	0
Harry Sydney	Green Bay	16/0	51	163	2	49	384	1
Scott Lockwood	New England	4/0	35	162	0			
Leroy Thompson	Pittsburgh	15/1	35	157	1	22	278	0
Keith Henderson	S.F./Minn.	15/0	44	150	1	5	64	0
Merril Hoge	Pittsburgh	16/12	41	150	0	28	231	1
Larry Centers	Phoenix	16/1	37	139	0	50	417	2
Ken Clark	Indianapolis	13/2	40	134	0	5	46	0
Steve Smith	L.A. Raiders	16/15	44	129	0	28	217	1
Todd McNair	Kansas City	16/0	21	124	1	44	380	1
Robert Delpino	L.A. Rams	10/4	32	115	0	18	139	1
Fred McAfee	New Orleans	14/1	39	114	1	1	16	0
Mark Green	Chicago	15/0	23	107	2	7	85	0
Sammie Smith	Denver	4/1	23	94	0			
Erric Pegram	Atlanta	16/1	21	89	0	2	25	0
Gary Brown	Houston	16/0	19	87	1	1	5	0
Anthony McDowell	Tampa Bay	12/8	14	81	0	27	258	2
Rueben Mayes	Seattle	16/0	28	74	0	2	13	0
Brian Mitchell	Washington	16/0	6	70	0	3	30	0
Johnny Hector	N.Y. Jets	5/0	24	67	0	2	13	0
Anthony Thompson	Phox./Rams	8/0	19	65	1	5	11	0
Daryl Johnston	Dallas	16/16	17	61	0	32	249	2
Eric Ball	Cincinnati	16/14	16	55	2	6	66	2
Tommie Agee	Dallas	16/0	16	54	0	3	18	0
Robert Green	Washington	15/0	8	46	0	1	5	0
James Brooks	Clev./T.B.	6/2	18	44	0	2	-1	0
Marc Logan	San Francisco	16/1	8	44	1	2	17	0
A.B. Brown	N.Y. Jets	7/1	24	42	0	4	30	0
Troy Stradford	Rams/Det.	8/0	12	41	0	2	15	0
Kevin Turner	New England	16/1	10	40	0	7	52	2
Eddie Fuller	Buffalo	8/0	6	39	0	2	17	0
Bernie Parmalee	Miami	10/0	6	38	0			
Randy Baldwin	Cleveland	15/0	10	31	0	2	30	0
Ottis Anderson	N.Y. Giants	13/0	10	31	0			
Scottie Graham	N.Y. Jets	2/0	14	29	0			
Tracy Johnston	Seattle	16/0	3	26	0			
Stanford Jennings	Tampa Bay	11/0	5	25	0	9	69	1

Alonzo Highsmith	Tampa Bay	5/2	8	23	0	5	28	0
Ostell Miles	Cincinnati	11/0	8	22	0			
Ed Tillison	Detroit	6/0	4	22	0			
Buford McGee	Green Bay	4/3	8	19	0	6	60	0
Lewis Tilman	N.Y. Giants	16/0	6	13	0	1	15	0
Tony Paige	Miami	16/16	7	11	1	48	399	1
Dexter McNabb	Green Bay	16/0	2	11	0			
Derrick Gainer	Raiders/Dal.	7/0	2	10	0			
Sheldon Canley	N.Y. Jets	1/0	4	9	0			
Maurice Carthon	Indianapolis	16/6	4	9	0	3	10	0
Dexter Carter	San Francisco	3/0	4	9	0	1	43	1
Aaron Craver	Miami	6/0	3	9	0			
Sam Gash	New England	15/0	5	7	1			
James Saxon	Miami	16/0	4	7	0	5	41	0
Darrin Nelson	Minnesota	16/0	10	5	0			
Vai Sikahema	Philadelphia	16/0	2	2	0	13	142	0
Ron Wolfley	Cleveland	15/0	1	2	0	2	8	1
Kimble Anders	Kansas City	11/2	1	1	0	5	65	0
Spencer Tillman	Houston	16/0	1	1	0			
Warren Williams	Pittsburgh	16/0	2	0	0	1	44	0
Bob Perryman	Denver	4/1	3	-1	0	2	15	0

1992 Wide Receivers

Player	Team	GP/GS	RECEIVING			RUSHING		
			REC	YDS	TD	ATT	YDS	TD
Sterling Sharpe	Green Bay	16/16	108	1461	13	4	8	0
Andre Rison	Atlanta	15/13	93	1113	11			
Haywood Jeffires	Houston	16/16	90	913	9			
Jerry Rice	San Francisco	16/16	84	1201	10	9	58	1
Curtis Duncan	Houston	16/16	82	954	1			
Michael Irvin	Dallas	16/14	78	1369	7	1	-9	0
Mike Pritchard	Atlanta	16/15	77	827	5	5	37	0
Anthony Miller	San Diego	16/13	72	1060	7	1	-1	0
Brett Perriman	Detroit	16/16	69	810	4			
Eric Martin	New Orleans	16/11	68	1041	5			
Fred Barnett	Philadelphia	16/16	67	1083	6	1	-15	0
Ernest Givins	Houston	16/16	67	787	10	7	75	0
Andre Reed	Buffalo	16/16	65	913	3	8	65	0
Reggie Langhorne	Indianapolis	16/12	65	811	1	1	-7	0
Gary Clark	Washington	16/14	64	912	5	2	18	0
Lawrence Dawsey	Tampa Bay	15/12	60	776	1			
Ricky Proehl	Phoenix	16/14	60	744	3	3	23	0
Drew Hill	Atlanta	16/14	60	623	3			
Randal Hill	Phoenix	16/14	58	861	3	1	4	0
Chris Burkett	N.Y. Jets	16/5	57	724	1			
Mark Carrier	Tampa Bay	14/11	56	692	4			
Irving Fryar	New England	15/14	55	791	4	1	6	0
Wendell Davis	Chicago	16/16	54	734	2	4	42	0
Cris Carter	Minnesota	12/12	53	681	6	5	15	0
Jessie Hester	Indianapolis	16/16	52	792	1			
James Lofton	Buffalo	16/15	51	789	6			
Herman Moore	Detroit	12/11	51	966	4			
Ricky Sanders	Washington	15/5	51	707	3	4	-6	0
Rob Moore	N.Y. Jets	16/15	50	726	4	1	21	0
Jeff Graham	Pittsburgh	14/10	49	711	1			
Tim Brown	L.A. Raiders	15/12	49	693	7	3	-4	0
Ed McCaffrey	N.Y. Giants	16/3	49	610	5			
Michael Haynes	Atlanta	14/14	48	808	10			
Mark Jackson	Denver	16/13	48	745	8	3	-1	0
Michael Jackson	Cleveland	16/14	47	755	7	1	21	0
Henry Ellard	L.A. Rams	16/15	47	727	3			
Tom Waddle	Chicago	12/12	46	674	4			
Art Monk	Washington	16/14	46	644	3	6	45	0
Mark Duper	Miami	16/16	44	762	7			
Bill Brooks	Indianapolis	14/10	44	468	1	2	14	0
Mark Clayton	Miami	13/13	43	619	3			
J.J. Birden	Kansas City	16/10	42	644	3			
Calvin Williams	Philadelphia	16/15	42	598	7			
Anthony Carter	Minnesota	16/14	41	580	2	16	66	1
Webster Slaughter	Houston	12/9	39	486	4	3	20	0
Willie Anderson	L.A. Rams	15/8	38	657	7			
Mike Sherrard	San Francisco	16/8	38	607	0			
Ernie Jones	Phoenix	13/5	38	559	4	2	-3	0
Willie Davis	Kansas City	16/14	36	756	3	1	-11	0
Alvin Harper	Dallas	16/13	35	562	4	1	15	0
Leonard Harris	Houston	14/7	35	435	2	1	8	0
Greg McMurtry	New England	16/15	35	424	1	2	3	0

Tim McGee	Cincinnati	16/16	35	408	3			
Nate Lewis	San Diego	15/10	34	580	4	2	7	0
Dwight Stone	Pittsburgh	15/13	34	501	3	12	118	0
Willie Green	Detroit	15/13	33	596	5			
Don Beebe	Buffalo	12/8	33	554	2	1	-6	0
Tony Martin	Miami	16/3	33	553	2	1	-2	0
Kelvin Martin	Dallas	16/1	32	359	3	2	13	0
Al Toon	N.Y. Jets	9/8	31	311	2			
Quinn Early	New Orleans	16/16	30	566	5	3	-1	0
Ernie Mills	Pittsburgh	14/4	30	383	3	1	20	0
Shawn Jefferson	San Diego	16/2	29	377	2			
Jeff Chadwick	L.A. Rams	14/2	29	362	3			
Willie Gault	L.A. Raiders	16/16	27	508	4	1	6	0
Mark Ingram	N.Y. Giants	12/12	27	408	1			
Tommy Kane	Seattle	11/11	27	369	3			
Chris Calloway	N.Y. Giants	16/1	27	225	1			
Arthur Marshall	Denver	16/1	26	493	1	11	56	0
Carl Pickens	Cincinnati	16/10	26	326	1			
Michael Timpson	New England	16/2	26	315	1			
Lawyer Tillman	Cleveland	11/9	25	498	0	2	15	0
John Taylor	San Francisco	9/8	25	428	3	1	10	0
Tim Barnett	Kansas City	12/3	24	442	4			
Vance Johnson	Denver	11/7	24	294	2			
Torrance Small	New Orleans	13/1	23	278	3			
Fred Banks	Miami	16/0	22	319	3			
Terance Mathis	N.Y. Jets	16/1	22	316	3	3	25	1
Hassan Jones	Minnesota	9/5	22	308	4	1	1	0
Joe Johnson	Minnesota	15/6	21	211	1	4	26	0
Courtney Hawkins	Tampa Bay	16/5	20	336	2			
Louis Clark	Seattle	10/9	20	290	1			
Brian Blades	Seattle	6/5	19	256	1	1	5	0
Reggie Rembert	Cincinnati	9/4	19	219	0			
Brian Brennan	Cin./S.D.	15/0	19	188	1			
Fred Jones	Kansas City	14/5	18	265	0			
Wesley Carroll	New Orleans	16/5	18	292	2			
Aaron Cox	L.A. Rams	10/3	18	261	0			
Stephen Baker	N.Y. Giants	13/11	17	333	2			
Tony Hargain	Kansas City	13/0	17	205	0			
Sanjay Beach	Green Bay	16/11	17	122	1			
Jeff Query	Cincinnati	10/2	16	256	3	1	1	0
Willie Drewrey	Tampa Bay	9/2	16	237	2			
Mike Farr	Detroit	14/9	15	115	0			
Anthony Morgan	Chicago	12/4	14	323	2	3	68	0
Anthony Edwards	Phoenix	16/2	14	147	1			
Tony Jones	Atlanta	10/4	14	138	1			
Rob Carpenter	N.Y. Jets	16/0	13	161	1	1	2	0
Ron Lewis	S.F./G.B.	9/4	13	152	0			
Cedric Tilman	Denver	9/1	12	211	1			
Alexander Wright	Dal./Raiders	13/1	12	175	2			
Derek Russell	Denver	12/6	12	140	0			
Robert Brooks	Green Bay	16/1	12	126	1	2	14	0
Dennis Gentry	Chicago	15/0	12	114	0	5	2	0
Robb Thomas	Seattle	15/0	11	136	0	1	-1	0
Sam Graddy	L.A. Raiders	7/1	10	205	1			
Odessa Turner	San Francisco	16/0	9	200	2			
Aubrey Matthews	Detroit	13/0	9	137	0			

Charles Davenport	Pittsburgh	15/1	9	136	0			
Mervyn Fernandez	L.A. Raiders	15/2	9	121	0			
Jeff Campbell	Detroit	12/2	8	155	1			
Roy Green	Philadelphia	9/0	8	105	0			
Doug Thomas	Seattle	12/4	8	85	0	3	7	0
Brad Lamb	Buffalo	7/0	7	139	0			
Jake Reed	Minnesota	16/0	6	142	0			
Emile Harry	K.C./Rams	11/0	6	58	0	1	27	0
George Thomas	Atlanta	5/1	6	54	0			
David Daniels	Seattle	13/1	5	99	0			
Rico Smith	Cleveland	10/1	5	64	0			
Eric Wright	Chicago	13/0	5	56	0			
Floyd Turner	New Orleans	2/2	5	43	0			
Vernon Turner	L.A. Rams	12/0	5	42	0	2	14	0
Reggie Barrett	Detroit	8/6	4	67	1			
Ron Morris	Chicago	4/0	4	44	0			
Jason Phillips	Atlanta	12/0	4	26	1			
Walter Stanley	S.D./N. E.	14/0	3	63	0			
Robert Clark	Miami	3/0	3	59	0			
Joey Smith	N.Y. Giants	16/1	3	45	0			
Mike Williams	Miami	15/0	3	43	0			
Mark Didio	Pittsburgh	2/0	3	39	0			
Clarence Verdin	Indianapolis	16/0	3	37	0			
Floyd Dixon	Philadelphia	7/0	3	36	0			
Milt Stegall	Cincinnati	16/0	3	35	1			
Shawn Collins	Cleveland	9/2	3	31	0			
James Milling	Atlanta	5/0	3	25	0			
Pat Newman	New Orleans	10/0	3	21	0			
Desmond Howard	Washington	16/1	3	20	0	3	14	0
Kitrick Taylor	Green Bay	10/0	2	63	1			
Jamie Holland	Cleveland	4/2	2	27	0			
Al Edwards	Buffalo	7/0	2	25	0	1	8	0
Steve Tasker	Buffalo	15/2	2	24	2	1	9	0
Pat Coleman	Houston	14/0	2	10	0			
Corey Harris	Hou./G.B.	15/0	2	10	0			
Mike Barber	Tampa Bay	2/0	1	32	0			
Barry Wagner	Chicago	1/0	1	16	0			
Robert Claiborne	San Diego	8/0	1	15	0			
Mike Young	Denver	3/0	1	11	0			
Keenan McCardell	Cleveland	2/0	1	8	0			
Glen Kozlowski	Chicago	4/0	1	7	0			
Marcus Dowdell	New Orleans	4/0	1	6	0			
John Jackson	Phoenix	6/0	1	5	1			
Yancey Thigpen	Pittsburgh	11/0	1	2	0			
Louis Lipps	New Orleans	2/0	1	1	0			

1992 Tight Ends

Player	Team	GP/GS	RECEIVING REC	YDS	TD	RUSHING ATT	YDS	TD
Jay Novacek	Dallas	16/16	68	630	6			
Keith Byars	Philadelphia	16/16	56	502	2	41	176	1
Jackie Harris	Green Bay	16/11	55	595	2			
Shannon Sharpe	Denver	16/11	53	640	2	2	-6	0
Marv Cook	New England	16/15	52	413	2			
Keith Jackson	Miami	13/11	48	594	5			
Brent Jones	San Francisco	15/15	45	628	4			
Kerry Cash	Indianapolis	16/16	43	521	3			
Ron Hall	Tampa Bay	12/11	39	351	4			
Derrick Walker	San Diego	16/16	34	393	2			
Jim Price	L.A. Rams	15/3	34	324	2			
Ethan Horton	L.A. Raiders	16/16	33	409	2			
Pete Metzelaars	Buffalo	16/7	30	298	6			
Steve Jordan	Minnesota	14/12	28	394	2			
Howard Cross	N.Y. Giants	16/16	27	357	2			
Rodney Holman	Cincinnati	16/13	26	266	2			
Mark Bavaro	Cleveland	16/16	25	315	2			
Keith Jennings	Chicago	16/14	23	264	1			
Terry Orr	Washington	16/7	22	356	3			
Pat Carter	L.A. Rams	16/16	20	232	3			
Ben Coates	New England	16/2	20	171	3	1	2	0
Pete Holohan	Cleveland	9/1	20	170	0			
Craig Thompson	Cincinnati	16/3	19	194	2			
Mark Boyer	N.Y. Jets	16/16	19	149	0			
Johnny Mitchell	N.Y. Jets	11/3	16	210	1			
Adrian Cooper	Pittsburgh	16/14	16	197	3			
Andrew Glover	L.A. Raiders	16/1	15	178	1			
Eric Green	Pittsburgh	7/6	14	152	2			
Keith McKeller	Buffalo	11/8	14	110	0			
Charles Arbuckle	Indianapolis	16/3	13	152	1			
Butch Rolle	Phoenix	16/13	13	64	0			
Hoby Brenner	New Orleans	15/14	12	161	0			
Keith Cash	Kansas City	15/8	12	113	2			
Ron Heller	Seattle	16/11	12	85	0			
Jim Riggs	Cincinnati	12/2	11	70	0			
Reggie Johnson	Denver	15/7	10	139	1	2	7	0
Ferrell Edmunds	Miami	10/5	10	91	1			
Frank Wainright	New Orleans	13/4	9	143	0			
Jonathan Hayes	Kansas City	16/16	9	77	2			
Paul Green	Seattle	4/4	9	67	1			
Pat Beach	Philadelphia	16/7	8	75	2			
Tyji Armstrong	Tampa Bay	15/8	7	138	1			
Jamie Williams	San Francisco	16/1	7	76	1			
Clarence Kay	Denver	16/13	7	56	0			
Ron Middleton	Washington	16/12	7	50	0			
Jimmie Johnson	Detroit	16/5	6	34	0			
Tim Jorden	Pittsburgh	15/4	6	28	2			
Walter Reeves	Phoenix	16/16	6	28	0			
Mike Tice	Minnesota	12/9	5	65	1			
Kelly Blackwell	Chicago	16/2	5	54	0			
Scott Galbraith	Cleveland	14/2	4	63	1			
Brent Novoselsky	Minnesota	16/1	4	63	0			

Robert Awalt	Buffalo	14/1	4	34	0
Derek Brown	N.Y. Giants	16/7	4	31	0
Ed West	Green Bay	16/8	4	30	0
Don Warren	Washington	11/10	4	25	0
Tommie Stowers	New Orleans	12/0	4	23	0
Alfredo Roberts	Dallas	16/4	3	36	0
Mike Hinnant	Detroit	15/1	3	28	0
Trey Junkin	Seattle	16/1	3	25	1
Greg Baty	Miami	16/0	3	19	1
Mike Jones	Seattle	4/1	3	18	0
David Jones	L.A. Raiders	16/0	2	29	0
Maurice Johnson	Philadelphia	11/3	2	16	0
Jeff Thomason	Cincinnati	4/0	2	14	0
Thomas McLemore	Detroit	11/1	2	12	0
Derek Tennell	Minnesota	3/2	2	12	0
Ken Whisenhunt	N.Y. Jets	10/6	2	11	0
Troy Sadowski	N.Y. Jets	6/2	1	20	0
Derek Ware	Phoenix	15/0	1	13	0
Jeff Parker	Tampa Bay	3/0	1	12	0
Dave Moore	Mia./T.B.	5/2	1	10	0
Mike Dyal	Kansas City	3/0	1	7	0
Danta Whitaker	Minnesota	6/2	1	4	0

1992 Kickers

Player	Team	GP	XP	XPA	FG	FGA	PCT	PTS
Pete Stoyanovich	Miami	16	34	36	30	37	81.1	124
Morten Anderson	New Orleans	16	33	34	29	34	85.3	120
Chip Lohmiller	Washington	16	30	30	30	40	75.0	120
Lin Elliott	Dallas	16	47	48	24	35	68.6	119
Steve Christie	Buffalo	16	43	44	24	30	80.0	115
Gary Anderson	Pittsburgh	16	29	31	28	36	77.8	113
John Carney	San Diego	16	35	35	26	32	81.3	113
Mike Cofer	San Francisco	16	53	54	18	27	66.7	107
Nick Lowery	Kansas City	15	39	39	22	24	91.7	105
Al Del Greco	Houston	16	41	41	21	27	77.8	104
Fuad Reveiz	Minnesota	16	45	45	19	25	76.0	102
Chris Jackie	Green Bay	16	30	30	22	29	75.9	96
Jason Hanson	Detroit	16	30	30	21	26	80.8	93
Norm Johnson	Atlanta	16	39	39	18	22	81.8	93
Matt Stover	Cleveland	16	29	30	21	29	72.4	92
Kevin Butler	Chicago	16	34	34	19	26	73.1	91
Roger Ruzek	Philadelphia	16	40	44	16	25	64.0	88
Jim Beech	Cincinnati	16	31	31	19	27	70.4	88
David Treadwell	Denver	16	28	28	20	24	83.3	88
Tony Zendejas	L.A. Rams	16	38	38	15	20	75.0	83
Matt Bahr	N.Y. Giants	12	29	29	16	21	76.2	77
Jeff Jaeger	L.A. Raiders	16	28	28	15	26	57.7	73
Dean Biasucci	Indianapolis	16	24	24	16	29	55.2	72
Greg Davis	Phoenix	16	28	28	13	26	50.0	67
Cary Blanchard	N.Y. Jets	11	17	17	16	22	72.7	65
Ken Willis	T.B./Giants	15	27	27	10	16	62.5	57
John Kasay	Seattle	16	14	14	14	22	63.6	56
Charlie Baumann	New England	16	22	24	11	17	64.7	55
Eddie Murray	K.C./T.B.	8	13	13	5	9	55.6	28
Jason Staurovsky	N.Y. Jets	4	6	6	3	8	37.5	15
Brad Daluiso	Denver	16	0	0	0	1	0.0	0
Lee Johnson	Cincinnati	16	0	0	0	1	0.0	0
Rich Camarillo	Phoenix	16	0	1	0	0	—	0

Appendix

1993 NFL Schedule

(All times local)

WEEK 1

SUNDAY, SEPTEMBER 5

ATLANTA AT DETROIT	1:00
CINCINNATI AT CLEVELAND	1:00
DENVER AT NEW YORK JETS	1:00
KANSAS CITY AT TAMPA BAY	1:00
LOS ANGELES RAMS VS. GREEN BAY (at MILW.)	12:00
MIAMI AT INDIANAPOLIS	12:00
MINNESOTA AT LOS ANGELES RAIDERS	1:00
NEW ENGLAND AT BUFFALO	1:00
NEW YORK GIANTS AT CHICAGO	3:00
PHOENIX AT PHILADELPHIA	1:00
SAN FRANCISCO AT PITTSBURGH	1:00
SEATTLE AT SAN DIEGO	1:00
HOUSTON AT NEW ORLEANS	7:00

MONDAY, SEPTEMBER 6

DALLAS AT WASHINGTON	9:00

WEEK 2

SUNDAY, SEPTEMBER 12

BUFFALO AT DALLAS	3:00
CHICAGO AT MINNESOTA	12:00
DETROIT AT NEW ENGLAND	1:00
INDIANAPOLIS AT CINCINNATI	1:00
KANSAS CITY AT HOUSTON	12:00
NEW ORLEANS AT ATLANTA	1:00
NEW YORK JETS AT MIAMI	4:00
PHILADELPHIA AT GREEN BAY	12:00
PHOENIX AT WASHINGTON	1:00
PITTSBURGH AT LOS ANGELES RAMS	1:00
SAN DIEGO AT DENVER	2:00
TAMPA BAY AT NEW YORK GIANTS	1:00
LOS ANGELES RAIDERS AT SEATTLE	5:00

MONDAY, SEPTEMBER 13

SAN FRANCISCO AT CLEVELAND	9:00

WEEK 3

SUNDAY, SEPTEMBER 19

ATLANTA AT SAN FRANCISCO	1:00
CINCINNATI AT PITTSBURGH	1:00
CLEVELAND AT LOS ANGELES RAIDERS	1:00
DETROIT AT NEW ORLEANS	12:00
HOUSTON AT SAN DIEGO	1:00
LOS ANGELES RAMS AT NEW YORK GIANTS	1:00
SEATTLE AT NEW ENGLAND	1:00
WASHINGTON AT PHILADELPHIA	1:00
DALLAS AT PHOENIX	5:00

MONDAY, SEPTEMBER 20

DENVER AT KANSAS CITY	8:00

OPEN DATES: AFC EAST EXCEPT NEW ENGLAND, NFC CENTRAL EXCEPT DETROIT

WEEK 4

SUNDAY, SEPTEMBER 26

CLEVELAND AT INDIANAPOLIS	12:00
GREEN BAY AT MINNESOTA	12:00
LOS ANGELES RAMS AT HOUSTON	12:00
MIAMI AT BUFFALO	1:00
PHOENIX AT DETROIT	1:00
SAN FRANCISCO AT NEW ORLEANS	3:00
SEATTLE AT CINCINNATI	4:00
TAMPA BAY AT CHICAGO	12:00
NEW ENGLAND AT NEW YORK JETS	8:00

MONDAY, SEPTEMBER 27

PITTSBURGH AT ATLANTA	9:00

OPEN DATES: AFC WEST EXCEPT SEATTLE, NFC EAST EXCEPT PHOENIX

WEEK 5

SUNDAY, OCTOBER 3

ATLANTA AT CHICAGO	12:00
DETROIT AT TAMPA BAY	1:00
GREEN BAY AT DALLAS	12:00
INDIANAPOLIS AT DENVER	2:00
LOS ANGELES RAIDERS AT KANSAS CITY	12:00
MINNESOTA AT SAN FRANCISCO	1:00
NEW ORLEANS AT LOS ANGELES RAMS	1:00
PHILADELPHIA AT NEW YORK JETS	4:00
SAN DIEGO AT SEATTLE	1:00
NEW YORK GIANTS AT BUFFALO	8:00

MONDAY, OCTOBER 4

WASHINGTON AT MIAMI	9:00

OPEN DATES: AFC CENTRAL, NEW ENGLAND, PHOENIX

WEEK 6

SUNDAY, OCTOBER 10

CHICAGO AT PHILADELPHIA	1:00
CINCINNATI AT KANSAS CITY	12:00
DALLAS AT INDIANAPOLIS	12:00
MIAMI AT CLEVELAND	1:00
NEW ENGLAND AT PHOENIX	1:00
NEW YORK GIANTS AT WASHINGTON	1:00
NEW YORK JETS AT LOS ANGELES RAIDERS	1:00
SAN DIEGO AT PITTSBURGH	1:00
TAMPA BAY AT MINNESOTA	12:00
DENVER AT GREEN BAY	6:30

MONDAY, OCTOBER 11

HOUSTON AT BUFFALO	9:00

OPEN DATES: NFC WEST, DETROIT, SEATTLE

WEEK 7
THURSDAY, OCTOBER 14
LOS ANGELES RAMS AT ATLANTA	7:30

SUNDAY, OCTOBER 17
CLEVELAND AT CINCINNATI	1:00
HOUSTON AT NEW ENGLAND	1:00
KANSAS CITY AT SAN DIEGO	1:00
NEW ORLEANS AT PITTSBURGH	1:00
PHILADELPHIA AT NEW YORK GIANTS	1:00
SAN FRANCISCO AT DALLAS	3:00
SEATTLE AT DETROIT	1:00
WASHINGTON AT PHOENIX	1:00

MONDAY, OCTOBER 18
LOS ANGELES RAIDERS AT DENVER	7:00

OPEN DATES: AFC EAST EXCEPT NEW ENGLAND, NFC CENTRAL EXCEPT DETROIT

WEEK 8
SUNDAY, OCTOBER 24
ATLANTA AT NEW ORLEANS	12:00
BUFFALO AT NEW YORK JETS	1:00
CINCINNATI AT HOUSTON	12:00
DETROIT AT LOS ANGELES RAMS	1:00
GREEN BAY AT TAMPA BAY	1:00
NEW ENGLAND AT SEATTLE	1:00
PHOENIX AT SAN FRANCISCO	1:00
PITTSBURGH AT CLEVELAND	1:00
INDIANAPOLIS AT MIAMI	7:30

MONDAY, OCTOBER 25
MINNESOTA AT CHICAGO	8:00

OPEN DATES: AFC WEST EXCEPT SEATTLE, NFC EAST EXCEPT PHOENIX

WEEK 9
SUNDAY, OCTOBER 31
CHICAGO AT GREEN BAY	12:00
DALLAS AT PHILADELPHIA	1:00
KANSAS CITY AT MIAMI	1:00
LOS ANGELES RAMS AT SAN FRANCISCO	1:00
NEW ENGLAND AT INDIANAPOLIS	1:00
NEW ORLEANS AT PHOENIX	2:00
NEW YORK JETS AT NEW YORK GIANTS	1:00
SAN DIEGO AT LOS ANGELES RAIDERS	1:00
SEATTLE AT DENVER	2:00
TAMPA BAY AT ATLANTA	1:00
DETROIT AT MINNESOTA	7:00

MONDAY, NOVEMBER 1
WASHINGTON AT BUFFALO	9:00

OPEN DATES: AFC CENTRAL

WEEK 10
SUNDAY, NOVEMBER 7
BUFFALO AT NEW ENGLAND	1:00
DENVER AT CLEVELAND	1:00
LOS ANGELES RAIDERS AT CHICAGO	3:00
MIAMI AT NEW YORK JETS	4:00
NEW YORK GIANTS AT DALLAS	12:00
PHILADELPHIA AT PHOENIX	2:00
PITTSBURGH AT CINCINNATI	1:00
SAN DIEGO AT MINNESOTA	12:00
SEATTLE AT HOUSTON	12:00
TAMPA BAY AT DETROIT	1:00
INDIANAPOLIS AT WASHINGTON	8:00

MONDAY, NOVEMBER 8
GREEN BAY AT KANSAS CITY	8:00

OPEN DATES: NFC WEST

WEEK 11
SUNDAY, NOVEMBER 14
ATLANTA AT LOS ANGELES RAMS	1:00
CLEVELAND AT SEATTLE	1:00
GREEN BAY AT NEW ORLEANS	12:00
HOUSTON AT CINCINNATI	1:00
KANSAS CITY AT LOS ANGELES RAIDERS	1:00
MIAMI AT PHILADELPHIA	1:00
MINNESOTA AT DENVER	2:00
NEW YORK JETS AT INDIANAPOLIS	4:00
PHOENIX AT DALLAS	12:00
SAN FRANCISCO AT TAMPA BAY	1:00
WASHINGTON AT NEW YORK GIANTS	1:00
CHICAGO AT SAN DIEGO	5:00

MONDAY, NOVEMBER 15
BUFFALO AT PITTSBURGH	9:00

OPEN DATES: DETROIT, NEW ENGLAND

WEEK 12
SUNDAY, NOVEMBER 21
CHICAGO AT KANSAS CITY	12:00
CINCINNATI AT NEW YORK JETS	1:00
DALLAS AT ATLANTA	1:00
DETROIT VS. GREEN BAY (at MILW.)	12:00
HOUSTON AT CLEVELAND	1:00
INDIANAPOLIS AT BUFFALO	1:00
LOS ANGELES RAIDERS AT SAN DIEGO	1:00
NEW ENGLAND AT MIAMI	1:00
NEW YORK GIANTS AT PHILADELPHIA	4:00
PITTSBURGH AT DENVER	2:00
WASHINGTON AT LOS ANGELES RAMS	1:00
MINNESOTA AT TAMPA BAY	8:00

MONDAY, NOVEMBER 22
NEW ORLEANS AT SAN FRANCISCO	6:00

OPEN DATES: PHOENIX, SEATTLE

WEEK 13
THURSDAY, NOVEMBER 25
CHICAGO AT DETROIT	12:30
MIAMI AT DALLAS	3:00

SUNDAY, NOVEMBER 28
BUFFALO AT KANSAS CITY	3:00
CLEVELAND AT ATLANTA	1:00
DENVER AT SEATTLE	1:00
LOS ANGELES RAIDERS AT CINCINNATI	1:00
NEW ORLEANS AT MINNESOTA	12:00
NEW YORK JETS AT NEW ENGLAND	1:00
PHILADELPHIA AT WASHINGTON	1:00
PHOENIX AT NEW YORK GIANTS	4:00
SAN FRANCISCO AT LOS ANGELES RAMS	1:00
TAMPA BAY AT GREEN BAY	12:00
PITTSBURGH AT HOUSTON	7:00

MONDAY, NOVEMBER 29
SAN DIEGO AT INDIANAPOLIS	9:00

WEEK 14
SUNDAY, DECEMBER 5
ATLANTA AT HOUSTON	12:00
DENVER AT SAN DIEGO	1:00
GREEN BAY AT CHICAGO	12:00
INDIANAPOLIS AT NEW YORK JETS	1:00
KANSAS CITY AT SEATTLE	1:00
LOS ANGELES RAIDERS AT BUFFALO	1:00
LOS ANGELES RAMS AT PHOENIX	2:00
MINNESOTA AT DETROIT	1:00
NEW ENGLAND AT PITTSBURGH	1:00
NEW ORLEANS AT CLEVELAND	1:00
NEW YORK GIANTS AT MIAMI	4:00
WASHINGTON AT TAMPA BAY	1:00
CINCINNATI AT SAN FRANCISCO	5:00

MONDAY, DECEMBER 6
PHILADELPHIA AT DALLAS	8:00

WEEK 15
SATURDAY, DECEMBER 11
NEW YORK JETS AT WASHINGTON	12:30
SAN FRANCISCO AT ATLANTA	4:00

SUNDAY, DECEMBER 12
BUFFALO AT PHILADELPHIA	1:00
CHICAGO AT TAMPA BAY	1:00
CINCINNATI AT NEW ENGLAND	1:00
CLEVELAND AT HOUSTON	12:00
DALLAS AT MINNESOTA	3:00
DETROIT AT PHOENIX	2:00
INDIANAPOLIS AT NEW YORK GIANTS	1:00
KANSAS CITY AT DENVER	2:00
LOS ANGELES RAMS AT NEW ORLEANS	12:00
SEATTLE AT LOS ANGELES RAIDERS	1:00
GREEN BAY AT SAN DIEGO	5:00

MONDAY, DECEMBER 13
PITTSBURGH AT MIAMI	9:00

WEEK 16
SATURDAY, DECEMBER 18
DALLAS AT NEW YORK JETS	4:00
DENVER AT CHICAGO	11:30

SUNDAY, DECEMBER 19
ATLANTA AT WASHINGTON	1:00
BUFFALO AT MIAMI	1:00
HOUSTON AT PITTSBURGH	1:00
LOS ANGELES RAMS AT CINCINNATI	1:00
MINNESOTA VS. GREEN BAY (at MILW.)	12:00
NEW ENGLAND AT CLEVELAND	1:00
PHOENIX AT SEATTLE	1:00
SAN DIEGO AT KANSAS CITY	3:00
SAN FRANCISCO AT DETROIT	4:00
TAMPA BAY AT LOS ANGELES RAIDERS	1:00
PHILADELPHIA AT INDIANAPOLIS	8:00

MONDAY, DECEMBER 20
NEW YORK GIANTS AT NEW ORLEANS	8:00

WEEK 17
SATURDAY, DECEMBER 25
HOUSTON AT SAN FRANCISCO	2:30

SUNDAY, DECEMBER 26
ATLANTA AT CINCINNATI	1:00
CLEVELAND AT LOS ANGELES RAMS	1:00
DETROIT AT CHICAGO	12:00
INDIANAPOLIS AT NEW ENGLAND	1:00
LOS ANGELES RAIDERS AT GREEN BAY	12:00
NEW ORLEANS AT PHILADELPHIA	1:00
NEW YORK GIANTS AT PHOENIX	2:00
NEW YORK JETS AT BUFFALO	1:00
PITTSBURGH AT SEATTLE	1:00
TAMPA BAY AT DENVER	2:00
WASHINGTON AT DALLAS	3:00
KANSAS CITY AT MINNESOTA	7:00

MONDAY, DECEMBER 27
MIAMI AT SAN DIEGO	6:00

WEEK 18
FRIDAY, DECEMBER 31
MINNESOTA AT WASHINGTON	3:00

SUNDAY, JANUARY 2
BUFFALO AT INDIANAPOLIS	1:00
CHICAGO AT LOS ANGELES RAMS	1:00
CINCINNATI AT NEW ORLEANS	3:00
CLEVELAND AT PITTSBURGH	1:00
DALLAS AT NEW YORK GIANTS	1:00
DENVER AT LOS ANGELES RAIDERS	1:00
GREEN BAY AT DETROIT	1:00
MIAMI AT NEW ENGLAND	1:00
PHOENIX AT ATLANTA	1:00
SAN DIEGO AT TAMPA BAY	4:00
SEATTLE AT KANSAS CITY	12:00
NEW YORK JETS AT HOUSTON	7:00

MONDAY, JANUARY 3
PHILADELPHIA AT SAN FRANCISCO	6:00

POSTSEASON
SATURDAY AND SUNDAY, JANUARY 8-9
AFC and NFC wild-card playoffs
SATURDAY AND SUNDAY, JANUARY 15-16
AFC and NFC divisional playoffs
SUNDAY, JANUARY 23
AFC and NFC conference championships
SUNDAY, JANUARY 30
Super Bowl XXVIII at Georgia Dome, Atlanta

Fantasy Football Schedules

Six-Team League

Team #	1	2	3	4	5	6
Week #						
1	2	1	4	3	6	5
2	3	6	1	5	4	2
3	4	5	6	1	2	3
4	5	3	2	6	1	4
5	6	4	5	2	3	1
6	2	1	4	3	6	5
7	3	6	1	5	4	2
8	4	5	6	1	2	3
9	5	3	2	6	1	4
10	6	4	5	2	3	1
11	2	1	4	3	6	5
12	3	6	1	5	4	2
13	4	5	6	1	2	3
14	5	3	2	6	1	4
15	6	4	5	2	3	1
16	Playoffs					
17	Championship Game					
18	(Season Over)					

Eight-Team League

Team #	1	2	3	4	5	6	7	8
Week #								
1	2	1	4	3	6	5	8	7
2	3	4	1	2	8	7	6	5
3	4	8	6	1	7	3	5	2
4	5	6	8	7	1	2	4	3
5	6	5	7	8	2	1	3	4
6	7	3	2	5	4	8	1	6
7	8	7	5	6	3	4	2	1
8	2	1	4	3	6	5	8	7
9	3	4	1	2	8	7	6	5
10	4	8	6	1	7	3	5	2
11	5	6	8	7	1	2	4	3
12	6	5	7	8	2	1	3	4
13	7	3	2	5	4	8	1	6
14	8	7	5	6	3	4	2	1
15	2	1	4	3	6	5	8	7
16	3	4	1	2	8	7	6	5
17	Playoffs							
18	Championship Game							

10-Team League

Team #	1	2	3	4	5	6	7	8	9	10
Week #										
1	2	1	4	3	10	7	6	9	8	5
2	4	5	8	1	2	9	10	3	6	7
3	6	3	2	5	4	1	8	7	10	9
4	9	10	6	7	8	3	4	5	1	2
5	2	1	5	9	3	7	6	10	4	8
6	5	7	4	3	1	10	2	9	8	6
7	10	6	7	8	9	2	3	4	5	1
8	4	3	2	1	10	9	8	7	6	5
9	3	5	1	9	2	8	10	6	4	7
10	5	4	8	2	1	10	9	3	7	6
11	8	9	10	6	7	4	5	1	2	3
12	7	8	9	10	6	5	1	2	3	4
13	3	7	1	5	4	8	2	6	10	9
14	6	4	5	2	3	1	9	10	7	8
15	10	6	7	8	9	2	3	4	5	1
16	Playoffs									
17	Championship Game									
18	(Season Over)									

12-Team League

Tm #	1	2	3	4	5	6	7	8	9	10	11	12
Wk #												
1	2	1	4	3	6	5	8	7	10	9	12	11
2	3	4	1	2	7	8	5	6	11	12	9	10
3	4	3	2	1	8	7	6	5	12	11	10	9
4	5	6	11	12	1	2	9	10	7	8	3	4
5	6	7	9	10	11	1	2	12	3	4	5	8
6	12	11	8	6	9	4	10	3	5	7	2	1
7	11	10	6	5	4	3	12	9	8	2	1	7
8	7	8	12	9	10	11	1	2	4	5	6	3
9	8	9	7	11	12	10	3	1	2	6	4	5
10	10	12	5	7	3	9	4	11	6	1	8	2
11	9	5	10	8	2	12	11	4	1	3	7	6
12	2	1	4	3	6	5	8	7	10	8	12	11
13	3	4	1	2	7	8	5	6	11	12	9	10
14	4	3	2	1	8	7	6	5	12	11	10	9
15	5	6	11	12	1	2	9	10	7	8	3	4
16	6	7	9	10	11	1	2	12	3	4	5	8
17	Playoffs											
18	Championship Game											

Index

About the Author

Rick Korch is the managing editor of *Pro Football Weekly* and one of the foremost pro football historians in the country.

He has spent 16 years in and around the National Football League. Korch was previously the public relations director for the NFL Alumni association and a public relations assistant for the Miami Dolphins.

Korch is the author of three other books and is co-author of *The Sports Encyclopedia: Pro Football, The Modern Era*. He is also a researcher for HBO's "Inside the NFL" television program.

Korch has won five awards from the Professional Football Writers of America, including best feature story in 1990. That story, a nine-part series, has been turned into a book, *The Truly Great*, to be published this year. He is married and lives in Arlington Heights, Illinois.

Suggestions

Anyone wishing to write to the author with comments or suggestions for next year's edition of this book, please do so. Write to:

Rick Korch
P.O. Box 1542
Northbrook, Illinois 60065-1542